Taking English Planning Law Scholarship Seriously

Taking English Planning Law Scholarship Seriously

Edited by
Maria Lee and Carolyn Abbot

First published in 2022 by
UCL Press
University College London
Gower Street
London WC1E 6BT

Available to download free: www.uclpress.co.uk

Collection © Editors, 2022
Text © Contributors, 2022
Images © Contributors and copyright holders named in captions, 2022

The authors have asserted their rights under the Copyright, Designs and Patents Act 1988 to be identified as the authors of this work.

A CIP catalogue record for this book is available from The British Library.

Any third-party material in this book is not covered by the book's Creative Commons licence. Details of the copyright ownership and permitted use of third-party material is given in the image (or extract) credit lines. If you would like to reuse any third-party material not covered by the book's Creative Commons licence, you will need to obtain permission directly from the copyright owner.

This book is published under a Creative Commons Attribution-Non-Commercial 4.0 International licence (CC BY-NC 4.0), https://creativecommons.org/licenses/by-nc/4.0/. This licence allows you to share and adapt the work for non-commercial use providing attribution is made to the author and publisher (but not in any way that suggests that they endorse you or your use of the work) and any changes are indicated. Attribution should include the following information:

Lee, M. and Abbot, C. (eds). 2022. *Taking English Planning Law Scholarship Seriously*. London: UCL Press. https://doi.org/10.14324/111.9781800082885

Further details about Creative Commons licences are available at https://creativecommons.org/licenses/

ISBN: 978-1-80008-290-8 (Hbk.)
ISBN: 978-1-80008-289-2 (Pbk.)
ISBN: 978-1-80008-288-5 (PDF)
ISBN: 978-1-80008-291-5 (epub)
DOI: https://doi.org/10.14324/111.9781800082885

Contents

List of figures	viii
List of legislation	ix
Table of cases	xvi
List of contributors	xxiii
Acknowledgements	xxvi
List of abbreviations	xxvii
Executive summaries	xxix

Part I: Introduction — 1

1. The importance of taking English planning law scholarship seriously — 3
   Maria Lee

2. English planning law: An outline — 10
   Maria Lee

Part II: Place shaping, place framing — 33

Introduction to Part Two — 33
Carolyn Abbot and Maria Lee

3. Backstreet's back alright: London's LGBT+ nightlife spaces and a queering of planning law and planning practices — 35
   Steven Vaughan and Brad Jessup

4. The highway: A right, a place or a resource? — 64
   Antonia Layard

| 5 | Marine planning for sustainability: The role of the ecosystem approach | 85 |

Margherita Pieraccini

Part III: Participation — 109

Introduction to Part Three — 109
Carolyn Abbot and Maria Lee

| 6 | Place, participation and planning law in a time of climate change | 111 |

Chiara Armeni

| 7 | Planning inquiries and legal expertise: A fair crack of the whip? | 133 |

Carolyn Abbot

Part IV: Time and scale — 155

Introduction to Part Four — 155
Maria Lee and Carolyn Abbot

| 8 | Futurescapes of planning law: Some preliminary thoughts on a timely encounter | 157 |

Elen Stokes

| 9 | Slippery scales in planning for housing | 180 |

Maria Lee

Part V: Planning at the intersections — 205

Introduction to Part Five — 205
Maria Lee and Carolyn Abbot

| 10 | Contracting affordable housing delivery? Residential property development, section 106 agreements and other contractual arrangements | 207 |

Edward Mitchell

11 Embracing the unwanted guests at the judicial review
    party: Why administrative law scholars should take
    planning law seriously   229
    Joanna Bell

12 Provoking McAuslan: Planning law and property rights   249
    Kim Bouwer and Rachel Gimson

13 Concluding thoughts   268
    Carolyn Abbot and Maria Lee

Index   272

List of figures

7.1 Proposal site in the context of the Bolton Adopted
 Development Plan 142

List of legislation

UK Primary Legislation

Acquisition of Land Act 1981	
section 12	264
Cities and Local Government Devolution Act 2016	14
Compulsory Purchase Act 1965	257
section 5	264
Countryside and Rights of Way Act 2006	128, 189
Criminal Justice and Courts Act 2015	
section 84	24
Deregulation Act 2015	
section 108	29
Energy Act 2016	
section 78	128
Environment Act 1995	225
Environment Act 2021	
section 102	29
section 103	29
Equality Act 2010	46, 58, 75
section 149	29, 38, 56, 58
European Union (Withdrawal) Act 2018	104, 199
Extradition Act 2003	
section 27(3)	243
Freedom of Information Act 2000	
section 10	80
Gender Recognition Act 2004	160
Greater London Authority Act 1999	13, 56
section 334	17
Greater London Authority Act 2007	56
Highways Act 1980	
section 41	80, 82
section 58	82
section 137	80

section 263	81
section 265	81
section 328	80
section 329	80
Housing Act 1996	245
section 204	245
Human Rights Act 1998	240
Land Compensation Act 1961	259
section 5	265
section 6	265
section 14	265
section 17	265
section 18	265
Land Registration Act 2002	
Schedule 1	81
Schedule 3	81
Law of Property Act 1925	
section 78	253
Local Democracy, Economic Development and Construction Act 2009	14
Local Government Act 1972	12, 27
section 111	216
Local Government Act 1988	
section 28	38, 56
Local Government Act 1992	27
Local Government Act 2000	28
Local Government and Public Involvement in Health Act 2007	13, 27, 28
Local Land Charges Act 1975	
section 3	225
Localism Act 2011	13, 14, 22, 28, 29, 41, 56, 167, 190, 245, 265
section 1	215, 216, 225
section 17	265
section 95	57
section 96	57
section 232	265
section 240	265
Schedule 9	245
Marine and Coastal Access Act 2009	85, 86, 94, 96
section 44	94, 104
section 46	104
section 47	104

section 48	104
section 50	104
section 51	94
section 52	104
section 53	104
section 54	104
section 58	95, 104
section 61	104
schedule 6	104
Medical Act 1980	
sections 40-40A	243
National Heritage Act 1983	151
National Parks and Access to the Countryside Act 1949	128
Natural Environment and Rural Communities Act 2006	
section 40	29
Planning Act 2008	18, 27, 29, 104, 109, 116, 117, 118, 125, 150, 244, 245, 271
section 13	243
section 31	127
section 35	175
section 41	175
section 42	127
section 43	127
section 47	127
section 49	127
section 56	127
section 60	127
section 87	128
section 88	127
section 90	127
section 93	127
section 104	125, 129
section 106	128
section 107	127
section 122	264
section 216	223
schedule 13	265
Planning and Compulsory Purchase Act 2004	11, 13, 21, 23, 190, 245
section 15	29
section 17	29
section 18	29
section 19	29, 175

section 20	29, 30, 199
section 21	30
section 23	30
section 27	30, 175
section 33A	30
section 34	29, 30
section 38	18, 21, 29, 136, 174, 188, 199, 200, 281
section 38A	199
section 39	29
section 113	243
Planning (Listed Buildings and Conservation Areas) Act 1990	41
section 1	41
section 8	41
section 66	57
section 69	42
section 72	57
Public Bodies Act 2011	56
Road Traffic Act 1984	
section 17	80
section 38	82
Road Traffic Regulation Act 1984	
section 9	80
section 60	80
Roads (Scotland) Act 1984	
section 151	80
Senior Courts Act 1981	
section 31	242
Town Planning Act 1909	242
Town and Country Planning Act 1947	11, 231
Town and Country Planning Act 1990	18, 27, 117, 245, 258, 271
section 49	265
section 54A	29, 151
section 55	17, 242
section 56	145
section 57	28, 174, 223
section 58	17
section 61	28
section 62	225
section 62A	30, 198
section 62B	30, 198
section 70	58, 136, 174, 223
section 72	243

section 77	29, 151, 169, 175
section 78	29, 45
section 79	29, 175
section 92	225
section 106	19, 207, 216, 225
section 137	264
section 138	264
section 149	264, 265
section 150	264, 265
section 168	265
section 226	264
section 260	
section 266	264
section 268	264
section 288	26
section 319A	29
section 336	80, 265
section 366	264
Schedule 4B	30
Schedule 6	29, 199, 200
Schedule 13	26, 265
Traffic Management Act 2004	
section 16	81
section 31	81
Tribunals Courts and Enforcement Act 2007	
section 15	243, 245

UK Delegated Legislation

Assets of Community Value (England) Regulations 2012 SI 2012/2421	
Regulation 2	57
Regulation 4	57
Regulation 5	57
Regulation 12	57
Regulation 13	57
Regulation 14	57
Schedule 3	57
Civil Procedure Rules 1998 SI 1998/3132	243, 245
Community Infrastructure Levy Regulations 2010 SI 2010/948	144
Regulation 59	223
Regulation 122	208

Conservation of Habitats and Species Regulations 2017 SI 2017/1012	104
Environmental Assessment of Plans and Programmes Regulations 2004 SI 2004/1633	104
Infrastructure Planning (Onshore Wind Generating Stations) Order 2016 SI 2016/306	128
Marine Environment (Amendment) (EU Exit) Regulations 2018 SI 2018/1399	104
Part 3	96
Marine Strategy Regulations 2010 SI 2010/1627	96, 104
Regulation 5	96
Motorways Traffic (England and Wales) Regulations 1982 SI 1982/1163	80
Practice Direction 54D	
Rule 3.2	245
Rule 3.4	245
Town and Country Planning (Consultation) (England) Direction 2009	141
Town and Country Planning (Determination of Appeals by Appointed Persons) (Prescribed Classes) Regulations 1997 SI 1997/420	29
Town and Country Planning (Development Management Procedure) (England) Order 2010 SI 2010/2184	
Article 36	225
Town and Country Planning (Development Management Procedure) (England) Order 2015 SI 2015/595	28, 30, 245
Article 2	225
Article 5	225
Article 7	225
Article 15	29
Article 18	29
Article 31	175
Article 40	225
Schedule 4	29
Town and Country Planning (Environmental Impact Assessment) Regulations 2017 SI 2017/571	144, 242
Town and Country Planning (General Permitted Development) (England) Order 2015 SI 2015/596	17, 28, 199, 245
Town and Country Planning (Inquiries Procedure) (England) Rules 2000 SI 2000/1624	
Rule 6	151

Rule 15	151
Town and Country Planning (Local Planning) Regulations 2012 SI 2012/767	29
Town and Country Planning (Mayor of London) Order 2008 SI 2008/580	28, 56
Schedule 1	56
Town and Country Planning (Use Classes) Order 1987 SI 1987/764	17, 28, 191, 199, 245

European Legislation

Directive 2001/42/EC on the assessment of the effects of certain plans and programmes on the environment [2001] OJ L 197/30	127
Directive 2008/56/EC establishing a framework for community action in the field of marine environmental policy [2008] OJ L 164/19	96, 104
Article 1	104
Article 9	96
Directive 2011/92/EU on the assessment of the effects of certain public and private projects on the environment (codification) [2012] OJ 2012 L 26/1	127
Directive 2014/89/EU establishing a framework for maritime spatial planning [2014] OJ L 257/135	96, 97, 101, 103, 104

International conventions and agreements

Aarhus Convention on Access to Information, Public Participation in Decision-Making and Access to Justice in Environmental Matters 1998	115, 127
Convention Concerning the Protection of the World Cultural and Natural Heritage 1972	119, 128
Convention for the Protection of the Marine Environment of the North-East Atlantic 1992	104
Convention on Biological Diversity 1992	91, 92, 97, 102, 104
Convention on the Conservation of Antarctic Marine Living Resources 1980	104
Johannesburg Declaration on Sustainable Development 2002	87
Rio Declaration on Environment and Development 1992	88
Transforming Our World: the 2030 Agenda for Sustainable Development 2015	88

Table of cases

Domestic Cases

Aberdeen City and Shire v Elsick Development Company [2017] UKSC 66; [2017] PTSR 1413 ... **30**

Austerberry v Oldham Corp (1885) 29 ChD 750 ... **263**

Barbone v Secretary of State for Transport [2009] EWHC 463 (Admin); [2009] Env LR D12 ... **128**

Barnwell Manor Wind Energy Limited v East Northamptonshire District Council & Ors [2014] EWCA Civ 137; [2015] 1 WLR 45 ... **128**

Baroness Cumberlege of Newick and another v Secretary of State for Communities and Local Government and another [2017] EWHC 2057 (Admin); [2017] WLR(D) 549 ... **129**

BDW Trading Ltd. v Secretary of State for Communities and Local Government [2016] EWCA Civ 493; [2017] PTSR 1337 ... **58**

Bedford Borough Council v Secretary of State for Communities and Local Government, Nuon UK Ltd [2013] EWHC 2847 (Admin) ... **129**

Bestzone Ltd v London Borough of Tower Hamlets [2019] APP/E5900/W/18/3204874 ... **57**

Bolton Metropolitan District Council and Others v Secretary of State for the Environment and Others [1995] 1 WLR 1176 ... **129**

Bradford Corpn v Pickles [1895] AC 587 (HL) ... **263**

Bushell v Secretary of State for the Environment [1981] AC 75 (HL) ... **128**

Burgos v Secretary of State for Housing, Communities and Local Government [2019] EWHC 2792 (Admin) ... **261, 265, 266**

Catesby Estates Ltd v Steer [2018] EWCA Civ 1697; [2018] JPL 1375 ... **120, 128**

Cheatle v General Medical Council [2009] EWHC 645 (Admin) ... **246**

Citizens UK v Secretary of State for the Home Department [2017] EWHC 2301 (Admin); [2018] 4 WLR 123 ... **243**

City of Edinburgh v Secretary of State for Scotland [1997] UKHL 38; [1997] 1 WLR 1447 ... **29**

Council of Civil Service Unions v Minister for the Civil Service [1985] AC 374 (HL) ... **244**

Cuckmere Brick v Mutual Finance [1971] EWCA Civ 9; [1971] Ch 949 ... **263**

Derbyshire Waste Ltd v Blewett [2004] EWCA Civ 1508; [2005] Env LR 15 ... **244**

DHN Food Distributors v Tower Hamlets LBC [1976] 1 WLR 852 ... **265**

Dimes v Proprietors of Grand Junction Canal 10 ER 315 (HL) ... **244**

DLA Delivery Ltd v Baroness Cumberledge of Newick [2018] EWCA Civ 1305; [2018] PTSR 2063 ... **246**

Dover District Council v CPRE [2017] UKSC 79; [2018] 1 WLR 108 ... **28, 181, 182, 184, 185, 189, 191, 192, 193, 197, 241, 243, 245, 246**

DPP v Jones (Margaret) and Another (1999) 2 AC 240 ... **81**

DPP v Ziegler and others [2021] UKSC 23; [2021] 3 WLR 179 ... **80**

Duncan v Lounch (1845) 6 QB 904 ... **263**

Fairmount Investments Ltd v Secretary of State for the Environment [1976] 1 WLR 1255 (HL) ... **150**

Federated Homes Ltd v Mill Lodge Property Ltd [1980] 1 All ER 371 (CA) ... **253–4, 263**

Fletcher Estates Ltd v Secretary of State for the Environment [2000] 2 AC 307 (HL) ... **265**

Fuller v Secretary of State for Communities and Local Government [2015] EWHC 142 (Admin) ... **243**

Gladman Developments Ltd v Secretary of State for Housing, Communities and Local Government and Corby Borough Council [2021] EWCA Civ 104 ... **30, 199, 200**

Glencore Energy UK Ltd v HMRC [2017] EWHC 1476 (Admin); [2017] STC 1824 ... **243**

Grampian Regional Council v Secretary of State for Scotland [1983] 1 WLR 1340 (HL) ... **265**

Gregory v London Borough of Camden [1966] 2 All ER 196 (QB) ... **242**

Gregory with *Walton v Scottish Minister* [2012] UKSC 44; [2013] PTSR 51 ... **243**

Hallam Land Management Ltd v Secretary of State for Communities and Local Government [2018] EWCA Civ 1808; [2019] JPL 63 ... **246**

Halliburton Company v Chubb Bermuda Insurance Ltd [2020] UKSC 48; [2020] 3 WLR 1474 ... **244**

Harrison v Duke of Rutland [1893] 1 QB 142 (CA) ... **81**

Health and Safety Executive v Wolverhampton City Council [2012] UKSC 34; [2021] 1 WLR 2264 ... **129**

Hopkins Homes Ltd v Secretary of State for Communities and Local Government [2017] UKSC 37; [2017] 1 WLR 1865 … 20, 24, 29, 30, **138, 151, 175, 188, 198, 199, 200, 244, 246**

Hossain v Secretary of State for the Home Department [2015] EWCA Civ 207 … **245**

Hussain v Sandwell Metropolitan Borough Council [2017] EWHC 1641 (Admin); [2018] PTSR 142 … **225**

International Tea Stores v Hobbes [1903] 2 Ch 165 … **263**

Kennedy v Charity Commission [2014] UKSC 20; [2015] AC 455 … **241, 246**

Kensington and Chelsea RLBC v Secretary of State for Communities and Local Government [2010] EWCA Civ 1466 (also known as *Vannes KFT v Kensington and Chelsea RLBC*)

Lever (Finance) Ltd v Westminster Corporation [1970] 3 All ER 496 (CA) … **224**

Locabail v Bayfield Properties Ltd [2000] QB 451 (CA) … **244**

Local Government Board v Arlidge [1914] AC 120 (HL) … **243**

London Borough of Southwark and another (Respondents) v Transport for London (Appellant) [2018] UKSC 63; [2018] 3 WLR 2059 … **67, 81**

Mansell v Tonbridge and Malling Borough Council [2017] EWCA Civ 1314; [2019] PTSR 1452 … **244**

Miller v Prime Minister [2019] UKSC 41; [2020] AC 373 … **242**

Mounsey v Ismay (1865) 3 H&C 486 … **263**

Newbury DC v Secretary of State for the Environment [1981] AC 578 (HL) … **29, 244**

North Wiltshire DC v Secretary of State for the Environment (1993) 65 P & CR 137 (CA) … **246**

Nzolameso v Westminster CC [2015] UKSC 22; [2015] 2 All ER 942 … **246**

Oxton Farm v Harrogate BC [2020] EWCA Civ 805 … **244**

Palmer v Herefordshire Council and Another [2016] EWCA Civ 1061; [2017] WLR 411 … **152**

Parkhurst Road Ltd v Secretary of State for Communities and Local Government [2018] EWHC 991 (Admin); [2019] JPL 855 … **224**

Paul Newman New Homes Ltd v Secretary of State for Housing, Communities and Local Government [2021] EWCA Civ 15; [2021] PTSR 1054 … **175**

Peel Investments (North) Ltd v Secretary of State for Housing, Communities & Local Government [2020] EWCA Civ 1175; [2021] 2 All ER 581 … **175**

Phipps v Pears [1965] 1 QB 76 (CA) … **251, 263**

Prest v Secretary of State for Wales (1982) 81 LGR 193 … **264**

R v Amber Valley DC, ex parte Jackson [1985] 1 WLR 298 (QB) … **29, 244**

R v Bow Street Metropolitan Stipendiary Magistrate, ex parte Pinochet [2000] 1 AC 119 (HL) ... **244**

R v Chadwick [1975] Crim LR 105 ... **82**

R v Inland Revenue Commissioners, ex parte MFK Underwriting Agents Ltd [1990] 1 WLR 1545 (QB) ... **246**

R v Inland Revenue Commissioners, ex parte Unilever [1996] STC 681 (CA) ... **246**

R v Rochdale MBC ex parte Milne (2001) 81 P&CR 27 (QB) ... **58**

R v Somerset County Council, Ex p Fewings [1995] 1 WLR 1037 (CA) ... **29**

R v Westminster City Council ex parte Monahan [1989] 1 PLR 188 (CA) ... **129**

R (Albion Water Ltd) v Water Services Regulation Authority [2012] EWHC 2259 (Admin) ... **246**

R (Alconbury Developments Ltd) v Secretary of State for the Environment [2001] UKHL 23; [2003] 2 AC 295 ... **246**

R (Cart) v Upper Tribunal [2011] UKSC 28; [2012] 1 AC 663 ... **245**

R (ClientEarth) v Secretary of State for Business, Energy and Industrial Strategy [2021] EWCA Civ 43; [2021] PTSR 1400 ... **244**

R (Corbett) v Cornwall Council [2020] EWCA Civ 508; [2020] JPL 1277 ... **245**

R (Din) v Secretary of State for the Home Department [2018] EWHC 1046 (Admin) ... **244**

R (Friends of the Earth) v Heathrow Airport Ltd [2020] UKSC 52; [2021] 2 All ER 967 ... **18, 29, 243**

R (Fylde Coast Farms Ltd) v Fylde BC [2021] UKSC 18; [2021] 1 WLR 2794 ... **243**

R (G) v Immigration Appeal Tribunal [2004] EWCA Civ 1731; [2005] 1 WLR 1445 ... **245**

R (Gallaher Group Ltd) v Competition and Markets Authority [2018] UKSC 25; [2019] AC 96 ... **240, 241, 246**

R (Greenpeace) v Secretary of State for Trade and Industry [2007] EWHC 311 (Admin); [2007] JPL 1314 ... **128**

R (Gullu) v London Borough of Hillingdon [2019] EWCA Civ 682; [2019] PTSR 1738 ... **245**

R (Help Refugees) v Secretary of State for the Home Department [2017] EWHC 2727 (Admin); [2018] 4 WLR 168 ... **243**

R (Hillingdon LBC) v Secretary of State for Transport [2010] EWHC 626 (Admin); [2010] JPL 976 ... **128**

R (Holborn Studios Ltd) v London Borough of Hackney [2020] EWHC 1509 (Admin); [2021] JPL 17 ... **244**

R (Iqbal) v Secretary of State for the Home Department [2015] EWCA Civ 838; [2016] 1 WLR 582 ... **245**

R (Island Farm Development Ltd) v Bridgend County BC [2006] EWHC 2189 (Admin) ... **244**

R (Keyu) v Secretary of State for Foreign and Commonwealth Affairs [2015] UKSC 69; [2016] AC 1355 ... **242**

R (Kind) v Secretary of State for the Home Department [2021] EWHC 710 (Admin); [2021] ACD 66 ... **244, 246**

R (Lancashire CC) v Secretary of State for the Environment, Food and Rural Affairs & another [2019] UKSC 58; [2021] AC 194 ... **243**

R (Lewis) v Redcar and Cleveland BC [2008] EWCA Civ 746; [2009] 1 WLR 83 ... **244**

R (Lumba) v Secretary of State for the Home Department [2011] UKSC 12; [2012] 1 AC 245 ... **243, 246**

R (Millgate Developments Ltd) v Wokingham Borough Council [2011] EWCA Civ 1062; [2012] 3 EGLR 87 ... **223**

R (Monkhill) v Secretary of State for Housing, Communities and Local Government and Waverley Borough Council [2021] EWCA Civ 74; [2021] JPL 1178 ... **199**

R (Mynydd Y Gwynt Ltd) v Secretary of State for Business, Energy and Industrial Strategy [2016] EWHC 2581 (Admin); [2017] Env LR 14 ... **129**

R (Mynydd Y Gwynt Ltd) v Secretary of State for Business, Energy and Industrial Strategy) [2018] EWCA Civ 231; [2018] WLR(D) 117 ... **129**

R (Nicklinson & another) v Ministry of Justice [2014] UKSC 38; [2015] AC 657 ... **242**

R (Patel) v General Medical Council [2013] EWCA Civ 327; [2013] 1 WLR 2801 ... **246**

R (Privacy International) v Investigatory Powers Tribunal [2019] UKSC 22; [2020] AC 491 ... **245**

R (Reprotech (Pebsham) Ltd) v East Sussex CC [2002] UKHL 8; [2003] 1 WLR 348 ... **246**

R (Rights: Community: Action) v Secretary of State for Housing, Communities and Local Government [2020] EWHC 3073 (Admin); [2021] JPL 843 ... **245**

R (Rights: Community: Action) v Secretary of State for Housing, Communities and Local Government [2021] EWCA Civ 1954; [2022] JPL 843 ... **28, 200**

R (Sainsbury's Supermarkets Ltd) v Wolverhampton City Council [2010] UKSC 20; [2011] 1 AC 437 ... **264**

R (Samuel Smith Old Brewery (Tadcaster)) v North Yorkshire CC [2020] UKSC 3; [2020] 3 All ER 527 ... **24**
R (SB (Ghana)) v SSHD [2020] EWHC 668 (Admin) ... **244**
R (Wandsworth) v Secretary of State for Transport [2005] EWHC (Admin) 20; [2006] 1 EGLR 91 ... **128**
R (John Watson) v London Borough of Richmond upon Thames LBC [2013] EWCA Civ 513 ... **129**
R (Wilbur Developments Ltd) v Hart DC [2020] EWHC 227 (Admin); [2020] PTSR 1379 ... **244**
R (Williams) v Powys County Council [2017] EWCA Civ 42; [2018] 1 WLR 439 ... **128**
R (Wright) v Resilient Energy Severndale Ltd and Forest of Dean District Council [2019] UKSC 53; [2019] 1 WLR 6562 ... **29, 30, 58, 243**
Re Ellenborough Park [1955] 3 WLR 91 (Ch) ... **254, 264**
Re Ellenborough Park [1956] Ch 131 (CA) ... **254, 263**
Regency Villas Title Ltd v Diamond Resorts (Europe) Ltd & Others [2018] UKSC 57; [2019] AC 553 ... **254–5, 264**
Rhone v Stephens [1994] UKHL 3; [1994] 2 AC 310 ... **263**
Ridge v Baldwin [1964] AC 40 (HL) ... **244**
Secretary of State for Communities and Local Government v Hopkins Development Ltd [2014] EWCA Civ 470; [2014] PTSR 1145 ... **244**
Secretary of State for the Home Department, ex parte Khan [2016] EWCA Civ 137; [2016] 4 WLR 56 ... **236, 245**
Secretary of State for Transport v Curzon Park and others [2021] EWCA Civ 651; [2022] JPL 22 ... **265**
Simplex GE (Holdings) Ltd v Secretary of State for the Environment [1988] 3 PTSR 1041 (CA) ... **243**
Singh v Secretary of State for the Home Department [2015] EWCA Civ 74 ... **245**
SM v Hackney [2021] EWHC 3294 (Admin) ... **82**
Smith v Castle Point BC [2020] EWCA Civ 1420; [2021] Env LR 20 ... **243**
Smith v East Elloe Rural District Council [1956] AC 736 (HL) ... **242**
South Buckinghamshire DC v Porter [2004] UKHL 33; [2004] WLR 1953
St Modwen Developments Ltd v Secretary of State for Communities and Local Government [2017] EWCA Civ 1643; [2018] PTSR 746
Steer v Secretary of State for Communities and Local Government & Ors [2017] EWHC 1456 (Admin); [2017] JPL 1281
Stringer v Minister of Housing and Local Government [1970] 1 WLR 1281 ... **29, 58, 129, 244**
Suffolk Coastal District Council v Hopkins Homes Ltd and another [2017] UKSC 37; [2017] WLR 1865

TABLE OF CASES   xxi

Tapling v Jones (1865) 11 HL Cas 290 ... **263**

Tesco Stores Ltd v Dundee City Council [2012] UKSC 13; [2012] PTSR 983 (HL) ... **24, 30, 244**

Tesco Stores Ltd v Secretary of State for the Environment [1995] 1 WLR 759 (HL) ... **29, 30, 129, 151, 240, 246**

Thamesmead Town Ltd v Allotey (2000) 79 P&CR 557 ... **263**

Thilakawardhana v Office for Independent Adjudicator for Higher Education [2018] EWCA Civ 13 ... **246**

Thorpe Hall Leisure Ltd v Secretary of State for Housing, Communities and Local Government [2020] EWHC 44 (Admin) ... **244**

Tithe Redemption Commission v Runcorn Urban District Council [1954] Ch 383 ... **81**

Transport for London v Spirerose Ltd [2009] UKHL 44; [2009] 1 WLR 1797 ... **265**

Trump International Golf Club Scotland Ltd v Scottish Ministers [2015] UKSC 74; [2016] 1 WLR 85 ... **244**

Tulk v Moxhay (1848) 2 Philips 774 ... **253, 263**

Tunbridge Wells Corp v Baird [1896] AC 434 ... **72, 81**

United Trade Action Group v Transport for London [2021] EWHC 72 ... **69, 81**

United Trade Action Group v Transport for London [2021] EWCA Civ 1197 ... **81**

Wainhomes (North-West) v Secretary of State for Housing, Communities and Local Government [2020] EWHC 2294 (Admin) ... **246**

Walton v Scottish Minister [2012] UKSC 44; [2013] PTSR 51 ... **243**

Waters v Welsh Development Agency [2004] UKHL 19; [2004] 1 WLR 1304 ... **265**

Westminster City Council v Great Portland Estates [1985] AC 661(HL) ... **29, 129**

European Court of Human Rights

Bryan v UK (1995) 21 EHRR 342 ... **246**
James v UK [1986] ECHR 2; (1986) 8 EHRR 123 ... **256**

United States Cases

People v Harriet New York Judicial Repository 265-66 (1819) ... **82**

List of contributors

Carolyn Abbot is Professor of Environmental Law at the University of Manchester and Co-Director of the Manchester Centre for Regulation, Governance and Public Law. Carolyn's research centres broadly on environmental regulation. Her focus, in recent years, has been on the role of non-state actors in shaping environmental regulation and decision-making. Most recently, she has considered how environmental groups use legal expertise to influence decision-making, with a particular emphasis on legal mobilisation outside the courtroom. She is currently turning her attention to the role of legal expertise in the context of planning law.

Chiara Armeni is Associate Professor at Université Libre de Bruxelles (ULB), where she holds the Chair of Environmental Law at the Faculty of Law and Criminology. She is interested in the legal aspects of environmental protection, planning and climate change governance. Her research focuses on the role of law and public participation in environmental decision-making. Chiara holds a PhD in Law from UCL. Before joining ULB, Chiara was Lecturer in Environmental and EU law at University of Sussex, School of Law, Politics and Sociology (2016–20) and Research Associate at University College London, Faculty of Laws (2009–16).

Joanna Bell is Associate Professor and Jeffrey Hackney Tutorial Fellow in Law at St Edmund Hall, University of Oxford. She specialises in English and Welsh administrative law, especially judicial review, and related legal fields including planning, environmental and constitutional law. Her published works include *The Anatomy of Administrative Law* (Hart 2020) and various articles published in leading academic journals. She is part of the authorial team which updates the leading practitioner textbook *De Smith's Judicial Review*. Her publications have been cited on multiple occasions in the UK Supreme Court.

Kim Bouwer is Assistant Professor in Tort Law at Durham Law School. She holds a PhD from UCL and has held a number of academic and professional posts globally, including at the University of the Witwatersrand (Johannesburg), UCL (London and Adelaide) and the EUI (Florence). Kim's research falls within the broad sphere of environmental law, where she focuses mainly on litigation in the context of climate change. In her work, she examines the structures of private law, questioning in particular the role property interests play in shaping the law.

Rachel Gimson is Lecturer in Law at the University of Exeter. Prior to starting at Exeter she was a Lecturer in Law at the Mauritius branch of the University of Aberystwyth. She completed her PhD at the University of Sussex. Her specialism is trial by social media and perceptions of justice in the digital age. As a result of teaching land law for a number of years, she is increasingly interested in theories of land law and how private and public property rights develop and intersect.

Brad Jessup is Senior Lecturer at Melbourne Law School at the University of Melbourne. He is a former planning and environment lawyer who worked on planning matters from local to transjurisdictional scales. His teaching includes environmental law and law and sexualities and involves supervising students tackling planning matters for emergent businesses in the green economy. Brad's research focuses on local environmental and planning conflicts, adopting legal geography approaches and exploring them through concepts of environmental justice, notions of sustainability and ideas of community.

Antonia Layard is Professor of Law at the University of Oxford and Tutorial Fellow in Law at St Anne's College. Antonia's research interests are in law and geography where she explores how law, legality and maps construct space, place and 'the local'. She has particular interests in 'urban law' as well as the legal provisions and practices involved in highways, mobilities and buses.

Maria Lee has been Professor of Law at University College London since 2007, and was director and co-director of UCL's Centre for Law and the Environment for over a decade. Maria's research interests lie in the ways we make decisions on environmental matters, including in areas of high technological complexity and controversy. She concentrates on the governance of decision-making, examining the ways in which law implicates issues like the use of expertise and public participation. In recent years, she has been particularly interested in the ways these issues play out in planning law.

Edward Mitchell is Lecturer in the School of Law at the University of Essex. His recent research includes an empirical examination of the contractual arrangements between local authorities and private sector property developers that often underpin the compulsory purchase and redistribution of private land. His other recent work has examined financial viability modelling and legal processes in the context of local authority decision-making related to property development on large urban sites. Edward is also presently working on a project looking at the use of technology enhanced learning in legal education.

Margherita Pieraccini is Professor of Law at the University of Bristol, UK. She is a socio-legal scholar specialising in environmental matters. In particular, her current research interests include marine conservation law and governance, the commons and sustainability. She has published on legal pluralism, nature conservation, common pool resources governance, sustainability and marine governance. Her books include *Contested Common Land: Environmental Governance Past and Present* (with Rodgers, Straughton and Winchester, Earthscan 2011), and *Legal Perspectives on Sustainability* (co-edited with Novitz, University of Bristol Press 2020). She has recently completed a monograph, *Regulating the Sea: A Socio-Legal Analysis of English Marine Protected Areas* (Cambridge University Press, forthcoming).

Elen Stokes is Professor of Law at Cardiff Law School. Her primary areas of interest are environmental law and policy, with particular points of focus on the regulation of new technologies, and the relationship between law and the future. Her recent work draws on interdisciplinary futures research to understand the various roles of law in mediating, enacting and regularising conceptions of the future that achieve powerful effects in the present. Elen is a co-founder of Cardiff University's Centre of Environmental Law and Politics.

Steven Vaughan is Professor of Law and Professional Ethics at the Faculty of Laws, University College London, and former Co-Director of the UCL Centre for Law and the Environment and of qUCL (UCL's queer research network). Interested in regulation and governance broadly framed, Steven's scholarship covers two primary fields: environmental law; and lawyers' ethics. Keen that his work engages with an audience beyond the academy, Steven has spoken at the Hay Festival of Literature and Arts, regularly blogs, and has written for a number of media outlets (including *The Times, The Guardian* and *The Lawyer*).

Acknowledgements

We are very grateful to all our contributors, and we have both learned a great deal from new friends and old. This group of legal scholars has been extremely generous with their time and energy, making the whole experience genuinely enjoyable and collaborative.

For most of us, presenting our draft chapters at our workshop in September 2021 was our first big trip out after lockdown – it could not have been a better reintroduction to academic life, and indeed the world. The generous and rigorous feedback on each paper was enormously valuable. We took an editorial decision that none of us would thank each other in our chapters – but the gratitude is real and expressed here.

Beyond the authors, we are grateful to Professor Jane Holder, Dr Lucy Natarajan and Professor Yvonne Rydin for their support of this project. For all that we discuss a neglect of planning law scholarship in this volume, we were lucky to be able to count on the expertise of this established UCL community of planning scholars.

We would also like to thank the SLS Small Projects and Events Fund for supporting our workshop; Cat Balogun, Lisa Penfold and Tatjana Wingender at UCL and Val Lenferna at Manchester for their help with the workshop and management of this project; and Mia Morris for her help with referencing and bibliographies. We are grateful to all at UCL Press for their hard work, and for the privilege of being able to publish open access.

And, last but not least, we want to thank each other. As ever, working together has been a joyful and intellectually rewarding experience. What next?!

Maria Lee and Carolyn Abbot
London and Manchester

List of abbreviations

A1P1	Article 1, Protocol 1 European Convention on Human Rights
AJR	Application for Judicial Review
ANPR	Automatic Number Plate Recognition
AONB	Area of Outstanding Natural Beauty
BLUF	Breeches and Leather Uniform Fanclub
BOAT	Byways Open to All Traffic
CA	Combined Authority
CAAD	Certificate of Appropriate Alternative Development
CBD	Convention on Biological Diversity
CIL	Community Infrastructure Levy
CPRE	The Countryside Charity
DBEIS	Department for Business, Energy and Industrial Strategy
DCLG	Department for Communities and Local Government
DCO	Development Consent Order
DDC	Dover District Council
DECC	Department for Energy and Climate Change
Defra	Department for Environment, Food and Rural Affairs
DfT	Department for Transport
DLUHC	Department for Levelling Up, Housing and Communities
DMPO	Town and Country Planning (Development Management Procedure) (England) Order
DVLA	Driver and Vehicle Licensing Agency
ECHR	European Convention on Human Rights
ECtHR	European Court of Human Rights
EN-1	Overarching National Policy Statement for Energy (NPS EN-1)
ETO	Experimental Traffic Order
ExA	Examining Authority
GDPO	Town and Country Planning (General Development Procedure) (England) Order 1995
GLA	Greater London Authority
GPDO	Town and Country Planning (General Permitted Development) Order 2015
HEART	Hulton Estate Area Residents Together
IP	Interested Party
LBCA Act	Planning (Listed Buildings and Conservation Areas) Act 1990

LGBTQIA+	Lesbian, gay, bisexual, transgender, queer/questioning, intersex, asexual and others
LCA	Land Compensation Act
LIR	Local Impact Report
LPA	Local Planning Authority
LTN	Low Traffic Neighbourhood
MBC	Metropolitan Borough Council
MCA Act	Marine and Coastal Access Act
MHCLG	Ministry of Housing, Communities and Local Government
MMO	Marine Management Organisation
MPS	Marine Policy Statement
NGO	Non-Governmental Organisation
NP	National Park
NPPF	National Planning Policy Framework
NPS	National Policy Statement
NSIP	Nationally Significant Infrastructure Project
ODPM	Office of the Deputy Prime Minister
OUV	Outstanding Universal Value
PCPA	Planning and Compulsory Purchase Act 2004
PINS	Planning Inspectorate
PPG	Planning Practice Guidance
RPG	Registered Park and Garden
RTRA	Road Traffic Regulation Act 1984
RVT	Royal Vauxhall Tavern
SDGs	Sustainable Development Goals
SI	Statutory Instrument
SLVI	Seascape, Landscape, and Visual Impact
SOCC	Statement of Community Consultation
TCPA	Town and Country Planning Act
TfL	Transport for London
UK	United Kingdom
UN	United Nations
UNECE	United Nations Economic Commission for Europe
VED	Vehicle Excise Duty
WHS	World Heritage Site

Executive summaries

Part One: Introduction

Chapter 1 The Importance of Taking English Planning Law Scholarship Seriously

This chapter explores the genesis and development of this volume, which lies largely in the relative neglect of planning by legal scholars. Planning is central to the response to many of the significant challenges of our time (from the climate and environmental crises to social and economic inequalities); and planning law raises some of the most fundamental questions faced by legal scholars (from the legitimacy of authority to the relationship between public and private rights and interests). This book aims to contribute to stimulating conversations about planning law, and to create a space for planning law scholarship in all its variety, and for curiosity about law in all its complexity.

Chapter 2 English Planning Law: An Outline

This introductory chapter outlines English planning law, focusing on the Local Planning Authority (LPA) system of developing plans and dealing with applications for planning permission. It would be impossible to do justice to the complexity and detail of planning law (and we might even wonder whether there is such 'a' single thing as 'planning law'); the aim is to ease progress through the rest of the book (for authors and readers), and to provide just a hint of the fascination of planning law. The outline incorporates a discussion of four things: the identity of the ubiquitous but underexplored figure of the LPA; decision-making on applications for planning permission; the making and role of development plans; and the relationship between policy and law. This chapter concludes with a brief overview of current and uncertain plans for reform, suggesting that planning law may be as difficult to reform as it is to summarise.

Part Two: Place Shaping, Place Framing

Chapter 3 Backstreet's Back Alright: London's LGBT+ Nightlife Spaces and a Queering of Planning Law and Planning Practices

Spaces, typically out of view and often architecturally modest, have long been valued by queer folk, and the construction by and dependence of queers on space has been the subject of much research. Yet the role of planning law in the production and maintenance of queer spaces remains underexplored. This chapter part-fills that gap and analyses the legal and political happenings of three London queer spaces in 2019: (i) XXL (a men-only, 1,500 capacity gay club near London Bridge which closed in September 2019 because of a £1.3bn apartment, hotel and office development); (ii) The Royal Vauxhall Tavern (a queer pub in Vauxhall whose supporters have generated what they label a 'quadruple lock' against redevelopment, including Grade II listing and the designation of the space as an Asset of Community Value); and (iii) Backstreet (a small fetish (leather and rubber) club in London's East End which was 'saved' by Tower Hamlets Development Committee from redevelopment). The authors argue that the ways in which these spaces have intersected with planning law demonstrate the heteronormativity and queer invisibility of planning laws and an ignorance of the connection between place and sexualities, even when LGBT+ people are identified as being present in those places. The authors' energising premise is that planning law and practices should recognise queer spaces and consider queerness as deserving of protection in relation to space and location. What their work shows is that the architecture of planning law and current planning practices creates a structure and opportunities for both possibilities and non-possibilities for negotiating and protecting queer spaces.

Chapter 4 The Highway: A Right, A Place or A Resource?

Highways can be understood as a right to passage, a place or, as this chapter suggests, as a resource to be allocated and governed. Using the example of Low Traffic Neighbourhoods (LTNs), the chapter suggests that while both the right to passage and place are relevant to legal formulations, neither fully explain how highways operate. While highways are often framed as a right to passage, these universal rights cannot exist in isolation. They require the allocation and governance of roadspace so that some forms of passage, notably by motor vehicles, do not dominate.

Drawing on the concepts of spatial imaginaries and spatial particularism, the chapter next explains how highways have become a regulatory category of place, predicated on an often quite particular spatial imaginary of vehicular mobility and flow. Such spatial assumptions are open to challenge, particularly by local residents in LTNs who prefer 'their' streets to be available for walking and cycling as well as play and connection. While understanding the highway as a place matters, LTNs illustrate how allocation and governance decisions are required to determine how different highways operate.

Highways are, the chapter suggests, best understood as a resource, incorporating a universal right to passage as well as place-thinking. Drawing on Maria Lee's concept of a 'prior institutional knowledge claim', the chapter explains how an understanding of what a highway 'is' underpins institutional knowledge of how to govern the highway. Framing a highway as a 'right', a 'place' or even property blurs regulatory understanding, inhibiting governance based on the 'prior institutional knowledge claim'. Improving our understanding of what highways are will improve governance, even if, as we all know, sharing is hard.

Chapter 5 Marine Planning for Sustainability: The Role of the Ecosystem Approach

Sustainable development is at the core of planning law. However, sustainable development is a ubiquitous concept, with multiple definitions which lead to different planning outcomes. Narrowly understood, sustainable development consists in a trade-off between separate spheres (economy, environment, society). Understood more widely, sustainable development is a process of integration and openness to plural views and values. When sustainable development is conceptualised narrowly, the risk is that environmental and economic considerations are subject to a cost-benefit analysis which may lead to planning for growth. Which of these two visions of sustainable development is present in marine spatial planning? Marine spatial planning has emerged around the world as a key process for addressing sustainability challenges, following an ecosystem-based approach. The ecosystem approach, as defined in international law, points to holistic and integrated management of interconnected social-ecological systems and emphasises procedural inclusiveness too. Hence, it has the potential to foster a wide understanding of sustainability. The extent to which this is reflected in domestic settings is considered in this chapter. Focusing on English marine spatial planning, the chapter discusses how the ecosystem approach has been conceptualised in selected marine planning documents and what vision of sustainable marine planning it contributes to. The conclusion is that the ecosystem approach, as defined in English marine policy documents, falls short of contributing to a wide vision of sustainability because it is either defined narrowly on environmental terms only and divorced from social considerations, or because it is linked to economic issues and a growth-oriented planning agenda.

Part Three: Participation

Chapter 6 Place, Participation and Planning Law in a Time of Climate Change

A place is a complex frame through which we understand the world. Climate change is progressively transforming familiar places not only by affecting their morphological and ecosystem characteristics, but also through the siting of new energy infrastructure. The way in which infrastructure development 'fits' with people's experience of places is at the centre of a rich academic enquiry, but is relatively underexplored by legal scholars. Yet law is important as places are 'made' and transformed – although not exclusively – through legal and regulatory processes and the normative choices underpinning them. Lay public concern over experience of places is regularly reflected in the public participation process on planning consent.

This chapter aims to put place experience on the legal agenda. First, it locates place experience in the academic literature and explains why it is important for planning decisions. Secondly, it looks at how place experience is dealt with in the consenting of offshore wind energy Nationally Significant Infrastructure Projects in England, illustrating the example of the examination of the Navitus Bay proposal. In that context, place experience claims were received by the regulatory process, but their recognition as a basis for the decision was limited by a comfortable reliance on technical assessment and a strong policy commitment to climate mitigation. Thirdly, the chapter contends that, although handling experience is difficult for decision-makers, planning law does not represent a necessary barrier to it. The author suggests that a broader interpretation of the notion of material considerations could help decision-makers to be more confident in recognising place-based arguments as a legitimate basis for a planning consent decision, even in the urgency of the climate crisis.

Chapter 7 Planning Inquiries and Legal Expertise: A Fair Crack of the Whip?

The merits of public participation in planning are well-rehearsed. All planning applications must be advertised and members of the public can submit their views to the local planning authority. These views must be taken into account in determining individual planning applications. More extensive opportunities are provided where, for example, applications are determined by planning inquiries. And yet, despite multiple attempts to ensure meaningful participation, there remain significant challenges around the extent to which these mechanisms are effective in ensuring that the local voice is heard. This chapter focuses on one particular challenge for local groups, namely the legal complexity of the planning framework, both in terms of substance and process.

It argues that legal experts, in their role as knowledge providers, skilled advocates and legal practitioners, can help local community groups represent their interests on a more equal footing with others. With a particular focus on planning inquiries, the chapter investigates what legal experts *do* using an example of a recently called-in planning application in Bolton, in the Northwest of England. Peel Holdings, the Northwest's largest private landowner, submitted a planning application to build a championship golf course and over 1,000 residential houses on green belt land and in Hulton Park, a Registered Park and Garden. Through an analysis of written documents associated with the planning inquiry, the chapter shines a light on how access to legal expertise helped Hulton Estate Area Residents Together (HEART), a local group formed to oppose the application, get a 'fair crack of the whip'.

Part Four: Time and Scale

Chapter 8 Futurescapes of Planning Law: Some Preliminary Thoughts on A Timely Encounter

The concept of the future has been studied in many different disciplines but has not received the same detailed attention in legal scholarship. This is especially curious in a field like planning law, which has a strong and obvious future-orientation. The author's aim in this chapter is to make a case for treating planning law more seriously as an important site of future-making, and to encourage more systematic thinking about the role of law in determining how the future is engaged in the present. One way of achieving this is by introducing a 'futurescapes' perspective to legal analysis, to capture the different temporal features of law that shape how the future comes to be understood, legitimated and acted upon. Forging those links helps to address the future not as a backdrop to law but as a key means through which law operates. The discussion illustrates the kinds of questions that might usefully be asked about how law never simply represents the future but actively produces the futures it then seeks to govern.

Chapter 9 Slippery Scales in Planning for Housing

Housing is an extraordinarily complex social and legal challenge, which is frequently at the centre of planning and planning reform. It has also been at the heart of contests over the appropriate scale of planning, including scale-shifting 'regionalism' and 'localism', and the fluctuating and contested relationship between local and central government. As well as the complexity and dynamism of scale, housing illustrates both instrumental uses of scale to find 'right' answers, and the limitations of such approaches. This chapter explores scale in the law of planning for housing, and the slipperiness of the authority allocated through both casual and self-conscious legal and institutional scaling and re-scaling. Neither central nor local is innately better qualified to deliver either inclusive or socially and environmentally progressive outcomes. But housing highlights the need for opportunities to contest determinations of development need, and many of those opportunities are found in local planning. If planning is a space not just for implementing a pre-defined vision of the public interest, but also for working out that public interest, a powerful (but not all-powerful) local is important.

Part Five: Planning at the Intersections

Chapter 10 Contracting Affordable Housing Delivery? Residential Property Development, Section 106 Agreements and Other Contractual Arrangements

Recent town planning and legal scholarship has considered controversies surrounding the provision of 'affordable housing' for people who would otherwise be unable to access homes of an acceptable standard via the private housing market. The current practice in England is to seek to secure the construction of affordable housing through 'planning obligations' made by agreement between property developers and local planning authorities pursuant to section 106 of the Town and Country Planning Act 1990. However, there has been relatively little attention afforded to either the key contract terms in these section 106 agreements or the way these contracts work in practice. This chapter examines the interlinked section 106 agreements created for affordable housing delivery for three residential development projects. These projects are unremarkable developments that happen all the time, everywhere in England. However, the section 106 agreements made for these developments are highly formal and highly technical contractual documents. The chapter draws upon Ian Macneil's relational contract theory to consider why local planning authorities and property developers create such formal and detailed contractual arrangements. The chapter thus provides an empirical analysis of key contract terms and underlying contractual behaviour and shows how well-connected developers can use these contractual arrangements to create a type of 'one-sided flexibility' that enables them to choose when, where and how they fulfil their obligations to deliver affordable housing. Consequently, the author offers new perspectives on the nature of opportunism and the pursuit of control in the contracts used for town planning processes.

Chapter 11 Embracing the Unwanted Guests at the Judicial Review Party: Why Administrative Law Scholars Should Take Planning Law Seriously

This edited collection draws attention to the neglect of planning law by legal scholars. Despite the large degree of practical overlap between the two fields, administrative law scholars have generally been as guilty of neglecting planning law as others. This chapter identifies three reasons why administrative law scholars would benefit from engaging more deeply with planning law case law. First, the planning regime is one of the most established, developed and commonly litigated areas of administration in England and Wales. Courts have had ample opportunity to develop judicial review doctrine in this field. Planning case law therefore offers a useful case study, revealing valuable insights into what highly developed judicial review doctrine looks like. Secondly, planning law judicial reviews are not peculiar. Many of the features of planning case law which perhaps deter closer intellectual engagement are widespread features of much administrative law adjudication. Scholars must take these characteristics seriously and factor them into their understanding of judicial review. Thirdly, planning judicial reviews are a proven source of broader judicial review principle. It continues to be important to look to planning judicial reviews for potential legal developments which may have application in other areas. The chapter concludes with a more general call to administrative law scholars to more warmly embrace the 'vertical' as well as the 'horizontal' dimensions of judicial review.

Chapter 12 Provoking McAuslan: Planning Law and Property Rights

The law governing land and property relations has traditionally been classified as 'private', being concerned with rights and priority interests in estates in land as fundamentally constitutive of private property relations. In contrast, administrative regimes, such as those involving planning and environmental issues, are typically defined as 'public'. These public regimes are commonly seen as presenting an incursion on private rights, rather than as being part of an intertwined and complementary body of property law principles. Indeed, seminal work by McAuslan suggests that public and private ideologies in the planning regime are fundamentally opposed.

The authors interrogate his thesis from two directions. They suggest that a strictly private approach to property law does not take account of the implicit recognition of the social usefulness of land that runs through the cases. They highlight a number of ways in which the public interest is embedded in land law. Second, they focus on one area of the planning regime – compulsory purchase and compensation – and question the extent to which the way this operates now can be said to be in the public interest. While they do not dispute McAuslan's thesis entirely, the authors argue that the public and private aspects of property governance are more entangled – and, at times, more complementary – than he suggests.

Part I
Introduction

1
The importance of taking English planning law scholarship seriously

Maria Lee[*]

Planning ('development', 'land use', 'town and country' planning[1]) is at the heart of the response to many of the significant challenges of our time, from the climate and environmental crises to social and economic inequalities. It is embedded in, as well as partially constituting, our democratic systems, so that the challenges of democratic decision-making in a complex society cannot be avoided when thinking about planning. Planning *law* raises some of the most fundamental questions faced by legal scholars, from the legitimacy of authority to the relationship between public and private rights and interests. And yet, planning has been relatively neglected by legal scholars in recent decades.

Law matters in planning. The vastness of the legislation and case law is stunning, and frames every part of planning. Policy (by contrast with law) is strong and impactful, and there may be substantial questions around the relative strength of law; but that occasional thinness of law in the face of power, politics and policy may be significant in itself. Despite the relative absence of legal academics in the field, there is no shortage of planning law literature: as well as the patchwork of legal scholarship, planning scholars from other disciplines often have a sophisticated appreciation of law; and a densely legal planning literature is produced by and for practitioners. Legal scholarship also matters in planning, as will be demonstrated throughout the following chapters.

This introductory chapter explores the genesis and development of this volume, which lies largely in the sense that the academic community has something to offer planning law – and, vice versa, that planning law has something to offer legal scholarship. I will not outline the content of the individual chapters, summaries of which can be found at the beginning of this volume, but I will refer to the chapters.

Although many legal scholars have done important work, the picture is partial and fragmented. The reasons for the relative neglect of planning by legal scholars are undoubtedly complex. The twin difficulties of dense detail and constant change are pursued throughout this volume, especially in the next introductory chapter. They may simply make planning law seem off-putting, dreary. But as Elen Stokes puts it in her chapter, when scholars take planning law seriously, we resist the notion that the technicalities of planning law are subjects suitable only for practice and not theory. She cites Anneliese Riles, who distinguishes between 'cultural' and 'instrumental' approaches to law (overlapping in many cases), law as the 'repository of social meanings', or law as a means to a stated end.[2] Planning law is not *just* a means to an end.

This volume implies an assumption that legal academics have something to add to the vast, sophisticated literatures by and for planning law practitioners and by planning scholars from other disciplines. Whilst planning scholars do not need lessons on planning law, there are glimpses in their literature of an understandable neglect of the significance and implications of legal frameworks. For example, limited initial appreciation of the significance of Brexit for planning may suggest a lack of interest in the origin (and hence bindingness and stickiness) of planning law. Even exceptional scholarship can reinforce this sense of neglect. For example, the insight that certain interests dominate planning, sidelining other issues of greater local concern, is crucial,[3] but the role played by legal frameworks in determining what matters is under-explored. A discussion of planning practice refers to the 'framework of legislation that is constantly changing', and reaches the slightly alarming conclusion that 'planning education necessarily shies away from arming its students with knowledge that is likely to be out of date once they graduate'.[4] This is a strong hint of a narrow view of law, uninterested (perhaps understandably) in broader and more sustained legal values and legal approaches.

The often-erudite legal practitioner literature is generally focused on problem-solving, be that using law as a tool to solve problems of the built environment, or solving internal legal questions, for example of interpretation or consistency. This is a valuable exercise. But it will rarely capture broader perspectives, as Martin Loughlin put it, of 'law as a fluid, reflexive phenomenon with its peculiar traditions, values and tensions'.[5] Further, what interests practitioners is likely to be shaped at least in part by their work, and hence by the interests of their clients. Although much of the planning bar works for a variety of actors (central and local government, affected communities, NGOs), the developer interest is strong. This is not to suggest bias, or a lack of concern for the public interest. It is simply to observe that, however 'objective' the legal analysis, our 'conceptual frameworks', our way of understanding the world, shape our approach.[6]

Planning law scholarship would be much the poorer without practitioners and without legal analysis by 'non-legal' scholars; but it is also poorer without legal scholars. A sustained focus, uninterrupted by the latest legal development or client, and a holistic appreciation of broader legal and institutional frameworks, should be a feature of good legal scholarship.[7]

A practitioner orientation is likely to be instrumentalist in Riles' terms, law seen predominantly as a tool or instrument for manipulating the world; similarly for non-legal scholars, law is an instrument in their own scholarly or policy endeavour.[8] Although legal values that seem to 'get in the way' must be acknowledged and valued for what they are, as must 'the complexity of law and what it is doing',[9] asking the instrumental questions – how a legal framework contributes positively to good, democratic place-making, environmental enhancement, spatial justice, climate mitigation – is a perfectly legitimate scholarly (as well as policy) endeavour. And when law is used as an instrument by those who seek to deploy it through legislation, policy or courts, it is right to scrutinise that. But planning law does have deeper roots than this.

Law creates process and substantive obligations,[10] and it is often impossible to separate the two. Its normative and substantive input is generated in part by substantive standards for decisions, including by using the frameworks of planning law (especially the requirement to seek planning permission) to implement legal obligations found elsewhere, for example on habitat protection or air quality.[11] The bulk of planning law, of legislative provisions and case law, is about process. And yet, planning law is more than 'just a scaffolding to support a process'.[12] When planning law tells decision-makers where and how to look and listen, legally defined institutional arrangements enable and constrain the availability and use of particular decision-making resources. Law directly and indirectly prioritises who, and which interests and values, are most likely to be heard and able to influence decisions, and how.

However significant the power, the politics and the policy around planning, however considerable the discretion of central and local government, it is not a free-for-all. Law provides substantive frameworks and limits on action, as planning and its objects are brought into the broader legal order.[13] Law is supportive of, but also frames and goes beyond, 'planning judgment'. Law shapes, although rarely determines, outcomes.

One of the impacts of a lack of planning law scholarship is the absence of much discussion of how we understand planning (law) as a scholarly community. What planning is has become highly politicised and ideological. We disagree about planning law because we disagree about the role of the state and the market, about where politics and democracy should happen (and how), about what equality means and demands, about the pace and method of environmental improvement. When we talk about planning law, we talk about all of these things, and more.

Descriptively, planning shapes the nature and location of infrastructure, from wind energy to waste facilities, the need for and manner of transport, the energy efficiency and flood exposure and resilience of homes. It shapes the presence and accessibility of high-quality green and blue space and built environment, the accessibility of food, education, work, recreation and health and healthcare. In fact, planning is 'concerned with everything that makes a successful place', in a physical and a social sense.[14] Planning, or its failure, is broad and all embracing. A major review (the Raynsford Review) commissioned by the Town and Country Planning Association refers to the 'vilification of the planning process in mainstream political discourse' and the fragmentation of 'broader civil society consensus around the need for planning'.[15] These comments are compelling, and meaningful as we try to make sense of law and law reform. Waves of planning reform have purported to 'fix' the system, 'on the grounds that it is a chronic obstacle to growth'.[16] The Government's 2020 White Paper *Planning for the Future* describes a supposedly 'outdated and ineffective' system,[17] which government blames squarely for 'long-term and persisting undersupply of housing'.[18] These decades of criticism and reform leave us with a widely shared 'vision in which planning choreographs development rather than representing genuine regulatory control';[19] let alone representing any striving for democratic consideration of place-based public interest.

Planning for the Future does see a positive purpose for planning, which is 'central to our most important national challenges', from 'combating climate change' to 'rebalancing our economy';[20] the market alone is not enough. Even a much-loved planning system could take many forms, however, and a regime for the choreography of development surely dominates.

As editors, Carolyn and I have not tried to impose a single vision of planning law, of scholarship, or of planning law scholarship on this volume. We have organised the chapters loosely around four substantive parts (Place Shaping, Place Framing; Participation; Time and Scale; Planning at the Intersections), reflecting simply a combination of our own interests, the interests of our contributors, and so we believe also some of the key concerns of the academy in this area. There are gaps, most obviously in terms of many of the elements of planning – particular processes or tools – but not least around race and gender.[21] We have deliberately limited our contributors to legal scholars, notwithstanding the value of cross-disciplinary work and of engagement with practitioners. And we are focusing only on English law; planning is a devolved matter, and so the other countries of the United Kingdom have different legal arrangements. The authors cover a range of issues from diverse perspectives, take diverse approaches and rely on excitingly diverse literatures. We hope that this is the starting point, and the gaps will turn out to be opportunities.

Our methodologies and perspectives in this collection are not uniform: we used doctrinal, theoretical, contextual approaches. All of the work is basically desk-based, perhaps due to the time and space constraints of an edited collection. Some chapters (Joanna Bell, Kim Bouwer and Rachel Grimson) discuss planning in the round; many focus on particular objects of planning, from energy (Chiara Armeni, Stokes) to highways (Antonia Layard). Some of the chapters (especially Bell) carefully analyse a range of case law, including the lower-level decisions that tell us a lot about what animates planning law. The case study features heavily (especially Carolyn Abbot, Edward Mitchell, Margherita Pieraccini and Steven Vaughan and Brad Jessup), as does the use of a heavily worked example or illustration to find insight (for example Layard and Maria Lee). And although desk-based, many of the chapters rely heavily on detailed empirical exploration of dozens of planning documents: not just cases, legislation and local and central policy, but also planning applications, environmental statements, consultation responses, developers' promotional materials, clauses in contracts, officers' reports, decisions; all read with an eye on the legal framework within which these documents perform their roles. This methodology is laborious, but ultimately rewarding. Coupled with the case law and legislation, it provides considerable insight into the meanings and impacts of law in all its detailed technicalities. As is perhaps intimated by the reference to examples and illustrations, as well as case studies, our methodologies are very open. Methodology should not be a constraint on our imagination. Methodological clarity allows us to see what a scholar is doing and why, and consider how it affects our work.

The group of contributors to this volume came together around the time of England's third lockdown, January 2021. Perhaps presumptuously, Carolyn and I wondered whether our feelings of isolation and distraction might be shared, and invited the contributors to four interim (voluntary) zoom get-togethers. Professor Yvonne Rydin very generously joined us for one of these meetings to talk about the Raynsford Review, of which she was a member. In the other meetings we discussed the early plans for each of our chapters, a very early and partial draft of this chapter and the next, and the 2020 White Paper. These meetings may have been one of the few benefits of lockdown. We learned a great deal, and began our chapters even before we were quite putting pen to paper. We also began to get to know each other, and came to our in-person workshop at UCL in September 2021 having already built a certain amount of trust for this collaborative exercise. This workshop was mainly limited to contributors, but Dr Lucy Natarajan generously gave her time to chair part of it. At this workshop, drafts of each chapter were commented on by another contributor, with lively and useful discussions of each paper among the whole group.

Liz Fisher's insistence that 'there is a need for scholars in . . . planning law to take law more seriously' is powerful,[22] notwithstanding the relentless focus on legal detail in the practitioner-focused literature and the strong history and brilliant individuals working in planning law scholarship. We would like this book to contribute to stimulating conversations about planning law, and to create a space for planning law scholarship in all its variety, and for curiosity about law in all its complexity.

Notes

* I am grateful to Jane Holder and UCL Press's anonymous reviewer for comments on this chapter. Note that we have taken an editorial decision that none of our chapters will thank either editors or other contributors – we take the collaboration as read.
1. For current purposes these terms can be used interchangeably.
2. Riles 2005, 973.
3. In a wonderful project, Aitken et al 2008 attribute the dominance of 'ornithology' to campaign groups deeming it to be 'less subjective' than other issues, with only incidental reference to law.
4. Tomaney and Ferm 2018, 3, again in a wonderful collection.
5. Loughlin 1986, 31.
6. Rubin 1993, 749.
7. Aagaard 2018 discusses the role of legal scholarship in environmental law.
8. For Riles 2005, consistently with science and technology studies, tools have their own agency, and 'changes in seemingly mundane tools can lead to fundamental epistemological shifts' (986), so that examining the tools of law does more than it seems.
9. Fisher 2018.
10. Lee et al 2018; Fisher 2018; McAuslan 1980.
11. Fisher, Lange and Scotford 2018.
12. Booth 2007, 143.
13. Also Fisher 2018.
14. Town and Country Planning Association 2018, 12; Rydin 2011.
15. Town and Country Planning Association 2018, 23.

16. Lord and Tewdwr-Jones 2014, 346.
17. Ministry of Housing, Communities and Local Government (MHCLG) 2020, 6.
18. MHCLG 2020, 13; the simplification of the housing crisis is discussed in Lee's chapter below.
19. Lord and Tewdwr-Jones 2014, 349.
20. MHCLG 2020, 10.
21. Colomb and Raco 2018 review the literature on ethnicity and diversity in planning theory; see Beebeejaun 2016 on gender in planning theory and practice.
22. Fisher 2018. We had not knowingly borrowed our initial title from Liz's great paper (or indeed self-consciously from Dworkin), but it presumably resonated with us for a reason.

References

Aagaard, Todd S. (2018). 'What Legal Scholarship Can Contribute to Environmental Law'. In *Perspectives on Environmental Scholarship: Essays on Purpose, Shape and Direction*, edited by Ole W. Pedersen, 10–25. Cambridge: Cambridge University Press.

Aitken, Mhairi, Seonaidh McDonald and Peter Strachan (2008). 'Locating "Power" in Wind Power Planning Processes: The (Not So) Influential Role of Local Objectors', *Journal of Environmental Planning and Management* 51: 777–99.

Beebeejaun, Yasminah (2017). 'Gender, Urban Space, and the Right to Everyday Life', *Journal of Urban Affairs* 2: 323–34.

Booth, Philip (2007). 'The Control of Discretion: Planning and the Common Law', *Planning Theory* 6: 127–45.

Colomb, Claire and Mike Raco (2018). 'Planning for Diversity in an Era of Social Change'. In *Planning Practice: Critical Perspectives from the UK*, edited by Jessica Ferm and John Tomaney, 174–88. Abingdon: Routledge.

Fisher, Elizabeth (2018). 'Law and Energy Transitions: Wind Turbines and Planning Law in the UK', *Oxford Journal of Legal Studies* 38: 528–56.

Fisher, Elizabeth et al (2018). *Environmental Law: Text, Cases, and Materials*. Oxford: Oxford University Press.

Lee, Maria et al (2018). 'Techniques of Knowing in Administration: Co-production, Models, and Conservation Law', *Journal of Law and Society* 45: 427–56.

Lord, Alex and Mark Tewdwr-Jones (2014). 'Is Planning "Under Attack"? Chronicling the Deregulation of Urban and Environmental Planning in England', *European Planning Studies* 22: 345–61.

Loughlin, Martin. 'Planning Law Textbooks Through the Texts Darkly' (1986), *Planning Practice and Research* 1: 31–3.

McAuslan, Patrick (1980). *Ideologies of Planning Law*. Oxford: Pergamon Press.

Ministry of Housing, Communities and Local Government (2020). *White Paper: Planning for the Future*.

Riles, Anneliese (2005). 'A New Agenda for the Cultural Study of Law: Taking on the Technicalities', *Buffalo Law Review* 53: 973–1033.

Rubin, Edward L (1993). 'Thinking Like a Lawyer, Acting like a Lobbyist: Some Notes on the Process of Revising UCC Articles 3 and 4', *Loyola of LA Law Review* 26: 743–88.

Rydin, Yvonne (2011). *The Purpose of Planning: Creating Sustainable Towns and Cities*. Bristol: Policy Press.

Tomaney, John and Jessica Ferm (2018). 'Introduction: Contexts and Frameworks for Contemporary Planning Practice'. In *Planning Practice: Critical Perspectives from the UK*, edited by Jessica Ferm and John Tomaney, 1–19. Abingdon: Routledge.

Town and Country Planning Association (2018). *Planning 2020: Raynsford Review of Planning in England*.

2
English planning law: An outline
Maria Lee[*]

Introduction

The contributors to this book make good the argument in the previous chapter that planning and planning law are at the heart of the greatest challenges of our time, that planning raises key conundrums for legal scholars, and that planning law scholarship has a lot to offer the study of planning. This chapter outlines English planning law (different approaches apply in the other countries of the United Kingdom), focusing on the Local Planning Authority (LPA) and its role in the development of plans and determination of applications for planning permission. The aim is to ease progress through the rest of the book (for authors and readers), and to provide just a hint of the fascination of planning law. An outline of planning law is far from straightforward, however. Perennial change, combined with crushing detail, may have inhibited sustained scholarship (as discussed in the previous chapter); these factors also inhibit successful summary. Invidious as the task might be, it is a necessary starting point.

The outline in this chapter begins with the ubiquitous figure of the LPA. English planning is part of an extraordinarily complex local government framework, which has evolved inconsistently. The complexity and the contestability of the shape and content of English local government, the generally 'bewildering picture',[1] is flattened by generalising (as is probably necessary) about 'the' LPA. The democratic credentials and broader role of local government are hard to grasp, and inherently tied up with their relationship with place and planning. I make no claims to be able to unpick the huge constitutional questions associated with English local government, but I am intrigued by how rarely they are asked by legal scholars.

I then explore planning ('development', 'land use', 'town and country' planning[2]) as operated by this elusive and yet taken-for-granted LPA, starting with the obligation under the much-amended Town and Country Planning Act (TCPA) 1990 to seek planning permission for 'development'. This apparently banal regulatory measure has the potential to decide the quality and evolution of an area as a place to live, play and work. It is, however, partial. An LPA can use its permitting powers to prevent development, or to influence the way that development takes place; but the LPA has limited capacity to make development happen.

Next I turn to plan-making, largely governed by the (also much-amended) Planning and Compulsory Purchase Act (PCPA) 2004. The plan is in principle the LPA's vision for its area, with exciting opportunities to imagine and begin to construct the prospects for a place. Again, it is inherently limited. Implementation is largely in the hands of private-sector developers, and the plan plays an uncertain role in applications for planning permission. The weaknesses of LPA planning are plain to see throughout this book, and it is easy to tell a story of decline. But its potential is enormous.

This chapter then turns to the perennially tricky relationship between policy and law, and the role of legal frameworks in the practical significance of policy. Planning law is found in multiple dense and lengthy pieces of primary and secondary legislation, and subject to voluminous case law. The profound significance of central policy (especially the National Planning Policy Framework (NPPF))[3] and local policy (especially the development plan) to planning practice and legal analysis adds a deep layer of complication to any analysis.

And finally, the burden of working with dense and difficult law and policy is amplified by what the Raynsford Review (a 'holistic appraisal of the kind of planning system that England will need', commissioned by the Town and Country Planning Association) calls a 'bewildering rate of change'.[4] Although the legal structure remains recognisable from the TCPA 1947, planning has been subject to almost constant reform, including sweeping statutory changes to the making and implementation of plans, and less high-profile, but equally significant, changes to consenting.

I conclude this chapter with a brief overview of current plans for reform. The government seems to have backed away from the 'radical' reform promised (not for the first time) in *Planning for the Future*,[5] a 2020 White Paper. Planning law may be as difficult to reform as it is to summarise. Planning law scholarship cannot wait for a period of stability.

Local Planning Authorities and local government

The planning literature generally talks about 'the' LPA as if it does not matter who *does* planning: elected or appointed, and by whom; well-resourced and autonomous, or scrappy and dependent; with broad powers beyond planning, or not. Of course, few doubt that who does planning does matter.

A patchwork of local government provides the framework on which both planning and England's local democracy depend. Planning law and its structures and processes both sit in and partially construct local government and local democracy. Planning creates moments for democratic activity, in decision-making by elected representatives and through pervasive legal obligations to consult, as well as opportunities for more ambitious public participation. The constant reform of planning law frequently manifests as, or arises out of (or both), profound institutional change to local government. Taking 'the' LPA as our agent in discussion of planning law is a significant, perhaps necessary, reduction of complexity. But it merits a little pulling apart before we proceed.

The NPPF defines the LPA in England prosaically, as

> the public authority whose duty it is to carry out specific planning functions for a particular area. All references to local planning authority include the district council, London borough council, county council, Broads Authority, National Park Authority, the Mayor of London and a development corporation, to the extent appropriate to their responsibilities.[6]

Local government in England is formed basically of local councils with locally elected councillors, and has one of two basic structures – a two-tier or a unitary system. The Local Government Act 1972 introduced two-tier councils across England (with the exception of London), dividing responsibilities between district councils (responsible for most planning matters) and county councils (responsible for transport, minerals and waste planning). Unitary authorities, which include metropolitan districts, London boroughs and some city councils,[7] were introduced in the early 1990s[8] and do not divide these responsibilities. In a foretaste of what follows, the creation of a unitary authority is 'frequently ... contingent on Government policy, or local initiative, at a given time, rather than any rationale relating to local economy, geography or identity'.[9]

District, county and unitary authority members (councillors) are elected. Turnout for local elections is consistently low – nearly 35 per cent in 2018, varying between local authorities.[10] The leader of a local (district, county or unitary) authority is generally chosen by other council members, so not directly elected. A number of referenda on the adoption of a directly elected mayor by local authorities were held in 2012, and the results for all, bar Bristol City Council, were negative.[11] Subsequently, the need for a referendum was removed by statute,[12] and a small number of local authorities have introduced a directly elected mayor.[13]

Parish or town councils operate at a lower level, and can be established under the Local Government and Public Involvement in Health Act 2007.[14] Parish councils do not have statutory duties, and do not cover the whole country. Where there is no parish council, a neighbourhood planning forum can seek designation from the LPA to take on certain planning powers. The forum must be open to individuals who live, work or are elected councillors in the neighbourhood area and be composed of at least 21 such individuals, and must be established 'for the express purpose of promoting or improving the social, economic and environmental well-being of an area'.[15] For our purposes,[16] the most significant power of parish councils and neighbourhood fora is to develop a 'neighbourhood plan' under the Localism Act 2011, discussed further below.

This relatively simple, if ad hoc, picture of local government has been much complicated by multiple reforms over decades. At the end of the twentieth century, devolution in the UK led to new national authorities, responsibilities and democratic arrangements in Scotland, Wales and Northern Ireland, and a new pan-London system. This left London (the subject of Steven Vaughan and Brad Jessup's and Antonia Layard's chapters below) with a different local democratic, governance and planning system from the rest of England. The Greater London Authority Act 1999 created the Greater London Authority (GLA), comprised of a directly elected London Mayor and a directly elected scrutinising body, the London Assembly. The GLA sits above London's unitary authorities (the London boroughs and the City of London). The London Mayor has a number of planning responsibilities. The mayor prepares a 'spatial development strategy' (the London Plan), which provides the framework for London planning.[17] The boroughs must refer all applications of 'potential strategic significance' to the Mayor, who can make comments, direct refusal, or take the decision as LPA for the application.[18]

Outside London, Regional Spatial Strategies, drawn up by new Regional Assemblies under the PCPA 2004, replaced the 'structure plans' that had been prepared by county councils on strategic issues since the 1960s. Regional planning had been intended to form part of a broader English devolution agenda, which was stalled by the rejection of directly elected Regional Assemblies and city mayors in referenda.[19] Regional planning and Regional Assemblies were abolished on change of government through the Localism Act 2011.

The rearrangement of English local government has continued in a low-key, and anything but systematic, way. The loss of the democratic element to regional planning, and the subsequent abolition of regional planning, raised unresolved territorial conundrums around the relationship between England and the rest of the UK, and left a gap in 'more than local' government and planning. This gap was filled initially by non-statutory efforts at coordination and collaboration between local authorities, put on a statutory footing by the introduction of 'combined authorities' (CAs) by the Local Democracy, Economic Development and Construction Act 2009. CAs provide for formal statutory joint working between local authorities in England (excluding London), generally building on pre-existing collaborative arrangements. The Cities and Local Government Devolution Act 2016 allowed CAs to adopt a system of directly elected mayors (often called Metro-mayors), without the referenda that had previously derailed these developments.[20] The mayor chairs the CA, made up of the leaders of each of the constituent local authorities; each member including the chair has one vote, and different issues require different levels of agreement.

The precise powers of CAs vary according to individual 'deals' struck with central government.[21] The deal is negotiated between central government and the leaders of constituent local authorities in private. This establishes central government control at the outset, and there are 'questions about how much [CAs] take devolved powers from the top rather than "suck up" powers from local authorities'.[22] The deal has to be agreed by all local authorities in the CA, but their lack of involvement in the negotiations means that councils (and local people) are presented with a package which it may be difficult to reject, and almost impossible to influence. The final deal is put in place by an order under the 2009 Act (with the exception of powers that are not statutory). Many of the deals include the power to create a spatial plan, which must however be agreed by the mayor and all members of the CA.[23]

Mayoral CAs, with their perceived greater democratic accountability, tend to have greater powers. The 'strong-leader' model implied[24] by the preference for mayoral CAs belies, however, their very limited executive powers[25] and their practical dependence on collaboration with many other partners at both local and national levels.[26] The complexity of local government means that even the basic question of who speaks for a place is not necessarily resolved.[27] Moreover, central government continues to exercise control, not only through the 'deal', but also through discretionary funding, as discussed below.[28]

The chaotic structure of English local government lacks consistency and predictability. There seems to have been limited considered attention to what local or sub-national governance, authority and democracy should look like.[29] Instead, we have a historical accumulation of different bits and pieces,[30] and various political initiatives for one model or another of local economies, communities and democracies, and the different understandings of society associated with those models. This lack of strategic consideration of what local government should be and should do intensifies the instability and fragmentation of planning law, as different political priorities come and go. The way various models of local government function will anyway depend on the context.[31] As I write (January 2022), a long-awaited 'levelling-up' White Paper is expected, with potential further development;[32] somebody somewhere may have a vision for local government, but so far without broader public debate.

Local responsibility, and even local democracy, was one of the key features of the post-1947 planning regime: 'the responsibility of the local community for managing its own environment is integral to the system'.[33] This idea of local community/democratic responsibility goes along with discretion. At the same time as democratic accountability confers legitimacy on the exercise of discretion, discretion provides an ability to respond to local needs. Most decisions are taken in principle by local elected officials (even if the input of appointed expert officials might be determinative[34]) as well as being subject to some form of participation or information and consultation. The exercise of discretion by elected politicians must comply with legal requirements, for example as to equalities or environmental assessment. The legal framework also, as discussed below and throughout this volume, provides multiple opportunities for central policy and supervision to displace local discretion.

Compliance with law and policy, as well as the exercise of planning judgment, is likely to be a priority for the officers advising members. They have professional experience and expertise in both planning and related matters such as design or biodiversity. Elected members are not bound by professional advice, but disagreement with officers is often a source of surprise, and may indicate that fuller reasons are required for a decision.[35] The difficulty of bringing expert and political decision-making together is a pervasive issue across government and administration, and far from unique to planning.[36] It reflects, however, an important divide in the understanding of planning, which might be seen as predominantly a technocratic process, or as predominantly democratic. The ways in which planning implements the public interest as defined by experts,[37] or works out democratically what the public interest might be, is one of the fascinations of the area.

As statutory institutions, the powers and role of local authorities can be easily amended. Martin Loughlin argues that, 'once utilised in ways which irritate the central state, the powers of local authorities will either be severely restricted or altogether removed from local government'.[38] He wrote these words in the wake of the ideological conflict of the 1980s between central and local government, Thatcherism and municipal socialism. In planning specifically, the 1980s led to increased centralisation, but combined with elements of deregulation and a more market-led approach;[39] complex trends that continued through subsequent changes of government.

Equally importantly, central government exercises considerable financial power over local authorities, who have suffered severe funding cuts over recent years.[40] Government can place limits on local authority powers to raise their own funds, and exercises control over grants to local authorities. Financial power is routinely used to control local authority autonomy,[41] and the notoriously complicated nature of local authority funding renders this difficult to observe from the outside. Specifically on CAs, Mark Sandford argues that there is 'no prospect of local electoral accountability offsetting any inclination by combined authorities to prioritise upward accountability towards the providers of their funds', in the absence of more meaningful transparency around funding, including the sources and destinations of potential funding.[42]

The discussion in this section begs broader questions about what local government should be, and the proper extent of local government powers and autonomy. Normative choices about democratic systems constitute as well as reflect different communities and different ideas of democracy.[43] Mark Sandford, whose work (including for the House of Commons Library) is important to this outline, identifies two 'broad traditions of thought': a division between 'local government [as] principally a delivery vehicle for public services provided according to nationally-set legal entitlements'; and 'local governments as governments, with a broader responsibility for the wellbeing of their electorates'.[44] Central government seems to regard local authorities largely as 'an administrative arm of central government',[45] 'providers of care rather than active custodians of towns and cities'.[46] Local authorities, and the individuals who constitute them, may contest this through local politics and local identity and community building, to different degrees.

Planning powers and responsibilities are shared in complicated and often ad hoc ways between different scales, as discussed in a number of chapters below, but especially those by Maria Lee and Elen Stokes. The fundamentally meaningful shift of planning powers away from local actors through apparently technical legal change is concerning. It should not be thought, however, that local is always and necessarily 'better'. The local can operate to exclude 'outsiders' and has incentives to ignore broader impacts or consequences for other localities;[47] further, values imposed by the centre might include critical values around environmental protection and equalities.

Development control and planning permission

The planning system turns around the statutory prohibition on 'development' in the absence of planning permission.[48] The scope of planning regulation, and so the shaping of space, is therefore determined by the very broad statutory definition of 'development' in section 55(1) TCPA 1990: 'the carrying out of building, engineering, mining or other operations in, on, over or under land, or the making of any material change in the use of any buildings or other land'. Section 55(2) excludes certain operations, including (notoriously from an environmental perspective) the use of land for agriculture or forestry. Section 55(2)(f) provides that changes of use within the same class do not constitute development, so that amending the Town and Country Planning (Use Classes) Order 1987[49] to place activities in the same class takes changes between those activities out of the planning system. Section 58 further provides that planning permission can be granted by a 'development order'. The General Permitted Development Order (GPDO) 2015 grants permitted development rights to categories of development, so that individual planning permission is not needed.[50] In addition to conventional use for low-impact developments, these two mechanisms provide the opportunity to reduce regulation of particular types of development. As discussed further in Lee's chapter below, creating housing has been a government priority for some years, and coordinated changes to the Use Classes Order and the GPDO allow for the conversion of various categories of property (office, retail) to residential without planning permission (although 'prior approval' of certain limited issues is sometimes still required).[51]

The ease with which the very *scope* of planning can be restricted is striking. Statutory instruments are largely in the hands of government, with only limited parliamentary scrutiny,[52] and their technical appearance means that they often receive limited public attention. In addition to the deregulatory restriction of the very category of 'development', whole areas of development have been transferred for ministerial decision under the Planning Act 2008. There seems to be little if any analysis or consistency around where the development control system in general, or LPA resources in particular, should be focused.

The grant or refusal of planning permission is also largely governed by the TCPA 1990.[53] Applications for development are made to the LPA; the application must be publicised, along with information on how to respond, and various statutory consultees (such as the Environment Agency) must be consulted,[54] providing a lay and expert information-gathering exercise, as well as an opportunity for public participation.

Under section 70, the LPA 'shall have regard to' the provisions of the development plan (the key space for LPAs to set out their vision for an area, discussed below) and any other material considerations.[55] This is the centre of the discretionary regulatory approach of English planning. Material considerations, discussed in a number of chapters below, is an open category, and in law 'any consideration which relates to the use and development of land' is capable of being a material consideration.[56] The law draws a 'clear distinction' between whether something is material, and how much (if any) weight is given to a material consideration; the former is a matter of law, the latter a matter of planning judgment for the decision-maker.[57] The Supreme Court in the *Heathrow* case highlights three categories of material consideration:

> First, those clearly (whether expressly or impliedly) identified by the statute as considerations to which regard must be had. Second, those clearly identified by the statute as considerations to which regard must not be had. Third, those to which the decisionmaker may have regard if in his judgment and discretion he thinks it right to do so.[58]

The court may also identify issues 'so obviously material' that a failure to have regard to them would be unlawful.[59]

This most basic question of 'material considerations' in planning highlights not only the significance of discretion, but also the valuing of discretion by the courts, alongside judicial oversight of the scope of that discretion. The courts recognise and provide space for the democratic and political nature of the LPA: although there is a duty 'to be fair and carefully to consider the evidence', being 'politically pre-disposed' on a matter is not unlawful.[60]

The broad section 70 discretion was apparently tightened by the introduction of section 38(6) PCPA 2004,[61] providing that 'If regard is to be had to the development plan', any determination 'must be made in accordance with the plan unless material considerations indicate otherwise'. The intention of this provision was to prioritise the plan (act in accordance with, rather than have regard to), but the House of Lords quickly confirmed that any such prioritisation is neither 'governing' nor 'paramount'.[62] The plan is the 'starting point' for decision-making[63] – but, given the scope of material considerations that may 'indicate otherwise', and the continuing obligation to have regard to all material considerations, not the end point.

LPAs can refuse planning permission, or grant planning permission subject to 'such conditions as they think fit'.[64] Well-established case law constrains this discretion to impose conditions, requiring conditions to be imposed for a planning (rather than any other) purpose and to 'fairly and reasonably relate to the permitted development', as well as to be *Wednesbury* reasonable.[65]

Whether the uplift in land value from a grant of planning permission can or should be shared with LPAs, and the slightly less controversial question of whether developers should contribute to the public infrastructure needs generated by their development, create major challenges. There are two key mechanisms for 'planning gain' in English law. Planning obligations or planning agreements, provided for by section 106 TCPA 1990, are negotiated case-by-case between developers and the LPA, to provide benefits such as infrastructure or a money payment to the LPA. One such case is discussed in detail in Edward Mitchell's chapter below, indicating vividly the complexity of the negotiation and the difficulty of scrutiny, both suggestive of an advantage for well-resourced developers.[66] The Community Infrastructure Levy (CIL), which provides for LPA infrastructure costs, on a fixed scale, was introduced to avoid the protracted, complex and often secretive negotiations over individual section 106 agreements or obligations.[67] The majority of LPAs have not adopted a CIL scheme; those that have are predominantly in high land value areas.[68] More generally, the National Audit Office has concluded that 'local authorities now rely more on sources of income that are dependent on local economic conditions',[69] exacerbating geographical inequalities.[70]

Central government plays a very significant role in local planning. The scalar questions raised by the relationship between central and local government are the subject of Lee's chapter below, while the temporal elements are addressed by Stokes. No particular scale is necessarily the 'best' scale for decision-making;[71] but the relative absence of considered debate on the English territorial constitution is striking. In addition to, and reinforcing, the policy-making role discussed below, central government plays a direct supervisory role in development control. A disappointed applicant (only) has the right to appeal to the Secretary of State on the merits,[72] for a complete rehearing of the case.[73] The appeal is usually decided by the Planning Inspectorate (PINS) acting 'instead of' the Secretary of State,[74] or it is occasionally 'recovered' to be made personally by the Secretary of State (to whom PINS provides a report and recommendations). PINS is an executive body of the Department for Levelling Up, Housing and Communities (DLUHC), accountable to the Secretary of State, who in turn is accountable for its work to Parliament. The Supreme Court in *Hopkins Homes* describes PINS as acting independently, and being 'in some ways analogous to . . . expert tribunals'.[75] Appeals can take the form of written representations, an inquisitorial hearing or a formal inquiry.[76] They are subject to statutory review before the courts,[77] not judicial review, although statutory review and judicial review are sufficiently similar for current purposes.

Third parties who object to the grant of planning permission have no right of appeal on the merits, and must turn to the more limited potential of judicial review. The Secretary of State may also call-in applications from the LPA for a ministerial decision (again PINS provides a report and recommendations), a process discussed in more detail by Carolyn Abbot and by Stokes below.[78] Call-in is subject to judicial review only. The significance of judicial review for planning law scholarship is discussed in detail in Joanna Bell's chapter below.

The NPPF applies a 'presumption in favour of sustainable development', discussed further by Margherita Pieraccini below, where she explores the more open potential of sustainable development in the marine planning environment.[79] Whether the notion of sustainability really adds much to 'development' in the NPPF is questionable, and does not mean that all development must be 'sustainable' in any ecological sense.[80] The presumption implies swift approval of applications 'that accord with an up-to-date development plan'. Permission is not usually granted if it conflicts with an up-to-date plan.[81] The question of whether a plan is up-to-date is, however, more complicated than it sounds, especially for housing, and a very recently adopted plan could be out-of-date. In the absence of an up-to-date plan, the 'tilted balance' in favour of development applies.[82] These provisions, and the resulting diminution of LPA control over development, are discussed by Abbot and by Lee, below.

Plan-making

Applications for planning permission are made in the context of the development plan. Planners might see plan-making as more creative than the regulatory side of planning, assembling, alongside communities, a vision for the future of an area. In the absence of significant powers for local authorities to develop land and run services, much of the implementation of plans is dependent on private-sector decisions, or at least collaboration between local government and private developers. The ability to grant and refuse planning permission becomes a key tool in achieving a plan.

The role of the plan in applications for planning permission is discussed above; non-statutory local policy (which might also be called a local plan) is likely to be a material consideration in planning decisions,[83] but the discussion here is of the statutory plan. The process for making a plan is largely governed by the much-amended PCPA 2004.[84] The LPA is explicitly required to have regard to 'national policies and advice contained in guidance issued by the Secretary of State' when making its plan.[85] The development plan should be prepared in consultation with local communities: the LPA must prepare and comply with a 'statement of community involvement', setting out its policy on involvement of those with an interest in the development of the area.[86]

The development plan is constituted by the adopted development plan documents for an area, as well as any neighbourhood plan.[87] LPAs must prepare a 'local development scheme', specifying matters including 'the local development documents which are to be development plan documents'.[88] The local development documents must 'set out the authority's policies . . . relating to the development and use of land in their area', including policies to address the LPA's strategic priorities.[89] The NPPF provides that 'strategic' policies should look ahead at least 15 years and 'set out an overall strategy for the pattern, scale and design quality of places', and 'make sufficient provision' for a number of issues, such as housing, infrastructure, community facilities, conservation and enhancement of the natural and built environment.[90] Strategic policies should 'provide for objectively assessed needs for housing and other uses', other than in defined circumstances.[91] Lee's chapter below explores the highly contentious process of allocating land for housing.

In addition to these specific policy obligations, the LPA must by statute have various issues in mind when making the plan. All powers under the relevant Part of the PCPA 2004 must be exercised 'with the objective of contributing to the achievement of sustainable development'.[92] The local development policies must 'contribute to the mitigation of, and adaptation to, climate change'.[93] The LPA is required to have regard to 'the resources likely to be available for implementing the proposals in the document'.[94] The LPA must also comply with various general '(due) regard' duties, such as the biodiversity duty,[95] the equality duty[96] (on which see Vaughan and Jessup below) and the growth duty.[97] An appraisal of sustainability is mandatory.[98]

LPA development plan documents are submitted to the Secretary of State for 'independent examination' (carried out by PINS).[99] Any person can request the opportunity to appear at an open hearing.[100] The purpose of the examination is to determine whether the plan documents satisfy the statutory obligations and whether the plan 'is sound'.[101] Soundness is not defined in the statute, but the NPPF provides more detailed criteria,[102] establishing considerable scope for central intervention and control of this creative space for LPAs. The inspector can recommend adoption or non-adoption of the plan or make recommendations for alteration. The LPA can only adopt a plan if that is the recommendation of the inspector, or with the modifications recommended by the inspector.[103] In addition, the Secretary of State has broad powers to direct an LPA to modify a local development document if s/he 'thinks that [it] is unsatisfactory', or to direct withdrawal of a plan prior to its adoption.[104] There are also default powers to prepare or revise a development plan document, or issue directions, 'if the Secretary of State thinks that a local planning authority is failing or omitting to do anything it is necessary for them to do'.[105]

The neighbourhood plan is a voluntary layer of planning introduced by the Localism Act 2011.[106] A neighbourhood plan is developed by a parish council or neighbourhood forum. It must be developed in consultation with the local community and is put to a local referendum before adoption by the LPA. It forms part of the development plan for the area, taking priority over an LPA's non-strategic policies, but limited by an obligation to be consistent with national policy and strategic policies; neighbourhood plans 'should not promote less development' than the LPA's strategic policies.[107] Examination in public, before the referendum, allows PINS to scrutinise compliance with these requirements.

The process for adopting local plans is difficult and under-resourced,[108] and many LPAs are without an up-to-date plan, diminishing its impact in decision-making. The land allocation and other distributive issues inherent in creating a plan are politically sensitive. There are also many ways in which a plan can 'fail' at examination stage, from a failure to cooperate with neighbouring authorities[109] to a failure to allocate sufficient land to meet the assessment of housing need. Plans that are successfully adopted may very quickly become out-of-date, again often because of central government obligations in respect of housing land.

Policy and law

The role and status of planning policy, and its relationship with planning law, is a central conundrum for lawyers.[110] The strong influence of policy is a constant refrain in almost every chapter that follows. Policy can be made at the local (including development plan) level or central (including NPPF) level. The Secretary of State's policy-making powers are 'derived, expressly or by implication, from the planning Acts which give him overall responsibility for oversight of the planning system'.[111] The case law is tricky and interesting. But perhaps more knotty for lawyers is the mismatch between the legal and the practical import of central government policy. In law, central government policy is not determinative; in practice, it is treated 'as essentially gospel'.[112] This practical effect is however very much influenced by broader legal frameworks, especially for central government supervision of LPAs.

Policy cannot render an immaterial consideration material in law,[113] and policy remains subordinate to the legislative language.[114] But government has enormous discretion around setting policy, and when it chooses to can create very powerful incentives or pressures for or against particular forms of development.

The PCPA 2004 requires LPAs to have regard to Secretary of State guidance when making plans,[115] but there is no similar explicit requirement when considering applications for planning permission. In both cases, relevant policy is clearly a material consideration, and it would be unlawful to fail to have regard to it. Provided that it has regard to government guidance when it is material, however, an LPA may lawfully choose to give it no weight as a matter of planning judgment (provided that would not be irrational in law).

The ways in which the *legal* framework provides for central government oversight of the LPA reinforce central government policy.[116] To depart from national policy when refusing planning permission (or imposing conditions) creates a significant risk of appeal.[117] That appeal is a fresh hearing of the merits. There is an expectation that the Secretary of State and PINS, acting 'instead of' the Secretary of State on appeal,[118] will apply central policy, and inspectors certainly see their role as in part to ensure the correct application of ministerial policy.[119] The Supreme Court has described inspectors as being 'required to exercise their own independent judgment . . . within the framework of national policy as set by government'.[120] Failure to apply policy in *granting* planning permission creates the risk of call-in (rarely exercised) by the Secretary of State. Given that objectors to development cannot instigate a merits appeal (only judicial review), there is a pro-development slant to this legal framework.

'Planning by appeal' reduces the LPA's ability to plan its area, and a desire to avoid appeals understandably makes LPAs and their professional officers cautious.[121] This caution is reinforced by so-called 'special measures': the Secretary of State can 'designate' an LPA that is 'not performing adequately', so that applications for certain planning permissions can be made directly to PINS (on behalf of the Secretary of State).[122] One of the criteria for designation is a very particular approach to 'quality', assessed by reference to successful appeals; if 10 per cent or more of an LPA's decisions are overturned on appeal, the LPA is eligible for designation.[123]

Legal frameworks therefore reinforce the strong practical impact of central government policy. Legal questions also arise in respect of disagreement about the meaning or impact in any particular case of central or local policy. It is a 'firmly settled' principle of planning law that the *application* of policy (including the weight of policy pulling in different directions) to facts is a matter of planning judgment for the decision-maker, subject only to rationality review, but the interpretation of policy is a matter of law for the courts.[124]

The Supreme Court in *Tesco Stores v Dundee City Council* emphasises the need for LPAs to proceed on the basis of a 'proper understanding' of (in this case local plan) policy.[125] Rather than a rationality review of the LPA interpretation, the court interprets policy itself, 'objectively in accordance with the language used, read as always in its proper context'.[126] Courts have expressed their frustration with 'excessive legalism' related to the interpretation of policy[127] and the danger of 'over-legalisation of the planning process'.[128] *Hopkins Homes*, developed in *Samuel Smith* (both concerning the NPPF), limits the scope of *Tesco* by contrasting the 'relatively specific language' of the policy at issue in *Tesco* with policies 'expressed in much broader terms, [which] may not require, nor lend themselves to, the same level of legal analysis'.[129] We see some deference to the expertise of planners (explicitly PINS), including a presumption that inspectors have understood policy correctly.[130] The relationship between interpretation and application of the policy might be as important as the broad or specific nature of the policy. In *Tesco*, the question of textual interpretation was 'a logically prior question as to the issue to which planning judgment requires to be directed'; in cases like *Hopkins Homes*, 'Even where there are disputes over interpretation, they may well not be determinative of the outcome'.[131] None of this is easy to put into practice.

Reform

Planning has been subject to almost constant reform, piecemeal and yet dramatic, virtually since its modern post-war beginnings. In the 2020 *Planning for the Future* White Paper, the Prime Minister (using the extended metaphor of planning as an old building) promised to 'tear it down and start again'.[132] Considerable disquiet about the proposed reforms, most influentially among backbench Conservative MPs,[133] has led to delay and possible retreat on some issues (certainly on the rhetoric). A Planning Bill promised in the 2021 Queen's Speech may now not happen in that form, and a politically influential Secretary of State, Michael Gove, has been placed in charge of planning at the renamed DLUHC.[134] So as we write, the future of planning law is deeply uncertain. One of the things we seek to emphasise through this collection, however, is that planning law scholarship must be undaunted in the face of perennial legal change. Even as change opens new avenues for planning law scholarship, the issues and structures addressed here and throughout this book, and the approaches we take, will continue to speak to legal and policy analysis.

But even as a historical document (and it is not that), the pressures behind the White Paper have not gone away, and it highlights the ways in which planning might proceed. The most obviously profound proposal in the White Paper is a move from the discretionary consideration of planning applications by LPAs, described above, to a zoning system (although that word is never used), under which local plans would place land into three sparsely explained categories: growth areas 'suitable for substantial development'; renewal areas 'suitable for some development'; and protected areas.[135] Only in protected areas would planning permission be required, as a result of the particular environmental and/or cultural characteristics. This raises all sorts of questions, not least about the variety and complexity of zoning around the world,[136] by contrast with the presumed self-evidence and simplicity of the discussion in the White Paper. Further, the loss of the discretion and public participation at the permitting stage would be difficult (at best) to replace during plan-making, especially alongside the tight deadlines proposed in the White Paper. These zoning proposals prompted considerable public controversy and the Government seems to have backed away from them in particular.

The White Paper contains many other proposals.[137] Just to take two, first, it is proposed that planning 'should be based on data, not documents' and that 'Local Plans should be visual and map-based, standardised, based on the latest digital technology, and supported by a new template'. This is presented in the White Paper as a simple technical improvement to planning.[138] Such a turn to technology is always political, however, and digitisation has the potential to change planning in ways that are yet to be explored.[139] Placing a digitised map at the centre of a plan may for example reduce the role of context and contestation, and shift power towards those responsible for and best able to engage with the necessary technology. The White Paper's enthusiasm for the industry sector referred to as 'PropTech' may hint at further marketisation, if not deregulation, of planning. A second proposal is in the White Paper's promise of a 'fast-track for beauty', through various procedural and institutional reforms.[140] The relationship between 'beauty' and broader questions of design is unclear.[141] Nor is 'beauty' a simple matter, and at the (local?) implementation level is likely to require complex processes for (sufficient) consensus and implementation.

Given the possible retreat from a stand-alone Planning Bill, we should remember that major reform of the planning system commonly occurs without legislative drama, or indeed any legislation at all, including through apparently small, technical changes. We should also note the potential for the easier implementation of changes to approaches formerly protected by EU law, such as certain rights to participate, or strict habitats protection in some areas.

Conclusion

Any outline sacrifices complexity and an assessment of how things might be otherwise, and that risk is particularly great in respect of planning, where detail can be decisive. The flawed outline above necessarily underplays the complexity and crucial detail of planning law, which is however confronted throughout this volume.

The density and extent of the legal and policy materials mean that representing or drawing conclusions about 'planning law' as a single thing is probably impossible. We might ask whether there is such 'a' thing as 'planning law', and even the depiction of LPA planning as central inevitably glosses over the complexity of the allocation of authority or power in planning. Perhaps LPA planning is subject to such a range of variations and exceptions that it is more residual than core. The LPA system sometimes applies in a distinctive way, for example using the planning permission system to implement the statutory protection of certain interests such as landscape (discussed in the chapters below by Chiara Armeni and by Lee), registered parks and gardens (Abbot), 'heritage' (Vaughan and Jessup), and compulsory purchase (Kim Bouwer and Rachel Gimson). A number of planning regimes apply completely beyond the LPA system. Marine planning is separate from the TCPA system, which applies only to land, as is the system of development consent orders for 'nationally significant infrastructure projects' under the Planning Act 2008, discussed respectively in Pieraccini's and Armeni's chapters. Law relating to the 'highway', separate from planning, but around which planning happens, is discussed in Layard's chapter. The LPA can partially 'escape' the confines of planning regulation by using its land assembly powers to stimulate (private sector) property (re-)development.[142] Other special regimes have been set up over the years, in an effort to stimulate economic development through various (mainly fiscal) measures, sometimes including bespoke planning regimes. Development corporations, for example, are designed for the regeneration of whole areas, and as well as having powers to buy and develop land have planning powers, side-stepping the LPA. The nineteenth-century approach of making land use decisions by statute is now rare, but remarkably persistent.[143]

The hope is that this chapter has provided a glance at the meaningfulness of planning law, to be pursued in later chapters. If the density and detail of planning law are off-putting for legal scholars, the uneven impact of complexity on those using the system is raised throughout this volume, most explicitly in Abbot's chapter. Developers large and small will have different relationships with legal complexity, in turn different from LPAs (see also Mitchell below), and from the publics and public interest groups whose locality is the subject of planning law. We should also recall the 'open hostility from the political elite' towards planning over decades,[144] and consider the effect this might have on the development (and indeed stability) of the law.

Notes

* I am grateful to Jane Holder and UCL Press's anonymous reviewer for comments on this chapter.
1. Roberts 2020.
2. For current purposes these terms can be used interchangeably.
3. Ministry of Housing, Communities and Local Government (MHCLG) 2021a.
4. Town and Country Planning Association 2018, 6 and 7, Annex 2.
5. MHCLG 2020b, Prime Minister's Foreword.
6. MHCLG 2021a, Annex 2. National Park Authorities, whose members are appointed by constituent local authorities from their elected members, have planning powers in the National Parks (and Norfolk Broads).
7. Some 'city' councils are simply honorific.
8. Local Government Act 1992, amending Local Government Act 1970. The creation of unitary authorities is governed by the Local Government and Public Involvement in Health Act 2007.

9. House of Commons Library 2020b, 4.
10. Electoral Commission 2019.
11. House of Commons Library 2021a.
12. Local Government and Public Involvement in Health Act 2007, removing the referendum required under the Local Government Act 2000.
13. There were 15 directly elected local authority mayors in 2021 (House of Commons Library 2021a). Lord Mayor is a ceremonial position.
14. See House of Commons Library 2019.
15. TCPA 1990, section 61F, introduced by the Localism Act 2011; Neighbourhood Plan (General) Regulations 2012 SI 2012/637.
16. On 'assets of community value' see Vaughan and Jessup below.
17. Greater London Authority Act 1999, section 334.
18. Town and Country Planning (Mayor of London) Order 2008 SI 2008/580.
19. Starting with the North East in 2004; see House of Commons Library 2021a.
20. Special issue *Local Economy* [2019] (34) 2; House of Commons Library 2021a.
21. For more detail on the 'deals', see House of Commons Library 2020a.
22. Roberts 2020.
23. The London Mayor does not have to revert to the boroughs in the same way.
24. And sometimes explicit: Gove 2021, Q27, Q30.
25. See e.g. Roberts 2020.
26. Sandford 2019b.
27. Roberts 2020.
28. Sandford 2019a.
29. The instrumental use of referenda is also striking.
30. The echo of Deirdre Curtin's analysis of the Maastricht Treaty on European Union 1992 is apposite: Curtin 1993.
31. Roberts 2020.
32. Gove 2021, Q30. Published in February (Department for Housing, Levelling Up and Communities 2022), promising local devolution (not for the first time), and more mayors with more powers.
33. *South Bucks District Council v Porter and another* [2003] UKHL 26; [2004] WLR 1953, [11].
34. Marshall 2021, 109.
35. *Dover District Council v Council for the Protection of Rural England* [2017] UKSC 79; [2018] 1 WLR 108.
36. Marshall 2021, introduction.
37. McAuslan's ideology of public interest: McAuslan 1980; Owens and Cowell 2011.
38. Loughlin 1996, 170. Also Tewdwr-Jones 1999.
39. Tewdwr-Jones 1999.
40. See House of Commons Library 2021b; generally on local authority funding see National Audit Office 2021.
41. Sandford 2019a.
42. Sandford 2019b, 115.
43. Eckersley 2017.
44. Sandford 2019b, 2; Loughlin 1996.
45. Roberts 2020, 996.
46. Bruff and Kumi-Ampofo 2019, 169.
47. Purcell 2006; Lee below.
48. TCPA 1990, section 57.
49. Town and Country Planning (Use Classes) Order 1987 SI 1987/764.
50. Town and Country Planning (General Permitted Development) (England) (Order) SI 2015/596.
51. See *R (on the application of Rights: Community: Action) v Secretary of State for Housing, Communities and Local Government* [2021] EWCA Civ 1954, a useful review of how these provisions fit together. This case was an unsuccessful judicial review of SIs 2020/755, 756 and 757; the Court of Appeal found that the measures did not need to be subjected to strategic environmental assessment. Ferm et al 2020 highlight the negative consequences of the loss of planning control.
52. See King 2020.
53. The detailed procedure largely governed by the Town and Country Planning (Development Management Procedure) Order (DMPO) 2015 SI 2015/595.

54. DMPO 2015, regulations 15, 18 and Schedule 4.
55. The brief list of considerations in section 70 directs that attention be paid to particular issues (such as local government finance) and removes any doubt as to whether they can be material.
56. *Stringer v Minister of Housing and Local Government* [1970] 1 WLR 1281; *R (on the application of Wright) v Resilient Energy Severndale Ltd and Forest of Dean District Council* [2019] UKSC 53; [2019] 1 WLR 6562.
57. *Tesco Stores Ltd v Secretary of State for the Environment* [1995] 1 WLR 759 (HL).
58. *R (Friends of the Earth) v Heathrow Airport Ltd* [2020] UKSC 52; [2021] 2 All ER 967, [116], citing Simon Brown LJ in *R v Somerset County Council, ex parte Fewings* [1995] 1 WLR 1037 (CA), 1049. See also *R (Samuel Smith Old Brewery (Tadcaster)) v North Yorkshire CC* [2020] UKSC 3; [2020] 3 All ER 527.
59. *Heathrow*, [117]–[127].
60. *R v Amber Valley DC, ex parte Jackson* [1985] 1 WLR 298 (QB), discussed in Endicott 2021, 198–9. See also Bell in this volume.
61. Formerly section 54A TCPA 1990.
62. *City of Edinburgh v Secretary of State for Scotland* [1997] UKHL 38; [1997] 1 WLR 1447.
63. *Hopkins Homes Ltd v Secretary of State for Communities and Local Government* [2017] UKSC 37; [2017] 1 WLR 1865, [11], citing the NPPF.
64. Section 70(1).
65. *Newbury DC v Secretary of State for the Environment* [1981] AC 578 (HL). The Supreme Court in *Wright v Resilient Energy* rejected the invitation to 'update' the law.
66. He also discusses agreements under the Localism Act 2011.
67. Planning Act 2008, Part 11.
68. Town and Country Planning Association 2018.
69. National Audit Office 2021, 35.
70. On which see UK2070 Commission 2020.
71. Lee below; Purcell 2006.
72. TCPA 1990, section 78.
73. TCPA 1990, section 79.
74. TCPA 1990 Schedule 6; Town and Country Planning (Determination of Appeals by Appointed Persons) (Prescribed Classes) Regulations 1997 SI 1997/420.
75. *Hopkins Homes*, [25].
76. TCPA 1990, section 319A, amended by section 20 Business and Planning Act 2020.
77. TCPA 1990, section 288.
78. TCPA 1990, section 77.
79. MHCLG 2021a.
80. Upton 2018.
81. MHCLG 2021a, [12].
82. MHCLG 2021a, [11].
83. *Westminster City Council v Great Portland Estates* [1985] AC 661 (HL).
84. And the Town and Country Planning (Local Planning) Regulations 2012 SI 2012/767.
85. PCPA 2004, section 34(1).
86. PCPA 2004, sections 18 and 19(3).
87. PCPA 2004, section 38.
88. PCPA 2004, section 15.
89. PCPA 2004, sections 17 and 19(1C).
90. MHCLG 2021a, [20]–[23].
91. MHCLG 2021a, [11], discussed further by Lee below.
92. PCPA 2004, section 39. The NPPF approach to sustainable development is not demanding: Upton 2018; MHCLG 2021a.
93. Section 19(1A).
94. Section 19.
95. Natural Environment and Rural Communities Act 2016, section 40, filled out by Environment Act 2021, sections 102 and 103.
96. Equality Act 2010, section 149.
97. Deregulation Act 2015, section 108.
98. PCPA 2004, section 19.
99. PCPA 2004, section 20.
100. PCPA 2004, section 20(6).

101. PCPA 2004, section 20(5).
102. MHCLG 2021a, [35].
103. PCPA 2004, section 23.
104. PCPA 2004, section 21.
105. PCPA 2004, section 27.
106. Part 6 introducing Schedule 4B TCPA. Neighbourhood Plan (General) Regulations 2012 SI 2012/637.
107. MHCLG 2021a, [29].
108. Local government spending on planning and development fell by 35.7 per cent between 2010 and 2020: National Audit Office 2021.
109. PCPA 2004, section 20(5)(c), singling out section 33A for scrutiny.
110. See also Fisher, Lange and Scotford 2018, chapter 8; Ruiz-Tagle 2020.
111. *Hopkins Homes*, [21].
112. Marshall 2004, 456.
113. *Wright v Resilient Energy*.
114. *Hopkins Homes*; *Gladman Developments Ltd v SSHCLG & Corby BC & Uttlesford DC* [2021] EWCA Civ 104; Lee below.
115. Section 34.
116. The DMPO provides that certain decisions should be notified to the Secretary of State.
117. See e.g. *Aberdeen City and Shire v Elsick Development Company* [2017] UKSC 66; [2017] PTSR 1413, [53], Lord Hodge.
118. TCPA 1990, Schedule 6, 1(1).
119. See e.g. the interviews in Hickman and Boddy 2020.
120. *Hopkins Homes*, [21].
121. Bradley 2021, 395; Ferm and Raco 2020.
122. TCPA 1990, sections 62A and 62B; introduced by the Growth and Infrastructure Act 2013, amended by the Housing and Planning Act 2016.
123. MHCLG 2020a. The other criterion is 'speed', i.e. a failure to meet statutory time limits for deciding applications.
124. *Tesco v Secretary of State*, [57] per Lord Hoffmann.
125. *Tesco Stores Ltd v Dundee City Council* [2012] UKSC 13; [2012] PTSR 983 (HL), [17] per Lord Reed.
126. *Tesco v Dundee*, [18].
127. Cosgrove and du Feu 2019 on the Court of Appeal.
128. *Hopkins Homes*, [23]–[34]; *Samuel Smith*, [21], both per Lord Carnwath. See also *Tesco v Dundee*, on avoiding a 'legalistic approach to the interpretation of development plan policies', [34], per Lord Hope.
129. See Ruiz-Tagle 2020. *Hopkins Homes*, [24]; *Samuel Smith*, [21].
130. *Hopkins Homes*, [25].
131. *Hopkins Homes*, [24], [25].
132. MHCLG 2020b, 17.
133. The surprise 2021 Cheshunt and Amersham by-election loss for the government was partially attributed to proposed planning reform.
134. On Gove's role in post-Brexit environmental law see Abbot and Lee 2021.
135. MHCLG 2020b, 20.
136. On the variety and complexity of approaches to zoning see Royal Town Planning Institute 2020.
137. The White Paper is extensive: note also proposals for significant reform of the processes for funding infrastructure, and of local plan-making. Other consultations were launched at the same time (see e.g. House of Commons Library 2021c) and others are in train, e.g. on nationally significant infrastructure (Department for Business, Energy and Industrial Strategy 2021).
138. MHCLG 2020b, 18 and 38. Gove 2021, Q79, places 'digitisation' in the category of reforms that 'everyone agrees are sensible'.
139. Chapman et al 2020. More generally Harlow and Rawlings 2020.
140. MHCLG 2020, 52.
141. MHCLG 2021b.
142. Mitchell 2020; Layard 2010.
143. See e.g. Crossrail Act 2008.
144. Lord and Tewdwr-Jones 2018.

References

Abbot, Carolyn and Maria Lee (2021). *Environmental Groups and Legal Expertise: Shaping the Brexit Process*. London: UCL Press, https://www.uclpress.co.uk/products/155996 (accessed 12 June 2022).

Bradley, Quintin (2021). 'The Financialisation of Housing Land Supply in England', *Urban Studies* 58: 389–404.

Bruff, Garreth and Felix Kumi-Ampofo (2019). 'Housing, Growth and Infrastructure: Supporting the Delivery of New Homes in the Sheffield City Region, UK', *Local Economy* 34: 167–80.

Chapman, Kiera et al (2020). 'What Role Should Technology Play in Planning?'. In *The Right Answers to the Right Questions?*, 46–50, Town and Country Planning Association, available at https://tcpa.org.uk/resources/the-right-answers-to-the-right-questions/ (accessed 12 June 2022).

Colomb, Claire and Mike Raco (2018). 'Planning for Diversity in an Era of Social Change'. In *Planning Practice: Critical Perspectives from the UK*, edited by Jessica Ferm and John Tomaney, 174–88. Oxford: Routledge.

Cosgrove, Tom and Ben du Feu (2019). 'Interpreting Planning Policy: A Judicial Plea for Simplicity and an End to Excessive Legalism that is Likely to Fall on Deaf Ears', *Journal of Planning and Environmental Law*: 444–55.

Curtin, Deirdre (1993). 'The Constitutional Structure of the Union: A Europe of Bits and Pieces', *Common Market Law Review* 30: 17–69.

Department for Business, Energy and Industrial Strategy (2021). *Planning for New Energy Infrastructure Draft National Policy Statements for Energy Infrastructure*.

Department for Housing, Levelling Up and Communities (2022). *Levelling Up the United Kingdom*.

Eckersley, Robyn (2017). 'Geopolitan Democracy in the Anthropocene', *Political Studies* 65: 983–99.

Electoral Commission (2019). *Results and Turnout at the 2018 May England Local Elections*. https://www.electoralcommission.org.uk/who-we-are-and-what-we-do/elections-and-referendums/past-elections-and-referendums/england-local-council-elections/results-and-turnout-2018-may-england-local-elections (accessed 12 June 2022).

Endicott, Timothy (2021). *Administrative Law*. Oxford: Oxford University Press.

Ferm, Jessica and Mike Raco (2020). 'Viability Planning, Value Capture and the Geographies of Market-Led Planning Reform in England', *Planning Theory & Practice* 21: 218–35.

Ferm, Jessica et al (2020). 'Emerging Problematics of Deregulating the Urban: The Case of Permitted Development in England', *Urban Studies* 1–19.

Fisher, Elizabeth et al (2018). *Environmental Law: Text, Cases, and Materials*. Oxford: Oxford University Press.

Harlow, Carol and Rick Rawlings (2020). 'Proceduralism and Automation'. In *The Foundations and Future of Public Law: Essays in Honour of Paul Craig*, edited by Elizabeth Fisher, Jeff King and Alison Young, 275–97. Oxford: Oxford University Press.

House of Commons Library (2019). *Parish and Town Councils: Recent Issues*.

House of Commons Library (2020a). *Devolution to Local Government in England*.

House of Commons Library (2020b). *Local Government in England: Structures*.

House of Commons Library (2021a). *Directly Elected Mayors*.

House of Commons Library (2021b). *Council Tax Increases 2020–21*.

House of Commons Library (2021c). *Planning for the Future: Planning Policy Changes in England in 2020 and Future Reforms*.

King, Jeff (2020). 'The Province of Delegated Legislation'. In *The Foundations and Future of Public Law: Essays in Honour of Paul Craig*, edited by Elizabeth Fisher, Jeff King and Alison Young, 145–71. Oxford: Oxford University Press.

Layard, Antonia (2010). 'Shopping in the Public Realm: A Law of Place', *Journal of Law and Society* 37: 412–41.

Layard, Antonia (2019). 'Planning by Numbers: Affordable Housing and Viability in England'. In *Planning and Knowledge: How New Forms of Technocracy are Shaping Contemporary Cities*, edited by Mike Raco and Frederico Savini, 213–24. Bristol: Bristol University Press.

Lee, Maria et al (2018). 'Techniques of Knowing in Administration: Co-production, Models, and Conservation Law', *Journal of Law and Society* 45: 427–56.

Lord, Alex and Mark Tewdwr-Jones (2014). 'Is Planning "Under Attack"? Chronicling the Deregulation of Urban and Environmental Planning in England', *European Planning Studies* 22: 345–61.

Loughlin, Martin (1996). *Legality and Locality. The Role of Law in Central-Local Government Relations*. Oxford: Clarendon Press.

McAuslan, Patrick (1980). *Ideologies of Planning Law*. Oxford: Pergamon Press.

Marshall, Tim (2004). 'Regional Planning in England: Progress and Pressures since 1997', *The Town Planning Review* 75: 447–72.

Marshall, Tim (2021). *The Politics and Ideology of Planning*. Bristol: Bristol University Press.

Ministry of Housing, Communities and Local Government (2020a). *Improving Planning Performance: Criteria for Designation*.

Ministry of Housing, Communities and Local Government (2020b). *White Paper: Planning for the Future*.

Ministry of Housing, Communities and Local Government (2021a). *National Planning Policy Framework*.

Ministry of Housing, Communities and Local Government (2021b). *National Design Code: Planning Practice Guidance for Beautiful, Enduring and Successful Places*.

Mitchell, Edward (2020). 'Financial Viability Modelling in Urban Property Development', *Northern Ireland Legal Quarterly* 71: 35–55.

National Audit Office (2021). *The Local Government Finance System in England: Overview and Challenges HC 858*.

Purcell, Mark (2006). 'Urban Democracy and the Local Trap', *Urban Studies* 43: 1921–41.

Riles, Anneliese (2005). 'A New Agenda for the Cultural Study of Law: Taking on the Technicalities', *Buffalo Law Review* 53: 973–1033.

Roberts, Jane (2020). 'The Leadership of Place and People in the New English Combined Authorities', *Local Government Studies* 46: 995–1014.

Royal Town Planning Institute (2020). *Planning Through Zoning*.

Ruiz-Tagle, Samuel (2020). '*Samuel Smith* and Judicial Review of Policy Interpretation: A Middle Way in the Law and Policy Divide', *Journal of Environmental Law* 32: 577–87.

Sandford, Mark (2019a). 'Money Talks: The Finances of English Combined Authorities', *Local Economy* 34: 106–22.

Sandford, Mark (2019b). *Two Masters: The Dilemma of Central-Local Relations in England*, Report prepared for UK2070 Commission. *Make No Little Plans* (UK2070 Commission, 2020) available at http://uk2070.org.uk/wp-content/uploads/2020/04/08-Central-local-relations-web.pdf (accessed 12 June 2022).

Tewdwr-Jones, Mark (1999). 'Discretion, Flexibility, and Certainty in British Planning: Emerging Ideological Conflicts and Inherent Political Tensions', *Journal of Planning Education and Research* 18: 244–56.

Tomaney, John and Jessica Ferm (2018). 'Introduction: Conexts and Frameworks for Contemporary Planning Practice'. In *Planning Practice: Critical Perspectives from the UK*, edited by Jessica Ferm and John Tomaney, 1–19. Oxford: Routledge.

Town and Country Planning Association (2018). *Planning 2020: Raynsford Review of Planning in England*.

Upton, William (2019). 'What is the Purpose of Planning Policy? Reflections on the Revised National Planning Policy Framework 2018', *Journal of Environmental Law* 31: 135–49.

UK2070 Commission (2020). *Make No Little Plans: Acting at Scale for a Fairer and Stronger Future*.

Part II
Place shaping, place framing
Carolyn Abbot and Maria Lee

Planning is 'concerned with everything that makes a successful place'[1] in a physical and a social sense. The purpose of this part is to shine a light on the scope and variety of planning as a scholarly activity, from Steven Vaughan and Brad Jessup's account of the role of planning law in contributing to the production and sustaining of queer spaces, to Antonia Layard's analysis of highways as a resource, to Margherita Pieraccini's assessment of the potential for an ecosystem approach to be integrated into marine spatial planning. Given our sense that legal scholars contribute less than they might to our understanding and appreciation of planning, this volume seeks to highlight the very broad potential of planning law scholarship, rather than pinning the contributors down to a particular approach to, or aspect of, planning law. Our contributors to Part 2 put this into practice beautifully.

The three contributions in this part reveal multiple ways in which planning law can contribute to shaping and framing our understanding of place. They take us beyond the traditional legal focus on development consent, and highlight the multitude of tools and approaches used in planning law, from heritage listing, to compulsory purchase, to the designation of low-traffic neighbourhoods. They also highlight the significance of our *understandings* of place. A highway is more than a right of passage, an LGBTQ+ venue is more than bricks and mortar. Both Layard's and Vaughan and Jessup's chapters highlight the contestation and disagreement over what particular places are, and who they are for. And whilst the progressive and ambitious intellectual underpinnings of sustainable development are all but forgotten in the drive for 'development' on land, Pieraccini opens up the potential for fresh ambition in the context of marine planning.

Note

1. Town and Country Planning Association 2018, 12.

Reference

Town and Country Planning Association (2018). *Planning 2020: Raynsford Review of Planning in England.*

3
Backstreet's back alright: London's LGBT+ nightlife spaces and a queering of planning law and planning practices

Steven Vaughan and Brad Jessup[*]

Introduction

Across the period 1986 to 2016, over 200 individual LGBT+ nightlife spaces (bars, pubs, nightclubs etc) operated in London. That number has varied over time. London LGBT+ nightlife spaces enjoyed a steady increase in number from 1986 to 2001, a slight drop from 2001 to 2006, and then recent and significant intensification in closures.[1] From 2006 to 2017, the number of London LGBT+ nightlife spaces plummeted from 121 to 51. This drop is much greater than that for nightlife spaces more generally.[2] These types of LGBT+ nightlife spaces – typically out of view, generally architecturally modest, and often obscured to the wider public – have long been valued by queers. For many, they have deep meaning related to their identities: as places of coming out; of finding communities; of being safe. The construction of space by queers and the value of queer space to queer people has been the subject of much research in geography, sociology and history.[3] Yet, the role of planning law in the production, maintenance and protection of queer spaces remains underexplored. This chapter seeks to partly fill that gap.

In what follows, we analyse the legal and political happenings of three London LGBT+ night-time spaces. The first, The Royal Vauxhall Tavern, is a queer pub in Vauxhall. Supporters have generated what they label as a 'quadruple lock' against redevelopment, including Grade II listing and the designation of the space as an Asset of Community Value.

The second, Backstreet, is a small fetish (leather and rubber) club. Located in London's East End, it was 'saved' by Tower Hamlets Development Committee from redevelopment. The third, XXL, a men-only, 2,000 capacity bear[4] club near London Bridge, closed in September 2019 because of a £2.5bn development scheme.[5]

We argue that the ways in which these spaces have intersected with planning law demonstrate the heteronormativity of planning laws and an ignorance of the connection between place and sexualities, even when LGBT+ people are identified (by developers, planners and others) as being present in those places. We are curious as to what might become of planning law if it were informed by queer legal theory. This includes the idea that the law should be less binarised and especially inclusive of alternative ways of living and experiencing; and ideas of how the law should disrupt dominant power and cultural relations and give agency and recognition to the particular marginalities of LGBTQIA+ people on their own terms.[6] This kind of analysis adds to the already critical view of planning law as being driven by individualistic and what some might frame as neoliberal perspectives,[7] an antithesis of a queer approach.

This chapter asks a series of questions about planning practices and offers thoughts on possible ways forward, especially precipitated by legal change. Our energising premise is that planning law and practices should recognise queer spaces and consider queerness as deserving of protection in relation to space and location. What we will see is that the architecture of planning law creates a structure and opportunities for both possibilities and non-possibilities for negotiating and protecting queer spaces. Those spaces are physical instantiations of a history which has too often been rendered invisible through homophobia or an antagonism to queerness.

Our chapter unfolds in five parts. We begin with our methodology and then turn to a snapshot of the various planning law regimes that are relevant to the spaces we discuss. After setting out the ambits of existing research on queer spaces, we offer a set of narratives about our three case studies and how they have intersected with planning law. We conclude with what we see as useful ways forward for LGBTQIA+ people in, and a queering of, planning law. Here, we suggest that there are various ways in which planning can be better attentive to queer culture, needs, histories and theory through the ways in which queer spaces are produced, maintained and protected through planning law. Law is of especial importance. It is through law that development and destruction occur, observable to communities of interest. We hope with this work to make contributions to the material practices of planning as well as to queer theory. And so we suggest, for example, that the law might be better reflective of the lived history of heritage rather than the material embodiment of heritage.

Methodology

We use three 'different but related' case studies in this chapter to look for similarities and differences within and between specific instances in which queer spaces in London have engaged with planning law.[8] The three sites were chosen for our project because: they are subject to the same planning regimes and policy architectures (all three being in London); they each intersected with planning law in (differing) significant ways in 2019; the outcome in each case is different (one space lost, one 'saved', one still fighting); and even though they are generally viewed as spaces for gay men, they do represent some variety in queer nightlife spaces (a queer pub, a fetish bar and a bear club).

Case studies are used to develop as full as possible an understanding of the happening under review; to examine that happening 'in its natural setting, recognizing its complexity and its context'.[9] Indeed, context is said to be one of the key elements separating the use of case studies from other similarly thick, detailed, qualitative work.[10] As such, case studies are thought to be particularly useful in responding to *how?* and *why?* questions (here, for example, how does planning law recognise the relationship between place, community and sexuality?; and why might planners not be able to fully value that relationship?).[11] We have chosen this approach for our project because case studies are, and our approach to the material is, part analytical/doctrinal and part narrative,[12] this tack suiting one of our aims which is to make more public, and to a more diverse set of audiences, the stories of queer spaces.

We are open about the simple facts that our data set is small (n=3), our geographic focus is limited (to London),[13] we are interested primarily in a snapshot in time (what happened in 2019), we have preferenced the urban over the rural,[14] and that while to some extent different in their form and function, our queer spaces are each nightlife venues and each (primarily; one exclusively) spaces for gay men. While some reflexivity is required about stepping unthoughtfully into generalisations from one or a handful of case studies,[15] there is nothing necessarily problematic about the use of case studies to offer thoughts about broader topics,[16] especially if such broader sense-making is done sensitively (which we aim to do).[17]

Like many other case studies, we draw on a range of disparate documentary materials and sources in what follows.[18] For each queer space we examine, we have looked at the relevant planning regimes, documents on local authority and the Greater London Authority (GLA) websites (including planning decisions, minutes of committee meetings, consultations and consultation responses, policy documents, and so on), articles on those spaces in the mainstream and queer media, comments and items on community and activist group web pages, and chat rooms and other online discussion fora (Twitter, Facebook, etc). This documentary digging and reflection for the purpose of storytelling and doctrinal analysis, engaging with hundreds of planning-related documents, took place between August 2019 and August 2021.

The relevant legal space

Our cases touch upon a diversity of dynamic planning regimes (and associated policies) which have become layered over time. These are: regimes which shape plan-making at local, regional and national levels; regimes which direct and shape planning permission; regimes which allow planning authorities to bargain certain benefits from developers by way of obligations linked to the grant of planning permission (known as section 106 agreements); regimes which are designed to protect certain places and areas from (re)development (through heritage listings, 'local listings' and Conservation Area designations);[19] regimes which give groups a first refusal to buy certain types of spaces on their proposed sale (so-called 'assets of community value'); regimes which are intended to keep a check on spaces changing their current use to future different uses; and regimes which set out what those categories of use are and how they can be assessed.[20] Legal regimes on the compulsory purchase of land by the state are also relevant, although did not arise in our three case studies.[21]

There is then the Equality Act 2010 and its public sector equality duty, which says that public bodies (such as planning authorities) must give due regard to eliminating unlawful discrimination, to advancing equality of opportunity, and to encouraging good relations; all in the context of a list of 'protected characteristics' (including sexual orientation).[22] This positive duty is a marked departure from section 28 of the Local Government Act 1988, which stipulated (until its repeal in 2003) that local governments must abstain from 'intentionally promoting homosexuality'.[23] Because each of our three case studies is located in London, the GLA, led by the Mayor of London, is also relevant. Established in

2000,[24] the GLA is neither a devolved body, like the Welsh Government, nor a conventional local authority, but something in-between.[25] While most planning matters are for Greater London's 35 individual planning authorities (local councils and boroughs),[26] the Mayor has step-in rights and must be sent applications of 'potential strategic importance' for consideration.[27] These include developments with more than 150 houses, flats, or houses and flats and buildings more than 30 metres high outside the City.[28] The effect of the GLA's planning responsibility is to add a further scalar dimension to planning,[29] discussed in more detail by Maria Lee in this volume, and also has generated additional planning policy that overlays the local and sometimes challenges national plans.

Queer spaces and their demise

Alan Collins writes of four stages of change in queer spaces, starting with the initial presence of a single gay bar and then, in the second stage, a greater mass of LGBT+-friendly services.[30] In the fourth stage, we see a shift 'from celebrated gayborhood [the third stage] to lucrative investment opportunity'.[31] This fourth stage, in which our case studies are situated, brings with it the influx of affluence to a space which often forces out its prior residents and communities, said to be part of 'neoliberal strategies of urban governance'.[32] With physical changes to queer spaces also come the potential for changes in identity and values. As Olimpia Burchiellaro puts it, 'Gentrification rendered (un)intelligible those queer and working-class ways of being which challenge the spatio-temporal logics of capitalist normativity, unveiling the "straightening" effects of inclusion within a process of capital accumulation'.[33] In this way, others have argued that difference can be included (via planning law) only to the extent that a sanitised and straight-sanctioned version of queerness is acceptable,[34] and where planning law straightens out the 'wonkiness' and unacceptability of the queer.[35] As Samuel Douek puts it, 'not only does the city observe a transition of physical amenity from democratic to commodified, but the notion of queer identity moves towards conformist respectability'.[36] We come back to this below.

Turning now to London and its queer nightlife spaces, our focus shifts to two seminal studies undertaken by Ben Campkin and Lo Marshall which chart the period from 1986 to 2017 (noted in our Introduction).[37] When Campkin and Marshall explored why London LGBT+ venues had closed (down in number from 121 to 51 between 2006 and 2017), the most common reason was redevelopment.[38] A significant number had been forced to close because of large-scale infrastructure projects in London (including Crossrail and the Channel Tunnel Link).[39] Few, a mere 5 per cent, closed because of financial problems.[40] Similar closures of queer spaces, and for the same reasons, have been seen in North America[41] and Australia.[42] Campkin and Marshall also conducted a survey with 239 members of the queer community about their experiences of and views on nightlife spaces. That survey showed high levels of anxiety around the LGBT+ nightlife closures and a desire for 'safe spaces', 'havens' and 'substitute homes';[43] places 'in which diverse gender identities and sexualities are affirmed, accepted and respected'.[44] In more recent work, Campkin and Marshall have argued that 'real estate-led global city competitiveness is affecting our capacity to secure the heritage of queer publics, and for them to keep a foothold in the spaces they have historically occupied'.[45] We would agree, with one slight gloss; namely that it is a combination of 'real estate-led global city competitiveness' and also the framing and practices of our current planning law regimes that is affecting our capacity. With that in mind, we now turn to our case studies.

Case study 1 – The Royal Vauxhall Tavern

The Royal Vauxhall Tavern (RVT) (372 Kennington Lane) was built in 1863 at Spring Gardens on land which was originally part of the Vauxhall Pleasure Gardens (a space for public and alternative entertainments thought to have been used since the 1660s). From the later parts of the nineteenth century, the RVT was recognised as a drag and cabaret venue.[46] The RVT became known as an LGBT+ space from at least the 1960s.[47] While much of the surrounding area in Vauxhall was redeveloped in the 1970s and 1980s, the RVT managed to escape demolition.[48] The pub has been, and continues to be, the home for many famous drag artists (including Lily Savage) and has been a welcoming space for many (including, it is said, Diana, Princess of Wales, who went there dressed in men's clothes, accompanied by Freddy Mercury and Kenny Everett).[49] It has also been an important site for LGBT+ activism and campaigning, and avowedly queer in recent years.[50]

James Lindsay took over the RVT in 2005. The business, Vauxhall Tavern London Limited, was restructured in both 2014 and 2019, with the freehold property sold, in 2014, by Lindsay to Austrian property developer Immovate.[51] A 20-year lease renewal was signed between Lindsay and Immovate in October 2018. The sale to Immovate prompted the creation of the RVT Future campaign, 'made up of Tavern performers, promoters and regulars . . . fighting to secure the future of the Royal Vauxhall Tavern as an LGBTQ pub and queer performance space'.[52] What happened over the following five years is striking, making the RVT both an outlier as regards queer spaces and a fascinating case study choice. Work by RVT Future campaigners led to what they term a 'quadruple lock' to protect the RVT. First, RVT Future, as a community interest company, and considered to have a 'local connection' to the venue, succeeded in having the property designated by Lambeth Council under the Localism Act 2011 as an 'Asset of Community Value' in October 2014 (and redesignated for another five years in October 2019). As a consequence of this designation, the RVT has a 'Community Right to Bid' should the property be put up for sale (including a statutory six-month period for community fund-raising).[53] Lambeth Council keeps a document listing each of its community assets of value.[54] It says about the RVT that is it home to 'A range of community activities including performance arts, cabaret, musical and burlesque'.[55] Nothing is said here about the RVT being a queer space. In June 2018, RVT Future set up and registered the Vauxhall Tavern Community Benefit Society Limited with the Financial Conduct Authority. This would be the vehicle used for any community buy-out of the RVT and was made possible as part of a fund-raising campaign which saw over 800 RVT supporters donate £31,331, far below the anticipated sale price of the building of over £2,500,000.

As the second part of the 'quadruple lock', RVT Future had an idea that they described as 'more ambitious': to get the RVT heritage-protected under English planning law.[56] Here, the relevant policy seeks to protect 'heritage assets' (broadly defined in the National Planning Policy Framework (NPPF) and given further substance via a set of Good Practice Advice Notes and other planning practice guidance), with the Planning (Listed Buildings and Conservation Areas) Act 1990 (the LBCA Act 1990) the main piece of legislation. Under section 1 of the LBCA Act 1990, the relevant Secretary of State is required to compile a list of 'buildings of special architectural or historic interest'. The criteria for 'special interest' are found primarily in a guidance document published by the Department for Digital, Culture, Media and Sport, titled 'Principles of Selection for Listing Buildings'. An enhanced consent process exists for alterations to or the demolition of any buildings so listed (section 8 LBCA Act 1990). Interestingly, *anyone* can apply for any building to be included on the National Heritage List for England, which is managed and maintained by Historic England (formerly known as English Heritage). Historic England advises the Secretary of State on listing and solicits nominations for listing direct from any community member or group, unfiltered by local planning authorities (LPAs).

In January 2015, RVT Future submitted a listing application to English Heritage. A 'lukewarm interim report' was received.[57] Concerned that the listing application might not be successful, a revised application was submitted on 8 June 2015 (double the length of the first application), including letters of support from 'eminent types', including artists, Sir Ian McKellen, three MPs and local vicars. A month later, in July 2015, Immovate published an open letter regarding the RVT and the listing process, suggesting that the RVT would likely close if listed (due to increased insurance and other costs) and that any such closure would be the fault of RVT Future.[58] A Grade II listing decision was nevertheless taken in September 2015, 'making the Royal Vauxhall Tavern the first ever British building listed for its importance to LGBTQ heritage'.[59] The listing application was made possible primarily because of the efforts of Ben Walters (also known as Dr Duckie, after a popular weekly RVT event). Walters' listing applications put forward a compelling case for the diversity of events taking place at the RVT and the importance of those events to a wide range of queer communities, rather than, as is typical in applications for heritage listing, an exclusive focus on the architectural interest of the building.[60]

The Historic England listing entry for the RVT says this about the pub's 'historic interest':

> the building has historic and cultural significance as one of the best known and longstanding LGB&T venues in the capital, a role it has played particularly in the second half of the C20. It has become an enduring symbol of the confidence of the gay community in London for which it possesses strong historic interest above many other similar venues nationally.

In the Mayor of London's 'A–Z of Planning and Culture', published in October 2015, it is said that the listing of the RVT 'raises interesting questions about what cultural value means, and to whom, and how we protect informal assets that have acquired heritage value over time'.[61] The RVT was the first building to be listed *because* of its queer heritage; because a queer community of longevity and geographic plurality could be attached to the place embodied by the RVT.[62] This is both unusual and significant. As Gail Dubrow and others remind us, speaking about queer spaces in the USA, 'The few landmarks of queer heritage that made their way onto landmark registers did so for incidental reasons, such as their architectural significance'.[63] This is a similar experience in the UK, which we highlight below.

As the third aspect of the 'quadruple lock', the Vauxhall Conservation Area has been expanded to include the RVT.[64] Section 69 of the LBCA Act

1990 requires local authorities to identify 'areas of special architectural or historic interest the character and appearance of which it is desirable to preserve or enhance' and to then designate those spaces as Conservation Areas. Once so designated, Conservation Areas are subject to enhanced planning controls (including on demolition requests, extensions and certain alterations).[65] In its Conservation Area Statement, Lambeth Council states that the RVT 'has become a recognised lesbian, gay, bisexual and transgender (LGBT) venue and a flagship for the gay community' and that 'Its presence, along with the availability of inexpensive premises locally has allowed LGBT bars and clubs to flourish'.[66]

Finally, and as the fourth aspect of the 'quadruple lock', RVT Future had the pub designated as mixed use *sui generis* (a mix of pub, nightclub and cabaret/performance space) via a planning application for a Certificate of Lawful Development (Existing) to Lambeth Council which was granted in January 2017.[67] As co-chair of RVT Future Rob Holley frames it, this mixed use designation 'means the Tavern's use must be balanced between these activities, and a new buyer couldn't parachute in a chain franchise or convert the top floors into private residential'.[68] This is not quite right, as applications for change of use would be possible, albeit any such application would be reviewed against Lambeth's Local Plan.

Before we turn to our second case study, it is worth saying a little more about the people behind RVT Future. The eight-strong group includes, in addition to Dr Duckie, Amy Lamé and Richard Heaton. Their bios are framed on the RVT Future website by reference to their connection with the RVT. What is not explained on the RVT Future website is the positions of influence that they hold. Lamé is the Mayor of London's 'Night Czar', appointed in 2016 to champion London's nightlife both in the UK and internationally, and Heaton is Sir Richard Heaton, the Permanent Secretary to the Ministry of Justice between 2015 and 2020 and now Warden of Robinson College Cambridge. RVT Future has both substantial political clout and significant legal expertise in its leadership, resonating with Carolyn Abbot's discussion of expertise in this volume.

Despite the 'quadruple lock', RVT Future is clear with its supporters that the RVT is not 'saved'. The pub was put up for sale in July 2021.

Case study 2 – Backstreet

Backstreet opened in 1985 and is London's 'longest running leather bar'.[69] A few steps from Mile End Tube station in the east of London, the bar operates a strict dress code (rubber, leather, 'executive'/suits, and so on, depending on the fetish night). As Claire Colum notes, the East End of London has traditionally been home to activities not welcomed inside the city walls.[70] One of the poorest parts of London, the East End had been able to resist gentrification until the early 2010s.[71] On 13 April 2016, Galliard Homes submitted a planning application to Tower Hamlets Council seeking approval to demolish the existing site and to build a 12-storey tower comprising residential units, some commercial space and a nightclub. As part of the application, Stephen Levrant Heritage Architecture Ltd authored a 'Heritage Statement, Townscape and Visual Impact Assessment' dated March 2017. Backstreet is not mentioned in this assessment.

The decision-maker, the Tower Hamlets Strategic Development Committee, met on 16 February 2017. From that meeting, we learn that Galliard Homes had agreed to a 'relocation strategy' for Backstreet plus up to £10,000 of relocation costs as part of a section 106 agreement linked to the development application. This is some change in tune, given Backstreet was initially told the bar would have 12 months to vacate the site if the planning permission was granted. Despite support from the Planning Officer, the Tower Hamlets Strategic Development Committee did not approve the April 2016 application by Galliard Homes. The Committee minutes detail various reasons for the lack of approval, primarily linked to the 'height and bulk' of the proposal. Backstreet was also a consideration, but a minor one. Interestingly, 'the Committee asked questions about the loss of the club and why this was considered acceptable. [Planning] Officers felt that it could invite a conflict with the residential use in terms of the amenity impact.' This is not surprising, David Bell and Jon Binni having noted that 'as areas become more "respectable", so gay commercial spaces are forced out'.[72] We come back to this below.

Following the February 2017 refusal, Galliard Homes revised its application, and the documents came back to the same Committee. More is said this time round about Backstreet. As part of site notices and letters sent to locals about the application, we are told that 'A number of representations received attest to the fact that it [Backstreet] is an important and renowned LGBT venue, both within London and further afield'.[73] In his report for the Committee meeting on 25 April 2017, Case Officer Brett McAllister sets out that:[74]

> The existing nightclub serving a particular part of the gay community can be considered to be of some public value, given that sexual orientation is a protected characteristic under the Equalities Act 2010, and it could be held to be [a] local community facility in policy terms. However, for the reasons set out within the report, the

harm resulting from the loss of this facility, to allow for the provision of housing and commercial space in a sustainable location, is justified in planning terms.

In his report, the Case Officer also noted Policy 3.1 of the London Plan which set out that development 'should protect and enhance facilities and services that meet the needs of particular groups and communities'.[75] Despite concluding that Backstreet contributed 'community infrastructure' and serviced a local and translocal queer community,[76] the Case Officer recommended that the planning application be approved (given the high residential quality of the proposal, the feeling that the proposal would 'relate well' with the local area, and that any amenity or heritage impacts would be minor/acceptable). For eight different reasons (one of which was the loss of Backstreet), the Tower Hamlets Strategic Development Committee refused the revised application.[77]

Skip forward four months and a (re)revised application from Galliard Homes comes back to the Committee. This (re)revised application includes a proposed nightclub in the basement of the space, with the offer of a planning obligation via a section 106 agreement to provide 'first refusal' on that nightclub to the Backstreet owner.[78] The Backstreet owners were said to be content with this way forward. No other aspects of the application had changed (on height, bulk, density, massing, air quality impacts, etc). The Committee refused the (re)revised application. In a 20 November 2017 letter, the Mayor of London set out that he did not see any need to 'take over' the application for his own determination.[79] In a GLA planning report accompanying the Mayor of London's letter,[80] reference was made to the offer in the (re)revised application to give Backstreet first refusal on the basement nightclub: 'The proposed revisions are strongly supported in line with London Plan Policy 4.6 and the Culture and Night Time Economy Supplementary Planning Guidance, and should be secured as part of any future planning permission.' This report also notes the 'long standing' presence of Backstreet, 'a well-established and unique community facility at a time when such venues are coming increasingly under threat'.[81]

An appeal against a further decision in December 2017 by Tower Hamlets to refuse the development was lodged on 13 June 2008, under section 78 of the Town and Country Planning Act 1990 and requesting a planning inquiry.[82] In her Appeal Decision of 9 August 2019, rejecting the appeal, Planning Inspector Julia Gregory made some interesting observations about Backstreet. One was that, because Backstreet served 'a national and even international clientele', it did not fall within the Tower Hamlets provisions that spoke to the need to protect the 'local community'.[83] Like the Development Committee, Inspector Gregory was also concerned about possible future conflict between the future owners of the development's apartments and the users of Backstreet should the development be permitted.[84] She came to the view that 'much of the charm of the club may be hard to replicate' and felt 'the future of the club is at this time in significant peril'.[85] How Inspector Gregory went on to frame the 'Conclusions' in the appeal is also worth exploring. She stated that 'all the benefits [of the proposed development] would be at the expense of the character and appearance of the area more generally, and the tall building would be contrary to the scale of buildings envisaged in the development plan for this location'. Backstreet, and its future, is only relevant in the Conclusions in the penultimate paragraph: 'Furthermore, I am not satisfied that the future of the club is protected.'[86] We come back to this 'Furthermore' below.

On 16 August 2019, the *Guardian* published a piece titled 'London Council Saves Gay Fetish Club from Redevelopment'.[87] Even allowing for some journalistic licence, the way in which the *Guardian* framed what happened with the space at 562 Mile End Road is striking. One would be forgiven, reading this piece, for thinking that Backstreet's presence (and its possible futures) was the *only* reason for why planning permission was refused and why the planning appeal failed. The Deputy Mayor of Tower Hamlets, Councillor Rachel Blake, is quoted in the *Guardian* as saying that Backstreet is 'an important community asset'. As such, the Council was 'going the extra mile . . . to protect safe spaces for our diverse community. It is the last true gay fetish club, and diversity matters to us,' she said. 'This kind of venue really matters to us, it matters to Tower Hamlets and to the whole of London. It is very important to have safe spaces for the whole community.'[88]

The sincerity of these words is not doubted. However, what the above wider narrative makes clear is that Backstreet was one of a *number* of reasons why planning permission was refused by the Council and, notwithstanding the presence of the Equality Act or planning policy about the importance of community facilities or a campaign led by the Breeches and Leather Uniform Fanclub (BLUF), the queer community at issue and their connection to place was at best a minor consideration for the Planning Inspector in the denied planning appeal.

Case study 3 – XXL

Twenty years ago, and borne out of boredom with London's gay scene, which was especially centred around Soho and the West End, Mark Ames created XXL, a club night dedicated to bears. By 2002, XXL had a permanent home in The Arches, close to London Bridge, and began to spread to club nights in other parts of the UK and the USA, and then to develop a large number of associated Pride events. XXL is one of the world's most recognisable bear movements, with 'over 100,000 members around the world'.[89] As part of an expansion, XXL moved to Pulse Nightclub in 2012, where it hosted nights catering to 2,000 bear clubbers and their admirers. It is here where our planning story begins. It is also a complex story and much of the detailed insight in what follows comes from a detailed response to an 18 July 2019 FOI request made to City Hall.[90]

In 2014, Southwark Council granted planning permission for a large-scale redevelopment of space bounded by Blackfriars Road, Southwark Street, Hopton Street and the River Thames; a £2.5 billion scheme of almost 500 new flats through nine new buildings ranging from five to 49 storeys to be known as Bankside Yards.[91] Pulse Nightclub, at 1 Invicta Plaza, was within this scheme. The Mayor of London, in his review of the planning application, had noted the need for an equalities impact assessment under the Equalities Act 2010 given that the 'proposal would involve the loss of a gay nightclub'.[92] What happens next is not especially clear, but it seems (from a letter from XXL's solicitors) as though Southwark then refused planning permission for the continued operation of Pulse and, after that, proceeded to review the Bankside Yards application.[93] The effect of the refusal was to discard the need for an equalities impact assessment because XXL no longer had permission to operate. As the XXL solicitor puts it, 'In effect they could and did pretend you didn't exist, for the purposes of whether they needed to do a diversity report or not'.[94] What is striking is that, in setting out their reasons for refusing to grant planning permission for Pulse's continued use, Southwark explicitly noted the 'changing residential character of the area' due to another redevelopment (No. 1 Blackfriars) and as a result of the current Bankside Yards application. Put together:[95]

> It was felt that the harm to existing residents (such as those within River Court and Rennie Court) as well as future residents was significant and in the absence of suitable controls and mitigation, would be of detriment to the existing and future residents of the surrounding area.

The logic of this argument escapes us. XXL appealed the Pulse refusal and won.

The Bankside Yards developer appears to have made no effort to include XXL's continued operation in its plans. The October 2013 report prepared for the Southwark Planning Committee as part of the planning application deliberations notes that plans were shown to provide new uses in place of the nightclub.[96] There is then a gap between 2014 (the grant of the Bankside Yards planning permission) and 2017 when, we think, XXL was able to continue to operate as normal as other parts of the Bankside Yards development carried on around but did not disturb Pulse nightclub. Native Land bought the site in 2015. In the spring of 2017, Native Land indicated to XXL that the club would shortly be served with a six-month eviction notice.[97] By way of response, XXL asked the Mayor of London, in May 2017, to intervene in the redevelopment. James McNeil and Mark Ames (XXL's owners) suggested that 'What is actually taking place is a social cleansing of the neighbourhood so they [Native Land] can maximise their price on each unit by not having a gay nightclub there'. The GLA Public Liaison Officer replied to McNeil and Ames to (rightly) note that the 2013 planning application had been reviewed by the previous Mayor of London, Boris Johnson, that authority had been delegated to Southwark to make the decision at that time, and that it would not now be possible to unpick that planning decision.

XXL was not evicted in 2017 (again, for reasons which are unclear to us) and continued to operate. Skip ahead two years and on 24 June 2019, XXL was served with a three-month eviction notice by Native Land.[98] XXL appealed the notice but was unsuccessful. A change.org petition to the Mayor of London to save XXL collected just under 6,000 signatures, but also led nowhere.[99] Various meetings took place between XXL, Southwark and the Mayor of London's office in the summer of 2019. Relations between XXL's owners and Amy Lamé, the Night Czar, seem complex; an 8 July 2019 email from Amy to Mark and James, for example, asked why a petition had been created to seek her support when she had already been giving it 'since 2017'.

At a July 2019 Southwark Council Members' Questions meeting, Councillor David Nokes asked the leader of the council what support the council had given to XXL. The council leader's response is worth setting out in full:

> The council is committed to provide full assistance to XXL to either remain in their current location or find alternative premises.
> The loss of LGBTQ+ venues is a pan-London issue and one which we take very seriously. To this end meetings have been hosted by Councillor Johnson Situ with XXL, the Mayor's Night Czar, Arch Co and Native Land.

Further meetings are planned with Arch Co and XXL, as well as Native Land, in order to see if a solution can be found.

What seems to be lost in this response is any sense of historic responsibility on the part of Southwark Council. The council that gave the planning permission for the redevelopment (in 2014), and which had incorrectly refused the planning permission for the continued operation of Pulse nightclub, had contributed to the decline across London of queer spaces, not sought to redress it. XXL was evicted and the final XXL club night at Pulse took place on 21 September 2019.

Queering planning law

Jason Prior argues that 'formal urban planning processes and regulations are increasingly used as mechanisms to govern sexuality within later 20th century Western cities'.[100] In this section, we want to reflect on our three case studies and what they suggest about current planning practices and regimes, and how those practices and regimes might be better attentive to queer people, culture, needs and histories. Let us begin by talking about plans. Campkin and Marshall argue that there should be a 'requirement for local authorities to recognise the importance of LGBTQ+ venues in their borough plans'.[101] We agree, and it is obvious that work needs to be done, including to better address the histories of those venues. Thinking about the locales of our three case studies, neither the Tower Hamlets Local Plan 2013 nor the Southwark Plan, adopted in 2007 and due for revision, mentions queer spaces or queer people at all. The Lambeth Local Plan, adopted in September 2015, is a little better, with two references, noting for example that 'Vauxhall is renowned for its nightlife, with various lesbian, gay, bisexual and transgendered (LGBT) and other venues'.[102] We wonder if a certain kind of queerness and a certain kind of space – the RVT being a very visible pub in a part of London with an accepted recent history of homosexuality – is more likely to feature in local plans than other spaces (such as, for instance, an underground fetish bar in the East End). Away from our case studies, Planning Out (a forum for LGBT+ planning professionals) makes reference to a 'pioneering' level of 'explicit promotion and protection of LGBT+ places' in Westminster's City Plan in relation to Soho,[103] overlooking the predominance of venues for gay men in that part of London (the concept of the 'gay village' often criticised for its lack of inclusivity),[104] and hiding altogether places and experiences of queer people lacking abdominal muscles: Backstreet and

XXL among them. Recalling queer theory, local plans across London do little to dissolve categories and challenge understandings of queer and they fail to recognise LGBT+ largely beyond the LGB (and often only the G). The London Plan 2021 makes no explicit reference to queer spaces and their importance, the Strategy simply noting that 900,000 LGBT+ people live in London. Nor are queer people or queer spaces mentioned anywhere in the Integrated Impact Assessment prepared by Arup as part of the London Plan's development. The approach by Westminster with Soho is laudable, but it should not take the location of a gay village for an LPA to reflect on the presence and importance of queer spaces in its area (and to speak to the value of those places, and the need to protect them, in their local plans). Inclusion and recognition in a plan will not, by itself, be enough of course. This is because the plan may contain multiple and contradictory provisions, something repeatedly noted in the relevant case law.[105]

Whether or not local plans have specific focus on queer spaces, we would also encourage LPAs to be more explicit, when granting or refusing planning permission which would impact a queer space, about how they have considered that queer space and its queer clientele in their decision-making. This could come from a reframing of, or addition to, what LPAs understand as 'other material considerations', to which they have a duty to have regard.[106] These can be broad if they have a 'proper planning purpose';[107] and 'any consideration which relates to the use and development of land is capable of being a planning consideration'.[108] Social and economic factors have previously been held to be relevant considerations.[109] Yet the consideration of such factors can depend on communities raising concerns as part of the planning process. While RVT Future, led by privileged folk familiar with planning politics, found planning law devices through which to insert their concerns in a manner that the planning system could recognise, that was not the case our other spaces. With Backstreet, BLUF and its director Nigel Whitfield ran a series of 'Backstreet: How you can help save it' blogposts on the BLUF website. These posts contained detailed information on how BLUF members could and should write to Tower Hamlets expressing their support for the continued operation of Backstreet. Initially, BLUF members were specifically encouraged *not* to object to the Backstreet redevelopment *solely* on the grounds of its importance as a queer space:[110]

> It may be worth mentioning the importance of The Backstreet as a venue for the gay community, but remember that is not one of

the specific points on which the application will be judged, so you should refer to some of those above.

BLUF felt unable to advise its members to frame their objections to the proposed development around sexuality.[111] The practice of the law operated to disguise and further marginalise those members. The bar (and its history and importance) was ultimately a part of Tower Hamlets' decision-making, and it featured in the appeal heard by the Planning Inspector, but we can do better than the space being a 'Furthermore' in a reasoned decision. Queer spaces – their histories, uses, contributions, value, and so on – are capable of being material. This was highlighted by local politicians who saw, at least in their comments to the *Guardian*, Backstreet as part of the fabric of Mile End. Planners, and planning inspectors, should have the confidence to engage with queer spaces centrally and head on. Backstreet and XXL both show the ways in which new developments have the potential to crowd out existing queer uses of space by bringing (quiet, clean, gentrified) residential development to places that had noisier, dirtier, less sanitised uses. We are not, to be clear, of the view that a place's essence as a queer space should automatically trump all other considerations, but we are in favour of some central guidance which offers some better protection for queer spaces and which can support LPAs in putting the materiality of queer spaces at the heart of their decision-making about those spaces.

Building on our concern about planning-driven queer sanitation, we have mixed feelings about the use of section 106 agreements, only reinforced by Edward Mitchell's chapter below. These agreements can constitute a privatisation of planning decision-making, creating opportunities for planning authorities to divest responsibility for realising public outcomes to developers.[112] Such agreements are also prone to be used as a point of leverage with developers, with negotiation occurring opaquely and out of public view. With Backstreet, while the Tower Hamlets' planning officers recognised the services the bar offered to the queer fetish community, those officers were also of the view (given their recommendations that planning approval be granted) that the space could easily be replicated, via a section 106 agreement, with a new basement venue in the redeveloped space. Recall that the Planning Inspector, however, saw this differently, questioning how simple it would be to replicate 'the charm of the club'.[113] With XXL, having served the queer club an eviction notice, Native Land went on, in August 2019, to commit to putting an 'LGBT+ occupier' into a new 'cultural space' as part of Bankside Yards, having 'listened to the concerns raised by Southwark Council, City Hall and London's LGBT+ community at the loss of a dedicated venue'.[114] In January 2020, Southwark entered into a planning agreement with Native Land for a new queer space to open by the end of 2022. But it will not be a space for XXL. Councillor Johnson Situ commented that:[115]

> While the new space will not be a like for like replacement, this agreement ensures it will provide a safe place for people to meet, socialise and celebrate the diverse LGBTQ+ population in our borough.

Queer spaces are not fungible and section 106 agreements may give the impression that those spaces are being 'saved' when in fact they are not. In her year-long ethnographic fieldwork on a community campaign to save The Joiners Arms (a queer pub in East London), Burchiellaro writes that 'the [section 106] agreement mobilized "diversity" as something not simply compatible with but that actually legitimated and justified the process of redevelopment'.[116] Reflecting on queer theory for a moment, and the experience of XXL and Backstreet alongside The Joiners Arms, what we see occurring through proposals to replicate venues are attempts to homogenise queerness just at a time when the diversity of queerness is being unhidden to a wider community. Campaigners against the Joiners Arms section 106 agreement objected to the developer's plans to restyle the venue. Rather than the facade being unremarkable and modest – the venue identified in part by its 'dicey atmosphere', 'permanently flooded toilets' and a 'haggard rainbow flag'[117] – its proposed replacement (with floor to ceiling windows) would, as one campaigner put it, resemble 'a fucking gastro-pub'.[118] In this regard, we might think of queer places as part of a 'counter-cultural response to marketed cosmopolitanism'.[119]

The foregoing discussion reveals that queer space replacements via section 106 agreements may be inappropriate and that planning authorities (including their case officers) should think carefully about how those agreements are deployed. It is entirely possible that planners using section 106 agreements to 'protect' queer spaces feel they are doing the right thing; saving something that might otherwise be lost. This is a risk of 'good planning' – that is, the risk that policies and processes and laws which are drafted in order to promote inclusivity end up threatening what is special and important about queer spaces. So, for example, the 'successes of Manchester's gay village led to an influx of heterosexual people to the village and a decrease in feelings of safety among queer people in the gay village'.[120] The Mayor of London's Culture and the Night-Time Economy Supplementary Planning Guidance states that:[121]

> Facilities that meet the needs of particular groups (for example, LGBT+ community) should be protected. The loss of these facilities should be resisted.

But what does 'protection' mean? And is replacement the same as protection? On the latter, we think probably not in many cases.

This question of protection also arises in respect of listing regimes which, we feel, are not sufficiently attentive to queer heritage. Alois Riegl wrote the first substantial work on heritage in 1903; on how we might go about creating a schema of, and then deploying, heritage values. His work was exclusively about 'physical values and their physical preservation'.[122] More recently, and particularly in the last 20 years, a body of work on critical heritage studies has emerged which asks hard questions about the socio-political complexities that are associated with heritage theory and practice.[123] What we see with our case studies, and queer spaces more generally, is that time as an energising factor, for listing may serve to diminish the potential of the law to protect queer spaces.[124] As Historic England frames it: 'The older a building is, and the fewer the surviving examples of its kind, the more likely it is to be listed.'[125] Longevity and scarcity are key. Historic England also says that:

> Particularly careful selection is required for buildings from the period after 1945. Buildings less than 30 years old are not normally considered to be of special architectural or historic interest because they have yet to stand the test of time.[126]

This may prove challenging for queer spaces. Historic England explains that for older buildings with some notable physical fabric quality there should also be an interest in them that is connected with the 'nation's social, economic, cultural, or military history and/or [they should] have close historical associations with nationally important people'. What does this mean, then, for queer spaces with short or poorly documented histories? Or for queer spaces with a long history where the 'physical fabric' of those spaces is otherwise unremarkable? In September 2016, Historic England began to respond to these, and other, questions. In *Pride of Place: A Guide to Understanding and Protecting Lesbian, Gay, Bisexual, Transgender and Queer (LGBTQ) Heritage*, Historic England states that it aims to 'uncover new locations associated with England's LGBTQ past, and to revisit existing heritage sites and consider their LGBTQ significance'.[127] It is an important and praiseworthy piece of work by Historic England (in association with academics at Leeds Beckett University) but it is not immediately clear what outcomes *Pride of Place* has delivered.

While the exact number of listed buildings is not known (as single entries on the National Heritage List for England can cover multiple properties), it is thought that around 400,000 to 500,000 buildings are listed.[128] Only one, the Royal Vauxhall Tavern, has been listed *because* of its queer heritage. As part of *Pride of Place*, a handful of residential listed spaces have been relisted to have their queer heritage made (more) public. In 2016, for example, five buildings had their listing entries amended to include reference to their queer pasts (such as Oscar Wilde's house in Tite Street, London).[129] These additions to the list are valuable, and similar projects have taken place in the USA.[130] The RVT, however, is exceptional: in its history, in the diversity of uses across the queer community, in the expertise deployed to protect it. The RVT's exceptionality, especially contrasted with Backstreet and XXL, both supports the reasons for its Grade II listing but may also set a worryingly high bar for other queer spaces to be similarly protected. As Amin Ghaziani reminds us, 'Acts of queer cultural preservation and resistance make sense as life-saving, identity-affirming and community building'.[131] Listing could, and we think should, play a greater role in relation to the protection of queer spaces.[132] Perhaps, then, a different standard for listing, a less rigid set of understandings of a place being historic or not, and a greater sensitivity to the experiences of a community of people to a place should be applied by Historic England when it reviews listing applications for queer spaces.

Our calls for greater sensitivity probably speak to a need for education. Queer heritage is not homogenous. This is important to recall and also offers a practical hurdle to overcome. On the latter, and as Petra Doan has noted, the fluidity of 'queer' may pose some challenges to planning regimes and planners. This is both because the identities, interests and needs of the LGBT+ community are wide and diverse (and planning regimes and planners may not be alive to that diversity); and also because queer spaces may be in flux and change rapidly (and planning and planners may struggle to keep up).[133] We (where the 'we' includes policymakers and planners) need to remember that the term 'queer spaces' is often a shorthand for spaces used by a certain group of privileged white gay men, and that the history of these spaces shows painful examples of exclusion for lesbians, Black, Asian and minority ethnic queers, the trans community, and disabled and working-class queers.[134] Acknowledging that history does not detract from the argument that planning needs to be more attentive to queers and queer spaces. Rather, it reinforces the need for nuance and reflexivity.

We want to end with a reflection on how our three case studies might inform the law's conception of the local or the community of planning. There have been repeated calls for greater participation, engagement and democratisation in planning, culminating in demands for clear rights, responsibilities and a 'real voice' to be given to communities.[135] Planning law has not achieved this.[136] Local development plans, and the processes through which they have been developed, have not necessarily resulted in policy being created to accord with local views and values. This is attributed in part to the standardised nature of local plans, and the privileging of certain voices in the development of neighbourhood plans – with a more micro-scale of planning acting to entrench already active people through the law.[137] We have been critical in this chapter of the lack of integration of equality considerations within planning law, seen in the experience of XXL's closure and the downplaying of the interests of Backstreet's clientele. We are concerned that RVT Future as a group, and how it was able to deploy multiple vehicles of protection through planning, should be treated as anything other than extraordinary. What happened with the RVT should not set an expectation as to the degree and extent of community involvement needed to influence planning decisions. At the same time, equality, diversity and queerness are concepts that offer potential for the advancement of planning law ideas of participation. They suggest to us that it is not enough for planning law to invite neighbourhood involvement into its processes or for local views or values to be elicited solely from notable groups in the evaluation of the impacts of a land use or proposal. Planning law must animate the material, and respond to the experience and the utility of everyday places (queer and non queer).[138] Planning law needs to render visible the multiple and sometimes messily constructed communities of a city like London and make sure that places of safety, meeting and entertainment are afforded to the diverse populations within the city. We think that a starting point for a queerer planning system would be to resist the increasingly dominant view of planning as being a forum to foreshadow private development and debate and realise government infrastructure needs.[139] A queerer planning system would be better attentive to queer culture, histories and theory through the ways in which queer spaces are produced, maintained and protected, and, more generally, would also seek to disrupt dominant power and cultural relations through giving agency and recognition to the particular marginalities of a range of communities on their own terms. Both are goals worth advancing.

Notes

* We are grateful to Alexander Laurence for his research assistance support with this piece and to Liz Fisher for comments on an earlier draft. The usual disclaimer applies.
1. Campkin and Marshall 2017, 6.
2. See, generally, Haslam 2015.
3. See e.g. Binnie and Valentine 2019; Lim and Browne 2009; Knopp 2017; Lewis 1994; Livermon 2010; Podmore 2020 and 2013; Reed 1996.
4. Bears being a gay subculture of larger-build, hairy, bearded men that emerged in the 1980s. Manley, Levitt and Mosher 2007; Wright 1997.
5. XXL's closure was the prompt for this paper. Steven had planned to take Brad to the club during Brad's 2019 sabbatical at UCL Laws (and was surprised to hear of its demise). It is worth noting our positionality at this point. The authors are professional, white cis gay men, occupying a place of privilege within the queer umbrella. Through this chapter we do not suppose to speak on behalf of any particular community, queer or otherwise. Undoubtedly, our interest in the cases explored, and our observations about the loss of queer spaces, have been informed and framed through our lived experience.
6. Desert 1997, 19.
7. Allmendinger and Haughton 2013, 8.
8. Holder and McGillivray 2017, 187.
9. Punch 2005, 144. See also Taylor 2016, discussing the case study approach in the context of queer parental experiences.
10. Goddard 2010.
11. Meyer 2001.
12. George and Bennett 2005.
13. For work on queer spaces in other UK cities see Moran and Skeggs 2003.
14. See Hubbard 2013.
15. See e.g. the discussions in Morgera and Parks 2014.
16. Mitchell 1983, 188.
17. Flyvbjerg 2006, 219.
18. Webley 2010.
19. On listing see Mynors 2006.
20. Certificates of Lawful Development (Existing).
21. On which see generally Mitchell 2021.
22. Equality Act 2010, section 149.
23. Local Government Act 1988, section 28.
24. Via the Greater London Authority Act 1999 with additional planning powers coming from the Greater London Authority Act 2007. Also relevant are the Public Bodies Act 2011 and the Localism Act 2011.
25. House of Commons Library 2018; Barclay 2012.
26. For a list see Mayor of London n.d.
27. Town and Country Planning (Mayor of London) Order 2008 SI 2008/580, as amended.
28. Town and Country Planning (Mayor of London) Order 2008 SI 2008/580, Schedule 1.
29. Jessup 2014.
30. Collins 2004.
31. Douek 2016.
32. Bell and Binnie 2004.
33. Burchiellaro 2021, 32.
34. Stockton 2019.
35. Ahmed 2006.
36. Douek 2016, 188.
37. Campkin and Marshall 2016 and 2017.
38. Campkin and Marshall 2017, 7.

39. Campkin and Marshall 2018.
40. Campkin and Marshall 2018.
41. Doan 2014.
42. See Context 2017 for the story of the queer venue demise in Melbourne.
43. Campkin and Marshall 2018.
44. Campkin and Marshall 2017, 9.
45. Campkin and Marshall 2018.
46. Andersson 2011.
47. Historic England n.d., 'Royal Vauxhall Tavern'.
48. Watt 2009.
49. Rocos 2021.
50. Clowes 2019.
51. Kurschel and Kriechbaum 2021.
52. Historic England n.d., 'Royal Vauxhall Tavern'.
53. See the Assets of Community Value (England) Regulations 2012 SI 2012/2421 (regulations 2, 4, 5, 12–14 and Schedule 3) and the Localism Act (sections 95 and 96).
54. In line with regulation 2 of the Assets of Community Value (England) Regulations 2012 SI 2012/2421.
55. Lambeth Council 2015.
56. Planning (Listed Buildings and Conservation Areas) Act 1990, section 66.
57. Historic England n.d., 'Royal Vauxhall Tavern'.
58. Kurschel and Kriechbaum, 2015.
59. Historic England n.d., 'Royal Vauxhall Tavern'.
60. Walters 2015, 17 and 30.
61. Mayor of London 2015.
62. Gorman-Murray 2007; Rushbrook 2002.
63. Dubrow et al 2011, 203.
64. It is not immediately clear to us whether or to what extent RVT Future pushed for this extension of the Conservation Area.
65. Planning (Listed Buildings and Conservation Areas) Act 1990, section 72.
66. Lambeth Council 2016, [2.22].
67. Lambeth Council, Planning Application PA16/04138/LDCE.
68. Gay Star News 2017.
69. The Backstreet n.d.
70. Colomb 2009.
71. Butler and Hamnett 2011.
72. Bell and Binnie 2004, 1817.
73. Tower Hamlets Council, Planning Application PA/16/00943, 18 [8.12].
74. Tower Hamlets Council, Planning Application PA/16/00943, 4 [2.7].
75. Tomer Hamlets Council, Planning Application PA/16/00943, 19 [8.15].
76. Tower Hamlets Council, Planning Application PA/16/00943, 19 [8.18].
77. Tower Hamlets Council, 'Minutes', April 2017.
78. Tower Hamlets Council, 'Agenda', August 2017.
79. Khan 2017.
80. Greater London Authority (GLA) 2017.
81. GLA 2017, [5.85].
82. *Bestzone Ltd v London Borough of Tower Hamlets* [2019] APP/E5900/W/18/3204874.
83. *Bestzone*, [53].
84. *Bestzone*, [60].
85. *Bestzone*, [61].
86. *Bestzone*, [72].
87. Neate 2019.
88. Neate 2019.
89. This figure is set out in a letter from XXL to the Mayor of London, disclosed as part of an 18 July 2019 FOI request.
90. GLA 2019.
91. Southwark Council 2013.
92. GLA 2012, 21.

93. Whilst planning permission for the nightclub was granted back in 2006 and again in 2008, Southwark did not consider that the use had become established as the first permission was never implemented and the second was unlawfully implemented as two pre-commencement conditions were not discharged. We think it arguable that an equalities impact assessment should have been carried out in relation to the decision not to grant the nightclub permission. While the Equality Act 2010 does not specifically require equalities impact statements to be undertaken, they are one (common) way of evidencing reflection on and compliance with the section 149 public sector equality duty.
94. GLA 2019.
95. Southwark Council 2013, 281.
96. Southwark Council 2013, 280.
97. GLA 2019.
98. XXL n.d.
99. Huck 2019.
100. Prior 2008, 340. See also Bauman 2002.
101. Campkin and Marshall 2017, 53.
102. Lambeth Council 2021, 11.12.
103. Planning Out 2019.
104. Dalgleish and Porter 2016.
105. See e.g. *BDW Trading Ltd v Secretary of State for Communities and Local Government* [2016] EWCA Civ 493, [21] Lindblom LJ; [2017] PTSR 1337; *R v Rochdale MBC, ex parte Milne* (2001) 81 P & CR 27.
106. Town and Country Planning Act 1990, section 70(2)(c). Such is likely also supported (query in some way required) by the public sector equality duty contained in the Equality Act 2010.
107. *R (on the application of Wright) (Respondent) v Resilient Energy Severndale Ltd and Forest of Dean District Council (Appellants)* [2019] UKSC 53; [2019] 1 WLR 6562.
108. *Stringer v Minister of Housing and Local Government* [1970] 1 WLR 1281.
109. See the discussion in Bowes 2019, 242 ff.
110. BLUF 2016.
111. This advice changed over time. One later post, for example, sets out 14 different arguments/points about Backstreet's value as a queer space that BLUF members could mention in letters to the Council.
112. See Morrison and Burgess 2014.
113. Morrison and Burgess 2014, 61.
114. News Shopper 2019.
115. Salisbury 2020.
116. Burchiellaro 2021, 31.
117. Andersson 2009, 64–65.
118. Burchiellaro 2021, 32.
119. Andersson 2009.
120. Binnie and Skeggs 2006; Moran et al 2001.
121. Mayor of London 2017.
122. Moayeri 2019, 4.
123. See, as a starting point, Winter and Waterton 2013.
124. See Elen Stokes' chapter in this collection.
125. Historic England n.d. 'Listed Buildings'.
126. Historic England n.d. 'Listed Buildings'.
127. Historic England 2016.
128. Historic England n.d. 'Listed Buildings Identification and Extent'.
129. Braidwood 2016.
130. Dubrow 2019.
131. Ghaziani 2014.
132. Listing is not, of course, a watertight solution. It does not help with rent increases, for example.
133. Doan 2007.
134. See Hemmings 2002; Manalansan 2005; Namaste 2000; Nero 2005; Nast 2002; Oswin 2008.
135. Town and Country Planning Association 2018.
136. Lee et al 2013.

137. Housing, Communities and Local Government Committee 2021.
138. Valverde 2012.
139. Natarajan et al 2019.

References

Ahmed, Sara (2006). *Queer Phenomenology: Orientations, Objects, Others*. Durham, NC: Duke University Press.
Allmendinger, Phil and Graham Haughton (2013). 'The Evolution and Trajectories of English Spatial Governance: "Neoliberal" Episodes in Planning', *Planning Practice & Research* 18: 6–26.
Andersson, Johan (2009). 'East End Localism and Urban Decay: Shoreditch's Re-Emerging Gay Scene', *The London Journal* 34: 55–71.
Andersson, Johan (2011). 'Vauxhall's Post-Industrial Pleasure Gardens: "Death wish" and Hedonism in 21st-Century London', *Urban Studies* 48: 85–100.
Barclay, Christopher (2012), *London Planning* (House of Commons Library Standard Note SN/SC/1416, 30 May).
Bauman, John F. (2002). 'Race, Class, Gender, and Sexuality in Planning History: Looking at Trends in Literature', *Journal of Planning History* 1: 225–9.
Bell, David and Jon Binnie (2004). 'Authenticating Queer Space: Citizenship, Urbanism and Governance', *Urban Studies* 41: 1807–20.
Binnie, Jon and Beverley Skeggs (2004). 'Cosmopolitan Knowledge and the Production and Consumption of Sexualized Space: Manchester's Gay Village', *The Sociological Review* 52: 39–61.
Binnie, Jon and Gill Valentine (1999). 'Geographies of Sexuality – A Review of Progress', *Progress in Human Geography* 23: 175–87.
BLUF (2016), 'Step Up to Save London's Leather Bar', *BLUF*, 8 June, available at https://www.bluf.com/local/london/news/567 (accessed 12 June 2022).
Bowes, Ashley (2019). *A Practical Approach to Planning Law*. Oxford: Oxford University Press.
Braidwood, Ella (2016). 'Historic England Reviews Listings to Include LGBTQ History', *Architects Journal*, available at https://www.architectsjournal.co.uk/news/historic-england-reviews-listings-to-include-lgbtq-history (accessed 12 June 2022).
Browne, Kath, Jason Lim and Gavin Brown (2009). *Geographies of Sexualities: Theory, Practices and Politics*. Farnham: Ashgate.
Butler, Tim and Chris Hamnett (2011). *Ethnicity, Class and Aspiration: Understanding London's New East End*. Bristol: Policy Press.
Campkin, Ben and Laura Marshall (2016). *LGBTQI Nightlife in London: from 1986 to the Present*, UCL Urban Lab, available at https://www.ucl.ac.uk/urban-lab/sites/urban-lab/files/LGBTQI_nightlife_in_London_from_1986_to_the_present_-_interim_findings.pdf (accessed 12 June 2022)
Campkin, Ben and Laura Marshall (2017). *LGBTQ+ Cultural Infrastructure in London: Night Venues, 2006–2017*, UCL Urban Lab, available at https://www.ucl.ac.uk/urban-lab/sites/urban-lab/files/executive-summary-lgbtq-cultural-infrastructure-in-london-night-venues.pdf (accessed 12 June 2022).
Campkin, Ben and Laura Marshall (2018). 'London's Nocturnal Queer Geographies', *Soundings* 70 (Winter): 82–96.
Clowes, Leon (2019). 'Got Any Gay Music? London's "Anti-Gay" Queer Clubs 1995–2000'. In *Nocturnes: Popular Music and the Night*, edited by Geoff Stahl and Giacomo Bottà. Berlin: Springer.
Collins, Alan (2004). 'Sexual Dissidence, Enterprise and Assimilation: Bedfellows in Urban Regeneration', *Urban Studies* 41: 1789–806.
Colomb, Claire (2009). 'Gentrification and Community Empowerment in East London'. In *Whose Urban Renaissance?: An International Comparison of Urban Regeneration Strategies*, edited by Libby Porter and Kate Shaw, 172–81. Abingdon: Routledge.
Context Pty Ltd (2017). *Greyhound Hotel Cultural Heritage Values Assessment: 1 Brighton Road, St Kilda*, available at https://www.portphillip.vic.gov.au/media/n0pp54kt/e28961-17-greyhound-hotel-cultural-heritage-values.pdf (accessed 12 June 2022).

Dalgleish, Jaime and Ella Porter (2016). *Inclusivity and Othering in Montreal's Gay Village*, available at https://ocpm.qc.ca/sites/ocpm.qc.ca/files/pdf/P87/8.3.1_mount_allison_final_research_project_paper_dalgleish_porter.pdf (accessed 12 June 2022).

Desert, Jean-Ulrick (1997). 'Queer Space'. In *Queers in Space: Communities, Public Places, Sites of Resistance*, edited by Gordon Brent Ingram, Anne-Marie Bouthillette and Yolanda Retter, 17–27. Seattle, WA: Bay Press.

Doan, Petra (2007). 'Queers in the American City: Transgendered Perceptions of Urban Spaces', *Gender, Place, and Culture* 14: 57–74.

Doan, Petra (2014). 'Regulating Adult Business to Make Spaces Safe for Heterosexual Families in Atlanta'. In *(Sub)Urban Sexscapes: Geographies and Regulation of the Sex Industry*, edited by Paul Maginn and Christine Steinmetz, 197–218. Abingdon: Routledge.

Douek, Samuel (2019). 'The Eradication of London's Democratic Queer Pubs'. In *A Gendered Profession: The Question of Representation in Space Making*, edited by James Benedict Brown, Harriet Harriss, Ruth Morrow and James Soane, 182–91. London: RIBA Publishing.

Dubrow, Gail (2019). 'Taking Action: An Overview of LGBTQ Preservation Initiatives'. In *Preservation and Place: Historic Preservation by and of LGBTQ Communities in the United States*, edited by Katherine Crawford-Lackey and Megan E. Springate, 85–131. New York: Berghahn Books.

Dubrow, Gail, Larry Knopp and Michael Brown (2011). 'Act Up versus Straighten Up: Public Policy and Queer Community-Based Activism'. In *Queerying Planning: Challenging Heteronormative Assumptions and Reframing Planning Practice*, edited by Petra L. Doan. Abingdon: Routledge.

Farrier, Stephen, Enoch Brater and Mark Taylor-Batty (2021). *Drag Histories, Herstories and Hairstories: Drag in a Changing Scene Volume 2*. London: Bloomsbury.

Flyvbjerg, Bent (2006). 'Five Misunderstandings About Case-Study Research', *Qualitative Inquiry* 12(2): 219–45.

Gay Star News (2017). 'London's Royal Vauxhall Tavern is Being Sold to New Owner', *Gay Star News*, 2 February, available at https://www.gaystarnews.com/article/londons-royal-vauxhall-tavern-sold (accessed 12 June 2022).

George, Alexander L. and Andrew Bennett (2005). *Case Studies and Theory Development in the Social Sciences*. Cambridge, MA: MIT Press.

Ghaziani, Amin (2014). *There Goes the Gayborhood*. Princeton, NJ: Princeton University Press.

Goddard, J. Tim (2010). 'Collective Case Study'. In *Encyclopaedia of Case Study Research*, edited by Albert J. Mills, Gabrielle Eurepos and Elden Wiebe. Oxford: Sage.

Gorman-Murray, Andrew (2007). 'Rethinking Queer Migration Through the Body', *Social & Cultural Geography* 8: 105–21.

Greater London Authority (2012). *Planning Report PDU/2942/01*.

Greater London Authority (2015). *An A–Z of Planning and Culture*.

Greater London Authority (2017). *Planning Report D&P/1755a/02*.

Greater London Authority (2019). FOI Request Response Reference MGLA180719-7961 (15 August).

Greater London Authority (2021). *London Plan 2021*, available at https://www.london.gov.uk/sites/default/files/the_london_plan_2021.pdf (accessed 12 June 2022).

Haslam, Dave (2015). *Life after Dark: A History of British Nightclubs & Music Venues*. New York: Simon and Schuster.

Hemmings, Clare (2002). *Bisexual Spaces: A Geography of Sexuality and Gender*. Abingdon: Routledge.

Historic England (2016). *Pride of Place: A Guide to Understanding and Protecting Lesbian, Gay, Bisexual, Transgender and Queer (LGBTQ) Heritage*, available at https://historicengland.org.uk/images-books/publications/pride-of-place-guide-to-understanding-protecting-lgbtq-heritage/pride-of-place/ (accessed 12 June 2022).

Historic England (n.d.). 'Listed Buildings', available at https://historicengland.org.uk/listing/what-is-designation/listed-buildings/ (accessed 12 June 2022).

Historic England (n.d.). 'Listed Buildings Identification and Extent', available at https://historicengland.org.uk/advice/hpg/has/listed-buildings/ (accessed 12 June 2022).

Historic England (n.d.). 'Royal Vauxhall Tavern', available at https://historicengland.org.uk/listing/the-list/list-entry/1426984 (accessed 12 June 2022).

Holder, Jane and Donald McGillivray (2017). 'Bringing Environmental Justice to the Centre of Environmental Law Research: Developing a Collective Case Study Methodology'. In *Research Methods in Environmental Law*, edited by Andreas Philippopoulos-Mihalopoulos and Victoria Brooks, 184–206. Cheltenham: Edward Elgar.

House of Commons Library (2018). *The Greater London Authority*.

Housing, Communities and Local Government Committee (2021). *The Future of the Planning System in England* (Final Report, 10 June).
Hubbard, Phil (2013). *Cities and Sexualities*. Oxford: Routledge.
Huck, Jonathan (2019). 'Stop this Major Popular Gay Club from Being Bulldozed and Turned into More Luxury Flats', available at https://www.change.org/p/sadiq-khan-stop-xxl-london-s-eviction-from-their-current-venue (accessed 12 June 2022).
Jessup, Brad (2014). 'Environmental Justice as Spatial and Scalar Justice: A Regional Waste Facility or a Local Rubbish Dump Out of Place?', *McGill International Journal of Sustainable Development Law & Policy* 9: 69–107.
Khan, Sadiq (2017). Letter to Owen Whalley, 20 November.
Knopp, Larry (2017). *From Lesbian and Gay to Queer Geographies: Pasts, Prospects and Possibilities*. Abingdon: Routledge.
Kurschel, Martin and Xaver Kriechbaum (2015). *RVT*, 8 July, available at http://www.rvt.community/wp-content/uploads/2015/07/Screenshot-2015-07-10-11.39.01.png (accessed 12 June 2022).
Lambeth Council (2015). 'Assets of Community Value – List of Successful Nominations', 27 May.
Lambeth Council (2016). Conservation Area Statement (September).
Lauria, Mickey and Lawrence Knopp (1985). 'Toward an Analysis of the Role of Gay Communities in the Urban Renaissance', *Urban Geography* 6: 152–69.
Lee, Maria, Chiara Armeni, Javier de Cendra et al (2013). 'Public Participation and Climate Change Infrastructure', *Journal of Environmental Law* 25: 33–62.
Lee, Maria, Lucy Natarajan, Simon Lock et al (2018). 'Techniques of Knowing in Administration: Co-production, Models and Planning Law' *Journal of Law and Society* 45: 427–56.
Lewis, Mark (1994). 'A Sociological Pub Crawl around Gay Newcastle'. In *The Margins of the City: Gay Men's Urban Lives*, edited by Stephen Whittle, 85–101. Aldershot: Arena-Ashgate.
Lindsay, James (2015). 'Our Response to Immovate's Threatening Open Letter', 10 July, available at http://www.rvt.community/letter/ (accessed 12 June 2022).
Livermon, Xavier (2010). 'Soweto Nights: Making Black Queer Space in Post-Apartheid South Africa', *Gender, Place & Culture* 21: 508–25.
McAuslan, Patrick (1980). *The Ideologies of Planning Law*. Oxford: Pergamon Press.
Manalansan, Martin Fajardo (2005). 'Race, Violence, and Neoliberal Spatial Politics in the Global City', *Social Text* 23: 141–55.
Manley, Eric, Heidi Levitt and Chad Mosher (2007). 'Understanding the Bear Movement in Gay Male Culture: Redefining Masculinity', *Journal of Homosexuality* 53: 89–112.
Mayor of London (2015). *A-Z of Planning and Culture*, available at https://www.london.gov.uk/sites/default/files/an_a-z_of_planning_and_culture.pdf (accessed 12 June 2022).
Mayor of London (2017). *Culture & the Night-Time Economy: Supplementary Planning Guidance*, available at https://www.london.gov.uk/sites/default/files/culture_and_night-time_economy_spg_final.pdf (accessed 12 June 2022).
Mayor of London (n.d.). 'London's Planning Authorities', available at https://www.london.gov.uk/what-we-do/londons-planning-authorities (accessed 12 June 2022).
Meyer, Christine Benedichte (2001). 'A Case in Case Study Methodology', *Field Methods* 13: 329–52.
Mitchell, Edward (2021). 'Compulsory Purchase and the State Redistribution of Land: A Study of Local Authority-Private Developer Contractual Behaviour', *Journal of Property, Planning and Environmental Law* 13: 1–16.
Mitchell, J. Clyde (1983). 'Case and Situation Analysis', *Sociological Review* 31: 187–211.
Moayeri, Paniz (2019). 'Toronto's Gay Village: Built-Form as Container for Social Heritage', *Journal of the Society for the Study of Architecture in Canada/Journal de la Société pour l'étude de l'architecture au Canada* 44: 3–20.
Moran, Leslie and Beverley Skeggs (2003). *Sexuality and the Politics of Violence and Safety*. Abingdon: Routledge.
Moran, Leslie et al (2001). 'Property, Boundary, Exclusion: Making Sense of Hetero-Violence in Safer Spaces', *Social & Cultural Geography* 2: 407–20.
Morgera, Elisa and Louisa Parks (2014). *An Inter-Disciplinary Methodology for Researching Benefit-Sharing as a Norm Diffusing in Global Environmental Law*, Edinburgh School of Law Research Paper No. 2014/42.
Morrison, Nicky and Gemma Burgess (2014). 'Inclusionary Housing Policy in England: The Impact of the Downturn on the Delivery of Affordable Housing through Section 106', *Journal of Housing and the Built Environment* 29: 423–38.

Mynors, Charles (2006). *Listed Buildings, Conservation Areas and Monuments*. London: Sweet & Maxwell.
Namaste, Viviane (2000). *Invisible Lives: The Erasure of Transsexual and Transgendered People*. Chicago, IL: University of Chicago Press.
Nast, Heidi J. (2003). 'Queer Patriarchies, Queer Racisms, International', *Antipode* 34: 874–909.
Natarajan, Lucy, Simon J. Lock, Yvonne Rydin et al (2009). 'Participatory Planning and Major Infrastructure: Experiences in REI NSIP Regulation', *Town Planning Review* 90: 117–38.
Neate, Rupert (2019). 'London Council Saves Gay Fetish Club from Redevelopment', *The Guardian*, 16 August, available at https://www.theguardian.com/world/2019/aug/16/london-council-saves-gay-fetish-club-from-redevelopment (accessed 12 June 2022).
Nero, Charles (2005). 'Why are Gay Ghettos White?' In *Black Queer Studies: A Critical Anthology*, edited by E Patrick Johnson and Mae Henderson, 228–49. Durham, NC: Duke University Press.
News Shopper (2019), 'New LGBTQ+ Occupier to be Found for Samson and Ludgate Development after XXL Eviction', 16 August, available at https://www.newsshopper.co.uk/news/17840566.new-lgbtq-occupier-found-samson-ludgate-development-xxl-eviction/ (accessed 12 June 2022).
Oswin, Natalie (2008). 'Critical Geographies and the Uses of Sexuality: Deconstructing Queer Space', *Progress in Human Geography* 32: 89–103.
Planning Out (2019), *LGBT+ Placemaking Toolkit*, available at https://res.cloudinary.com/fieldfisher/image/upload/v1574347193/PDF-Files/PDFs%20from%20old%20website/planning-out-placemaking-toolkit-2019_vxjryp.pdf (accessed 12 June 2022).
Podmore, Julie (2006). 'Gone "Underground"? Lesbian Visibility and the Consolidation of Queer Space in Montreal', *Social & Cultural Geography* 21: 595–625.
Podmore, Julie (2013). 'Critical Commentary: Sexualities Landscapes beyond Homonormativity', *Geoforum* 49: 263–7.
Prior, Jason (2008). 'Planning for Sex in the City: Urban Governance, Planning and the Placement of Sex Industry Premises in Inner Sydney', *Australian Geographer* 39: 339–52.
Punch, Keith F. (2005), *Introduction to Social Research*. Oxford: Sage.
Reed, Christopher (1996). 'Imminent Domain: Queer Space in the Built Environment', *Art Journal* 55: 64–70.
Rocos, Cleo (2013). *The Power of Positive Drinking*. London: Square Peg.
Rushbrook, Dereka (2002). 'Cities, Queer Space, and the Cosmopolitan Tourist', *GLQ: A Journal of Lesbian and Gay Studies* 8: 183–206.
Ruting, Brad (2008). 'Economic Transformations of Gay Urban Spaces: Revisiting Collins' Evolutionary Gay District Model', *Australian Geographer* 39: 259–69.
Salisbury, Josh (2020). 'New LGBT Space to Replace Former Southwark Gay Club XXL by 2022 after Development Row', *Southwark News*, 10 January, available at https://www.southwarknews.co.uk/news/xxl-london-lgbt-southwark/ (accessed 12 June 2022).
Southwark Council (2013). *Planning Committee Report 12/AP/3940* (8 October).
Southwark Council (2021). *Local Plan*.
Stockton, Kathryn Bond (2011). 'Rhythm: Secular Feelings, Religious Feelings'. In *Queer Times, Queer Becomings*, edited by E.L. McCallum and Miko Tuhkanen, 345–8. New York: SUNY Press.
Taylor, Yvette (2016). 'The "Outness" of Queer: Class and Sexual Intersections'. In *Queer Methods and Methodologies*, edited by Kath Browne and Catherine J. Nash, 69–84. Abingdon: Routledge.
The Backstreet (n.d.), available at https://thebackstreet.com/ (accessed 12 June 2022).
Tower Hamlets Council (2013), *Tower Hamlets Local Plan 2013*, available at https://www.towerhamlets.gov.uk/lgnl/planning_and_building_control/planning_policy_guidance/Local_plan/local_plan.aspx (accessed 12 June 2022).
Tower Hamlets Council (2017a). 'Agenda, decisions and minutes: Strategic Development Committee – Thursday, 16th February, 2017 7.00pm', available at https://democracy.towerhamlets.gov.uk/ieListDocuments.aspx?CId=360&MId=6758&Ver=4 (accessed 12 June 2022).
Tower Hamlets Strategic Development Committee (2017b). 'Agenda, decisions and minutes: Strategic Development Committee – Tuesday, 25th April, 2017 7.00pm', available at https://democracy.towerhamlets.gov.uk/ieListDocuments.aspx?CId=360&MId=6760&Ver=4 (accessed 12 June 2022).
Town and Country Planning Association (2018). *Planning 2020 – Raynsford Review of Planning in England*.

Valverde, Mariana (2012). *Everyday Law on the Street: City Governance in an Age of Diversity*. Chicago, IL: Chicago University Press.

Walters, Ben (2015). 'Supporting Statement for an Application to have the Royal Vauxhall Tavern Added to the National Heritage List for England', *RVT*, January, available at http://www.rvt.community/wp-content/uploads/2015/09/Initial-RVT-listing-application-January-2015.pdf (accessed 12 June 2022).

Watt, Paul (2009). 'Housing Stock Transfers, Regeneration and State-Led Gentrification in London', *Urban Policy and Research* 27: 229–42.

Webley, Lisa (2010). 'Qualitative Approaches to Empirical Legal Research'. In *The Oxford Handbook of Empirical Legal Research*, edited by Peter Cane and Herbet M. Kritzer, 926–51. Oxford: Oxford University Press.

Winter, Tim, and Emma Waterton (2013). 'Critical Heritage Studies', *International Journal of Heritage Studies* 19: 529–31.

Wright, Les (2013). *The Bear Book: Readings in the History and Evolution of a Gay Male Subculture*. Abingdon: Routledge.

XXL (n.d.). 'Save our Scene', available at https://www.xxl-london.com/saveourscene/ (accessed 26 January 2022).

4
The highway: A right, a place or a resource?

Antonia Layard[*]

Introduction

On 15 December 2020, the *Horrendous Hackney Road Closures* group delivered cabbages to Hackney Town Hall in East London, protesting against newly implemented low traffic neighbourhoods (LTNs). Campaigners emphasised both their opposition to closing residential streets to through traffic and their identity as 'born n bred' Londoners.[1] Despite the protest, Hackney Council went on to introduce 15 new LTNs, following government advice issued just after the first lockdown in 2020, when the Department for Transport called for a reallocation of roadspace for people walking and cycling, with an assumption that new initiatives would be made permanent.[2] Not all new LTNs have survived. In Ealing, West London, all but one of its nine new LTNs were removed a year later, following criticism and opposition by some residents. The arguments were extraordinarily fierce, with the longstanding Council Leader losing his job, breaches of freedom information requests[3] and even supporters of LTNs critical of the way consultation had been undertaken (with similar criticism directed at the following online consultation on whether the schemes should be removed).[4]

LTNs provide valuable illustrations of disputes over whether the highway is 'a right' of passage, 'a place' belonging in some sense to local residents rather than to motor vehicles driving through, or 'a resource' to be allocated and governed. This chapter argues that highways should be primarily understood as a resource, explaining that while the right of passage and place are undoubtedly relevant, they are not determinative in understanding what highways are. Once allocated (to pedestrians, cyclists, drivers and any other road users), highways are governed by highway authorities, both local and strategic, so that they can be shared between users. Other forms of governance also apply, including the behaviours and expectations of individuals on the road, often acting in accordance with local social norms; courts hearing cases in criminal and tort law; and physical infrastructure, often incorporating enforcement functions whether immediate, as with 'sleeping policemen',[5] or subsequent, as with enforcement fines. All these interventions govern shared use of highway space.

While expressing highways governance in terms of space is unfamiliar in law, highway space (usually called roadspace[6]) is the primary object of governance. Understanding this as a resource to be shared focuses on how we can all exercise rights to passage safely, encouraging mobility for all, whilst also respecting highways as places with diverse characteristics. To consider these aspects of highways governance, the chapter begins with an overview of LTNs before considering the highway first as a right, then as a place, and finally as a resource.

Low traffic neighbourhoods (LTNs)

LTNs build on both Dutch concepts of *woonerf* 'living street'[7] and post-war British concepts of 'environmental areas'.[8] Around 150 new LTNs have been introduced in England since 2020, benefiting from £2 billion in funding, both in response to the pandemic and to promote active travel, particularly walking and cycling.[9] The interventions restrict motor vehicle traffic in residential streets, using bollards, planters or automatic number plate recognition (ANPR) technology. They have been highly contested, not least because schemes can – at least initially – reallocate the traffic burden, impacting strategic roads (affecting residents there) as well as producing longer journeys for some drivers, thereby increasing carbon emissions. Increased congestion often disappears or reduces when drivers, aware of the new rules, change their habits so that traffic 'evaporates'.[10]

LTNs are both a product and a consequence of the system of governance of highways, calling for highways space, the resource, to be re-allocated, and so governed, differently. LTNs understand residential streets as quiet places suitable for active travel where noise, fumes and congestion do not predominate. The debates around their introduction recognise that although, spatially, there is wide variation between different types of places all labelled as highway – including pavements, verges, residential streets, A roads and motorways – legally, a highway is a single legal category. Each highway site is governed by similar rules subject to only limited exceptions, for instance prohibiting pedestrians and cyclists from motorways.[11] Challenging this regulatory homogeneity, LTNs emphasise spatial differences, calling for change in some streets but not others, asking for an area to be spatially enclosed as a distinct place of governance, applying different rules within than without.

LTNs are governed by a mixture of physical infrastructure, courtesy and good manners as well as enforcement fines if drivers insist on breaching the new rules of the road. Some road users resist change, sometimes resorting to litigation or campaigning, sometimes forcefully ripping up new planters at night. Such responses were not entirely unexpected: energetic opposition has long marked traffic interventions. 'Belisha beacons', marking new zebra crossings, were early targets for partygoers returning home in central London[12] while the avowedly pro-car Transport Minister, Ernest Marples, had a new parking meter thrown through a window at his house in protest at drivers having to pay to store their car on the road.[13] Similar difficulties were fictionalised in *Yes Minister*, where the newly minted Secretary of State, James Hacker, was made, in his words, 'Transport Supremo' before being quickly corrected by Sir Humphrey Appleby: 'I believe the Civil Service vernacular is Transport Muggins.'[14] Shared between national and local governments, transport policy affects passengers and voters who are quick to complain, dislike change, require reliability and are often used to the individual convenience of the car.

In 2020, given the circumstances of lockdown, Hackney, like many other councils, used 'experimental traffic orders' (ETOs) to propose LTNs, limiting consultation up front, before calling for input once the effects of experimental schemes could be assessed.[15] While such a use of trials to assess efficacy can be empirically valuable, this 'emergency' approach contrasts with conventional, more drawn-out consultation practices, so that, as one study has noted, 'people who were used to consultation prior to any decision being taken were shocked when works commenced on their doorsteps, sometimes with very little warning'.[16]

The greatest resistance to LTNs, however, has come from drivers whose transport choices have been curtailed, limiting, as some see it, their 'rights'. Assumptions about mobility – how long a journey takes by car or public transport – underpin choices about where to live, work or take children to school. It can be tempting, if not always plausible, to formulate these assumptions as rights – in particular to conflate 'a right of passage' with 'a right to drive'. As this chapter will illustrate, however, such a conflation is to misread highways law and governance, misunderstanding the highway as a regulatory category.

A right?

A highway is often understood as a way over which the public have rights of passage, whether on foot (a footpath), on foot or with animals (a bridleway or driftway), or on foot, with animals and with vehicles (a carriageway).[17] Yet while footpaths, bridleways and carriageways are all defined in legislation,[18] the term 'highway' (on which each of them depends) lacks statutory definition and has long been contested, particularly in its formulation as the 'King's highway'.[19] For example, while a 'road' is defined, this rests on a somewhat circuitous approach, being a 'highway (including a public path) and any other road, lane, footway, square, court, alley or passage (whether a thoroughfare or not) to which the public has access'.[20] 'Safe passage' is required if there is snow or ice,[21] while 'free passage' may not be obstructed,[22] yet there is no 'right' of passage in the English definition of a highway, unlike the Scottish definition of a road.[23]

The term is, however, often found in judicial decisions. In *DPP v Jones*, while Lord Irvine denied that a right of passage was the only right that could be exercised on a highway, holding that the highway was also a 'public place', he nevertheless acknowledged 'the primary right of the public to pass and repass'.[24] More recently, in *Southwark v Transport for London*, Lord Briggs mused that 'the innocent sounding word "highway" is itself capable of having a range of different meanings, dependent upon the context in which it is used' before defining a highway as 'a way over which the public have rights of passage, whether on foot, or horseback or in (or on) vehicles'.[25]

Lord Briggs in *Southwark* was reluctant to be pinned to a single definition, demonstrating that even if a right to passage is part of our understanding of a highway, it is not determinative. His Lordship concluded:

> There is in my view no single meaning of highway at common law. The word is sometime used as a reference to its physical elements. Sometimes it is used as a label for the incorporeal rights of the public in relation to the *locus in quo*. Sometimes, as here, it is used as the label for a species of real property. When used within a statutory formula, as here, the word necessarily takes its meaning from the context in which it is used.[26]

This modern formulation marks a change to earlier conceptions, focusing on multiplicity and rejecting a 'single meaning', particularly one based solely on a right to passage.

Certainly, the right has been longstanding. In the nineteenth century it was, according to Rachel Vorspan, 'arguably the only positive right recognized in English common law'.[27] In a legal system long preoccupied with easing and facilitating movement, particularly through the law of nuisance, a right preserved passage from obstruction. One recurring debate concerned whether the right was restricted to passing and repassing 'for the purpose of legitimate travel'[28] in accordance with 'reasonable and ordinary use' concepts that underwent considerable permutation and reinterpretation in response to changing historical circumstances. Nuisance doctrines predicated on the 'right to pass' developed in English law, particularly to limit industrial picketing, recreation (including 'annoying' football[29]), commercial activity and personal injury. Characterising the right to passage as 'a curious right – literal, physical, indeed in all senses pedestrian – . . . [protecting] travellers from annoyance, injury, inconvenience, or delay caused by physical impediments in the street',[30] Vorspan concludes that the right to passage had been central to nineteenth-century highways law.

Even then, however, this right to passage extended to all, requiring accommodation, as captured in early twentieth-century films showing distinctive pedestrian rhythms. Richard Hornsey notes how recordings show 'the jauntiness with which London's walkers trot along its pavements' as well as the 'the apparent disorder of their uncoordinated trajectories', snaking between flows of steady – if unregimented – largely horse-drawn traffic, producing 'a precarious and incomprehensible anarchy'.[31] David Rooney makes a similar observation, describing how pedestrians of the time 'crowd the junction, interweaving with vehicles, in ways which to modern eyes seem unruly, undisciplined and unsafe'[32] even at a time when the Highway Code exhorted pedestrians to use footpaths or, if none were available, to walk on the right of the carriageway in the face of oncoming traffic.[33] The right to passage was embodied, even though the potential for catastrophe was stark.

Given its historical origins, the right to passage was not, of course, conceived of as a right to drive. While pedestrians and slower users would have to get out of the way of faster and heavier modes of transport to avoid injury, the right belonged to all, regardless of the mode of transport employed. Once it was the carriage and the wagon, which pushed more vulnerable users out of the road;[34] with the rise of motor vehicles, it became increasingly clear that pedestrians and cyclists could no longer freely exercise their right to passage. Speaking in Parliament in 1938, MP

William Leach argued that 'the work of prohibiting access to the roads altogether to pedestrians and cyclists is very well advanced. Their right to the highway is now in positive danger. The motorist is winning this fight; the pedestrian and the cyclist are losing it.'[35]

Today the belief that drivers should have greater access to the road than pedestrians, cyclists or other users, as they pay a 'car tax', remains a common misconception. This is quite untrue. For while many vehicle owners pay a Vehicle Excise Duty (VED), this is an emissions tax, with some motorists –such as owners of electric cars – paying no VED, while low emission car owners pay lower rates. The Road Fund was set up in the 1909/10 Finance Act as part of Lloyd George's 'People's Budget'. It linked the revenues collected to road maintenance budgets, over 90 per cent of which went towards small-scale improvements in road surfaces. The Road Fund ended in 1937. Winston Churchill was one supporter of the change, arguing in 1925 against the idea that 'motorists are to be privileged for all time to have the whole yield of the tax on motors devoted to roads[.] Such contentions are absurd and constitute . . . an outrage upon common sense.'[36] Despite its abolition, 'road tax' remains a heady term, implying that the tax should be spent only on roads and that drivers have more right to roadspace than pedestrians and cyclists. No new roads were ever built using the Road Fund and today roads are funded out of local and general taxation. As the Driver and Vehicle Licensing Agency (DVLA) put it: 'There has been no direct relationship between vehicle tax and road expenditure since 1937.'[37]

An alternative, and more contemporary, claim to a right to the highway has been made by taxi drivers, including in *United Trade Action Group (UTAG) v TFL*, litigation challenging Transport for London's traffic orders made under their 2020 *Streetspace* scheme.[38] The taxi drivers attempted to argue that their ability to drive in bus lanes, withdrawn on some roads including the A10 thoroughfare, was a disproportionate interference by 'control of use' with their property rights, in breach of Article 1 of Protocol 1 to the European Convention on Human Rights (A1P1). This argument was swiftly dismissed at first instance, although there remains some recognition of taxis as having long-established status distinct from other cars, framed as a form of public transport. At first instance, while the judge held that A1P1 was engaged, in that the economic benefit deriving from a licence to carry on a particular economic activity constitutes a 'possession' within the meaning of A1P1, ultimately she concluded on a proportionality analysis that an interference with these possessions could not be established by control of use (a finding that was upheld in the Court of Appeal).[39]

A further attempt to encapsulate taxi driving as a right was to frame it as a 'legitimate expectation'. Again, this claim was rejected in *UTAG*, even though the Mayor's 2016 manifesto had expressly included a commitment to 'Retain the exclusive right of licensed black taxi drivers to use bus lanes and ply for hire'.[40] The Court of Appeal held that the taxi drivers did not have an expectation that met the requisite test of being 'clear, unambiguous, and devoid of relevant qualification', the claimants being unable to 'point to any clear, unambiguous and unqualified promise that every bus lane in London which taxis were permitted to use prior to the publication of the Plan and the Guidance would remain accessible to taxis for all time and in all circumstances'.[41] In the absence of bad faith, there was no breach of legitimate expectation here.[42]

Distinct from a right but with some similar discursive effects is the logic of pedestrianism, which proponents of LTNs are in part trying to promote, facilitating walking (and cycling) in streets devoid of cars. Described by Nick Blomley as a rationality of pedestrianism, this ability to travel on foot – a right to passage – is produced by engineers and local governments as well as by legal rules and practices regulating pavements (and so parts of highways).[43] Pedestrianism is, as Blomley suggests, an administrative logic on its own terms.

Despite these claims, and administrative rationalities, the right to passage is only one part of highways governance. The Supreme Court has been clear that the definition of a highway is not predicated solely on such a right.[44] And so while Vorspan's historical analyses lead to a conclusion that, historically, 'a highway was legally conceptualized not as a road, but as a right',[45] it is now more precise to say that while all have a right to passage, this contributes only one aspect of how we understand the highway today.

A place?

Highways are places, be they verges or pavements, A roads or motorways. Most highways governance makes only limited spatial distinctions between these different types of highways (apart from pavements, verges and motorways); on roads – whether quiet residential streets or major strategic networks – the rules on obstruction and expeditious movement of traffic apply. Obstructions are prohibited without reasonable excuse, even if such rules are enforced far more effectively on roads than on pavements blighted by parking.

This lack of spatial sensitivity in legal rules has led to a growing concern that setting matters, an argument taken up by proponents of

LTNs. There is growing recognition that although legally the category of highways is broadly consistent, spatially highways are not a homogenous category. This tension between legal order, spatial sensitivity and social norms lies at the heart of the disputes over LTNs as place-making initiatives.

Place is also, however, a central geographic concept increasingly relevant in legal analysis, particularly where administrative bodies designate places by identifying spatial categories. If space is what we move in, through which we connect, argue, live and work, and spatiality is space's effects, illustrating the impacts of location, context and relationships on environments, people and activities, then place is imbued with a characterisation, 'a collection of stories so far',[46] capable of being more effectively – if never definitively – legally enclosed and given a regulatory label. Categorising a piece of land as a particular type of place, in this case a highway, has legal and spatial consequences. Once mapped 'as' a highway,[47] places are governed by administrative authorities who implement spatial particularism, assuming that, once designated, each place within the category – that is, all highways – should be governed by shared principles, unless distinctions are made (as they are, for example, in respect of motorways).

One of the difficulties in legal place-making is that regulatory categorisation can be spatially particularistic, in that a designation can set out a rather singular version of how a place *should be*, even though other spatial imaginaries, understood as spatial assumptions, may exist for that place. For example, a highway may be assumed to prioritise motor vehicle flow rather than to be a space for active travel or neighbourly connection. If disputes arise between spatial imaginaries, the body with authority for the place can refer to the legal vision for the place and impose their spatial agenda. In this case, the highway authority could intervene, removing any obstructions and securing expeditious movement, even if, for example, a partially obstructive parklet or urban garden might be desired by residents in a street instead.

The idea that places are legally understood as they *should be* seems rather geographically dogmatic, and it is true that place designations can be difficult to integrate with more relational understandings of place. *DPP v Jones*, mentioned above, is the leading English and Welsh authority to conceptualise a highway as a place. Even here, however, movement is prioritised. Lord Irvine, refusing to find a protest on a verge near Stonehenge unlawful, held that the highway is a place which 'the public may enjoy for any reasonable purpose'.[48] However, this recognition was subject to an overriding requirement that there would be no obstruction inhibiting the 'primary right of the public to pass and repass', and that nothing is done on the highway – in this case a grass verge – that amounts to a public or private nuisance.[49] While the 'public right' to use the highway as a public place should not, the House of Lords held in *Jones*, be subject to 'any attempt to artificially restrict its scope',[50] even here passage remains the priority.

This raises the question: what kind of place is a highway? Can we identify several imaginaries rather than just one within a single legal category? In 2014, the Swedish artist Karl Jilg produced an image for the Swedish Road Administration representing the difficulties inherent in a single underpinning imaginary of rights of passage for motor vehicles that did not allow for those nearby, including those attempting to exercise their right to passage on foot. Jilg illustrated an urban intersection where roads are dug out as caverns, with a pedestrian perilously crossing the ravine on a rickety plank at the designated intersection.[51] The street scene lacks trees and flowerbeds, while the view is of tough concrete, where a dog strains on a leash and a young child gestures forwards into the chasm, a mother sharply pulling them back from the abyss. The picture captures calls by pedestrian and liveable streets activists for streets to be understood as spaces for all, particularly the most vulnerable, since, as the picture illustrates, while streets are understood as sites of mobility and flow, they are also sites of daily life. As Donald Appleyard noted in 1978: 'Since streets are where most of our children are reared, and where most housewives and old people spend their lives, they are, outside the home, the most important part of our urban environment.'[52]

DIY urbanists have long attempted to emphasise the 'place-ness' of highways, creating parklets after paying the meter, by installing a seating or green area for public use rather than parking a car.[53] This is not a particularly new practice. In 1915 Lyda Newman worked to close West 63rd Street in San Juan Hill, New York City, so that suffrage activists could work together while their children played safely outside.[54] The connection between place-making and highways also underpinned the 1896 decision in *Tunbridge Wells v Baird* on highways ownership. The Mayor and Tunbridge Wells urban authority, responsible for public health, had wanted to erect and maintain 'lavatories and places of convenience' under the town's Georgian walkway, the Pantiles.[55] When the court thwarted this desire, holding that the 'vesting of the street vests in the urban authority such property and such property only as is necessary for the control, protection, and maintenance of the street as a highway for public use',[56] and not for development of the subsoil, the Victorian place-making initiative failed, and the nearest toilets are now several minutes' walk away from the shopping area.

With the reduction in public spaces, many of which have been sold off and privatised,[57] new initiatives have started closing streets – for children to play out,[58] to revive the holding of street parties, to promote outside space for cafes and restaurants or to facilitate social distancing during a pandemic. All these initiatives have illustrated the capacity of highways – which make up between 15 and 30 per cent of London, for example, with higher proportions still in the city's centre[59] – to create spaces for connection and conviviality. Of course, despite their potential, highways are not ersatz public space, nevertheless they can balance mobility and flow with connection and accessibility, where some forms of travel, notably walking and slower cycling, do not push other users off the streets in the way that motor vehicles (or high-speed cycling) do.

LTNs are an attempt to change the spatial and legal understanding of what kind of place some highways – in this case designated residential streets – can be. The initiatives raise broader questions of 'whose streets', emphasising place, belonging and governance, and may require better forms of consultation and decision-making understanding how to share the roadspace in a locality. LTNs will be often contentious, particularly given embodied attachments to a right to passage or expectations of being able to drive. And so while 'place matters' in individual schemes, this cannot, by itself, explain the highway. Spatial specificity is one determinant of governance alongside a right to passage, yet allocation and governance need to be drawn together into a regulatory system.

A resource?

When a highway is dedicated at common law or by statute, legal, spatial and social consequences follow. Designation changes the nature of the site and how decisions can be made about it, labelling it as a particular type of place, as with landscape planning, heritage or national parks.[60] When assessing how to govern the highway, decision-makers can look to a raft of legislative and common law rules to determine road layout, apply traffic rules or close some streets to cars. Highways are a resource to be first allocated and then governed. This first step, determining where cars can drive and where they cannot and where, as a consequence, pedestrians and cyclists can move safely and where they cannot, is necessary before regulatory oversight of the roadspace can continue.

While there is some judicial authority that highways are a species of property, the better view is that ownership of the land underneath is not relevant to how the highway is governed above.[61] Conventionally, at common law, dedication does not require the transfer of ownership; instead the owner retains the freehold estate, subject to the right of the public to pass and re-pass over it.[62] Case law, often dealing with quite specific provisions of highways vesting or transfer in relation to local authorities, has developed a view that a freehold estate in what has been called the 'top two spits' of land[63] (two depths of a spade) or, to use a more modern expression, the 'zone of use',[64] can transfer when a highway vests or is transferred. As the landowner has little say about how the highway is governed, and, as the maxim goes, 'once a highway, always a highway', unless and until the highway is stopped up, the resource continues. The regulatory designation overlays land ownership, but until the highway comes to an end, the landowner's powers are in abeyance.

Once designated as highway, authorities have discretion as to how they manage this regulatory space. While they are subject to a 'network management duty' requiring them to secure 'expeditious movement of traffic' where 'reasonably practicable',[65] the legislative definition of 'traffic' includes pedestrians[66] and there is broad consensus that the term also includes cyclists.[67] Decisions to prioritise one type of passage over another on the network are legally possible and often quite pragmatic, as on motorways or in LTNs.

When making governance decisions about highways, the authority draws on a 'prior institutional knowledge claim'[68] of what a highway is, here said to be a resource rather than just a place or a right. A prior institutional knowledge claim is familiar throughout planning, notably in landscape planning (where Maria Lee developed the concept[69]) and in heritage. The claim rests on expertise, formulated as institutional knowledge so that once a site is designated, the designation precedes decision-making by providing shortcuts to govern the category. For instance, once a building is listed and recognised for its architectural and heritage qualities, the heritage designation has governance consequences, requiring decision-makers to act in particular ways that can only be removed by delisting. Similarly, a highway, once designated, is subject to a prior institutional knowledge claim that the piece of land should be governed as a highway, even if there is a lack of clarity as to what precisely the label 'highway' entails (that is, if people disagree over whether a highway is a right, place or resource).

This prior institutional knowledge claim informs how a site should be governed *as* a highway by conveying knowledge about what a highway *is* to decision-makers. Framing a highway as a 'right', a 'place' or even property blurs the regulatory understanding of the highway as a resource, so that the 'prior institutional claim' cannot govern as effectively as there is less agreement about what a highway 'is'. Understanding highways as primarily a resource to be allocated and governed, acknowledging rights to passage and the qualities of highways as both a regulatory spatial category and physical places, strengthens the effectiveness of the prior institutional knowledge, improving the governance that follows, particularly in times of change as with LTNs.

It is not just space that is shared; money is also shared. One reason why LTNs have been popular with local authorities is that by allocating space differently, and enforcing penalties if boundaries are infringed, LTNs can raise significant revenue to cover their costs, making them viable in times of austerity. Funding has long been critical to highways governance, with highways maintenance proving a significant financial liability, from the Tudor 'statute labour' system, 'performed with the utmost remissness' in the sixteenth and seventeenth centuries,[70] to the five-year £2.5 billion Potholes Fund today,[71] aiming in part to minimise litigation costs. Responsibility to maintain the highway is today premised on a highway authority's duty to maintain a highway[72] subject to a reasonableness defence.[73] Conventionally there has long been an argument, as in the Tudor 'statute labour' system, about whether the costs of road maintenance should be borne in the locality. In Hackney, London, £2.7 million was raised through LTN enforcement fines in 2021, with 82 per cent issued to drivers registered outside the borough.[74] This asks questions about who roads belong to, who should pay to use highway space and how we should balance residential needs with a desire to travel through neighbourhoods.

LTNs affect people outside the periphery, both those who can no longer enter as they wish as well as people who live on nearby boundary roads who may experience an increase in traffic after a scheme's introduction. Understanding highways as a resource, encourages local authorities to build an evidence base to underpin decisions on how to share roadspace. Such databases include information on changes in traffic, noise and air pollution both within and outside the periphery, though sometimes baseline data is missing.[75] Several cases have been brought against Hackney and other local authorities alleging a failure to comply with section 149 of the Equality Act 2010, the public sector equality duty, yet all have failed.[76] Judges have acknowledged the temporal contexts for ETOs, begun in the pandemic as well as their experimental nature, on occasion permitting 'rolling' assessments to complement formal and information consultation.[77] These defeats have prompted vocal criticism from LTN opponents, while other local authorities have delayed introducing LTNs to undertake new consultations. Many opponents continue to be unconvinced that LTNs are either fair or effective.

Such questions of how to allocate highways resource have long been contentious. One incident where road users insisted on exercising their 'rights' even though, legally, they had been curtailed arose in 1819 in New York where pig-keepers resisted a legal prohibition,[78] relying on 'social custom' to justify their continued practices for a further 30 years. Interpreting this American incident of highways law as 'as an arena of conflict, rather than as an unfolding text', Hendrik Hartog identified differing 'contending normative orders', where social pluralism was in tension with legal commands,[79] noting how law must interact with other factors. Conflicts between legal rules, social practices and local customs continue to dominate highways since sharing roadspace is hard, requiring a combination of rules and social negotiation.

This diversity of users has often required mechanisms to segregate people, vehicles and animals; rules could be straightforward or remarkably complex. In 1281, pigs were simply banned from the streets of the City of London, a famously meat-loving city, for sanitation reasons.[80] In 1720, in contrast, rules were often complicated, including one where 'Parliament enacted that not more than 12 sacks of meal, 12 quarters of malt, seven and a half cwt of bricks or one "chalder" of coals should be carried at one load, in a vehicle having iron tires, within ten miles of London or Westminster'.[81] Allocating and governing roadspace has a long history.

Historically, governance has proved particularly tricky when new highway users have been able to push others off the road by exercising their right to passage in a new physical form. Writing in 1913, when motor vehicles were venturing onto highways in increasing numbers, the Webbs noted that 'The first outcome of this new invasion of the roads was a storm of opposition, a persistent wail of complaint, from all who did not happen to use the new vehicles'.[82] This displacing of other users, notably in the 1910s and 1920s the newly arrived bicyclist, was a familiar pattern. Previously it had been the horse-drawn vehicle that, 'originally regarded as an intruder, had come to possess almost a monopoly of the King's Highway', when as herds and packs of animals were increasingly transported by train, commercial travellers no longer travelled on horseback and 'Even the foot passenger found himself increasingly relegated to side pavements or footpaths'.[83] Dominance of highway space has long limited the ability to exercise rights to passage on foot or on slower modes of transport.

With the advent of the 'automobile and the Motor Omnibus',[84] one innovative new mechanism to govern road use was the Highway Code, still today a living form of quasi-legislation that both captures social norms and prescribes behaviour. The first Highway Code of 1931 was a 'code of conduct' and 'good manners', lacking legal force, noting instead that: 'Good manners and consideration for others are as desirable and are as much appreciated on the road as elsewhere.'[85] The opening paragraph, however, stated in bold: 'Remember that all persons – pedestrians, cyclists, persons leading, riding or driving animals and the drivers of motor or horse drawn vehicles – have a right to use the highway and an obligation to respect the rights of others.' There was to be no hierarchy in favour of motor vehicles. The roadspace was to be allocated equitably, albeit resting on the 'good manners' of drivers.

The 1935 Highway Code, while more disciplinary in its approach, still emphasised universality in its opening provision: 'All persons have a right to use the road for the purpose of passage.'[86] By 1946, with the increase in motoring and the appalling death toll from vehicle accidents during the war (peaking at 9,169 deaths in 1940[87]), the opening presumption of rights for all users had disappeared. Instead, the Code was divided 'for convenience' into different classes of road users, while by 1954 there was no mistaking the tone for pedestrians. The opening paragraph states baldly: 'Where there is a pavement or footpath, use it.'[88] The Code no longer opened with a reminder that all persons have a right to use the highway.

Today, the driver's central position colours the Highway Code, which appreciates vulnerability but does not assert rights, an emphasis that has given rise to many calls for change. Breaching the code is not a criminal offence in its own right, and even a failure to observe a provision of the Highway Code will not render the driver liable to criminal or civil proceedings.[89] Any failure by the driver to adhere to the code can however be relied upon in proceedings by any party looking to establish liability.[90] The code has normative and moral functions as well as legal ones, still today acting as 'an unwritten code of good manners'.[91]

In January 2022, a new rule H1 came into force, revising the hierarchy of users to ensure that 'those road users who can do the greatest harm have the greatest responsibility to reduce the danger or threat they may pose to other road users'.[92] This new hierarchy places vulnerable road users before motorised vehicles, with pedestrians, particularly children, older adults and disabled people, at the top, followed by cyclists, horse riders and motor cyclists (in that order).[93] The Government suggests that the 'objective of Rule H1 is not to give priority to pedestrians, cyclists and horse riders in every situation, but rather to ensure a more mutually respectful and considerate culture of safe and effective road use that benefits all users. This does not detract from the requirement for everyone to behave responsibly.'[94] By changing the rules of hierarchy, the new Highway Code rule H1 can govern roadspace without requiring expensive alterations to infrastructure.

Such regulatory intervention is significant given that previous approaches to allocating roadspace have sometimes taken a far more invasive tack. In 1963, Colin Buchanan's *Traffic in Towns*, published for the Ministry of Transport, both warned of the damage caused by the motor car and provided suggestions to mitigate harm. In one famous image, cars dominate street level while escalators lead to pedestrian walkways above, adorned with neon signs against a backdrop of a housing tower. Clearly influenced by Corbusier, the figure is titled 'Vertical segregation' with the note that this 'illustrates vividly . . . the awkward truth that the motor vehicle is really demanding a radically new urban form'.[95] Vertical segregation and 'streets in the air'[96] were familiar ideas in 1960s Britain, particularly for modernist planners and architects,[97] yet vertically separating motor vehicles and pedestrians using flyovers was costly as well as complex in engineering and construction terms. Buchanan only proposed vertical segregation for a case study, yet the concept contributed to a broader conclusion that towns and cities would have to be comprehensively remodelled to make way for the 'universal motor-car', or as he also put it 'our beloved monster'.[98]

An alternative, horizontal segregation, much like LTNs today, was also included in the 1963 report. Envisaged as 'environmental areas' where traffic would be relegated to the boundary of a site, Buchanan drew on an earlier formulation of 'pedestrian precincts' advocated by Alker Tripp, a Commissioner of Police, who in 1942 had explained that once segregated, streets in precincts

> will then become town streets of the old-fashioned type. They will cease to be maelstroms of noise and confusion, and become companionable places, with an air of leisure and repose; such streets will provide a real promenade for the town dweller and a rest for jaded nerves. We shall get back to Merrie England.[99]

Taking up this lead, horizontal segregation was built into many communities in England, including on housing estates and in cul-de-sacs. Here, the road's physical infrastructure provided clear guidance to drivers on how to use the space. Today's LTNs use physical infrastructure that is less intrusive to communicate the new layout, including planters, signs and ANPR followed by fines in the post.

Yet using physical infrastructure to separate motor vehicles from more vulnerable road users is only one way to achieve segregation or co-existence.[100] As lawyers know well, it is often much cheaper and more effective to use legal rules to separate users, relying on self-governance, not least in fear of receiving a penalty or enforcement notice if the mandate is breached. If we understand the highway as a resource to be allocated between different users, including motorists and pedestrians, drafting legal rules accordingly, we can achieve horizontal segregation – sharing – at much lower public cost.

Conclusion: sharing is hard

Highways are dangerous places. Even during the pandemic in 2020–1, over 1,360 people died on British roads,[101] with normal death rates even higher at around 1,750.[102] Almost all fatalities are caused by driving, with car occupants suffering the highest proportion of fatalities (at 42%) followed by pedestrians (27%), motorcyclists (19%) and cyclists (6%). Deaths are most likely to occur on rural roads, though accidents are more frequent on urban streets with around 30,000 serious injuries a year.[103] Motorways, which limit sharing, are the safest form of highway.[104]

While mobility is undoubtedly critical for personal, social and economic reasons, people exercising their right to passage are putting others at considerable risk. To do this effectively, and as safely as possible whilst creating streets that are pleasant and provide opportunities for health-giving active travel, we need to be able to share. Highways are governed in multiple ways, by highway authorities, legislation and the common law, individual users' actions, social norms and infrastructure imbued with enforcement powers. With increasing rates of car ownership – expected to rise by up to 51 per cent over 2015 figures by 2050[105] – recognising highway space as a resource to be governed is increasingly critical.

LTNs provide useful illustrations to consider whether the highway is 'a right' of passage, 'a place' belonging in some sense to local residents rather than motor vehicles driving through, or 'a resource' to be allocated and governed. They illustrate why highways should be primarily understood as a resource, acknowledging the continued relevance of a right to passage for all, as well as the qualities of highways as both a regulatory spatial category and individual places. Cars can still enter if driven by residents, but through traffic can no longer cut through. The resource is not static; the spatial imaginaries LTNs propose would have been commonplace a hundred years ago, just as pigs seemed acceptable centuries before and the proliferation of motor vehicles seems conventional today. Spatial imaginaries can change over time, particularly for place-based regulatory concepts.

Understanding the highway as a resource also highlights the many similarities with planning, particularly if we understand 'development' as a spatial resource to be allocated rather than the right of individual landowners. In planning we are sharing space in very similar ways to highways. This was the fundamental insight of the Uthwatt Committee in 1943[106] with its call for the introduction of nationalised development rights, echoed in these war years by Alker Tripp's call for pedestrian precincts. As we have learned during the Covid pandemic, times of national crisis can provide fertile ground for reimagining our surroundings and their regulatory regimes, including the much-debated LTNs.

Notes

1. Smith 2020.
2. https://www.gov.uk/government/publications/reallocating-road-space-in-response-to-covid-19-statutory-guidance-for-local-authorities/traffic-management-act-2004-network-management-in-response-to-covid-19 (accessed 12 June 2022).
3. Freedom of Information Act 2000, section 10; Information Commissioner Decision Notices IC-62328-T8S4 and IC-68462-F9X2.
4. Hill 2021.
5. Latour 1994.
6. As 'highwayspace' is awkward, this chapter uses the word 'roadspace' instead.
7. Schepel 2005.
8. Buchanan 1964, 355.
9. Department for Transport (DfT) 2020a.
10. Laverty, Goodman and Aldred 2021; Aldred and Goodman 2020; Goodman, Urban and Aldred 2020; Aldred et al 2021.
11. Road Traffic Act 1984, section 17; Motorways Traffic (England and Wales) Regulations 1982.
12. Alexander 1977, 182–90.
13. Foster 2005, 39.
14. Lynn and Anthony 2011, 403.
15. Road Traffic Regulation Act (RTRA) 1984, section 9.
16. Local Government Association 2021.
17. Highways Act 1980, section 328.
18. Highways Act 1980, sections 328 and 329; Town and Country Planning Act (TCPA) 1990, section 336.
19. Cooper 2000.
20. RTRA 1984, section 60.
21. Highways Act 1980, section 41[1A].
22. Highways Act 1980, section 137. Note that section 137 must be read compatibly with the European Convention on Human Rights: see *DPP v Ziegler* [2021] UKSC 23; [2021] 3 WLR 179.
23. Roads (Scotland) Act 1984, section 151.

24. *DPP v Jones (Margaret) and Another* [1999] 2 AC 240, [257D].
25. *London Borough of Southwark and another v Transport for London* [2018] UKSC 63; [2018] 3 WLR 2059, [6].
26. *London Borough of Southwark,* [32].
27. Vorspan 1997, 923.
28. *Harrison v Duke of Rutland* [1893] 1 QB 142, [154].
29. Vorspan 2000, 905.
30. Vorspan 1997, 923.
31. Hornsey 2010, 105.
32. Rooney 2019.
33. Highway Code 1931, 4.
34. Webb and Webb 1913, V.
35. https://hansard.parliament.uk/Commons/1938-11-16/debates/6e0f0969-2447-4d74-bfcc-ad2dc579a3de/RoadAccidents (accessed 12 June 2022).
36. Shaw and Docherty 2014, 40.
37. https://www.whatdotheyknow.com/request/17118/response/41616/attach/html/2/Final%20reply.pdf.html (accessed 12 June 2022).
38. *United Trade Action Group v Transport for London* [2021] EWHC 72.
39. *United Trade Action Group v Transport for London* [2021] EWCA Civ 1197, [53].
40. *United Trade Action Group v Transport for London* [2021] EWCA Civ 1197.
41. *United Trade Action Group,* [74].
42. *United Trade Action Group v Transport for London* [2021] EWCA Civ 1197, [121].
43. Blomley 2010.
44. *London Borough of Southwark*.
45. Vorspan 1997, 927.
46. Massey 2005, 130.
47. These techniques are sometimes referred to as framing or bracketing: see Callon 1998; Blomley 2014. The term *mapping* is used here to denote both the legal and spatial categorisation: see Layard 2021.
48. *Jones,* [257D].
49. *Jones,* [257D].
50. *Jones,* [257E]. In *Jones* the Divisional Court questioned this construction but the Supreme Court [2021] UKSC 23 did not take this point up and overruled the Court of Appeal on different terms.
51. http://www.jilg.com/ (accessed 12 June 2022).
52. Appleyard, Gerson and Lintell 1976, 277.
53. Thorpe 2020.
54. Smithsonian 2020.
55. *Tunbridge Wells Corp v Baird* [1896] AC 434.
56. *Tunbridge Wells,* [44].
57. Kohn 2004; Layard 2019.
58. Layard 2012.
59. UN Habitat 2013.
60. Layard 2021.
61. See Lord Hope's disapproval of the lack of consideration for landowners' rights in his dissent in *Jones,* [277D].
62. Orlik 2012; public rights of passage are overriding interests in registered land: Land Registration Act 2002, Schedule 1(5) and Schedule 3(5).
63. *Tithe Redemption Commission v Runcorn UDC* [1954] Ch 383, 407, and see Orlik 2012.
64. Though see *London Borough of Southwark*. Lord Briggs held that a highway could be 'a species of real property', with maintenance obligations the *quid pro quo* for ownership. This appears to apply only to highways acquired under the Highways Act, section 265 ('transfer'), rather than under section 263 ('vesting').
65. Traffic Management Act 2004, section 16.
66. Traffic Management Act 2004, section 31.
67. *HHRC Ltd v Hackney Borough Council* [2021] EWHC 2440 (Admin) [43].
68. Lee 2017.
69. Lee 2017.
70. Webb and Webb 1913, 20.

71. https://www.gov.uk/government/news/funding-to-fix-equivalent-of-10-million-potholes-allocated-to-local-authorities (accessed 12 June 2022).
72. Highways Act 1980, section 41.
73. Highways Act 1980, section 58.
74. Dirnhuber 2021.
75. Bosetti et al 2022.
76. *SM v Hackney LBC* [2021] EWHC 3294 (Admin); *HHRC Ltd v Hackney LBC* [2021] EWHC 2440 (Admin); *R (Sheakh) v Lambeth London Borough Council* [2022] EWCA Civ 457.
77. *Sheakh* and *HHRC*.
78. *People v Harriet* New York Judicial Repository 265–6 (1819).
79. Hartog 1985, 900.
80. Velten 2013.
81. 6 George I. c. 6.
82. Webb and Webb 1913, 240.
83. Webb and Webb 1913, 238.
84. Webb and Webb 1913, v.
85. Highway Code 1931.
86. Highway Code 1935.
87. House of Commons Library 2012.
88. Highway Code 1954.
89. Road Traffic Act 1984, section 38.
90. *R v Chadwick* [1975] Crim LR 105.
91. Tennant et al 2021, 4.
92. DfT 2020b, 7.
93. DfT 2020b, 10.
94. DfT 2020b.
95. Buchanan 1964, 335.
96. Moran 2012.
97. Hebbert 1993.
98. Sir Roger Nugent citing Buchanan 1964 in 'Transport Debate', *Hansard HC Deb 08 July 1964 vol 698: cc425–542,* available at https://api.parliament.uk/historic-hansard/commons/1964/jul/08/transport (accessed 12 June 2022).
99. Cited in Saumarez Smith 2019, 43.
100. On the practice of shared space see Hamilton-Baillie 2008.
101. https://www.gov.uk/government/statistics/reported-road-casualties-in-great-britain-provisional-estimates-year-ending-june-2021 (accessed 12 June 2022).
102. DfT 2020c.
103. DfT 2020c.
104. DfT 2020c.
105. DfT 2018.
106. Uthwatt 1942.

References

Aldred, Rachel and Anna Goodman (2020). 'Low Traffic Neighbourhoods, Car Use, and Active Travel: Evidence from the People and Places Survey of Outer London Active Travel Interventions', *Findings*, available at https://findingspress.org/article/17128-low-traffic-neighbourhoods-car-use-and-active-travel-evidence-from-the-people-and-places-survey-of-outer-london-active-travel-interventions (accessed 12 June 2022).

Aldred, Rachel et al (2021). 'Equity in New Active Travel Infrastructure: A Spatial Analysis of London's New Low Traffic Neighbourhoods', *Journal of Transport Geography* 96: 103194.

Alexander, William (1977). 'The March of Time and the World Today', *American Quarterly* 29: 182–90.

Appleyard, Donald, Sue Gerson and Mark Lintell (1976). *Liveable Urban Streets: Managing Auto Traffic in Neighborhoods. Final Report.* Washington, DC: US Department of Transportation, Federal Highway Administration.

Blomley, Nicholas (2010). *Rights of Passage: Sidewalks and the Regulation of Public Flow*. Abingdon: Routledge.

Blomley, Nicholas (2014). 'Disentangling Law: The Practice of Bracketing', *Annual Review of Law and Social Science* 10: 133–45.

Bosetti, Nicolas et al (2022). *Street-Shift: The Future of Low-Traffic Neighbourhoods*. Centre for London, available at https://www.centreforlondon.org/publication/london-low-traffic-neighbourhoods/ (accessed 20 June 2022).

Buchanan, Colin (1964). *Traffic in Towns*. London: Penguin/HMSO.

Callon, Michael (1998). 'Introduction: The Embeddedness of Economic Markets in Economics', *The Sociological Review* 46: 1–57.

Cooper, Alan (2000). 'The King's Four Highways: Legal Fiction Meets Fictional Law', *Journal of Medieval History* 26: 351–70.

Department for Transport (2004). *Traffic Management Act 2004 Network Management Duty Guidance*.

Department for Transport (2018). *Road Traffic Forecasts 2018*.

Department for Transport (2020a). *Gear Change: A Bold Vision for Cycling and Walking*.

Department for Transport (2020b). *Cycling and Walking Investment Strategy: Safety Review Consultation on a Review of The Highway Code. Moving Britain Ahead*.

Department for Transport (2020c). *Reported Road Casualties Great Britain: 2019 Annual Report*, available at https://assets.publishing.service.gov.uk/government/uploads/system/uploads/attachment_data/file/928205/reported-road-casualties-gb-annual-report-2019.pdf (accessed 12 June 2022).

Dirnhuber, Jason (2021). *Council Raises £2.7m by Fining Drivers for Breaching LTNs*, available at https://www.hackneygazette.co.uk/news/local-council/hackney-fines-thousands-of-drivers-for-ltn-breaches-8098468 (accessed 12 June 2022).

Foster, Christopher (2005). *British Government in Crisis*. London: Bloomsbury.

Goodman, Anna, Scott Urban and Rachel Aldred (2020). 'The Impact of Low Traffic Neighbourhoods and Other Active Travel Interventions on Vehicle Ownership: Findings from the Outer London Mini-Holland Programme', *Findings*, available at https://findingspress.org/article/18200-the-impact-of-low-traffic-neighbourhoods-and-other-active-travel-interventions-on-vehicle-ownership-findings-from-the-outer-london-mini-holland-programme (accessed 12 June 2022).

Hamilton-Baillie, Ben (2008). 'Shared Space: Reconciling People, Places and Traffic', *Built Environment* 34: 161–81.

Hartog, Hendrik (1985). 'Pigs and Positivism', *Wisconsin Law Review*: 899–936.

Hebbert, Michael (1993). 'The City of London Walkway Experiment', *Journal of the American Planning Association* 59: 433–50.

Hill, Dave (2019). 'Ealing: What Next for Low Traffic Neighbourhoods?', *ON London*, available at https://www.onlondon.co.uk/ealing-what-next-for-low-traffic-neighbourhoods/ (accessed 12 June 2022).

Hornsey, Richard (2010). '"He Who Thinks, in Modern Traffic, Is Lost": Automation and the Pedestrian Rhythms of Interwar London'. In *Geographies of Rhythm: Nature, Place, Mobilities and Bodies*, edited by Tim Edensor, 99–112. Abingdon: Routledge.

House of Commons Library (2012). *Olympic Britain Social and Economic Change since the 1908 and 1948 London Games*.

Kohn, Margaret (2004). *Brave New Neighborhoods: The Privatization of Public Space*. Abingdon: Routledge.

Latour, Bruno (1994). 'On Technical Mediation', *Common Knowledge* 3: 29–64.

Laverty, Antony, Anna Goodman and Rachel Aldred (2021). 'Low Traffic Neighbourhoods and Population Health', *British Medical Journal* 372: 1–2.

Layard, Antonia (2012). 'Property Paradigms and Place-Making: A Right to the City; a Right to the Street?', *Journal of Human Rights and the Environment* 3: 254–72.

Layard, Antonia (2019). 'Privatising Land in England', *Journal of Property, Planning and Environmental Law* 11: 151–68.

Layard, Antonia (2021). 'Law, Place and Maps'. In *Handbook on Space, Place and Law*, edited by Robyn Bartel and Jennifer Carter, 129–40. Cheltenham: Edward Elgar.

Leach, William (1918). 'Road Accidents', [906], *House of Commons Hansard*, available at https://hansard.parliament.uk/Commons/1938-11-16/debates/6e0f0969-2447-4d74-bfcc-ad2dc579a3de/RoadAccidents (accessed 12 June 2022).

Lee, Maria (2017). 'Knowledge and Landscape in Wind Energy Planning', *Legal Studies* 3: 3–16.

Local Government Association (2021). *Stakeholder Engagement in an Emergency: Lessons from Low-Traffic Neighbourhoods.*

Lynn, Jonathan and Anthony Jay (2011). *The Complete Yes Minister*. London: Random House.

Massey, Doreen (2005). *For Space*. London: Sage.

Moran, Joe (2012). 'Imagining the Street in Post-War Britain', *Urban History* 39: 166–86.

Orlik, Michael (2012). 'Highway Boundaries and Local Searches', *Journal of Planning and Environmental Law* 6: 658–65.

Rooney, David (2019). *Spaces of Congestion and Traffic: Politics and Technologies in Twentieth-Century London.* Abingdon: Taylor & Francis.

Saumarez-Smith, Otto (2019). *Boom Cities: Architect Planners and the Politics of Radical Urban Renewal in 1960s Britain*. Oxford: Oxford University Press.

Schepel, Steven (2005). *Woonerf Revisited: Delft as an Example*, available at http://www.woonerfgoed.nl/int/Childstreet_files/StevenSchepel.pdf (accessed 12 June 2022).

Shaw, John and Iain Docherty (2014). *The Transport Debate*. Bristol: Policy Press.

Smith, Cachella (2020). *Anti-LTN Convoy Delivers Cabbages to Hackney Town Hall*, available at https://www.hackneygazette.co.uk/news/traffic/hackney-ltn-protesters-deliver-cabbages-to-town-hall-6754586 (accessed 12 June 2022).

Smithsonian (2020). *Was Childcare One Secret to Winning Suffrage?* https://www.youtube.com/watch?v=WaO__6iN82E (accessed 12 June 2022).

Tennant, Chris et al (2021). 'Code, Culture, and Concrete: Self-Driving Vehicles and the Rules of the Road', *Frontiers in Sustainable Cities* 3: 1–11.

Thorpe, Amelia (2020). *Owning the Street: The Everyday Life of Property*. Cambridge, MA: MIT Press.

UN Habitat (2013). *Streets as Public Spaces and Drivers of Urban Prosperity*. New York: UN Habitat.

Uthwatt, A.A. (1942). *Expert Committee on Compensation and Betterment: Final Report*. London: HMSO.

Velten, Hannah (2013). *Beastly London: A History of Animals in the City*. London: Reaktion Books.

Vorspan, Rachel (1997). 'Freedom of Assembly and the Right to Passage in Modern English Legal History', *San Diego Law Review* 34: 921–1046.

Vorspan, Rachel (1998). 'The Political Power of Nuisance Law: Labor Picketing and the Courts in Modern England, 1871-Present', *Buffalo Law Review* 46: 593–703.

Vorspan, Rachel (2000). 'Rational Recreation and the Law: The Transformation of Popular Urban Leisure in Victorian England', *McGill Law Journal* 45: 892–973.

Webb, Sydney and Beatrice Webb (1913). *English Local Government: The Story of the King's Highway*. London: Longmans.

5
Marine planning for sustainability: The role of the ecosystem approach

Margherita Pieraccini

Introduction

This chapter focuses on marine spatial planning in England, and its promise to achieve sustainable development. It does so by investigating the way in which the ecosystem approach, central to marine planning, is conceptualised in selected marine policy documents. Like land use planning,[1] the stated aim of marine spatial planning is sustainable development, as expressed in the Marine Policy Statement (MPS).[2] Whilst there has been considerable debate on the meaning of sustainable development in land use planning, with the presumption in favour of sustainable development eliciting much criticism for favouring 'growth-dependent' planning,[3] the meaning of sustainable development in English marine spatial planning has attracted less scholarly attention to date.[4] This can simply be explained by the fact that marine spatial planning is a much younger area of regulation, introduced under the Marine and Coastal Access (MCA) Act 2009.

Following the adoption of the MPS in 2011, a regional, phased approach to marine spatial planning has been implemented in England, with the individuation of 11 marine plan areas covering inshore and offshore regions. Because the MPS acts as the central framework for preparing the Marine Plans and for taking decisions affecting the marine environment, the study of both the MPS and the Marine Plans is necessary in order to analyse marine spatial planning in England.

Given that marine spatial planning is a nascent system, with the majority of Marine Plans adopted very recently, it is too early to provide a comprehensive assessment of how it has or has not delivered on its promise of sustainable development.[5] However, it is not too early to investigate how marine spatial planning frames and attempts to deliver sustainable development. To do so, this chapter looks at the core approach underpinning marine spatial planning – that is, the ecosystem approach – asking how it has been conceptualised and what role it has in marine planning for sustainability in English waters. As discussed below, in international environmental law, the ecosystem approach is a key legal strategy for integrated marine management, moving beyond the modernist foundations of much environmental and planning law, which are based on a nature/society binary, and championing epistemic pluralism. Thus, it has the potential to provide a novel approach to planning for sustainability. The extent to which this potential is fulfilled depends on how the ecosystem approach is conceptualised in English marine planning policy. To investigate such conceptualisation, a textual analysis of selected marine planning policy documents in England is provided, focusing on the MPS and the first two inshore and offshore marine plans adopted, namely the East and South Marine Plans. The East and South Marine Plans cover very diverse regions and areas, and present information in different ways. They are ideal for a comparative reading.

The chapter is structured as follow. The first section lays the conceptual foundations on which the paper is based by providing a critical investigation into the meanings of sustainable development and the ecosystem approach. The next section introduces the legal and policy framework for marine spatial planning in England. The MCA Act 2009 is the main Act for the regulation of the English marine environment, containing wide-ranging provisions related to marine conservation, licensing, fisheries, coastal access and of course marine planning, and establishing new bodies for the management of marine activities. The provisions related to marine spatial planning are to be found in Part III of the MCA Act 2009. Section 44 of the Act provides details for the preparation and adoption of the MPS, which states the general policies for contributing to the achievement of sustainable development in the UK marine area. The textual analysis of the MPS as well as East[6] and South England[7] Marine inshore and offshore Plans follows. In analysing the selected planning documents, the research question revolves around how the ecosystem approach has shaped the meaning of marine planning for sustainability. Two interrelated arguments are made. First, that the ecosystem approach as a concept has the potential to move sustainable development beyond a trade-off between separate categories, thereby pushing for a more holistic consideration of sustainable marine planning. Second, that despite the ecosystem approach being at the heart of marine planning for sustainability in England, the way in which it is defined in current planning documents falls short of fully achieving this potential. This is because the ecosystem approach is either defined quite narrowly in environmental terms or linked to economic issues and a neoliberal, growth-oriented planning agenda.

Conceptual foundations: sustainable development and the ecosystem approach

As stated in the introduction, English marine spatial planning is underpinned by the objective of sustainable development and by the ecosystem approach.[8] This is not confined to England. For example, in the EU, article 5(1) of the Marine Spatial Planning Directive states that 'when establishing and implementing maritime spatial planning, Member States shall consider economic, social and environmental aspects to support sustainable development and growth in the maritime sector, applying an ecosystem approach'.[9] However, the concepts of sustainable development and the ecosystem approach are ubiquitous and can be defined in multiple ways. Depending on the way they are conceptualised, they may lead to very different results for marine spatial planning. This section discusses the ways in which sustainable development and the ecosystem approach have been conceptualised in international law and policy, as this provides important ontological and epistemological reflections for the domestic assessment of marine spatial planning. The reason for focusing on the international law dimension first is that most of the conceptual development of both sustainable development and the ecosystem approach stems from this scale.

The history of the concept of sustainable development in international law and policy shows that, broadly speaking, there are two main definitions of sustainable development: one that views sustainable development as a trade-off between three separate pillars (the ecological, the economic and the social), and the other that understands sustainable development more holistically. The popular three pillars definition of sustainable development, articulated clearly in the Johannesburg Declaration 2002,[10] subscribes to a modernist logic and Cartesian division between nature and society. The three pillars (de facto two, as the social often disappears in the decision-making) are distinct and the aim of decision-making is to balance them against each other, thereby maintaining such divisions. If reconciliation between environmental protection and economic development is contemplated, it is conceptualised as the point of arrival, not the point of departure. Besides, this approach is concerned not with procedural issues but more with the balancing of distinct substantive concerns, primarily from an anthropocentric perspective, and it seldom problematises economic growth.

The other view of sustainable development is one that focuses more on holism and inclusiveness. The roots of this view are to be found in the Brundtland Report,[11] which spoke of interlocking crises due to the dissolution of the environment, economics, and society as separate compartments, and argued for acknowledging the interweaving of ecology and economy. It is also to be found in principle 4 of the Rio Declaration,[12] which provides that 'in order to achieve sustainable development, environmental protection shall constitute an integral part of the development process and cannot be considered in isolation from it'. More recently, Agenda 2030 promotes a holistic view of sustainable development, stating that the 17 Sustainable Development Goals (SDGs) are 'integrated and indivisible',[13] though also reiterating that they balance the three dimensions of sustainable development. Tellingly, the emphasis in these documents is not only on substantive factors but also on facilitating institutional processes that enable fulfilment of procedural rights such as participation, cooperation and access to justice.[14] This is key, as sustainable development understood in this way does not mean the achievement of a unified, fixed state of harmony, suppressing differences, but requires processes of negotiation, dialogue and openness to plural views and values. In a sense, it promotes bonding through difference. Although it is tempting to contrast this holistic and inclusive view with the balance approach to sustainable development, as Agenda 2030 shows with the reference to the three pillars approach, the two views can sit next to each other. Besides, the extent to which they move beyond an anthropocentric view of sustainable development is questionable. Inter-generational justice at the core of Brundtland is about human/social justice and some authors have argued that the Sustainable Development Goals (SDGs) do not overcome an anthropocentric bias.[15]

Ultimately, much depends on the way in which holism is understood. If it is understood as a way to integrate different pre-existing interests and reach a final consensus, then the modernist logic at the basis of sustainable development is not overcome even when this holistic view is championed. If holism is understood as indicative of a relational ontology, whereby relations between entities and interests are ontologically primary, rather than derivative and where the goal is not the suppression of difference, then we witness a clear departure from modernist assumptions.

Arturo Escobar, among others,[16] has emphasised the importance of relational ontology as a means of rethinking sustainable development. He defines relational ontology as an ontology 'in which *nothing preexist* [sic] *the relations that constitute it*. Said otherwise, things and beings are their relations, they do not exist prior to them.'[17] The problem with sustainable development is encountered when these relations are understood as and reduced to separate entities, be they nature/natural resources, society, the economy and so on, and efforts are made to balance or integrate these allegedly different entities to achieve the single goal of sustainable development. Drawing on indigenous cosmologies and transition movements, Escobar shows how there are alternative worldviews that do not neglect such relationality and speak about the co-constitution of nature and society. Their acknowledgement is important because it is a way to overcome ontological dualisms characteristic of modernity and to reclaim a space for difference. Escobar argues that:

> there are indeed relational worldviews or ontologies for which the world is always multiple – a pluriverse. Relational ontologies are those that eschew the divisions between nature and culture, individual and community, and between us and them that are central to the modern ontology . . . They point towards the pluriverse; in the successful formula of the Zapatista, the pluriverse can be described as "a world where many worlds fit".[18]

The task of sustainable development in this context is not to balance different elements to achieve a single goal, but to acknowledge the manifold relations and views that make up the world. It is not possible to speak about sustainable development in the singular. Relational ontology is indissolubly interlinked with epistemic plurality as relational views, 'worlds and knowledges otherwise',[19] are, for Escobar, to be acknowledged in decision-making fora. Relational ontologies challenge the epistemic foundation of modern politics, making space for different epistemologies and de facto pluralising the meaning of sustainability. Following a relational ontology, the meaning of holism in the discourse of sustainable development consists not in a move towards the suppression of difference in search of a unified and single sustainability, but in a movement towards plurality and recognition of multiple knowledges and ways of thinking and practising sustainability.[20]

These reflections on the ontological foundations of sustainable development and their epistemological implications are important because when sustainable development is conceptualised as a way to balance distinct substantive categories, with the economy disembedded from the social and separated from the environmental, there is the risk that certain interests are prioritised. This has been visible in land use planning in England, where 'growth-dependent' planning has predominated.[21] The presumption in favour of sustainable development for plan-making as well as decision-taking to be found in paragraph 11 of the National Planning Policy Framework (NPPF) has been criticised for favouring development and economic growth, at the expense of environmental and social factors.[22] The Raynsford Review of planning in England has pointed out that the presumption in favour of sustainable development makes it more difficult to reject an application. Raynsford also argues that the planning system needs to be refocused on long-term sustainable development, which requires a more accurate definition, encompassing core internationally agreed principles, such as the precautionary principle or inter-generational justice.[23] As Simon Bird has noted, the approach of the Secretary of State in planning law has been to treat the presumption in favour of sustainable development as a question of balance.[24] Thus, environmentally unsustainable development has been given the green light when economic benefits outweigh the environmental costs. A similar point has also been made in the Raynsford Review, which states that the poor definition of sustainable development 'creates space for the principles of sustainable development to be traded off against each other and so undermines any meaningful consideration of sustainable development in planning decisions', often favouring the economic needs of private interests over the wider public interest in social and environmental issues.[25] However, the recent *Planning for the Future* White Paper has done little to improve the situation, not explaining how it defines sustainable development and stating that 'the achievement of sustainable development is an existing and well-understood basis for the planning system'.[26] Treating sustainable development as a balancing, trade-off exercise is highly problematic because it runs counter to a more holistic understanding of sustainability.

The main problem with a trade-off approach occurs when economic growth is valued as outweighing environmental concerns. In those circumstances, environmentally and socially unsustainable development is favoured. In short, the sustainable development agenda in planning can end up sustaining capitalist modes of production and consumption at the expense of social and environmental aspects.

Moving to marine planning, what vision of sustainable development is to be found? Does marine planning for sustainability mean de facto planning for growth, and is sustainable development understood as a way to achieve a balance/trade-off between different substantive pillars? To answer these questions, it is essential to consider a key concept in marine planning (absent from land use planning), namely the ecosystem approach, and to investigate whether the ecosystem approach enables a shift towards a more relational view of sustainable development in marine planning.

The ecosystem approach has come to occupy a prominent place in international environmental law and governance, especially, but not exclusively, in relation to marine issues.[27] This is not surprising given that, as explained below, the concept of integration is at the core of the ecosystem approach, and it applies neatly to managing the interconnected systems to be found in the fluid and dynamic marine environment. The ecosystem approach has also been adopted as the primary framework for action under the Convention on Biological Diversity (CBD).[28]

There is no single definition of the ecosystem approach. It is an amorphous and potentially expansive concept. As Arie Troubworst has argued,[29] at its most basic, the ecosystem approach is about the holistic management of activities, following best available ecological knowledge aimed at satisfying human needs without compromising ecological integrity.

The holistic view inherent in the ecosystem approach derives from the concept of the ecosystem itself. An ecosystem is made up of the relationships between its biotic and abiotic components. Humans are not an external force operating on a natural resource base; they are an integral part of the ecosystem itself. In this way, the ecosystem approach avoids falling into the anthropocentric trap. Hence the modernist dichotomy between nature and society disappears. As defined in article 2 of the CBD, ecosystem means 'a dynamic complex of plant, animal, and microorganism communities and their non-living environment interaction as a functional unit'. The Guidance on the Ecosystem Approach produced by the Secretariat of the CBD explains well the holistic approach at the basis of the ecosystem approach:

> The ecosystem approach is based on the application of appropriate scientific methodologies focused on levels of biological organization, which encompass the essential structure, processes, functions and interactions among organisms and their environment. It also recognizes that humans, with their cultural diversity, are an integral component of many ecosystems . . . After all, all biomes . . . are interconnected in some way, and management action will likely have limited success if these connections are not taken into account.[30]

If integration is at the core of the concept, it is important to stress that it is a point of departure, rather than a point of arrival – by contrast with the approach to sustainable development discussed above – as the ecosystem approach assumes that relationships between living organisms and their physical environments are what primarily exist. Thus, the ecosystem approach is underpinned by a relational ontology, focussing on processes, functions and interactions.

Moreover, the ecosystem approach is not only about substantive integration but also provides important procedural openings by calling for the acknowledgement of different knowledges in decision-making. This is most explicit in the so-called Malawi principles, contained in Annex B to Decision V/6 of the CBD on the Ecosystem Approach.[31] Decision V/6 has been seminal in describing the ecosystem approach and spelling out the interlinked and complementary principles of the ecosystem approach, whose application is recommended. Principles 1, 11 and 12 are most relevant to the epistemological opening at play. Principle 1 states that 'the objectives of management of land, water and living resources are a matter of societal choice' and that different sectors of society view ecosystems in different ways, depending on their cultural, economic and societal needs. This emphasis on the plurality and diversity of perspectives on the objectives of management, which will enable the recognition of different worldviews, is reminiscent of the epistemic plurality advocated by scholars of pluriversality, such as Escobar. It also shows, as Vito De Lucia has argued, that ecosystems are not ontologically given, but are co-produced by social and ecological elements, thereby making a point on the political epistemology of nature.[32]

Malawi principle 11 states that the 'ecosystem approach should consider all forms of relevant information, including scientific and indigenous and local knowledge'. This is justified on instrumental grounds, stating that different sources can offer complementary information and enable a much better knowledge of ecosystem functions but also on more normative grounds by reference to the relevance of sharing information and checking decisions against available knowledge and views of stakeholders. Principle 12 states that 'the ecosystem approach should involve all relevant sectors of society and scientific disciplines'. The rationale behind this principle revolves around the complexity of biodiversity problems, involving many interactions so that necessary expertise at all levels of decision-making should be engaged.

For these reasons, the ecosystem approach is indicative of a paradigm shift in environmental law, as many authors have argued.[33] Rather than thinking about single species or habitats, or nature as a resource base for human activity, the ecosystem approach enables environmental law to focus on dynamic systems, in which each component (including human beings) is inter-linked in ecological processes of various temporal and spatial scales. Further, the focus on participatory processes shows that epistemic integration is an essential component of the ecosystem approach. Thus, the ecosystem approach has a transformative role, shifting sustainable management from a sectoral to a place-based holistic approach and holding the potential to increase environmental democracy.

However, it presents its challenges, especially regarding legal certainty because the concept of the ecosystem that is at its centre does not have clear-cut boundaries and cannot be reduced to precise elements and principles. As Dan Tarlock has discussed, although the concept of ecosystem has important implications for the future of environmental law, its translation into operational legal standards is not straightforward as the problem of scale is encountered.[34] When speaking about ecosystems, a unique spatial scale cannot be identified, as an ecosystem can refer to a single tree but also to a transnational landscape, and the temporal scales of management are not easily definable. For Tarlock, the solution is to move towards adaptive management that recognises that all ecosystem conservation is an experiment requiring constant adjustment in light of new knowledge.[35] Similarly, Niko Soininen and Froukje Platjouw discuss the importance of adaptive capacity for EU aquatic environmental law, embracing the ecosystem approach.[36] Interestingly, adaptive management appears in principle 9 of the Malawi principles, which states that 'the ecosystem approach must utilize adaptive management in order to anticipate and cater for such changes and events'.

Although adaptive management can be a useful concept to tackle scalar uncertainties and render ecological management responsive, this does not erase the fact that the ecosystem approach is underpinned by a complex and dynamic ecological concept, so that multiple and sometimes contested conceptualisations exist. This point has been well made in the work of De Lucia, who has traced, following a genealogical approach, how different and competing narratives of the ecosystem approach exist in international law and policy.[37]

These considerations have value for the present discussion on marine spatial planning. The ecosystem approach is all about holism, relational ontology and epistemic plurality, transcending modernist dichotomies between nature and society, and thereby able to move the goal of sustainable development away from a balance/trade-off approach and its anthropocentric orientations. However, due to its ubiquitous nature, more than one conceptualisation of the ecosystem approach exists. Thus, whether the ecosystem approach truly contributes to a relational orientation of sustainable development depends on the way in which English marine spatial planning law and policy defines it and engages with it. This question will be explored below, after providing an introduction to English marine spatial planning law.

An introduction to English marine spatial planning law

Marine spatial planning is a process which responds to growing and competing demands for marine spaces and resources by allocating spatial and temporal distribution of activities in marine areas to achieve sustainable development. Marine spatial planning does not focus on a single sector, be it marine conservation, fishing or renewables; it champions integrated and multi-functional management.[38] It is not surprising, then, that it has put at its core the holistic concept of the ecosystem approach. For some scholars, marine spatial planning is defined through the ecosystem approach, and is based on ecological principles articulating healthy and functioning ecosystems.[39] Policy too stresses the importance of implementing the ecosystem approach in marine spatial planning.[40]

Marine spatial planning legislation is gradually becoming more common around the world. As mentioned at the start of this chapter, in England, marine spatial planning was established under the MCA Act 2009, Part III. Therefore, its introduction is antecedent to the EU's legal efforts in this field, which date to 2014,[41] making the UK one of the leading countries in Europe to introduce legal requirements for marine planning.[42] The provisions relating to marine spatial planning contained in the MCA Act 2009 are very detailed, including the requirement to prepare the MPS under section 44, and the Marine Plans for each marine area under section 51. The MPS provides strategic environmental, social and economic considerations and policy objectives for key sectors, as well as detailing 22 high-level marine goals. The policies contained in the MPS are to contribute to the achievement of sustainable development in the UK marine area.[43]

Responsibility for preparing the Marine Plans lies with the Secretary of State in England[44] but it has been delegated to the Marine Management Organisation (MMO), an executive non-departmental public body established under Part I of the MCA Act 2009, with the general objective of contributing to the achievement of sustainable development and discharging many marine functions on behalf of the UK government. There are a total of 11 Marine Plans covering English inshore and offshore waters. The first Marine Plans were adopted in 2014 to cover the East inshore and offshore marine plan areas (East Inshore and East Offshore Marine Plans). They were followed by the South Inshore and Offshore Plans in 2018 to cover South of England inshore and offshore plan areas. The other Marine Plans, covering North East inshore and offshore, South East inshore, South West inshore and offshore and North West inshore and offshore, were adopted in Summer 2021.

If we were to draw an analogy with land use planning, we could say that the MPS sits on the same strategic plane as the NPPF or the National Policy Statements for major infrastructure, while Marine Plans operate at the level of local plans, though covering areas that are much more extensive.

Like local plans on land, Marine Plans are subject to a Habitats Regulation Assessment[45] and a Sustainability Appraisal[46] prior to their establishment. The MMO is also required to prepare a Statement of Public Participation,[47] setting out how and when interested persons will be engaged in the planning process. Once a draft plan is published, it is subject to consultation to allow public representations to be made. Under section 58 of the MCA Act 2009, public authorities must take authorisation or enforcement decisions in accordance with the appropriate marine policy documents within or affecting the marine area in question.[48] This includes decisions that require development consent, such as wind farms, and those that do not, such as shipping or fishing.[49] Thus, their remit is very wide and goes beyond development. Some discretion is afforded to the public authority if 'relevant considerations indicate otherwise'.[50] If a public authority takes an authorisation or enforcement decision otherwise than in accordance with the appropriate marine policy documents, the authority must state its reasons for doing so.[51] There is no obligation for public authorities to consult with the MMO.

Under section 58(3) of the MCA Act 2009, public authorities must have regard to the appropriate marine policy documents when taking a decision relating to the exercise of their functions capable of affecting the whole or part of the UK marine area, which is not an authorisation or enforcement decision.

Both the MPS and the Marine Plans are to be kept under review,[52] and can be amended and withdrawn if necessary.[53] There is also an obligation of periodic monitoring and reporting on implementation.[54] These provisions point to an adaptive management approach. As mentioned, the law is explicit in stating that the goal of marine planning is sustainable development and this is the stated objective for the policies of both the MPS and the Marine Plans.[55] No definition of sustainable development is given in the law, leaving the objective open-ended.

The next section analyses marine planning documents to investigate the way in which sustainable development is promoted, focusing on the way the ecosystem approach is conceptualised.

The ecosystem approach in the MPS

This section attempts to answer the research question the chapter is posing – namely how the ecosystem approach shapes the meaning of sustainable marine planning. It does so through a textual analysis of selected marine planning documents. Whilst, by contrast with the EU Marine Spatial Directive, the MCA Act 2009 is silent in relation to the ecosystem approach, its implementation documents place the ecosystem approach at the centre of marine planning. The UK MPS states that the process of marine planning will 'manage competing demands on the marine area, taking an ecosystem-based approach'.[56] In addition, one of its high-level marine objectives requires the UK governments to ensure that 'the use of the marine environment is spatially planned where appropriate and based on an ecosystem approach'.[57]

The interpretation of the ecosystem approach in the MPS is explicitly linked to regulation 5 of the UK Marine Strategy Regulations 2010,[58] which transpose the EU Marine Strategy Framework Directive into domestic law. This demonstrates the influence of EU environmental law on domestic marine planning. The Marine Strategy Framework is the environmental pillar of EU marine law, and it is very ecocentric in nature, establishing a framework within which Member States shall take the necessary measures to achieve or maintain good environmental status.[59] Under article 9, the Marine Strategy Framework Directive requires Member States to determine good environmental status for their marine areas on the basis of qualitative descriptors listed in Annex I. Such descriptors are of an ecological nature (for example maintenance of biological diversity, minimisation of human-induced eutrophication, exploitation of commercial fish and shellfish within biological safe limits) and no social descriptors are listed. In the post-Brexit context, the Marine Strategy Regulations 2010 are retained EU law,[60] having been amended by Part 3 of the Marine Environment (Amendment) (EU Exit) Regulations 2018 to ensure their operability after the UK's departure from the EU.[61]

Regulation 5 of the Marine Strategy Regulations 2010, as amended, specifies that the ecosystem approach ensures that the collective pressure of human activities remains compatible with the achievement of good environmental status and does not compromise the capacity of marine ecosystems to respond to human induced changes. The MPS also adds a third limb to Regulation 5's definition, stating that the ecosystem approach enables the sustainable use of marine goods and services.[62] This third limb is present in the EU Marine Strategy Directive's definition of the ecosystem approach under article 1(3), but not in the Marine Strategy Regulations, though the reference to present and future generations also found in article 1(3) of the Directive is absent from the definition presented in the MPS.

Turning now to assess the interpretation of the ecosystem approach in the MPS, several points can be made. First, it is evident that environmental considerations are predominant, reinforced by the fact that the good environmental status descriptors are only about environmental matters, not about humans. Second, procedural justice issues are not considered: participation and epistemic pluralism are absent from the definition. Further, not much attention is paid to intra- and intergenerational justice, demonstrated by the decision to remove from the MPS the reference to future generations found in article 1(3) of the Marine Strategy Framework Directive. Third, the dichotomous understanding between nature and society is present because ecosystems are framed and understood in purely environmental terms and human activities are solely defined as pressures on the marine environment, which is reduced to a resource base. The presence of the terms 'sustainable use' (rather than sustainable development) and 'goods and services' further indicate an emphasis on the economic aspects of sustainability. Finally, given that the ecosystem approach serves to 'manage competing demands in the marine area', a view of sustainable development that looks at balancing the needs of the various sectors, rather than a relational ontology, is promoted by the MPS.

Operationalising the ecosystem approach in Marine Plans: the MMO-commissioned framework

To support the operationalisation of the ecosystem approach to marine planning as required by the MPS, the MMO commissioned the writing of a practical framework.[63] This framework builds on CBD Malawi principles, suggesting a modified set of principles suitable for application in marine planning. It was published in 2014, and therefore could not influence the East Plans, adopted the same year, but could support the writing of the other Plans. However, as explained below, the way that it has influenced the South Plan in practice is negligible. Although the South Plan presents a more integrated approach, it does not show a wide understanding of the ecosystem approach.

Although the MMO-commissioned framework employs the definition of marine spatial planning to be found in the MPS, with all its limitations identified above, the endorsement of an adapted version of the Malawi principles helps to bring forth key elements of the ecosystem approach, pointing to a relational view. The conceptual discussion of the ecosystem approach in the previous section of this chapter highlighted three Malawi principles (principles 1, 11 and 12) that point to epistemological opening, essential for pluriversality, and also discussed principle 9 as key for recognising change and the need for adaptive management. Most, but not all, of these principles are to be found in the MMO-commissioned framework. Malawi principle 11 is copied into principle 4 of the MMO framework, which states that 'all forms of relevant information should be considered including scientific and local knowledge'; Malawi principle 12 is copied into MMO framework principle 5, which states that 'all relevant sectors of society and scientific disciplines should be involved', and a reference to the Statement of Public Participation as a way to implement these two principles is made. Principle 9 is reflected in principle 3 as well as principle 6, which respectively point to an acknowledgement of change and the endorsement of adaptive management. However, Malawi principle 1 is changed more drastically, with the revised MMO framework principle 1 stating that 'there should be clear long-term ecosystem objectives, ideally linked to targets and indicators, against which progress can be monitored'.[64] This change is justified on the basis that 'marine management objectives are relatively fixed' and that the Malawi principle underplayed the importance of setting clear ecosystem objectives. However, in doing so, the emphasis on the plurality of perspectives on management and the social (ecological) construction of these, fundamental to highlight the pluriversal epistemology of nature, is lost.

Thus, while the MMO-commissioned framework goes a step further than the MPS in endorsing openness to epistemic plurality, it does not present a complete relational shift as it falls short of thinking about the socio-ecological construction of the marine problem. Also, by simply invoking the Statement of Public Participation as a means to fulfil the requirements of Malawi principles 11 and 12, it does not provide a nuanced reading of participation, saying nothing about the terms of inclusion (for example consultative or deliberative) or how to account for different views and potential epistemic conflicts.

The Ecosystem approach in the East and South Marine Plans

Turning to the Marine Plans, different set-ups and approaches are noticeable between the East and the South Plans. As already mentioned, the East Plans were the first to be adopted in 2014 and the South Plans were adopted in 2018. Both contain inshore (from mean high water out to 12 nautical miles) and offshore (from the seaward limit of the territorial sea out to the 200 nautical mile boundary of the Exclusive Economic Zone) Plans. The East Plans cover an inshore area of 6,000 square kilometres stretching from Flamborough Head to Felixstowe and an offshore area of approximately 49,000 square kilometres, while the South Plan covers an area of around 20,000 square kilometres of water across 1,000 kilometres of coastline from Folkestone to the River Dart.

The phased adoption of the Plans is interesting in itself: plan-making is portrayed as an iterative process, with the newer plans learning from the previous ones, whilst adapting to local conditions. Besides, the legal requirement to have Plans reviewed every three years supports in principle such an iterative process, thereby displaying characteristics of adaptive management, an essential element for the success of the ecosystem approach. The extent to which adaptive management has happened in practice is more debatable. For example, the first three-year Report on the East Plans (2014–17) did not generate novel data but drew almost entirely on data gathered from other monitoring programmes, and did not review the East Plans' policies but only some (5 out of 11) of its objectives. This renders the added benefit of the review process questionable.[65] Improvements have been made with the second three-year Report (2017–20), with reporting across all objectives, assessment of policy effects, and consideration of policy effectiveness, though, as with the first three-year Report, most data is taken from existing monitoring programmes and data generated from MMO's marine licensing programme.[66] Given that data gaps were the reasons for avoiding explicit spatial policies in the East Plans as explained below, it is questionable why little attempt was made to gather new data for the monitoring Reports.

The main difference between the objectives and policies of the East Plans and the South Plan is that while the former are sector specific, the latter are more integrated, thus apparently displaying a stronger ecosystem approach to marine planning. Planning policies in the East Plans are structured around individual maritime sectors (for example aggregates, offshore renewables, fishing) and a series of objectives divided into economic, ecological and social categories. This seems indicative of a fragmented approach and an endorsement of the 'balance' view of sustainable development, whereby the natural elements are divorced from the social and economic ones. By contrast, the South Plan adopts a cross-sectoral approach. For example, objective 7 relates to supporting the reduction of the environmental, social and economic impacts of climate change. It encourages the implementation of mitigation and adaptation measures that avoid proposals' indirect contributions to greenhouse gas emissions, reduce vulnerability, improve resilience to climate and coastal change and consider habitats that provide ecosystem services. Thus, the South Plan seems to portray a more holistic understanding of sustainable development. However, the picture is more nuanced than this.

Despite their sectoral structure, the East Plans make an effort towards holism by stating that the objectives need to be considered alongside one another[67] and that 'the plan policies should not be read in isolation as more than one policy could apply to any proposal'.[68] However, the East Plans are silent on value prioritisation and negotiation between policies, leaving the choice regarding which policies are appropriate to a particular decision of the public authorities.[69] Such uncertainty regarding decision-making is exacerbated by the fact that the East Plans remain silent regarding how resources are going to be allocated. This is justified on the basis that there is lack of available data, hence prescriptive policies within the Plans cannot be formulated, rendering them more of a strategic guide than a spatial plan. This criticism is also applicable to the South Plan. Indeed, most policies do not have any specific spatial application and are not prescriptive, rendering very uncertain how the ecosystem approach will be implemented on the ground when choices regarding activities are made, and leaving much discretion in the hands of the public authorities. The Plans do not constitute helpful guidance to public authorities for consenting decisions, as they do not explain how the various policies are to be prioritised in case of conflict. The Plans put this in a positive light, as an endorsement of flexibility. However, their role as Plans to provide clarity and certainty for developers, sea users and public authorities is obviously watered down.

As regards the South Plan, despite its laudable cross-sectoral approach, it frames the ecosystem approach primarily around economic aspects. Indeed, the link between the ecosystem approach and economic issues is made from the very start, when it is specified that the Plan 'takes an ecosystem approach and reflects the benefit of clean and healthy seas and *natural capital* to provide *ecosystem goods and services*'.[70] Most of the subsequent references to ecosystem are to 'ecosystem services' and multiple mentions of natural capital are made, thereby embracing a functional/instrumental and economically oriented view of sustainable marine planning. The emphasis in the South Plan on natural capital reflects the UK Government's longstanding focus on this concept and again highlights the broader issue of the tension between international and domestic conceptualisations of sustainable development and the ecosystems approach. Such emphasis on the economic aspects is particularly problematic for affective values, or soft variables that are difficult to express in monetary terms or to quantify. Only calculable and quantifiable cultural ecosystem services such as tourism or recreational activities are represented, excluding other values such as place attachment, discussed by Chiara Armeni, below. Such a narrow representation of the ecosystem approach shows that the MMO-commissioned framework on the ecosystem approach did not have a strong influence on the drafting of the South Plan.

For some commentators, the East Plans are also indicative of a neoliberal ethos, with a strong focus on economic aspects of sustainability and an emphasis on reducing the bureaucratic burdens for industry, the promotion of resource exploitation and the translation of coastal well-being in economic terms, such as employment opportunities for coastal communities.[71] If the predominance of economic aspects of sustainability is clearly visible in the East Plans, it should be noted that when it comes to the discussion of the ecosystem approach in the East Plan, reliance on environmental/scientific information is predominant, rather than an economic discourse. However, such reliance on environmental knowledge is problematic in itself as other, more experiential, user-based knowledge is left out of the domain of legitimate knowledge in the East Plans. The explicit mention of the ecosystem approach is made in relation to the context of objective 6 (to have a healthy, resilient and adaptable marine ecosystem in the East marine plan areas). Like the MPS, multiple references are made to some[72] of the Marine Strategy Framework Directive's good environmental status descriptors to discuss how to manage the pressures of human activities on ecosystems. For example, noise and litter are singled out as two pressures that the ecosystem-based approach needs to manage and they are directly linked to the Marine Strategy Framework Directive requirements, respectively descriptor 11 and descriptor 10.[73] A clear distinction is made between the environment and human pressures, reinforcing the dichotomy between nature and society. No consideration of procedural aspects of the ecosystem approach, such as broad participation, is provided. Similarly, the South Plan does not say much regarding how different knowledges have been used and what place local knowledge should occupy when it comes to decision-taking. As Ralph Tafon put it, 'ecosystem-based management constitutes a discursive art of "herding" particular groups of people and their "alternative" ways of knowing and living with the marine environment towards achieving limited policy outcomes'[74] and it is far from neutral and adaptive. Participation under such circumstances would seem to be a co-opted discourse aimed at achieving a narrow consensus legitimising preconceived policy outcomes, not subject to societal debate.

Arguably, other sources of knowledges have been considered at early stages in plan-making, as explained in the Statements of Public Participation,[75] which detail the who, when and how of engagement, and the way in which comments and perspectives will be taken on board in the marine planning process. However, studies empirically exploring participation in marine spatial planning have found that, despite these legal requirements, the level of participation is tokenistic and centred on output-oriented legitimacy rather than input-oriented legitimacy.[76] For some, marine spatial planning is 'post-political', meaning that the space of contest and alternative readings of planning are discarded in favour of the adoption of consensual procedures within a neoliberal economic policy framework that is not subject to debate.[77] Also, for present purposes, it should be noted that the Statements of Public Participation do not make any reference to the ecosystem approach, thereby divorcing the discourse on ecosystem approach from that on participation.

Conclusion

This chapter has provided some reflections on the meaning of planning for sustainability, considering the case of English marine spatial planning. Like land use planning, marine planning's objective is sustainable development but, by contrast with land use planning, marine planning has the ecosystem approach at its core, playing a role in contributing to the way sustainable marine planning is framed and delivered. Indeed, the chapter has explored the way in which the ecosystem approach, as conceptualised in selected marine planning documents, is framing the meaning of sustainable marine planning. It has been argued that whilst the ecosystem approach, as defined in international environmental law (and more specifically the CBD's Malawi principles), is underpinned by a relational ontology and by epistemic pluralism, helping to shift the conceptualisation of sustainable development beyond a balance/trade-off exercise, this is not visible in the way it has been conceptualised in the domestic marine planning context. The textual analysis of the MPS and the East and South Marine Plans shows that the ecosystem approach has been interpreted in a narrower way, focusing on either environmental-only issues or economic ones. Both the MPS and the Marine Plans define the ecosystem approach by means of ecological indicators derived from the Marine Strategy Framework Directive that exclude the human dimensions and/or in terms of ecosystem services and natural capital. Environmental, social and economic issues are presented as separate. Although the Malawi principles, albeit revised, appear in the MMO-commissioned framework to operationalise the ecosystem approach, they do not seem to have greatly influenced the South Plan, which was adopted after the MMO-commissioned framework was developed. This means that the ecosystem approach as conceptualised in the marine policy documents analysed above does not contribute to a relational view of sustainable development. The risk of marine planning is that it follows the same pro-growth agenda as land use planning and, rather than presenting a radical alternative to the dichotomy between nature and society, retains modernist roots.

Notes

1. Ministry of Housing, Communities and Local Government (MHCLG) 2021, 5 [7].
2. Department for Environment, Food and Rural Affairs (Defra) 2011, 4.
3. Rydin 2013.
4. There is an emerging academic literature that investigates the relationship between sustainable development and marine spatial planning, but the majority is not legal literature, or it is not focused on England. Examples include Qui and Jones 2013; Gilek, Saunders and Stalmokaite 2019.
5. For an initial UK-wide assessment of the relationship between marine licensing decision-taking and marine plans, see Slater and Claydon 2020.
6. Defra 2014.
7. Defra 2018.
8. Defra 2011, 4 and 10.
9. Directive 2014/89/EU of the European Parliament and of the Council of 23 July 2014 establishing a framework for maritime spatial planning, OJ L 257/135 (Marine Spatial Planning Directive).
10. United Nations (UN) 2002.
11. World Commission on Environment and Development 1987.
12. UN 1992.
13. UN 2015, preamble, and [5].
14. UN 1992, principle 10; UN 2015 SDGs 16 and 17; World Commission on Environment and Development 1987, Annex I and principles 18, 20.
15. Kotze and French 2018.
16. For a similar perspective see Ingold 2011.
17. Escobar 2016, 18.
18. Escobar 2011, 139.
19. Escobar 2007.
20. Pieraccini and Novitz 2020.
21. Rydin 2013.
22. Bird 2013; Rydin 2013; Lees and Shepherd 2015; Field and Layard 2017.
23. Town and Country Planning Association 2018, 25 and 43.

24. Bird 2013.
25. Town and Country Planning Association 2018, 43.
26. MHCLG 2020, 30.
27. See e.g. Convention on the Conservation of Antarctic Marine Living Resources (adopted in 1980; in force in 1982) 19 ILM 841; Convention for the Protection of the Marine Environment of the North-East Atlantic (adopted in 1992, into force in 1998) 32 ILM 1069. At EU level see Marine Spatial Planning Directive; Directive 2008/56/EC establishing a framework for community action in the field of marine environmental policy, OJ L 164/19 (Marine Strategy Framework Directive).
28. Decision II/8, 'Preliminary Consideration of Components of Biological Diversity Particularly under Threat and Action Which Could Be Taken under the Convention' UNEP/CBD/COP/2/19.
29. Troubworst 2009.
30. Convention on Biological Diversity 2004, 1.
31. Decision V/6, 'Ecosytem Approach', UNEP/CBD/COP/5/23.
32. De Lucia 2019, 192.
33. Brooks et al 2002; Tarlock 2008; Galindo-Leal and Bunnel 1995.
34. Tarlock 2008, see also Westholm 2019.
35. Tarlock 2008.
36. Soininen and Platjouw 2019.
37. De Lucia 2015.
38. For an introduction to marine spatial planning see Douvere 2008; Slater 2012.
39. Douvere 2008; Foley et al 2010.
40. See e.g. Ehler and Douvere 2009.
41. Marine Spatial Planning Directive.
42. Earlier efforts at marine planning were made by Germany, the Netherlands and Belgium.
43. MCA Act 2009, section 44(1)(a).
44. MCA Act 2009, section 50(2).
45. Conservation of Habitats and Species Regulations 2017 SI 1012/2017, as amended.
46. Environmental Assessment of Plans and Programmes Regulations 2004 SI 1633/2004, as amended.
47. MCA Act 2009, Schedule 6.
48. MCA Act 2009, section 58(1).
49. See section 58(4) MCA Act 2009. It does not include any decision on an application for an order granting development consent under the Planning Act 2008. For those decisions, the only requirement is that the public authority must have regard to the appropriate marine policy documents.
50. MCA Act 2009, section 58(1).
51. MCA Act 2009, section 58(2).
52. MCA Act 2009, sections 46 and 54.
53. MCA Act 2009, sections 47–48, 52–53.
54. MCA Act 2009, section 61.
55. MCA Act 2009, section 44(1)(a) and section 51 (3)(b).
56. Defra 2011, 4.
57. Defra 2011, 12.
58. Marine Strategy Regulations 2010, SI 2010/1627, as amended.
59. Marine Strategy Framework Directive, article 1.
60. European Union (Withdrawal) Act 2018, section 8(1) enables a minister of the Crown to make such provisions as the minister considers appropriate to prevent, remedy or mitigate any failure of retained EU law to operate effectively, or any other deficiency in retained EU law arising from the UK withdrawal from the EU. Retained EU law is defined under sections 2–5 of the European Union (Withdrawal) Act 2018 and it includes EU-derived domestic legislation such as the Marine Strategy Regulations 2010.
61. Marine Environment (Amendment) (EU Exit) Regulations 2018 SI 2018/1399.
62. Defra 2011, 4 footnote 6.
63. MMO 2014.
64. MMO 2014, 13.
65. Defra 2017, 9.
66. Defra 2020, 14.

67. Defra 2014, [60].
68. Defra 2014, [9].
69. Defra 2014, [88].
70. Defra 2018, [17] (emphasis added).
71. Flannery and McAtree 2020.
72. As noted in the second Three-Year Report of the East Plans, there are too few policies covering too few elements of the ecosystem to support the broad scope of the objective. See Defra 2020, 41.
73. Defra 2014, [185].
74. Tafon 2018, 265.
75. MMO 2013 for the East Plan, and MMO 2015 for the South Plan.
76. Scarff et al 2015; Jones et al 2016; Smith and Jentoft 2017.
77. Flannery et al 2019; Clarke and Flannery 2020.

References

Bird, Simon (2013). 'The NPPF in Practice: Panacea, Pariah or Placebo?', *Journal of Planning Law* 12: OP82-99.
Brooks, Roger O., Ross Jones and Ross A. Virginia (2002). *Law and Ecology: The Rise of the Ecosystem Regime*. Aldershot: Ashgate.
Clarke, Jane and Wesley Flannery (2020). 'The Post-Political Nature of Marine Spatial Planning and Modalities For its Re-Politicisation', *Journal of Environmental Policy and Planning* 22: 170–83.
Convention on Biological Diversity (2004). *CBD Guidelines: The Ecosystem Approach*. Montreal: Secretariat of the Convention on Biological Diversity.
Department for Environment, Food and Rural Affairs (2011). *UK MPS*.
Department for Environment, Food and Rural Affairs (2014) *East Inshore and East Offshore Marine Plans*.
Department for Environment, Food and Rural Affairs (2017). *Three-year Report on the East Marine Plans*.
Department for Environment, Food and Rural Affairs (2018). *South Inshore and South Offshore Marine Plan*.
Department for Environment, Food and Rural Affairs (2020). *Three-year Report on the East Marine Plans*.
De Lucia, Vito (2015). 'Competing Narratives and Complex Genealogies: The Ecosystem Approach in International Environmental Law', *Journal of Environmental Law* 27: 91–117.
De Lucia, Vito (2019). *The 'Ecosystem Approach' in International Environmental Law: Genealogy and Biopolitics*. Abingdon: Routledge.
Douvere, Fanny (2008). 'The Importance of Marine Spatial Planning in Advancing Ecosystem-Based Sea Use Management', *Marine Policy* 32: 762–71.
Ehler, Charles and Fanny Douvere (2009). *Marine Spatial Planning: A Step-by-Step Approach Toward Ecosystem-Based Management*. Intergovernmental Oceanographic Commission and Man and the Biosphere Programme. IOC Manual and Guides No. 53, ICAM Dossier No. 6. Paris: UNESCO.
Escobar, Arturo (2007). 'Worlds and Knowledges Otherwise. The Latin American Modernity/Coloniality Research Programme', *Cultural Studies* 21 (2007): 179–210.
Escobar, Arturo (2011). 'Sustainability: Design for the Pluriverse', *Development* 54: 137–40.
Escobar, Arturo (2016). 'Thinking-Feeling with the Earth: Territorial Struggles and the Ontological Dimension of the Epistemologies of the South', *Revista de Antropologia Iberoamericana* 11: 11–32.
Field, Martin and Antonia Layard (2017). 'Locating Community-Led Housing within Neighbourhood Plans as a Response to England's Housing Needs', *Public Money and Management* 37: 105–12.
Flannery, Wesley, Jane Clarke and Benedict McAteer (2019). 'Politics and Power in Marine Spatial Planning'. In *Maritime Spatial Planning*, edited by Jacek Zaucha and Kira Gee, 201–17. Cham: Palgrave.
Flannery, Wesley and Ben McAteer (2020). 'Assessing Marine Spatial Planning Governmentality', *Maritime Studies* 19: 269–84.

Foley, Melissa M. et al (2010). 'Guiding Ecological Principles for Marine Spatial Planning', *Marine Policy* 34: 955–66.

Galindo-Leal, Carlos and Fred L. Bunnel (1995). 'Ecosystem Management: Implications and Opportunities of a New Paradigm', *The Forestry Chronicle* 71: 601–6.

Gilek, Michael Fred Saunders and Igne Stalmokaite (2019). 'The Ecosystem Approach and Sustainable Development in Baltic Sea Marine Spatial Planning: The Social Pillar, a "Slow Train Coming"'. In *The Ecosystem Approach in Ocean Planning and Governance*, edited by Langlet, David and Rosemary Rayfuse, 160–94. Leiden: Brill.

Ingold, Tim (2011). *Being Alive. Essays on Movement, Knowledge, and Description*. New York: Routledge.

Jones, Peter J., Louise M. Lieberknecht and W. Qiu (2016). 'Marine Spatial Planning in Reality: Introduction to Case Studies and Discussion of Findings', *Marine Policy* 71: 256–64.

Kotze, Louis J. and Duncan French (2018). 'The Anthropocentric Ontology of International Environmental Law and the Sustainable Development Goals: Towards an Ecocentric Rule of Law in the Anthropocene', *Global Journal of Comparative Law* 7: 5–36.

Lees, Emma and Edward Shepherd (2015). 'Incoherence and Incompatibility in Planning Law', *International Journal of Law in the Built Environment*, 7: 111–26.

Marine Management Organisation (2013). *East Inshore and East Offshore Marine Plan Areas: Statement of Public Participation*, revised August, available at https://assets.publishing.service.gov.uk/government/uploads/system/uploads/attachment_data/file/312377/east_final_spp_august2013.pdf (accessed 12 June 2022).

Marine Management Organisation (2014). *Practical Framework for Outlining the Integration of the Ecosystem Approach into Marine Planning in England. A report produced for the Marine Management Organisation.* MMO Project No. 1048.

Marine Management Organisation (2015). *South Inshore and South Offshore Marine Plan Areas: Statement of Public Participation*, revised February, available at https://assets.publishing.service.gov.uk/government/uploads/system/uploads/attachment_data/file/401300/Revised_South_Statement_of_Public_Participation.pdf (accessed 12 June 2022).

Ministry of Housing, Communities and Local Government (2020). *White Paper: Planning for the Future*.

Ministry of Housing, Communities and Local Government (2021). *National Planning Policy Framework*.

Pieraccini, Margherita and Tonia Novitz (2020). 'Sustainability and Law: A Historical and Theoretical Overview'. In *Legal Perspectives on Sustainability*, edited by Margherita Pieraccini and Tonia Novitz, 9–38. Bristol: University of Bristol Press.

Qiu, Wanfei and Peter J.S. Jones (2013). 'The Emerging Policy Landscape for Marine Spatial Planning in Europe', *Marine Policy* 39: 182–90.

Rydin, Yvonne (2013). *The Future of Planning: Beyond Growth Dependence*. Bristol: Policy Press.

Scarff, Gavin, Claire Fitzsimmons and Tim Gray (2015). 'The New Mode of Marine Planning in the UK: Aspirations and Challenges', *Marine Policy* 51: 96–102.

Slater, Anne-Michelle (2012). 'What is Marine Spatial Planning', *Environmental Law Review* 14: 1–5.

Slater, Anne-Michelle and Jim Claydon (2020). 'Marine Spatial Planning in the UK: A Review of the Progress and Effectiveness of the Plans and their Policies', *Environmental Law Review* 22: 85–107.

Smith, Glen and Svein Jentoft (2017). 'Marine Spatial Planning in Scotland. Levelling the Playing Field?', *Marine Policy* 84: 33–41.

Soininen, Niko and Froukje M. Platjouw (2019). 'Resilience and Adaptive Capacity of Aquatic Environmental Law in the EU: An Evaluation and Comparison of the WFD, MSFD, and Marine Spatial Planning'. In *The Ecosystem Approach in Ocean Planning and Governance,* edited by David Langlet and Rosemary Rayfuse, 17–79. Leiden: Brill.

Tafon, Ralph V. (2018). 'Taking Power to the Sea: Towards a Poststructuralist Discourse Theoretical Critique of Marine Spatial Planning', *Environment and Planning C: Politics and Space* 36: 258–73.

Tarlock, Dan (2008). 'Ecosystems' In *The Oxford Handbook of International Environmental Law*, edited by Daniel Jutta Brunnee Bodansky and Ellen Hey, 575–97. Oxford: Oxford University Press.

Town and Country Planning Association (2018). *Planning 2020: Raynsford Review of Planning in England*, available at https://www.tcpa.org.uk/Handlers/Download.ashx?IDMF=30864427-d8dc-4b0b-88ed-c6e0f08c0edd (accessed 12 June 2022).

Troubworst, Arie (2009). 'The Precautionary Principle and the Ecosystem Approach in International Law: Differences, Similarities and Linkages', *RECIEL* 18 (2009): 26–37.

United Nations (1992). *Rio Declaration on Environment and Development*, UN Doc A/CONF.151/26.

United Nations (2002). *The Johannesburg Declaration on Sustainable Development*, UN Doc A/CONF.199/20.

United Nations (2015). *Transforming Our World: The 2030 Agenda for Sustainable Development*, UNGA Res. 70/1.

Westholm, Aron (2019). 'Delimiting Marine Areas: Ecosystem Approach(es?) in EU Marine Management. In *The Ecosystem Approach in Ocean Planning and Governance*, edited by David Langlet and Rosemary Rayfuse, 117–39. Leiden: Brill.

World Commission on Environment and Development (1987). *Our Common Future*. Oxford: Oxford University Press.

Part III
Participation
Carolyn Abbot and Maria Lee

Much of the large legal literature on participation in England revolves in some way around the planning system. Only rarely, however, does it explicitly centre itself on planning law and planning questions. Many of the chapters in this volume raise the who, how and what of participation, and the role of legal frameworks in enabling or constraining participation. Our two chapters in this section address public participation directly. The democratic or substantive potential of participation, and its challenges and weaknesses[1] (intensified by an increasingly pro-development planning policy framework[2]), are well known. In their detailed exploration of particular cases (the Navitus wind farm and the Hulton Estate development), our contributors explore fresh facets of the participatory conundrum.

Whilst the division is not stark, and both authors see value in different understandings of participation, these chapters address public participation from different perspectives. Carolyn Abbot, in her evaluation of the potential contribution of legal experts to strengthening participatory opportunities for local community groups, tends to focus on the ability of participation to contribute to the quality of outputs. Chiara Armeni, on the other hand, looking at the approach to offshore wind energy under the Planning Act 2008, inclines more to the view that the participatory elements of planning are part of the democratic processes and structures of society.

Abbot's chapter highlights a particular dimension of the uneven distribution of opportunities to participate. As resource-rich participants in the planning system, developers are well-equipped to shape future land use (a theme also captured in Edward Mitchell's chapter); access by other participants to legal experts as knowledge providers, skilled advocates and experienced practitioners promotes *better* and more even participation. Armeni, as well as beautifully reinforcing the position of place experience on the legal agenda, argues that planning law does not prevent, and could even welcome, place-based arguments as a basis for planning decisions.

Notes

1. See e.g. Armeni and Lee 2021.
2. Beebeejaun 2018.

References

Armeni, Chiara and Maria Lee (2021). 'Participation in a Time of Climate Crisis', *Journal of Law and Society* 48: 549–72.
Beebeejaun, Yasminah (2018). 'Public Participation and the Declining Significance of Planning'. In *Planning Practice: Critical Perspectives from the UK*, edited by Jessica Ferm and John Tomaney, 85–100. Abingdon: Routledge.

6
Place, participation and planning law in a time of climate change
Chiara Armeni

Introduction

A place is a complex frame through which we understand the world.[1] Places are more than simply spatial locations, a point on the map, a potential development site. A place is a representation packed with relational, emotional, symbolic and metaphorical connotations. In a useful definitional effort, David Seamon describes it as 'any environmental locus in and through which individual or group actions, experiences, intentions, and meanings are drawn together spatially'.[2] Space becomes place when it feels 'familiar' and 'acquires definition and meaning'.[3] The way in which such acquisition of meaning occurs is at the centre of a rich academic enquiry mostly undertaken by geographers and philosophers, but is relatively underexplored by legal scholars.[4]

Yet law is an important part of this intellectual endeavour, as law constructs and is constructed by spatiality and placeness. Places are 'made' and transformed – although not exclusively – through legal and regulatory processes and the normative choices underpinning them. Planning law constantly prioritises and negotiates what interests and frames are taken into account in shaping place through development. At the heart of this exercise, planning law is confronted with how individuals and communities perceive, understand and accept infrastructure developments in and for a particular place. The *National Design Guide* 2021 clarifies that 'the identity or character of a place comes from the way that buildings, streets and spaces, landscape and infrastructure combine together and how people experience them. It is not just about the buildings or how a place looks, but how it engages with all of the senses.'[5]

How people experience places – and infrastructure within them – and what this means for planning decisions, are important questions for planning law.

These questions acquire an even greater significance in a time of climate crisis. Climate change is progressively transforming our familiar places not only by profoundly affecting their morphological and ecosystem characteristics, but also through the need for new, large-scale energy infrastructure.[6] The way in which this infrastructure 'fits' with people's relationships with places is complex and shapes public acceptance of projects. People's experience of places is reflected in the public participation process on planning consent, where wind energy infrastructure is often framed by participants as 'out of place' – as a threat or disruption to the place as it would be seen to 'industrialise' an otherwise rural place that is considered for its natural beauty and remoteness.[7] The climate change context in which consent decisions occur also usefully illustrates the tensions between technical evidence and democratic participation in planning decisions.[8]

This chapter's main purpose is to emphasise place experience in the legal agenda. First, the chapter locates the concept of place experience in the academic literature and explains why it is important for planning decisions. Secondly, it looks at how place experience is dealt with in the consent process for offshore wind energy Nationally Significant Infrastructure Projects (NSIPs) in England. Drawing on my earlier research, I discuss the examination of the Navitus Bay Wind Park project as an interesting example of how place experience claims are raised and handled in the process.[9] My central argument here is that place experience claims are received by the NSIP regulatory process, but their recognition as basis for the decision is limited by a comfortable reliance on technical assessment and a strong policy commitment to climate mitigation. Third, the chapter contends that, although handling experience is difficult for decision-makers, planning law does not represent a necessary barrier to it. I suggest that a broader interpretation of the notion of material considerations could help decision-makers be more confident in recognising place-based arguments as a legitimate basis for a planning consent decision, even in the urgency of the climate crisis.

Place experience

Places shape and are shaped by our experience. In his seminal work, Yi-Fu Tuan defines experience as 'a cover-all term for the various modes through which a person knows and constructs a reality. These modes range from the more direct and passive senses of smell, taste, and touch to active visual perception and the indirect modes of symbolization.'[10] For Tuan, through experience, places are a way to know the world. However, experience is problematic as feelings and aesthetic responses are difficult to express, explain or quantify in scientific terms.[11] Tuan argues that the physical sciences are inevitably blind to this experiential complexity: 'experiences are slighted or ignored because the means to articulate them or point them out are lacking'.[12]

Despite these barriers, place experience as knowledge remains a key framing. As Edward Casey explains, 'to live is to live locally, and to know is first of all to know the place one is in'.[13] A place is both the source and the object of knowledge. Tim Cresswell notes how 'place is . . . a way of seeing, knowing, and understanding the world. When we look at the world as a world of places, we see different things. We see attachments and connections between people and place. We see worlds of meaning and experience.'[14]

Place experience represents a mode of situated knowledge. Situated knowledges not only build on and define what people know, but 'they also shape the ways they interpret experiences *as* experiences'.[15] As knowledge is *conceptually* situated within one's experience, it is also *geographically* situated due to one's spatial relationship with a particular place. In this sense place experience is often equated to local knowledge. For Jason Corburn, as local knowledge is 'practical, collective and strongly rooted in a particular place', it constitutes an 'organized body of thought based on immediacy of experience'.[16] Place experience embeds a mixture of practical, sensory and emotional triggers. People develop their place experience through an indiscernible combination of actions (for example shopping,[17] playing, walking, cycling, bird-watching, fishing), sensory perceptions (for example the smell, sound or view of the landscape) and emotional connections (for example place attachment, sense of place, place identity). Each one of these elements is multidimensional and contested. Boundaries are difficult to draw. Seamon explains this through the 'place ballet': 'an interaction of individual bodily routines rooted in a particular environment that may become an important place of interpersonal and communal exchange, meaning, and attachment'.[18]

These overlying sensory and emotional characteristics of place experience are difficult to separate, making the boundary between place and other framings sometimes hard to recognise. Landscape is a good example. The traditional distinction between landscape and place focuses on the 'visual' and 'visuality'. Landscape is 'an intensely visual idea'.[19]

It implies a particular relationship with the viewer. From this perspective a landscape is not a place: 'We do not live landscapes – we look at them.'[20] But in some contexts, a landscape 'is more than "the view"'.[21] Jeff Malpas calls it 'the landscape problem', as 'landscape, while often understood in purely visual terms, is inadequately understood if construed as merely a "view"'.[22] Here the role of experience is crucial, bringing landscape and place to a closer, possibly overlapping, position. Casey understands landscapes as 'placescapes', 'congeries of places in the fullest experiential and represented sense'.[23] Landscape as passive view neglects the active experience of place from which view arises.[24]

Place experience is not only a useful frame to appreciate the richness of landscape as constructed and beyond 'the physical' and 'the visual.'[25] As Maria Lee suggests, people's lived experience represents the link between landscape and place attachment.[26] Place attachment refers to the 'bonding of people to places'.[27] This relationship is dynamic and socially constructed[28] as well as multidimensional.[29] Place attachment is 'a state of psychological well-being experienced by a person as a result of the mere presence, vicinity, or accessibility of the place'[30] or 'a positive affective bond between an individual and a specific place, the main characteristic of which is the tendency for the individual to maintain closeness to such a place'.[31] It can refer to both the process of attachment and the outcome of that process.[32] The feeling of attachment can originate 'with familiarity and ease, with the assurance of nurture and security, with the memory of sound and smells, of communal activities and homely pleasures accumulated over time'.[33] It encompasses 'the experience of living or spending time in a particular place'.[34] A sentiment of attachment can develop over time, as well as through intense and meaningful experiences. This notion is connected to other constructs or processes, such as place identity, sense of place, or place meaning, but there is a lack of consensus on the structure of such relationships and how to measure them.[35] Experiences of place attachment shape people's attitudes towards wind energy infrastructure. Place attachment can induce either public support or opposition to energy infrastructure development, depending on whether the technology is perceived as a threat or an opportunity to the locality.[36]

This deeper understanding of place experience is relevant to planning decisions. From the perspective of the substantive input, experience claims represent modes of situated knowledge.[37] While experiential evidence is always problematic for law, people's experience of doing, perceiving and feeling in a place are important complements of any other – far less questioned or scrutinised – form of knowledge (for example scientific, historical, economic, technical). Understanding the normative meaning and weight of these claims in the regulatory process for large-scale wind farms tells us about the values and type of input and knowledge underpinning planning decisions in this context. As this chapter submits, the extent to which these claims are recognised as evidence or material considerations for the decision is limited, not necessarily by law, but by technical and policy arguments. A reflection on these limitations opens up discussion on the space for lay public place experience claims in the participation process and the role of law in shaping that space. It engages more widely with the opportunities and challenges of public participation in planning decisions.

Participation in planning law

The right to participate in planning decisions constitutes a long-standing, ordinary feature of English planning law.[38] People have a right to have a say in decisions that affect their environment, by providing information and comments to the decision-making process. This legal commitment to participation derives from the idea that 'Planning shapes the places where people live and work' and 'So it is right that people should be enabled and empowered to take an active part in the process'.[39] Participatory requirements have been embedded in UK law since well before the negotiation of the Aarhus Convention,[40] but the legal incorporation of the provisions of the Convention within EU law has been a key driver to the entrenchment of the procedural environmental rights in English law.[41] The space for public consultation in the planning process is complemented by other specific occasions for participation through environmental assessment at strategic[42] and project level.[43]

There are multiple, well-known justifications for participation.[44] Participation enables better decisions.[45] As knowledge and information are dispersed and fragmented,[46] decisions based on wider sets of inputs, values and voices are more responsive to the problem and permit better environmental performance.[47] But participation is as much concerned with the democratic legitimacy of the outcome as it is with the quality of the decision. Whilst the merit of participation in guaranteeing the democratic legitimacy of planning decisions remains contested, a democratic decision cannot prescind from a participatory process.[48] Certainly, participation is challenging. Time, expert-framings and resources, inequalities in power and representation constitute well-known barriers to effective participation, even if the opportunity exists.[49] Nevertheless, it is through participation and contestation that knowledge claims are constructed through the regulatory planning process.[50] The debate on participation in planning has long been shaped by the 'practical preoccupation' of the planning enterprise, its reliance on technical assessment, 'professional planning knowledge'[51] and models.[52] This explains why the space for participation in planning is often framed as a contestation of – and at times in opposition with – expert knowledge, widely defined.[53]

In the current climate crisis, the tensions between technical expertise and democratic participation in decision-making have become severe.[54] We see emergency framings of the climate crisis increasingly used in various areas to justify the inevitability of technocratic decision-making, often leading to an erosion of legal rights and guarantees of participation.[55] This trajectory is not exclusive of decision-making in planning. Yet as the early work of Lee and colleagues illustrates, decisions on wind energy NSIPs in England are an example of this slow, incremental process of erosion in the light of climate objectives.[56] The legal recognition of the lay public's emotional and sensory experience of places is likely to be caught by this process.

Legal and policy framework for consenting offshore wind energy in England

In England, an offshore wind energy development with an overall energy generating capacity equivalent to or above 100MW is considered an NSIP under the Planning Act 2008. The siting of an NSIP requires a development consent order (DCO) from the Secretary of State for Business, Energy and Industrial Strategy.[57] The process is triggered when an application is accepted by the National Infrastructure Planning Unit at the Planning Inspectorate (PINS).

The consenting process

Before the application is formally submitted, the developer must carry out a public consultation on the project proposal.[58] A number of statutory consultees (for example Natural England, the Environment Agency and local planning authorities[59]), any relevant person with a right or interest in the land relevant to the proposed project, and the local community must be consulted during this phase.[60] The Local Planning Authority (LPA) must be consulted on the developer's draft Statement of

Community Consultation (SOCC), which constitutes the main document informing the consultation process with people living in the vicinity of the land where the project might be sited.[61] The applicant must take into account the responses to the consultation and publish the proposal, as well as the SOCC, with the application documents.[62]

Once the application is formally accepted for examination by PINS, an Examining Authority (ExA) is appointed. Before the examination, the public must register with PINS in order to submit representations.[63] During the examination, 'Interested Parties' (IPs) can make representations to the ExA.[64] The LPA can submit a Local Impact Report (LIR), giving details of the likely impact of the project on the LPA's area, and IPs are entitled to comment on it.[65] The examination is primarily based on written documents and evidence, but the ExA can ask questions, hold hearings and conduct site visits. Unlike the regime applicable to onshore wind infrastructure (governed by the Town and Country Planning Act 1990, described in Chapter 2 above), the Planning Act has abolished the possibility of conducting public inquiries during the examination of NSIPs.

After the examination is concluded, the ExA produces a report, including a summary of the process, the views expressed in the examination, its 'findings and conclusions' and the final recommendation to the Secretary of State as to whether the project should be authorised or rejected. The Secretary of State will then decide on the application by order within six months of the closure of the examination, having regard to the ExA report, any LIR and any other matters that the Secretary of State thinks are 'important and relevant' to the decision.[66] The decision on consent or refusal is subject to judicial review within six weeks of its notification.

National Policy Statements

The policy context is crucial in understanding the space for participation within the NSIP regime.[67] The Planning Act 2008 provides that the Secretary of State must decide the application for development consent for an NSIP 'in accordance with any relevant national policy statement' (NPS), unless he/she 'is satisfied that the adverse impact of the proposed development would outweigh its benefits'[68] or the proposed development is 'unlawful' under other (for example human rights) provisions.[69] The Overarching National Policy Statement for Energy (NPS EN-1) and the National Policy Statement for Renewable Energy Infrastructure (NPS EN-3) set the policy context for evaluating wind energy NSIPs applications.[70] NPS EN-1 builds on a narrative of 'need' and 'urgency' for new energy infrastructure in general, and of wind energy development in particular.[71] For this reason, the ExA 'should give substantial weight to the contribution which projects would make towards satisfying this need'.[72]

This policy explicitly embeds a 'presumption in favour of granting consent to applications for energy NSIPs'.[73] Notwithstanding subsequent governments' withdrawal of onshore wind from the NSIP regime,[74] NPS EN-1 notes that such a presumption in favour of development applies, 'unless any more specific and relevant policies set out in the relevant NPSs clearly indicate that consent should be refused'.[75] But the NPSs go deeper: they give precise indications to the ExA on how different technical, environmental and socio-economic considerations should be weighed. This means that in practice the NPSs 'anticipate many possible local objections, and often go on to explain why these various concerns need not (or less commonly cannot) outweigh the need for energy infrastructure development'.[76] Although the official intention was to move away from the government setting national priorities on individual decisions, Sheate argues that 'In reality, the NPS process allows the government to draw the decision-making framework very narrowly'.[77] This narrow approach has direct implications for the participation opportunities in decision-making and the ability to express different place experience claims.

The strong link between national policies and planning decisions on individual projects is not surprising.[78] To some extent it is conceived to provide certainty and consistency in the context of the government's ambition and commitment to the climate change agenda. But it is challenging when it comes to the scope for considering people's views and concerns.[79] First, participants in the consenting process for individual NSIPs cannot challenge the content of the national policy. As a decision on the need for this infrastructure has already been taken and is reflected in the NPS, the ExA 'may . . . disregard' representations that 'relate to the merits of policy set out in a national policy statement'.[80] Lee and colleagues note that although this is not a stringent legal requirement (that is, 'may . . . disregard'), 'the philosophy of the Planning Act is to emphasise strategic policy making over discretion in respect to individual projects'.[81] On this point, Richard Cowell and Patrick Devine-Wright argue that this approach is intended to produce 'a "planning cascade" for major infrastructure projects in which need is resolved before individual projects consents come forward, in order to reduce consenting processes to details of siting choices and impact'.[82]

Secondly, as the arguments made in the public consultation are weighted against the presumption in favour of development embedded in the NPSs, the scope for other considerations and values is limited. This includes place experience claims, as claims that question how the infrastructure 'fit' with the place experience would not align with the policy narrative of need, speed and urgency for new energy infrastructure development to address climate change. This is especially interesting when the presumption in favour of development potentially interacts with the legal and policy framework on nationally or internationally designated areas.

Law and policy on nationally and internationally designated areas

Nationally designated areas, such as national parks (NPs) and Areas of Outstanding Natural Beauty (AONBs), play an important role in shaping how people construct their experience of a place. National parks are areas designated by Natural England 'by reason of (a) their natural beauty, and (b) the opportunities they afford for open-air recreation, having regard both to their character and to their position in relation to centres of population'.[83] An AONB is land designated by Natural England 'for the purpose of conserving and enhancing the natural beauty of the area'.[84] The NPS EN-1 states that the Secretary of State 'should have regard' to the statutory purposes of these designated areas in her decision.[85] Importantly, 'conservation of the natural beauty of the landscape and the countryside should be given substantial weight by the [Secretary of State] in deciding on applications for development consent in these areas'.[86] In this context, a development can only be granted consent in exceptional circumstances.[87]

The impact of the development on designated World Heritage Sites (WHSs) is also relevant for the consent decision. The 1972 UNESCO Convention concerning the Protection of the World Cultural and Natural Heritage establishes a duty on Parties to 'ensure identification, protection, conservation, presentation and transmission to future generations of the cultural and natural heritage on its territory'.[88] The designation of a WHS carries 'no additional statutory controls', but its conservation and protection are provided for through the planning system and the other designations that relate to the site (for example listed buildings).[89] In England, protection of these sites is also reflected in energy NPSs,[90] the National Planning Policy Framework (NPPF)[91] and the Planning Practice Guidance (PPG).[92] NPS EN-1 states that particular consideration should be given to the value of heritage assets in order to 'avoid and minimise conflict between conservation of that significance and proposals for development' of energy infrastructure.[93] EN-1 establishes a 'presumption in favour of the conservation of designated heritage assets'.[94] On this basis, 'Any harmful impact on the significance of a designated heritage asset should be weighed against the public benefit of development' and the Secretary of State should refuse consent where the application will result in 'substantial harm to or total loss of significance of a designated heritage asset . . . unless it can be demonstrated that the substantial harm to or loss of significance is necessary in order to deliver substantial public benefits that outweigh that loss or harm'.[95]

Under the NPPF, the notion of heritage asset is broad: 'A building, monument, site, place, area or landscape identified as having a degree of significance meriting consideration in planning decisions, because of its heritage interest.'[96] Not only is the heritage asset protected, but its setting – that is, 'important views and other areas or attributes that are functionally important as a support to the site' – must also be considered.[97] The notion of setting of a heritage asset is not framed exclusively in terms of its physical and visual relationship with a heritage site, but includes the 'surroundings in which a heritage asset can be *experienced*'[98] as well as 'its local context, embracing present and past relationships to the adjacent landscape'.[99] This broad, experiential interpretation goes beyond the visual and is discussed in the case law. In *Steer* the High Court held: 'Whilst a physical or visual connection between a heritage asset and its setting will often exist, it is not essential or determinative . . . The word "experienced" [in the NPPF] has a broad meaning, which is capable of extending beyond the purely visual.'[100] However, the Court of Appeal in *Catesby Estates Ltd* framed it more narrowly, stating that 'The "surroundings" of the heritage asset are its physical surroundings, and the relevant "experience", whatever it is, will be of the heritage asset itself in that physical place'.[101]

Against this complex interplay between legal and policy framework, the rejection of the Navitus project offers an interesting example of how the place experience narrative is received and handled in the decision-making process.

The Navitus Bay Wind Park examination

The Navitus Bay Wind Park project was a proposal for an offshore wind energy NSIP to be located in the English Channel off the Dorset coast, to the west of the Isle of Wight. The proposal involved the construction of 194 wind turbines, up to three offshore substation platforms, and an onshore cable corridor connecting the project to a new onshore substation at Three Legged Cross, north of Ferndown. The examination began in September 2014 and was concluded with a rejection of the project in

March 2015. It was conducted through written evidence, eight issue-specific hearings, two open-floor hearings, a compulsory acquisition hearing and a number of site inspections. More than 2000 IP representations, of which the majority came from individuals and business representatives, were submitted to the ExA.[102]

The area identified for the project was of special environmental and heritage value. There were three types of designations potentially affected by the project: the Dorset and the Isle of Wight AONBs, the New Forest NP, and the Jurassic Coast WHS. I will focus on the Dorset AONB and the Jurassic Coast WHS, for which the Dorset AONB constitutes a heritage setting.

Experience of the Dorset AONB

The project was widely opposed by participants in the public consultation as 'simply unacceptable';[103] 'a disaster visually, economically and for the environment';[104] 'ecologically damaging and aesthetically unacceptable';[105] 'wanton vandalism of the natural landscape in the name of Environmentalism, purely for commercial gain';[106] and 'an unnatural and unattractive intrusion into an environmentally sensitive area'.[107] It was viewed as 'an illogical proposition'.[108]

Criticising a merely quantitative assessment of the Seascape, Landscape, and Visual Impact (SLVI) proposed by the applicant,[109] the ExA focused on the Dorset AONB characteristics and its linkages with the unique experience of the coast and its 'sense of place'.[110] The following passage in the ExA's report is indicative of this approach:

> Firstly, judgements of whether a project would compromise the special qualities of the designation cannot be bound by the sort of quantitative exercise deployed. Second, the Dorset AONB Management Plan confirmed that the AONB is a collection of fine landscapes *"each with its own characteristics and sense of place"*; in other words recognising that individual parts can as much reflect the qualities meriting the designation, as the Dorset AONB as a whole. Finally, the approach fails to recognise that the special and outstanding landscape qualities of this AONB are particularly well expressed on its coastal edge and in some instances can only be experienced on the coast.[111]

While the final assessment was a technical one, drawing on an expert framing through a mix of 'technical/expert', 'prior institutional' and 'professional planning' knowledge, the ExA here also looked at the role of experience of landscape.[112] In its report the ExA indulges in a lengthy, almost romantic description of the uniqueness of the coastal landscape, which defines people's experience of the AONB. It recalls the area's 'uninterrupted panoramic views' and 'views across to the open sea and Isle of Wight' as 'an integral part of the experience of the coastal landscape, adding to the sense of remoteness and tranquillity'.[113] This landscape offers 'opportunities for experiencing the dark skies and exceptional undeveloped coastline aspects of the AONB'.[114] The ExA did not focus on the physical changes to the landscape (which it agreed would not result from the project); rather it focused on 'the extent to which [Navitus] would undermine the experience or appreciation of the qualities of the AONB'.[115] In its conclusions, the ExA noted that 'the Application Project would have significant consequences for the "sensory perceptions" of the natural beauty of the Dorset AONB'.[116] The analysis of the potentially adverse impact on AONBs and NPs as inseparable heritage settings was, although not decisive, at least supportive of the rejection of the project.[117]

Experience of the Jurassic Coast WHS and its settings

The Dorset and East Devon coast – also known as the Jurassic Coast – was designated as a WHS in 2001.[118] While the Dorset and the Isle of Wight AONB and the New Forest NP were designated for their landscape and natural beauty, the Jurassic Coast WHS was designated because of the Outstanding Universal Value (OUV) of its 'outstanding combination of globally significant geological and geomorphological features', for which the Dorset AONB constituted an inseparable heritage setting.[119] The assessment of impact on the WHS and Heritage Assets in the project area was instrumental to the rejection of Navitus.

The Environmental Statement submitted by the applicant found that the impact of Navitus on the site's attributes would not be significant.[120] A large number of IP representations in the public consultation challenged these conclusions. Many participants focused on the idea of the infrastructure being developed in 'the wrong place' and 'not fitting' with its natural and heritage context. Due to the special heritage designation, participants saw this area as 'the wrong site for a windfarm'[121] and judged the project as being 'totally out of place'.[122] In other representations, this idea of siting a project in the 'wrong place' gave rise to calls for alternative locations and further distance from the coast to be considered.

Having evaluated the technical evidence and relevant IP representations, the ExA used the concept of 'immediate setting' to draw a link between the impact on the AONB and the impact on the WHS.[123] Here again the focus was on technical assessment of impact, but with consideration of the experience of landscape.[124] The ExA referred to the Management Plan for the Jurassic Coast WHS, stating that the 'setting should be regarded as the surrounding landscape and seascape and "concerns the quality of the cultural and sensory experience surrounding the exposed coasts and beaches" (experiential definition)'.[125]

The ExA emphasised the importance of the link between the quality of the AONB and the experience of the WHS. The following extract illustrates this approach:

> The Panel, however, fails to understand how the special qualities marking the coastal stretches of the AONB can be disassociated from the experiential aspects of the WHS. The overlapping of boundaries, for one, binds the AONB/Heritage Coast with the Site . . . [T]he high expectations of a tranquil setting comprising an exceptional undeveloped coastline and an open seascape is as much part of enjoying the WHS as it is a perceptual experience of the AONB or Heritage Coast. Similarly, appreciating the natural beauty of the AONB cannot be separated from appreciating it as a part of the WHS, especially for visitors wishing to experience the Site without detailed knowledge of its physical attributes. The same applies in reverse . . . [T]he WHS adds an extra dimension to the quality of the coastline.[126]

In reality, the applicant's Environmental Statement did not entirely dismiss the experiential value of the AONB setting. It noted that the 'dynamic nature' of the relationship between the surrounds of the asset and its experience is 'central to the OUV of the Jurassic Coast WHS'.[127] However, this acknowledgement of the interconnection between the AONB and the WHS – and their respective experience – did not amount to such a strong claim as in the ExA's report. The ExA was instead very clear on the significant implications of the functional linkage between the site and its settings, concluding that the harm caused to the view of the AONB would also affect the WHS.[128] It emphasised this in line with its detailed consideration of the experience of the place and its connection with the purpose of the national or international designation. And this is mixed with the dominant expert framing of the report. Even with mitigation measures in place, it was noted that 'the harm that would be caused to the setting of the Jurassic Coast WHS, and the harm to its OUV, carries significant weight against the decision to make the Order'.[129]

Place experience, planning law and decision-making

The example of the Navitus Bay Wind Park project offers some avenues for reflection on place experience and its weight in planning decisions. The Navitus examination nicely incorporates the tensions between landscape expectations, nature conservation and climate change mitigation objectives. But for those interested in place experience, I suggest that there is something more to read into the ExA approach to Navitus. The ExA shows considerable sympathy for issues of place experience as it engages with key aspects of the symbolism and of people's connection with a place and experience of landscape. But despite explicitly acknowledging its value, it has trouble wrapping place experience justifications into the reasoning for its decision. The final decision to reject the Navitus application was strictly technical, based on multiple types of knowledges and a technical assessment of SLVI of the project.[130] While engaging extensively with a narrative of place experience, the ExA was reluctant to give it weight as a determining factor for the decision. This mismatch between sympathy for the value of place experience and what finally counts in decision-making could be related to the reservations regarding experiential evidence in decision-making and the nature of the planning process.

As I illustrated earlier in the chapter, handling experience within the decision-making process is difficult as it often cannot be seen to 'fit' within the expectations of a technically justifiable decision. As a consistent body of scholarship has shown in recent years, the ability of lay public arguments, including concerns about place experience, to be taken into account in the final NSIP decision is limited by a policy presumption in favour of development and a comfortable reliance on technical assessments.[131] Unsurprisingly, the barriers to recognising place experience are in line with the limited scope for effective participation in NSIP regulatory practice,[132] the difficulty of translating lay public concerns into evidence,[133] and a 'dissonance' around the scope of lay public lived experience and technical evidence of impact in the consenting and post-consenting process.[134] But the planning process in general, and wind energy NSIP consenting in particular, are not purely technical processes, but rather profoundly 'political' decision-making moments as they inevitably deal with 'the ways in which artefacts, activities or practices become objects of contestation'.[135] The way in which place experience is handled by decision-makers poses a wider question on the role of law in shaping what counts in NSIP decision-making.

Given the complexity of experience, the extent to which the Secretary of State (and by implication the ExA) could be legally allowed to have regard to place experience in determining an NSIP application is not necessarily straightforward. However, I argue that planning law need not be – and indeed is not – a barrier to using place experience as a basis for decisions. Arguments based on place experience are at least capable of being considered good reasons for a decision. As I explained earlier, the Planning Act 2008 provides that in deciding on an NSIP application, the Secretary of State 'must have regard' to any relevant national policy statement, the appropriate marine policy documents, any local impact report, 'any matters prescribed in relation to development of the description to which the application relates', and *'any other matters which the Secretary of State thinks are both important and relevant to the Secretary of State's decision'*.[136] The Act does not define what 'important', 'relevant' and 'matter' mean. Nor is there clear judicial interpretation of those words.[137]

Nevertheless, it is plausible that the Court might resort to its long history of interpreting the meaning of 'material considerations' in planning, when required to interpret section 104 of the Planning Act.[138] As such a 'relevant' matter could be interpreted as 'material' in planning terms, while requiring it to be 'important' is an additional burden for the decision-maker.[139] Whether a material consideration is 'relevant' in the circumstances of determining a specific application is 'subject to review by the court on conventional public law grounds'.[140] The case law on material considerations suggests that planning law's difficulty in dealing with people's place experience discussed at the beginning of the chapter is not a legal necessity, but rather a matter of planning judgment. In planning law terms, nothing prevents place experience claims from being considered a *material* consideration in any particular case. However, the weight to be given to place experience as a material consideration is a question of planning judgment, shaped by political and policy considerations as discussed in Chapter 2.

Conclusions

Concerns about the space for people's place experience in the decision-making process might sound trivial in comparison to the scale and impact of climate change. Place experience is an ambiguous, multidimensional concept. What it means, how it enters the regulatory process and how planning decisions can take it into account are nuanced and complex questions. But place experience represents a valuable contribution to the crucial choices we make in and through law about infrastructure development in a time of climate change. Planning law has an important role to play in shaping the conversation about what values and experiences are to be enhanced and protected along the road.

The aim of putting place experience explicitly on the legal agenda is not simply and directly to highlight that this is an important area of legal analysis in planning law and decision-making. It is also to recognise that acknowledging the contribution of place experience to decision-making profoundly engages with the meaning and space for participation in planning decisions. Place experience claims are voiced in multiple ways by lay public participants. Certainly not every experience could or should be considered with the same intensity. But a place narrative always sits in the background of the decision-making process, reiterating the well-known complexity of handling expert and lay public evidence. In this context, acknowledging the contribution of place experience in decisions about climate change and its associated infrastructure constitutes an element of the effort towards taking planning law and participation seriously.

Notes

1. Agnew 1987.
2. Seamon 2014, 11.
3. Tuan 1977, 73 and 136.
4. But see Layard 2021 and Jessup 2020.
5. Ministry of Housing, Communities and Local Government (MHCLG) 2021, 14.
6. Devine-Wright and Quinn 2021.
7. Batel 2015.
8. Armeni and Lee 2021.
9. Armeni 2020.
10. Tuan 1977, 8 (referring to Tillich 1967, 29).
11. Tuan 1977, 200.
12. Tuan 1977, 201.
13. Casey 1996, 18.
14. Cresswell 2015, 18.
15. Lang 2011, 89.
16. Corburn 2005, 47.
17. Layard 2010.
18. Seamon 2014, 11.
19. Cresswell 2015, 17.
20. Cresswell 2015, 18.
21. Lee 2017, 10.
22. Malpas 2018, 7.
23. Casey 2002, 271.
24. Casey 2002, 271.
25. Lee 2017, 9 (references omitted).
26. Lee 2017, 19.
27. Altman and Low 1992, 2.
28. Di Masso, Dixon and Durrheim 2014.
29. Williams 2014.
30. Korpela 2012, 149 (references omitted).
31. Hidalgo and Hernández 2001, 274.
32. Giuliani 2003.

33. Tuan 1977, 159.
34. Bell et al 2013, 123.
35. Hernández, Hidalgo and Ruiz 2014, 125.
36. Devine-Wright 2008, 450. See also Carrus et al 2014.
37. Scott 2016.
38. McAuslan 1980.
39. Office of the Deputy Prime Minister (ODPM) 2004, Introduction.
40. UNECE Aarhus Convention on Access to Information, Public Participation in Decision-Making and Access to Justice in Environmental Matters 1998.
41. Participatory rights in English law have inevitably become more vulnerable to pressures and potential erosion since the UK left the EU.
42. Directive 2001/42/EC on the assessment of the effects of certain plans and programmes on the environment [2001] OJ L197/30.
43. Directive 2011/92/EU on the assessment of the effects of certain public and private projects on the environment (codification) [2012] OJ 2012 L 26/1.
44. Armeni and Lee 2021.
45. O'Brien 2000. See also Steele 2001.
46. Pieraccini 2015.
47. Irwin 1995.
48. Zakhour 2020.
49. Armeni and Lee 2021. See further Carolyn Abbot's chapter below.
50. Rydin et al 2018.
51. Lee 2017.
52. Lee et al 2018.
53. See e.g. Rydin 2007.
54. Armeni and Lee 2021.
55. Armeni and Lee 2021.
56. Lee et al 2013 and Rydin, Lee and Lock 2015. This is also more recently replicated in ordinary planning outside the climate emergency narrative: see e.g. MHCLG 2020.
57. Planning Act, section 31. Wind farms and associated infrastructure also need a lease from the Crown Estate, which owns all the seabed up to 12 nautical miles and has vested sovereign rights to explore and exploit the natural resources of the UK continental shelf (Planning Act 2008, section 135(a)).
58. Planning Act, section 42. See also Department for Communities and Local Government (DCLG) 2015.
59. Local Planning Authorities (LPAs) in England are District Councils, London Borough Councils, Broads Authorities, National Park Authorities and the Greater London Authority.
60. Planning Act, sections 42 and 43.
61. Planning Act, section 47.
62. Planning Act, section 49.
63. Planning Act, section 98(1).
64. Planning Act, sections 88, 90 and 93.
65. Planning Act, sections 56 and 60.
66. Planning Act, section 104. Section 107(1) provides for three months for the Planning Inspectorate to make recommendations and a further three months for the Secretary of State to make the decision.
67. As argued in Lee et al 2013 and Rydin, Lee and Lock 2015.
68. Planning Act, section 104(7).
69. Planning Act, section 104(4)–(6) and (8), as amended.
70. Department for Energy and Climate Change (DECC) 2011b, DECC 2011. EN-1 states that to reach its decision, the Secretary of State may include Development Plan Documents or other documents in the Local Development Framework, but in case of conflict with the NPSs, the latter prevails 'given the national significance of the infrastructure' [4.1.5]. Marine Policy Statements and marine plans are also relevant in offshore wind decisions, but in case of a conflict the NPS prevails [4.1.5]. It also clarifies that 'The energy NPSs have taken account of relevant Planning Policy Statements (PPSs) and older-style Planning Policy Guidance Notes (PPGs) in England and Technical Advice Notes (TANs) in Wales where appropriate' [4.1.6]. A revision of the 2011 energy NPSs was launched in 2020 and a public consultation was

conducted between September and November 2021 'to identify whether the revised energy National Policy Statements presented are fit for purpose' (Department for Business, Energy and Industrial Strategy (DBEIS) 2021, 4).
71. EN-1, [2.2.11] and [3.1.1].
72. EN-1, [3.1.4].
73. EN-1, [4.1.2].
74. Infrastructure Planning (Onshore Wind Generating Stations Order 2016 No 306). See also House of Commons: Written Ministerial Statement (HCWS42) – DCLG Written Statement made by Secretary of State for Communities and Local Government (Greg Clark), 18 June 2015. See further Energy Act 2016, section 78.
75. EN-1, [4.1.2].
76. Lee 2017, 6 referring to Lee et al 2013 and Rydin, Lee and Lock 2015.
77. Sheate 2017, 188.
78. On the contested relationship between policy and individual projects: *Bushell v Secretary of State for the Environment* [1981] AC 75, [1980] 3 WLR 22; *R (Wandsworth LBC) v Secretary of State for Transport* [2005] EWHC 20 (Admin), [2006] 1 EGLR 91; *R (Greenpeace Ltd) v Secretary of State for Trade and Industry* [2007] EWHC 311 (Admin), [2007] Env LR 29; *Barbone v Secretary of State for Transport* [2009] EWHC 463 (Admin), [2009] Env LR D12; *R (London Borough of Hillingdon & others) v Secretary of State for Transport* [2010] EWHC 626 (Admin), [2010] JPL 976. This case law is discussed in Lee et al 2013.
79. Lee et al 2013.
80. Planning Act, section 87(3). See also section 106(1).
81. Lee et al 2013, 57. This tendency is clearly a feature of the wider planning reform, in MHCLG 2020.
82. Cowell and Devine-Wright 2018, 508 (citing Owens 2004).
83. National Parks and Access to the Countryside Act 1949, section 5(2).
84. Countryside and Rights of Way Act 2000, section 82(1).
85. DECC, 2011b, [5.9.9].
86. DECC, 2011b, [5.9.9].
87. DECC 2011b, [5.9.10].
88. UNESCO Convention Concerning the Protection of the World Cultural and Natural Heritage 1972, article 4.
89. https://historicengland.org.uk/advice/hpg/has/whs/ (accessed 12 June 2022).
90. DECC 2011b and DECC 2011a.
91. MHCLG 2021.
92. DCLG 2012; DCLG 2016.
93. DECC 2011b, [5.8.12].
94. DECC 2011b, [5.8.14].
95. DECC 2011b, [5.8.15].
96. MHCLG 2021, 67.
97. Planning Inspectorate (PINS) 2015, [9.0.9].
98. MHCLG 2021, 71.
99. Historic England 2008, [76].
100. *Steer v Secretary of State for Communities and Local Government & others* [2017] EWHC 1456 (Admin) [64]; [2017] JPL 1281.
101. *Catesby Estates Ltd v Steer* [2018] EWCA Civ 1697; [2019] 1 P & CR 5 [29]. On setting, see also *Barnwell Manor Wind Energy Limited v East Northamptonshire District Council & others* [2014] EWCA Civ 137; [2015] 1 WLR 45 and *R (Williams) v Powys County Council* [2017] EWCA Civ 427; [2018] 1 WLR 439.
102. PINS 2015. All relevant representations were coded and listed at the end of the Examining Authority (EA) Report in Appendix C – REP-0015 to REP-2673.
103. REP-0187.
104. REP-0110.
105. REP-0111.
106. REP-0083.
107. REP-0250.
108. REP-0219.

109. PINS 2015, [7.1.132].
110. PINS 2015, [7.3.134].
111. PINS 2015, [7.3.134] (emphasis in the original).
112. Lee 2017.
113. PINS 2015, [7.3.136].
114. PINS 2015, [7.3.136].
115. PINS 2015, [7.3.138].
116. PINS 2015, [7.3.138].
117. See DECC 2015.
118. Nomination documents at https://whc.unesco.org/en/list/1029/documents/ (accessed 12 June 2022).
119. Outstanding Universal Value description at https://whc.unesco.org/en/list/1029 (accessed 12 June 2022).
120. PINS 2015, [9.2.3] also explaining the findings leading to this conclusion.
121. REP-0089.
122. REP-0153.
123. PINS 2015, [9.3.17].
124. Lee 2017.
125. PINS 2015, [9.3.18] as opposed to a functional definition which concerns the physical processes which the ExA did not explore.
126. PINS 2015, [9.3.20].
127. PINS 2015, [9.3.21].
128. PINS 2015, [9.3.23]. The ExA found this impact on the heritage assets 'less than substantive' (i.e. 'the impact would not be such as that "very much, if not all, of the significance was drained away"', [9.3.24] citing *Bedford Borough Council v Secretary of State for Communities and Local Government, Nuon UK Ltd* [2013] EWHC 2847 (Admin) [24]). However, it recognised that this is 'still an objection to some magnitude and requires the negative impact to be weighed against the public benefit of the development', [9.3.24].
129. PINS 2015, [9.3.26].
130. Lee 2017.
131. Lee et al 2013; Rydin et al 2015.
132. Rydin 2020; Rydin et al 2017.
133. Natajaran 2018; Natarajan 2019.
134. Natarajan 2021.
135. Barry 2001, 6.
136. Planning Act, section 104 (emphasis added).
137. Although some guidance could come from *R (Mynydd y Gwynt Ltd) v Secretary of State for Business, Energy and Industrial Strategy* [2016] EWHC 2581 (Admin); [2017] Env LR 14, [65], [54] and [61]. The subsequent Court of Appeal decision did not engage with 'material considerations' or 'important and relevant' matters. See *R (Mynydd y Gwynt Ltd) v Secretary of State for Business, Energy and Industrial Strategy* [2018] EWCA Civ 231; [2018] WLR(D) 117. This is also based on their purposive reading as elements to which the Secretary of State 'must have regard' in determining the decisions, in addition to any specific consideration to be taken into account by an enactment. *Baroness Cumberlege of Newick v Secretary of State for Communities and Local Government and another* [2017] EWHC 2057 (Admin); [2017] WLR (D) 549, [51].
138. Cook J in *Stringer v Minister of Housing and Local Government* [1970] 1 WLR 1281, 1294. In *Westminster City Council v Great Portland Estates* [1985] AC 66; [1984] 3 WLR 1035, Lord Scarman expanded the *Stringer* definition. See also *R v Westminster City Council, ex parte Monahan* [1989] 3 WLR 408; *Tesco Stores Ltd v Secretary of State for the Environment* [1995] 1 WLR 759; *R (Health and Safety Executive) v Wolverhampton City Council* [2012] UKSC 34; [2012] 1 WLR 2264 (where Lord Justice Carnwath held that '"material" in ordinary language is the same as "relevant"', [26]).
139. *Bolton Metropolitan District Council and Others v Secretary of State for the Environment and Others* [1995] 1 WLR 1176 [352]. Cf *R (John Watson) v London Borough of Richmond upon Thames LBC* [2013] EWCA Civ 513; [2013] CN 736.
140. *Baroness Cumberlege of Newick* [51].

References

Agnew, John (1987). *Place and Politics – the Geographical Mediation of State and Society*. Abingdon: Routledge (revised edn).

Altman, Irwin and Setha Low (1992). *Place Attachment*. New York: Springer.

Armeni, Chiara (2020). *Public Participation in Decision-making on Wind Energy Infrastructure: Rethinking the Legal Approach Beyond Public Acceptance*. Unpublished PhD thesis. University College London.

Armeni, Chiara and Maria Lee (2021). 'Public Participation in the Climate Crisis', *Journal of Law and Society* 48: 549–72.

Barry, Andrew (2001). *Political Machines: Governing a Technological Society*. London: Bloomsbury Academic.

Bell, Derek et al (2013). 'Revisiting the "Social Gap": Public Opinion and Relations of Power in the Local Politics of Wind Energy', *Environmental Politics* 22: 115–35.

Carrus, Giuseppe et al (2014). 'Place Attachment, Community Identification, and Pro-Environmental Engagement'. In *Place Attachment: Advances in Theory, Methods and Applications*, edited by Lynne C. Manzo and Patrick Devine-Wright, 154–64. Abingdon: Routledge.

Casey, Edward (1996). 'How to Get from Space to Place in a Fairly Short Stretch of Time'. In *Senses of Place*, edited by Steven Feld and Keith H Baso, 13–52. Santa Fe: School of Advanced Research Press.

Casey, Edward (2002). *Representing Place, Landscape Paintings and Maps*. Minneapolis, MN: University of Minnesota Press.

Corburn, Jason (2005). *Street Science: Community Knowledge and Environmental Health Justice*. Cambridge, MA: MIT Press.

Cowell, Richard and Patrick Devine-Wright (2018). 'A "Delivery-Democracy Dilemma"? Mapping and Explaining Policy Change for Public Engagement with Energy Infrastructure', *Journal of Environmental Policy and Planning* 20: 499–517.

Cresswell, Tim (2015). *Place – An Introduction*. Chichester: Wiley Blackwell, 2nd edn.

Department for Business, Energy and Industrial Strategy (2021). *Planning for New Energy Infrastructure: Draft National Policy Statements for Energy Infrastructure*.

Department for Communities and Local Government (2015). *Planning Act 2008: Guidance on the Pre-Application Process*.

Department for Energy and Climate Change (2011a). *National Policy Statement for Renewable Energy Infrastructure (EN-3)*.

Department for Energy and Climate Change (2011b). *Overarching National Policy Statement for Energy (EN-1)*.

Department for Energy and Climate Change (2015). *Planning Act 2008 – Planning Consent Application – Proposed Navitus Bay Wind Park*, 11 September.

Devine-Wright, Patrick (2008). 'Reconsidering Public Acceptance of Renewable Energy Technologies: A Critical Review'. In *Delivering a Low-Carbon Electricity System – Technologies, Economics and Policy*, edited by Michael Grubb, Tooraj Jamasb and Michael G. Pollitt, 443–61. Cambridge: Cambridge University Press.

Devine-Wright, Patrick (2014). 'Dynamics of Place Attachment in a Climate Change World'. In *Place Attachment: Advances in Theory, Methods and Applications*, edited by Lynne C. Manzo and Patrick Devine-Wright, 165–77. Abingdon: Routledge.

Di Masso Andrés, John Dixon and Kevin Durrheim (2014). 'Place Attachment as Discursive Practice'. In *Place Attachment: Advances in Theory, Methods and Applications*, edited by Lynne C. Manzo and Patrick Devine-Wright, 75–86. Abingdon: Routledge.

Fisher, Elizabeth (2018). 'Law and Energy Transition: Wind Turbines and Planning Law in the UK', *Oxford Journal of Legal Studies* 38: 528–56.

Fisher, Elizabeth, Bettina Lange and Eloise Scotford (2019). *Environmental Law: Text, Cases and Materials*. Cambridge: Cambridge University Press, 2nd edn.

Giuliani, Maria Vittoria (2016). 'Theory of Attachment and Place Attachment'. In *Psychological Theories for Environmental Issues*, edited by Mirilia Bonnes, Terence Lee and Marino Bonaiuto, 137–70. Abingdon: Routledge.

Hernández, Bernardo, M. Carmen Hidalgo and Cristina Ruiz (2014). 'Theoretical and Methodological Aspects of Research on Place Attachment'. In *Place Attachment: Advances in*

Theory, Methods and Applications, edited by Lynne C. Manzo and Patrick Devine-Wright, 125–38. Abingdon: Routledge.

Hidalgo, M. Carmen and Bernardo Hernández (2001). 'Place Attachment: Conceptual and Empirical Questions', *Journal of Environmental Psychology* 21: 273–81.

Historic England (2008). 'Conservation Principles, Policies and Guidance for the Sustainable Management of the Historic Environment', available at https://historicengland.org.uk/images-books/publications/conservation-principles-sustainable-management-historic-environment/conservationprinciplespoliciesandguidanceapril08web/ (accessed 12 June 2022).

Irwin, Alan (1995). *Citizen Science: A Study of People, Expertise and Sustainable Development*. Abingdon: Routledge.

Jessup, Brad (2020). 'Statues and Status. The Legal Geography of Landscape Values and Belonging', *University of Western Australia Law Review* 48: 140–69.

Korpela, Kalevi (2012). 'Place Attachment'. In *Oxford Handbook of Environmental and Conservation Psychology*, edited by Susan D Clayton, 148–63. Oxford: Oxford University Press.

Lang, James (2011). 'Epistemologies of Situated Knowledges: "Troubling" Knowledge in Philosophy of Education', *Educational Theory* 61: 75–96.

Layard, Antonia (2010). 'Shopping in the Public Realm: The Law of Place', *Journal of Law and Society* 37: 412–41.

Layard, Antonia (2021). 'Law, Place and Maps'. In *Handbook on Space, Place and Law*, edited by Robin Bartel and Jennifer Carter, 129–40. Cheltenham: Edward Elgar.

Lee, Maria (2017). 'Knowledge and Landscape in Wind Energy Planning', *Legal Studies* 37: 3–24.

Lee, Maria et al (2013). 'Public Participation and Climate Change Infrastructure', *Journal of Environmental Law* 25: 33–62.

Lee, Maria et al (2018). 'Techniques of Knowing in Administration: Co-Production, Models, and Conservation Law', *Journal of Law and Society* 45: 427–56.

McAuslan, Patrick (1980). *The Ideologies of Planning Law*. Oxford: Pergamon Press.

Malpas, John (2018). *The Place of Landscape: Concepts, Contexts and Studies*. Cambridge, MA: MIT Press.

Ministry of Housing, Communities and Local Government (2020). *White Paper: Planning for the Future*.

Ministry of Housing, Communities and Local Government (2021). *National Design Guide*.

Natarajan, Lucy (2018). 'Major Wind Energy and the Interface of Policy and Regulation: A Study of Welsh NSIPs', *Planning Practice and Research* 34: 1–17.

Natarajan, Lucy (2021). 'Citizen Monitoring of Environmental Regulation in England: The Post-Consent Stage'. In *Regulation and Planning. Pratices, Institutions, Agency*, edited by Yvonne Rydin et al, 163–73. New York: Routledge.

Natarajan, Lucy et al (2019). 'Participatory Planning and Major Wind Infrastructure: Experiences in REI NSIP Regulation', *Town Planning Review* 90: 117–38.

O'Brien, Mary (2020). *Making Better Environmental Decisions: An Alternative to Risk Assessment*. Cambridge, MA: MIT Press.

Office of the Deputy Prime Minister (2004). *Community Involvement in Planning: The Government's Objectives*.

Owens, Susan (2004). 'Siting, Sustainable Development and Social Priorities', *Journal of Risk Research* 7: 101.

Pieraccini, Margherita (2015). 'Rethinking Participation in Environmental Decision-Making: Epistemologies of Marine Conservation in South-East England', *Journal of Environmental Law* 27: 45–67.

Planning Inspectorate (2015). 'The Planning Act 2008 – Navitus Bay Wind Park – Examining Authority's Report of Findings and Conclusions and Recommendation to the Secretary of State for Energy and Climate Change'.

Rydin, Yvonne (2007). 'Re-examining the Role of Knowledge Within Planning Theory', *Planning Theory* 6: 52–68.

Rydin, Yvonne (2020). 'Silences, Categories and Black Boxes: Towards Analytics of the Relations of Power in Planning Regulation', *Planning Theory* 19: 214–33.

Rydin, Yvonne, Maria Lee and Simon Lock (2015). 'Public Engagement in Decision-Making on Major Wind Energy Projects', *Journal of Environmental Law* 27: 139–50.

Rydin, Yvonne et al (2018). 'Local Voices on Renewable Energy Projects: The Performative Role of the Regulatory Process for Major Offshore Infrastructure in England and Wales', *Local Environment* 23: 565–81.

Scott, Dayna N. (2016). 'We Are the Monitors Now': Experiential Knowledge, Transcorporeality and Environmental Justice', *Social & Legal Studies* 25: 261–87.

Seamon, David (2014). 'Place Attachment and Phenomenology: The Synergistic Dynamism of Place'. In *Place Attachment: Advances in Theory, Methods and Applications*, edited by Lynne C. Manzo and Patrick Devine-Wright, 11–22. Abingdon: Routledge.

Sheate, William R. (2017). '"Streamlining" the SEA Process'. In *The Strategic Environmental Impact Directive – A Plan for Success?*, edited by Gregory Jones and Eloise Scotford, 185–212. London: Hart Publishing.

Steele, Jenny (2001). 'Participation and Deliberation in Environmental Law: Exploring a Problem-Solving Approach', *Oxford Journal of Legal Studies* 21: 415–42.

Tillich, Paul (1967). *My Search for Absolutes*. New York: Simon and Schuster.

Tuan, Yi-Fu (1977). *Space and Place – The Perspective of Experience*. Minneapolis, MN: University of Minnesota Press.

Williams, Daniel (2014). '"Beyond the Commodity Metaphor" Revisited: Some Methodological Reflections on Place Attachment Research'. In *Place Attachment: Advances in Theory, Methods and Applications*, edited by Lynne C. Manzo and Patrick Devine-Wright, 89–99. Abingdon: Routledge.

Zakhour, Sherif (2020). 'The Democratic Legitimacy of Public Participation in Planning: Contrasting Optimistic, Critical, and Agnostic Understandings', *Planning Theory* 19: 349–70.

7
Planning inquiries and legal expertise: A fair crack of the whip?
Carolyn Abbot

Introduction

Public participation is an important feature of the planning system in England. All development proposals are made available to the public, and the public are legally entitled to make representations on any planning application. Local planning authorities (LPAs) must, by law, have regard to these representations when determining an application. More extensive participatory rights are provided for certain types of development.[1] As discussed further in Chiara Armeni's chapter in this volume, the value of public participation is well-rehearsed in the literature with both substantive (output legitimacy) and procedural (input legitimacy) arguments underpinning the inclusion of participatory processes in decision-making.[2] Meaningful public participation is, however, difficult to achieve. In this chapter, I focus on one challenge, namely the extent to which the public are able to engage effectively with the legally and procedurally complex nature of the planning system: 'Participation in planning currently doesn't feel like it is accessible to all. The systems are complex, and the language and systems seem to be from a bygone age.'[3]

I shine a spotlight on public participation in planning inquiries and explore the potential contribution that legal experts can make when supporting local community groups exercising their participatory rights in this forum.[4] Legal experts as knowledge providers, skilled advocates and experienced practitioners can, I argue, strengthen local community group participation in planning inquiries. The chapter builds upon a paper published in *Legal Studies* in which I explore, in general terms, how legal expertise can support local community groups in opposing planning applications.[5] I also draw upon my recently published co-authored monograph (with Maria Lee) in which we investigate how environmental non-governmental organisations (NGOs) used legal expertise in their lobbying and advocacy efforts to shape the post-Brexit environmental law landscape.[6]

The chapter explores legal expertise in planning using an example of a planning application called-in in July 2018 for development in Bolton in the Northwest of England.[7] The proposal was submitted by Peel Holdings, the Northwest's largest private landowner. With over 37,000 acres of land, including large areas of central Manchester and Liverpool, and a property portfolio worth over £2.3 billion,[8] Callum Ward and Erik Swyngedouw argue that through aggressive 'assetisation' and the 'capture' of local resources, Peel Holdings have shaped and influenced both regional and local governance structures and decision-making, including in the planning context.[9] The Peel Holdings proposal was to build a championship golf course (and associated buildings and infrastructure) and over 1,000 residential houses on Green Belt land and in Hulton Park, a Registered Park and Garden (RPG). It attracted considerable opposition. Members of the local community formed Hulton Estate Area Residents Together (HEART) who appeared at the planning inquiry, represented by a barrister. An analysis of written documents associated with the inquiry, including opening and closing statements, submissions of evidence and the Planning Inspector's report, provides a useful insight into what legal experts *do* when representing the local voice in the planning process.

Planning inquiries occupy an important place between administrative decision-making and the courts.[10] As such, they create demands for natural justice and fairness. They are also the means by which the most controversial development proposals are determined; developments that are often in conflict with local planning documents and, in some cases, national planning policy.[11] Developers, who have invested significant time and financial resource in designing and promoting a planning project, will use a planning inquiry as an opportunity to present their case for development in the strongest possible terms, mobilising their substantial resources and skills to influence an outcome that will serve their own interests. My starting premise is that if public participation in planning is to be more than ceremonial, local groups must be able to present their objections (or indeed support) as part of the planning inquiry process on an equal footing to others. Access to legal expertise gives these groups a 'fair crack of the whip'.[12]

Planning law is arguably one of the most complex regulatory systems in England and Wales. It is complex both procedurally and substantively, is underpinned by an ever-shifting framework of law and policy, and is embedded within a system of discretionary decision-making, leading to significant uncertainty for all those involved in the process. This chapter begins by exploring some of this complexity, focusing on decision-making. It then turns to a consideration of what legal experts *do* for local groups in planning inquiries. Two important points need to be made at the outset. First, I leave to one side the important question of what constitutes legal expertise and the rich and diverse literature that explores the complexity and contestedness of that expertise.[13] In this chapter, I evaluate the contribution of legal experts as knowledge providers, skilled advocates and experienced practitioners.[14] Examining the role of law and legal expertise through a lens of decision-making in planning law explicitly acknowledges 'the contingent and contested nature of legal arguments' in which developers and objectors are working, within the boundaries of the legal framework, to advocate opposing views as to the legality of the proposed development.[15] Second, I refer to legal experts rather than lawyers. What is clear is that whilst looking to professional identity (through qualification as a solicitor or barrister) may be a good indicator of legal expertise, it is by no means exclusive. As discussed by Abbot and Lee, expertise can be demonstrated in a multiplicity of ways.[16] This point is explicitly acknowledged in planning inquiry guidance which, as noted below, states that whilst it is customary for Rule 6 interested parties to be represented by an advocate, that advocate does not need to have legal qualifications.[17] Important knowledge, skill and experience may be held by those outside of the legal profession.

Layers of complexity in planning law

Recent empirical studies of participation in planning reveal that one of the core challenges in securing effective participation is the inherent complexity of planning law.[18] For instance, the use of esoteric terminology was identified as a particular barrier to participation in a recent empirical study of participation under the Nationally Significant Infrastructure Project (NSIP) process with Natarajan et al noting, as a typical comment, that 'the gobbledegook and the language were so complicated, I think it would have put most people off getting involved. You needed to be a Philadelphia lawyer [i.e. exceptionally competent] just to understand it.'[19] In this section, I explore legal complexity (both substantive and procedural) in determining planning applications.

In light of the rapid pace of change, the task of mapping out the planning law framework is 'like hitting a moving target'.[20] As noted by Lee in Chapter 2, development can only proceed if permission is granted by the state. Unlike most other countries, decision-taking (and indeed plan-making) is founded on a very much discretionary approach, within the context of an indicative as opposed to prescriptive policy framework.[21] This discretion is, of course, constrained by legal rules laid down in statute, planning policy, development plans and case-law. However, the uncertainty inherent in a case-by-case approach, combined with the sheer volume of material, has culminated, today, in a patchwork of laws and policies that frame what constitutes acceptable development. For all these reasons, this section cannot provide a detailed insight into the complexity of planning law. It will, however, reflect upon some examples, with a particular emphasis on the development consent process, and on some of the legal issues that lie at the heart of the case-study development proposal in Hulton Park.

Two legislative provisions are at the core of the development consent process, namely section 70(2) of the Town and Country Planning Act (TCPA) 1990, which states that 'regard must be had to the provisions of the development plan, so far as material to the application, and to any other material considerations', and section 38(6) of the Planning and Compulsory Purchase Act 2004, which provides that 'if regard is to be had to the development plan for the purpose of any determination to be made under the Planning Acts the determination must be made in accordance with the plan unless material considerations indicate otherwise'.[22] It would therefore seem that the development plan for the locality within which the planning proposal sits is pivotal, in that if the proposal complies with the provisions in the plan, then permission will be granted. This is not, however, the approach taken by the courts, who have determined that the development plan is the starting point for determining individual applications.[23] Planners and politicians have to balance provisions in the development plan with other 'material considerations'. And given that as of June 2020, only 50 per cent of local authorities had an up-to-date local development plan, the term 'material considerations' is at the heart of decision-making.[24] What constitutes a material consideration will vary from one application to another. Broadly speaking, it must be relevant to the specific development in question and must be something that can be controlled through the application of planning law. National planning policy is an important material consideration, and the National Planning Policy Framework (NPPF) sets 'the overall direction of the planning system, [and] provides the main planning policy for individual applications in the absence of an up-to-date development plan'.[25]

At over 70 pages in length, it sets out important policy statements on inter alia plan-making, decision-making, protecting green belt land and conserving and enhancing the natural environment.[26]

One of the most widely contested paragraphs of the NPPF is paragraph 11 (which also lies at the core of the Hulton Park decision-making process).[27] It states that 'plans and decisions should apply a presumption in favour of sustainable development'.[28] It goes on to say that for decision-taking this means:

> c) approving development proposals that accord with an up-to-date development plan without delay; or
> d) where there are no relevant development plan policies, or the policies which are most important for determining the application are out-of-date, granting permission unless
> > i) the application of policies in this Framework that protect areas or assets of particular importance provides a clear reason for refusing the development proposed; or
> > ii) any adverse impacts [of granting permission] would *significantly and demonstrably outweigh* the benefits, when assessed against the policies in this Framework taken as a whole.

Given the centrality of housing provision to planning (see further Lee's chapter), there is an explicit reference to the circumstances in which development plan policies on housing will be out-of-date where, for example the local authority cannot demonstrate a five-year supply of deliverable housing sites. The phrase 'policies in this Framework' (commonly referred to as 'footnote policies') is a reference to provisions on, for example, Green Belt and designated heritage assets, both of which are central to the Hulton Park decision. Paragraph 147 on development affecting the Green Belt, for example, states that 'inappropriate development is, by definition, harmful to the Green Belt and should not be approved except in very special circumstances'. Paragraph 148 goes on to say that 'substantial weight' should be given to Green Belt harm and that 'very special circumstances will not exist unless the potential harm to the Green Belt by reason of inappropriateness, and any other harm resulting from the proposal, is clearly outweighed by other considerations'.[29] Similar provisions on development proposals affecting heritage assets require decision-makers to assess, inter alia, the significance of the heritage asset and the extent to which potential harm is substantial harm or less than substantial harm to the significance of the heritage asset.[30]

Overall, paragraph 11 relates to what has been referred to as the 'tilted balance' to decision-making.[31] The burden placed on the public, local residents and local community groups in navigating this one, single component of the planning system is significant. The starting point is to consider whether the development plan is out-of-date and, if not, whether the development broadly accords with the policies in the plan. As discussed in the 2020 White Paper *Planning for the Future*, these plans

> have become lengthier documents of increasing complexity, in some cases stretching to nearly 500 pages; are underpinned by vast swathes of evidence base document, often totalling at least ten times the length of the plan itself and none of which are clearly linked, standardised, or produced in accessible formats; and include much unnecessary repetition of national policy.[32]

Not only do local community groups and other interested parties have to determine whether the development plan policies most important for determining the application are out-of-date, but in the event that they are, paragraph 11 of the NPPF triggers a series of complex balancing exercises that will ultimately determine whether the adverse impact of granting permission would significantly and demonstrably outweigh the benefits (referred to as the planning balance). Regional policy documents and secondary advice and guidance such as National Planning Practice Guidance and LPA Supplementary Planning Documents add further layers of complexity to decision-making. The ultimate check and balance is provided by the courts through judicial (or statutory) review, discussed further in Joanna Bell's chapter. Perhaps unsurprisingly given the significant resource invested in new proposals by developers, planning forms the third largest category of judicial review claims after immigration/asylum and prison cases.[33] Cases such as *Hopkins Homes* in the Supreme Court are indicative of the role of the courts in assessing the lawfulness of decision-making in planning law.[34] In assessing the planning balance, decision-makers are informed by expertise provided by town planners, scientists, economists and many others. Ultimately, the role of the legal expert is to understand the position this evidence occupies within a law and policy framework that is lengthy, dispersed and fraught with uncertainty.

Law and policy establish not only the framework within which decisions are taken, but also the process. Primary and delegated legislation, supported by lengthy guidance notes, establishes the procedural framework for participation. Where applications are called-in by the Secretary of State (as was the case in the Hulton Park development), a planning inquiry will be held.[35] Members of the public can apply for 'Rule 6' status which, if granted, entitles them to appear at the inquiry and places them in a position similar to that of the main parties.[36] It is, however, unusual for Rule 6 status to be granted to individuals; potential applicants who share similar views about a proposed development are encouraged to 'group together and elect a spokesperson to appear at the inquiry on the group's behalf'.[37] Groups applying for Rule 6 status must make a request to the Planning Inspectorate (PINS) outlining who they are, why they want Rule 6 status and, importantly, what they can bring to the inquiry that another party may not. If granted, the Rule 6 party must adhere to the detailed guidance on planning inquiries contained within multiple PINS documents.[38] They must produce a statement of case, they can be involved in the preparation of statements of common ground and they must submit proofs of evidence where they are intending to call another person to give evidence at the inquiry. Given the rather formal nature of the planning inquiry process, guidance notes that it is 'customary' for the main parties, including any Rule 6 parties, to be represented by an advocate, although, as noted above, the advocate does not need to hold any legal qualifications. Let us then turn to what legal experts *do* when representing local community groups, using the HEART and Hulton Park inquiry as an example.

HEART and Hulton Park

In this section, I explore the role of legal experts (and legal expertise) in supporting local communities (and their groups) in exercising their legal rights to participate in the planning process. It draws upon a methodological approach used by Abbot and Lee in their evaluation of the role of legal expertise in NGO advocacy outside the courtroom[39] and analyses publicly available documents that have been submitted as part of a called-in planning application, and the Planning Inspector's report. These documents are not only accessible, but also provide a coherent and extensive body of material which can be examined. In addition to examining written documents associated with the inquiry, I draw upon an informal conversation with a HEART representative where appropriate to enrich the written material. First, I begin by providing an overview of the proposed development, its legal and policy context and HEART's involvement.

The project and its legal context

The application, submitted by Peel Holdings, was a single hybrid planning application for both detailed and outline planning permission. Both Bolton Metropolitan Borough Council (MBC) and the applicant believed that it represented 'a unique opportunity to bring one of the greatest sporting events in the world (the Ryder Cup golf tournament) to Bolton and secure a lasting legacy which will endure for the long-term'.[40] As identified in the Principal Statement of Common Ground, there were three main elements to the application:

1. Detailed permission for restoration works to various historic structures within Hulton Park.
2. Detailed permission for a championship golf resource including the golf course, clubhouse and luxury hotel complex.
3. Outline permission for a residential development of up to 1,036 houses.

The development proposal is clear in saying that the proposed residential development is essential in cross-subsidising both the restoration of the RPG and the delivery of the golf course resort. In light of the Government's ambition to further advance the Northern Powerhouse agenda, both the applicant and LPA contended that

> the golf resort at Hulton Park would make a significant and unique contribution to these and other national and regional strategic growth objectives. It provides an opportunity to raise the international profile of the region and city region, to align activities with inward investment priorities across key economic sectors, and to boost local producer businesses linked to a growing visitor economy. It would provide a focal point for enhanced tourism and business development across the North West.[41]

The proposed development is significant, not just in terms of sheer scale (the project would take 20 years to complete), but also in terms of its complexity, diversity and impact on existing land use designations. The entire Peel Holdings development site is located within the adopted Greater Manchester Green Belt. If granted (and implemented) the measure of change that it would bring about to existing planning designations would require review in light of the development. Furthermore, the majority of the site is designated as a heritage asset (Hulton Park is a

Historic England Grade II RPG in Bolton in the Northwest of England).[42] Wide-ranging research into Hulton Park was undertaken as part of the planning inquiry. Much of this centred around the extensive landscape work that was completed in the eighteenth century by two well known English landscape gardeners, William Emes and his pupil John Webb.[43] Significant features of the park, including a Kitchen, Walled Garden and Pleasure Grounds, can still be specifically identified today, although 'all have been harmed by the absence of use and the significant passage of time and all are in danger of being lost as unmanaged nature takes hold'.[44] The larger area of planted parkland has also suffered, with many of the woodlands taken over by large areas of grassland. The earliest known hall on the site dates from the fourteenth century and in 1958 the badly damaged and vandalised hall was demolished. The estate was home to the Hulton family from around 1167 until 1993, when Sir Geoffrey Hulton died with no heir. The park was sold to Peel Holdings in 2010.

The application, submitted to Bolton MBC in May 2017, prompted significant local opposition. Over 1,100 objections relating, amongst other things, to environment, heritage, transport and highways, green belt and social/community benefits, were received to the initial public consultation comprising individual objection letters and pro-forma style objection letters.[45] One support letter was also received. In March 2018, Bolton MBC, in accordance with the recommendation of a Professional Officer, voted eight to seven in favour of granting permission, subject to a planning obligation and a detailed set of planning conditions. The application was referred to the Secretary of State under the Town and Country Planning (Consultation) (England) Direction 2009.[46] In July 2018, the application was called-in by the Secretary of State.[47] Such powers are used selectively in cases where, for example, the development is nationally significant or where the development deviates substantially from national policy.[48]

Many of the local community concerns were channelled through HEART, an association of residents from the Hulton area established to oppose the Hulton Park planning application. With over 800 signed-up members and around 2,000 followers on its social media accounts, HEART is a good example of a grassroots environmental group formed by residents objecting to a proposed development in the locality. For these local groups, 'the motivation for collective action is, at least in the first instance, usually based on a threat to individual members and their immediate locality as opposed to an ideological commitment to environmentalism'.[49] HEART were involved from the earliest stages of the decision-making process. The group submitted representations to

Figure 7.1 Proposal site in the context of the Bolton Adopted Development Plan.[50]

Bolton Planning Committee and appeared before that Committee (with legal representation). It hired legal representation to draft a letter to the Secretary of State requesting that the application be called in, and was granted Rule 6 status at the planning inquiry. Where this power is exercised, Rule 6 'interested parties' have the right to be heard at a public local inquiry or other hearing.[51] At the inquiry, the group were represented by a barrister from Exchange Chambers in Manchester. HEART raised over £40,000 to pay for both legal representation and expert witnesses at the inquiry. Around £10,000 of this was raised through the JustGiving crowd-funding website. The remaining 75 per cent was raised through locally organised events, including pub quizzes and yard sales.[52]

A full appraisal of the planning issues raised by the Hulton Park development and the Planning Inspector's report is outwith the scope of this chapter. By way of overview, the Inspector's 134-page report considers multiple questions in determining the planning balance, including the extent to which the proposal accords with Bolton MBC's development plan (and associated policies), the potential harm caused to Hulton Park as an RPG, a Green Belt analysis, the effect of the proposal on biodiversity, its socio-economic impacts and financial viability. All three main parties (namely the developer, Bolton MBC and HEART) agreed that the development plan for the provision of housing was out-of-date, thus triggering an assessment under paragraph 11(d) of the NPPF.[53] The relevant footnote policies for the purposes of the proposed development were those relating to designated heritage assets and Green Belt policies.

Both policies require certain matters to be taken into account, namely assessment of public benefits under heritage matters or other positive material considerations in the case of Green Belt balance. Additional benefits and harms, including a viability assessment, also had to be considered. In essence, HEART argued that the 'tilted balance' was not engaged as the harms of the proposed development (primarily to the Green Belt and Hulton Park as an RPG) significantly and demonstrably outweighed the benefits. Both Peel Holdings and Bolton MBC agreed that the proposed development would cause substantial harm to the Green Belt (as well as other harm) and should ordinarily be refused planning permission. They argued, however, that if the Ryder Cup were to be hosted at Hulton Park in either 2030 or 2034, 'very special circumstances' under paragraph 148 of the NPPF would exist and, on that basis, permission should be granted. The Inspector (and ultimately the Secretary of State) concluded that the material considerations in this case 'indicate a decision other than in accordance with the development plan – i.e. a grant of permission'[54] subject to specified conditions and a section 106 agreement. This agreement includes what has been termed the 'Ryder Cup Restriction'.[55] This restriction operates by way of a *Grampian* obligation (a negative obligation) that no form of development will be carried out on the site until the Ryder Cup has been awarded to Hulton Park.[56]

Planning inquiries: the role of legal expertise

Planning inquiries are generally very formal and similar to a law court. Proofs of evidence must be submitted, parties permitted to appear at the inquiry are entitled to call evidence, and there is a statutory right to cross-examine witnesses.[57] As noted above, there is no legal requirement that Rule 6 parties (or indeed any other party) be represented by a solicitor or barrister and it is by no means uncommon for Rule 6 parties to represent themselves.[58] Guidance does, however, encourage Rule 6 parties to have an advocate to present their case, with Inspectors assisting and advising inexperienced advocates on procedural matters where necessary.[59]

In the context of planning inquiries, we can conceive of legal experts as knowledge providers, skilled advocates and experienced practitioners. These features are of course interconnected; legal experts with experience of planning inquiries have the skills to ensure that their written and oral arguments are framed in terms that are legitimate and relevant in planning law and policy. Perhaps the most obvious contribution that legal experts make is in their detailed knowledge of the legal and policy framework within which decisions are taken.[60] Land conflict, 'once channelled into a public inquiry, is highly regulated in a way that defines arguments and evidence as legitimate or illegitimate, relevant or irrelevant'.[61] The wider legal and policy context within which decision-making sits limits the reasons that can be taken into account.[62] This body of knowledge is at the core of planning, and in the discussion above I provided a flavour of the complexity of substantive planning law rules as applied to decision-making.

So how important was expertise *in* the law in the case of HEART and Hulton Park? HEART's closing statement makes direct and explicit reference to one piece of legislation (namely the Community Infrastructure Regulations), one Court of Appeal decision[63] and one High Court decision.[64] There is much more significant emphasis placed on paragraphs of the NPPF (2019), including paragraphs 144 and 146 on proposals affecting the Green Belt and paragraph 189 on proposals affecting heritage assets. It would therefore be misleading to claim that HEART's opening and closing statements are law-heavy. They are not. They certainly contain more references to law than HEART's self-drafted objection to Bolton Planning Committee, which focuses, in terms of decision-making frameworks, on paragraphs of the NPPF, including an assessment of 'significant harm' to the RPG and the absence of 'very special circumstances' in relation to Green Belt policy.[65] But HEART's inquiry submissions are law-light. This is perhaps unsurprising given that there was little disagreement as to the applicable law and policy (and a legal expert is of course well-positioned to reach this conclusion). As indicated above, the applicant, Bolton MBC and HEART agreed that the development plan was out-of-date and so attention would turn to whether the footnote policies clearly established a reason for permission to be refused. The HEART submission can certainly be contrasted with Rule 6 party submissions at other planning inquiries, such as the objections lodged by Re-Form to the Whitechapel Bell Foundry development in London where reference to law, especially case-law, foregrounds the subsequent assessment of planning balance.[66]

Looking beyond HEART's written submissions, legal experts will also carry out a legal assessment of written documents submitted by the developer to ensure that they comply with a multitude of regulations, including Environmental Statements under the Town and Country Planning (Environmental Impact Assessment) Regulations 2017 and the Community Infrastructure Levy Regulations 2010,[67] both of which were in play in the Hulton Park inquiry. Legal experts can also advise on planning conditions and planning obligations, many of which are subject to constant redrafting throughout the inquiry process. Even where objections do not lead to a refusal of permission, the impact of arguments may be felt in different ways. For example, HEART succeeded in persuading the inspector that certain planning conditions should be reframed.[68] HEART also experienced a win in relation to the section 106 agreement[69] between Peel Holdings and Bolton MBC, the final version of which uses a *Grampian* obligation by which 'the owner of the site covenants that the development shall not be begun or initiated within the meaning of s.56 of the [Town and Country Planning Act 1990]' until the Ryder Cup has been awarded to Hulton Park.[70]

Whilst knowledge of substantive planning law is obviously important, legal experts can also offer a detailed understanding of the planning inquiry process, which is complex and lengthy, and involves a number of important milestones. In advance of the inquiry itself, there is a pre-inquiry meeting to discuss administrative and procedural arrangements. The Inspector will also lay out what evidence can be presented and how that evidence should be tested. Rule 6 parties must submit statements of case,[71] decide whether to agree to any statements of common ground, submit proofs of evidence and provide witness names. Complying with timescales and meeting the deadlines set by the Inspector are important in maximising the impact of opposition claims. The inquiry itself can last weeks (in the case of the Hulton Park inquiry, nine days). The formal oral sessions (at which cross-examination takes place) are only part of the process. As was the case in the Hulton Park inquiry, roundtable discussions may be used (to which Rule 6 parties are invited) to ventilate certain topics.[72] As one-shotters[73] (and here we see the connections between substantive knowledge and experience), community groups like HEART will have little understanding (and experience) of planning inquiries. Their knowledge is usually limited to the decision-making process at the local level, with its political complexities and nuances. Legal experts can guide groups like HEART through the process, giving them time and space to focus on maximising the influence of the objections to the proposed development.

Whilst HEART's legal representative clearly had to have knowledge of substantive law and legal process, I now turn to the role of legal experts as skilled advocates. My starting point is the simple observation that the primary purpose of planning inquiries is to provide 'for the investigation into, and formal testing of, evidence, usually through expert witnesses'.[74] As discussed in Armeni's examination of place experience in this volume, empirical studies of planning decision-making clearly point to a strong preference for technical as opposed to lay evidence, and yet, certainly in the initial stages of opposition, local group objections are often couched in lay terms.[75] Local knowledge can be crowded out by more formal, methodologically approved technical evidence claims. Expert witnesses, through the submission of witness statements and their presentation of evidence at the planning inquiry, form, in the words of Jane Holder and Donald McGillivray, 'the procedural and structural backbone of public inquiries'.[76] They play a crucial role in supporting the claims made by Rule 6 interested parties. In this regard, legal experts undertake important pre-inquiry work in providing advice on evidence.[77]

HEART's opposition to the Hulton Park development centred on four key areas:

(1) The harm to the RPG and the extent to which the development benefits the RPG.
(2) The economic viability of the proposal.
(3) The economic benefits of the proposal and the extent to which these were 'transformational'.
(4) The overall planning balance, including an assessment of whether the development would cause substantial harm to the Green Belt.

Unable to fund the cost of expert witnesses to address all four areas, HEART had to consider how best to spend their limited resource. The group was able to fund two expert witnesses to speak on their behalf, one speaking on Historic Landscape and Heritage matters,[78] with a second expert witness on planning and planning policy to address the central question of planning balance. In consultation with potential expert witnesses, legal experts can play a strategic role in advising on which witnesses should be called and what issues each of the witnesses should cover. As noted by Malcolm Pill (later Lord Justice Pill), 'the lawyer's training in identifying the important points and in detecting inconsistencies should be valuable at this stage'.[79] Evidential claims can be thoroughly tested in cross-examination, a matter to which I return below.

Turning to the contribution of lawyers as skilled advocates, advocacy is about persuasion; about persuading the Inspector that the planning balance lies in favour of the client (whether that be the developer or the local community group opposing the application). Although there is often some consensus between all parties as to the benefits and impacts of a development proposal, call-in applications will inevitably involve conflict and contention. The 'ability to present evidence, and have it rigorously tested through cross-examination' was identified as an important element of the inquiry process by respondents to the Rosewell Review.[80] Written and oral communication skills are obviously valuable and were a key factor in HEART's decision to seek formal legal representation at the inquiry.[81] Here we can draw heavily on Abbot and Lee's study of environmental NGO advocacy. Our interviews revealed that legal expertise in the presentation of arguments is important and – a point to which I shall return later – plays a role in ensuring that those arguments are taken seriously.[82] We also found that 'lawyers' expertise might include skills in putting arguments in the strongest adversarial form, or in managing disagreement in a collaborative way, or both simultaneously'.[83] Furthermore, legal training 'makes you very rigorous about how you analyse material . . . How you combine that with evidence … And then how you construct arguments.'[84] This is not necessarily a unique skill held by legal experts. But in the case of planning inquiries such as Hulton Park, with over 1,500 pieces of evidence, understanding that material in the context of a complex legal and policy framework lends further support to the contribution that legal experts can make in this regard.

The planning inquiry also provides a space for the cross-examination of witnesses – an 'essential tool in the advocate's armoury for persuasion of . . . his client's cause'.[85] Whilst cross-examination plays an important role in assisting the Planning Inspector, it has at its core the aim of persuading the Inspector as to the merits of the objector's case.[86] Legal experts, by virtue of professional training, are well-versed in the skills of cross-examination. In the Hulton Park inquiry, witnesses appearing for both Peel Holdings and Bolton MBC were cross-examined by HEART's barrister. HEART's closing submission uses evidence attained during cross-examination to, for example, challenge the extent to which the golf course hotel was designed with landscape conservation in mind. Cross-examination of the evidence provides a means of testing not only the substantive evidence itself, but also the methodology upon which that evidence is based. For example, the purpose of cross-examination on biodiversity gains in the Hulton Park inquiry was to test the sensitivity of the calculations to small adjustments, especially over the longer term. However, and here we return to the importance of expert evidence, HEART did not put forward an expert witness on biodiversity/ecology and so was unable to offer an alternative outlook on net gain. This was noted by the applicant:

> Two observations were made by HEART in relation to ecology. The first, was that if you altered the inputs, then the outputs of the model altered too. But since there was no evidence, or even suggestion, that the inputs were incorrectly identified, this position goes nowhere.[87]

The importance of challenging technical knowledge and presenting an alternative account of knowledge was noted by Lee in the context of an examination under the NSIP process where the objector, Challenge Navitus, 'understood the advantages of detailed critique of the applicant's technical case, and of providing its own competing technical material'.[88]

Finally, knowledge and skills are developed and deepened through experience both 'in terms of length of time an individual has spent developing their expertise . . . and in terms of practical hands-on experience'.[89] Experience combined with knowledge and skill makes for strong advocacy. In contrast with developers and LPAs, who are, adopting Marc Galanter's terminology, 'repeat players' with the backing of significant resource, local community groups like HEART are 'one-shotters' who only have recourse to participatory forums and the courts on occasion and for whom the stakes are high.[90] By bringing their experience to the inquiry, legal experts acting on behalf of groups like HEART can go some way to levelling the playing field:

> [By] knowing 'the rules of the game', community groups arguably gain an advantage when co-opting those with legal expertise irrespective of the merits of the case, especially in planning inquiries pursuant to the Secretary of State calling-in a planning application.[91]

An experienced legal expert will know which arguments are legally relevant (and importantly, irrelevant) as determined by the law and policy framework. She will know which arguments are likely to be the most (and least) influential in persuading the Planning Inspector as to a particular position. The importance of practical experience was also acknowledged by Abbot and Lee, with one interviewee stating:

> Unless you've been through one, or five or seven [judicial reviews] or whatever, or at least sat in a court or read the documents beforehand, so seen the type of submissions, but I think more important sat in the court . . .[92]

This particular quotation clearly resonates strongly in the context of planning inquiries. In short, whilst knowledge of process is obviously crucial, the experience gained by legal experts who have attended multiple inquires is invaluable to local group 'one-shotters' for whom planning inquiries are an unlived experience.

As noted in the introduction, I have focused in this chapter on the role of legal experts rather than lawyers, in recognition of the fact that professional legal qualifications are not a prerequisite for legal expertise.[93] In the context of planning inquiries, however, groups looking for representation will normally turn to the legal profession. This professional credentialing would seem to be important; a barrister would give their arguments and claims credibility in the eyes of both the Planning Inspector and opposition counsel.[94] This sense that arguments presented by a legal professional will be taken more seriously is echoed by both Abbot and Lee,[95] and Rebecca Sandefur, who states that 'lawyers appear to affect outcomes because their presence on a case acts as an endorsement of its merits.'[96]

Concluding thoughts

Planning inquiries are used to determine the most complex and controversial developments. If the merits of public participation are to be realised, then this participation must be meaningful and local communities must have a real opportunity to influence decision-making. Legal experts have an important role to play in representing local community groups like HEART. Whilst knowledge of law (and process) is important (more or less important depending on the extent to which there is disagreement as to the relevant legal rules), skill and experience are significant features of that expertise. This chapter has shone a light on the contribution that legal experts can make. Important empirical work should be undertaken to further explore legal expertise in planning inquiries in order to better understand how local groups can and should be supported in their participatory activities. This research could strengthen calls for more financial support.

However, there are strong indications that the sands may be shifting in the development consent process. White Paper proposals indicate that, in England at least, there may be a radical departure from our current discretionary approach to planning, with a move towards the use of zoning.[97] As discussed by Lee in the Introduction to this volume, the future of these proposals is uncertain. Under the 2020 proposals discussed in Chapter 2 above, local authorities (through their local plan) would allocate land into three (or possibly two) areas, namely growth areas, renewal areas and protected areas. Developers who wish to develop land would not need planning permission, provided their proposal complies with zoning provisions in the local plan. If such an approach were to be adopted, then public participation would shift to much earlier in the process (in the making of local plans and decisions relating to zones) and so too would the role of legal experts. Contention and conflict would occur at the plan-making (rather than decision-taking) stage. We have yet to see whether the 'local' voice would be as vocal under these new proposals (there is some evidence pointing to the fact that the public do not engage either with local plan-making or indeed with higher-level planning policy). What is certainly clear is that the zoning proposals are likely to be complex and couched in legally contestable terms. There will be much debate, and probably litigation. The focus of legal expertise will shift but, in all likelihood, it will be just as important, if not more so, if local communities are to have any influence on where and when development takes place.

Notes

1. See e.g. participatory rights for Nationally Significant Infrastructure Projects (NSIPs) under the Planning Act 2008.
2. See e.g. Lee and Abbot 2003.
3. Housing, Communities and Local Government (HCLG) Committee 2021, [64].
4. An analysis of recent planning inquiries reveals that some groups engage legal experts (most commonly barristers or solicitors) to represent them through the drafting and submission of written evidence and, in some cases, through representation at oral inquiries. For a discussion of the broader role that legal experts can play in achieving local community goals see Gordan 2007.
5. Abbot 2020.
6. Abbot and Lee 2021.
7. In September 2021 Peel Holdings submitted a fresh, revised application for development at Hulton Park. Many of the proposals mirror the application called-in in 2018, although in light of local opposition the new proposal has reduced the number of homes to be built on green belt land and includes more community facilities. On 14 January 2022, Bolton MBC received their planning officer's report in which approval was recommended. For details for the application see https://www.bolton.gov.uk/hultonpark (accessed 12 June 2022).
8. Shrubsole 2019.
9. Ward and Swyngedouw 2018.
10. For a history of planning inquiries see Hart 1997.
11. House of Commons 2019.
12. *Fairmount Investments Ltd v Secretary of State for the Environment* [1976] 1 WLR 1255 (HL), 1266.
13. See further Abbot and Lee 2021, chapter 4.
14. See further Fisher 2012, 48.
15. Abbot and Lee 2021, 81.
16. Abbot and Lee 2021, 87–9.
17. PINS November 2020, [13(1)].
18. See e.g. Natarajan et al 2019.
19. Natarajan et al 2019, 130.
20. Town and Country Planning Association 2020, 24. For an excellent account of UK planning reform see Prior 2005.
21. The majority of countries utilise some form of regulatory approach to development control through the use of zoning. For an interesting historical account of discretion in planning see Booth 2007.

22. Inserting a new section 54A into the TCPA 1990.
23. *Tesco Stores Ltd v Secretary of State for the Environment* [1995] 1 WLR 759 (HL).
24. Ministry of Housing, Communities and Local Government (MHCLG) 2020b, 12.
25. Upton 2019, 137.
26. MHCLG 2021.
27. The Hulton Park planning application was decided within the framework of NPPF 2019. The wording of paragraph 11 for decision-taking remains the same under NPPF 2021. Further references to the NPPF will be to the 2021 version unless otherwise stated.
28. The initial determination of the Hulton Park development was made with reference to the NPPF 2012. Department for Communities and Local Government (DCLG) 2012, [14].
29. Green belt planning policies have a long history and remain the subject of litigation in the highest courts. See e.g. *R (Samuel Smith Old Brewery (Tadcaster)) v North Yorkshire CC* [2020] UKSC 3; [2020] 3 All ER 527 for a recent discussion of the relevance of visual impacts of development on the openness of green belt land under (what is now) paragraph 146 of the NPPF.
30. MHCLG 2021, [189]–[208].
31. *Hopkins Homes Ltd v Secretary of State for Communities and Local Government* [2017] UKSC 37; [2017] 1 WLR 1865.
32. MHCLG 2020b, 26.
33. Bondy, Platt and Sunkin 2015.
34. *Hopkins Homes*.
35. The Covid-19 pandemic has had a significant impact on call-in inquiry procedures with, at times, an instruction that all inquiries be held remotely. PINS is currently conducting research as to the possible use of remote or hybrid inquiries moving forward as a matter of course. See further Phillips 2021.
36. The referral here is to Rule 6 of the Town and Country Planning (Inquiries Procedures) (England) Rules 2000.
37. PINS 2020b, [2].
38. See PINS 2020a and PINS 2020b.
39. Abbot and Lee 2021, chapter 5.
40. Statement of Common Ground [1.2], on file with author.
41. Statement of Common Ground [2.8], on file with author.
42. The National Heritage Act 1983 enabled English Heritage to establish a Register of Historic Parks and Gardens of Special Historic Interest. See further Pendlebury 1999.
43. See the Historic England official listing available at https://historicengland.org.uk/listing/the-list/list-entry/1001581?section=official-listing (accessed 12 June 2022).
44. MHCLG 2020a, [7.26].
45. Summary of Third Party Representations, on file with author.
46. Circular 02/2009. The 2009 Direction requires LPAs in England to consult the Secretary of State before granting permission for certain types of development.
47. TCPA 1990, section 77.
48. House of Commons 2019.
49. Abbot 2020, 272.
50. Planning Proof of Evidence by Jackie Copley, available at https://www.hearthulton.com/public-inquiry (accessed 12 June 2022).
51. See PINS 2020b.
52. For further details of HEART see Proof of Evidence submitted by Mr Paul Haworth, Chairman of HEART, available at https://www.hearthulton.com/public-inquiry (accessed 12 June 2022).
53. The Council did not have a five-year supply of housing land for the period 2018–2023. The identified supply was equivalent to 3.7 years.
54. MHCLG 2020a, [43].
55. For discussion see MHCLG 2020a, [8.3]–[8.12].
56. The current policy on Grampian conditions (and by implication Grampian obligations) is that they should only be avoided where 'there is no prospect at all of the action in question being performed within the time-limit imposed by the permission'. Department for Levelling Up, Housing and Communities (DLUHC) 2019, [009].
57. TCP (Inquiries Procedure) (England) Rules 2020, rule 15(5).
58. See e.g. a planning inquiry for mixed development (including outline planning permission for residential development) in West Yorkshire where the Burley Objectors Group was represented by eight group members, including a retired Parish Clerk and a retired town planner.

59. MHCLG 2020a, [13.1]. Albeit in a different planning process, Lee et al 2018 report the lengths that Examining Authorities in the NSIP process go to support lay participants at hearings.
60. Lisa Vanhala would describe this as 'legal stock', the body of substantive law within which local community groups can frame their opposition to proposed developments. Vanhala 2018.
61. Blackman 1991, 311.
62. Armeni 2016.
63. *Palmer v Herefordshire Council and Another* [2016] EWCA Civ 1061; [2017] WLR 411. In assessing the impact of the development on the significance of the asset, both the positive and negative impacts should be considered in order to determine the overall net effect.
64. [2013] EWHC 2847.
65. Provided to the author in personal correspondence with a HEART representative.
66. Available at https://re-form.org/uploads/images/WHITECHAPEL-BELL-FOUNDRY-RE-FORM-CLOSING-FINAL.pdf (accessed 12 June 2022).
67. SI 2010/968 as amended by Community Infrastructure Levy (Amendment) (England) (No 2) Regulations 2019 SI 2019/1103.
68. See e.g. MHCLG 2020a, [12.8] relating to the opening times of the proposed clubhouse.
69. As conveyed in informal conversation with a representative of HEART.
70. MHCLG 2020a, [8.7].
71. As opposed to formal objections which must be submitted by interested parties without Rule 6 status.
72. In the case of Hulton Park, roundtable discussions were used in relation to viability and highways matters.
73. Galanter 1974.
74. PINS 2020a, [B.4.1].
75. See also Lee 2017; Aitken 2010.
76. Holder and McGillivray 2018.
77. Pill 1986, 8.
78. The main source of disagreement between HEART and the applicant was that HEART's expert witness contended that there would be substantial harm to the heritage asset whereas the applicant argued that an overall benefit would accrue.
79. Pill 1986, 8.
80. MHCLG 2018, [2.14].
81. As conveyed in informal conversation with a representative of HEART.
82. Abbot and Lee 2021, 92.
83. Abbot and Lee 2021, 93.
84. Abbot and Lee 2021, 93.
85. Read 1997, 29.
86. For a discussion of the merits of cross-examination at a Planning Inquiry see Read 1997.
87. MHCLG 2020a, [7.101].
88. Lee 2017, 17.
89. Abbot and Lee 2021, 93.
90. Galanter 1974.
91. Abbot 2020, 279.
92. Abbot and Lee 2021, 94.
93. This was noted by Abbot and Lee 2021, 88.
94. In informal conversation with a HEART representative.
95. Abbot and Lee 2021, 119–20.
96. Sandefur 2015, 910.
97. MHCLG 2020b.

References

Abbot, Carolyn (2020). 'Losing the Local? Public Participation and Legal Expertise in Planning Law', *Legal Studies* 40: 269–85.
Abbot, Carolyn and Maria Lee (2021). *Environmental Groups and Legal Expertise: Shaping the Brexit Process*. London: UCL Press, available at https://www.uclpress.co.uk/products/155996 (accessed June 2022).

Aitken, Mhairi (2010). 'Wind Power Planning Controversies and the Construction of "Expert" and "Lay" Knowledges', *Science as Culture* 18: 47–64.

Armeni, Chiara (2016). 'Participation in Environmental Decision-Making: Reflecting on Planning and Community Benefits for Major Wind Farms', *Journal of Environmental Law* 28: 415–41.

Blackman, Tim (1991). 'Planning Inquiries: A Socio-Legal Study', *Sociology* 25: 311–27.

Bondy, Varda, Lucinda Platt and Maurice Sunkin (2015). *The Value and Effects of Judicial Review: The Nature of Claims, their Outcomes and Consequences*. London: Public Law Project.

Booth, Philip (2007). 'The Control of Discretion: Planning and the Common Law Tradition', *Planning Theory* 6: 127–45.

Department for Communities and Local Government (2012). *National Planning Policy Framework*.

Department for Levelling Up, Housing and Communities (2019). *PPG: Use of Planning Conditions*.

Fisher, Elizabeth (2012). 'The Rise of Transnational Environmental Law and the Expertise of Environmental Lawyers', *Transnational Environmental Law* 1: 43–53.

Galanter, Marc (1974). 'Why the "Haves" Come Out Ahead: Speculations on the Limits of Legal Change', *Law and Society Review* 9: 95–160.

Gordon, Jennifer (2007). 'The Lawyer is not the Protagonist: Community Campaigns, Law and Social Change', *California Law Review* 95: 2133–46.

Hart, Garry (1997). 'The Value of the Inquiries System', *Journal of Planning Law*: 8–13.

Holder, Jane and Donald McGillivray (2018). '"If This Were to be Lost": Relating Environmental Justice and an Ethic of Care in Everyday Shared Spaces', available at https://papers.ssrn.com/sol3/papers.cfm?abstract_id=3205109 (accessed 12 June 2022).

House of Commons Library Briefing Paper (2019), *Called-in Planning Applications (England)* No. 00930.

Housing, Communities and Local Government Committee (2021). *The Future of the Planning System in England First Report of 2021–2 HC 38*.

Howarth, David (2013). *Law as Engineering: Thinking About What Lawyers Do*. Cheltenham: Edward Elgar.

Lee, Maria (2017). 'Knowledge and Landscape in Wind Energy Planning', *Legal Studies* 37: 3–24.

Lee, Maria and Carolyn Abbot (2003). 'The Usual Suspects? Public Participation under the Aarhus Convention', *Modern Law Review* 66: 80–108.

Lee, Maria et al (2018). 'Techniques of Knowing in Administration; Co-Production, Models and Conservation Law', *Journal of Law and Society* 45: 427–56.

Lee, Maria et al (2018). 'Decision-Making for Major Renewable Energy Infrastructure', *Journal of Planning and Environment Law*: 507–12.

Ministry of Housing, Communities and Local Government (2018). *Independent Review of Planning Appeal Inquiries Report* (December).

Ministry of Housing, Communities and Local Government (2019). *National Planning Policy Framework*.

Ministry of Housing, Communities and Local Government (2020a). *Planning Inspectorate Report: Hulton Park Inquiry Ref: 3208426*, available at https://assets.publishing.service.gov.uk/government/uploads/system/uploads/attachment_data/file/905485/20-09-30_DL+IR_Hulton_Park.pdf (accessed 12 June 2022).

Ministry of Housing, Communities and Local Government (2020b). *White Paper: Planning for the Future*.

Ministry of Housing, Communities and Local Government (2021). *National Planning Policy Framework*.

Natarajan, Lucy et al (2019). 'Participatory Planning and Major Infrastructure: Experiences in REI NSIP Regulation', *Town Planning Review* 90: 117–38.

Pendlebury, John (1999). 'The Place of Historic Parks and Gardens in the English Planning System: Towards Statutory Controls?', *Town Planning Review* 70: 479–500.

Phillips, Rebecca (n.d.). 'Virtual Casework Events: Planning for the Future', available at https://planninginspectorate.blog.gov.uk/2021/11/11/virtual-casework-events-planning-for-the-future/ (accessed 12 June 2022).

Pill, Malcolm (1986). 'Public Inquiries and the Lawyer', *Bracton Law Journal* 18: 7–11.

PINS (2020a). *Called-in Planning Applications: Procedural Guide*, available at https://www.gov.uk/government/publications/called-in-planning-applications-procedural-guide (accessed 12 June 2022).

PINS (2020b). *Guide to Rule 6 for Interested Parties Involved in an Inquiry: Planning Appeals and Called-In Applications*, available at https://www.gov.uk/government/publications/apply-for-rule--status-on-a-planning-appeal-or-called-in-application/guide-to-rule--for-interested-parties-involved-in-an-inquiry-planning-appeals-and-called-in-applications (accessed 12 June 2022).

Prior, Alan (2005). 'UK Planning Reform: A Regulationist Interpretation', *Planning Theory and Practice* 6: 465–84.

Read, Lionel (1997). 'The Benefit and Purpose of Cross-Examination', *Journal of Planning and Environment Law*: 24–8.

Sandefur, Rebecca L. (2015). 'Elements of Professional Expertise: Understanding Relational and Substantive Expertise Through Lawyers' Impact', *American Sociological Review* 80: 909–33.

Shrubsole, Guy (2019). 'Who Owns the Country? The Secretive Companies Hoarding England's Lane', *The Guardian*, 19 April.

Town and Country Planning Association (2020). *Planning 2020 – Raynsford Review of Planning in England, Final Report*.

Upton, William (2019). 'What is the Purpose of Planning Policy? Reflections on the Revised National Planning Policy Framework 2018', *Journal of Environmental Law* 31: 135–49.

Vanhala, Lisa (2018). 'Is Legal Mobilization for the Birds? Legal Opportunity Structures and Environmental Nongovernmental Organizations in the United Kingdom, France, Finland, and Italy', *Comparative Political Studies* 51: 380–412.

Ward, Callum and Eric Swyngedouw (2018). 'Neoliberalisation from the Ground Up: Insurgent Capital, Regional Struggle, and the Assetisation of Land', *Antipode* 50: 1077–97.

Part IV
Time and scale
Maria Lee and Carolyn Abbot

Temporal and scalar questions are central to the legal analysis of planning. We see them throughout this volume: the opportunities afforded by time during Covid are apparent in Antonia Layard's discussion of low traffic neighbourhoods; the effort to bring all future possibilities into the present ('presentation') is a key question in Edward Mitchell's chapter; activists make instrumental calls on different scales of governance in Steven Vaughan and Brad Jessup's chapter; and Margherita Pieraccini's chapter brings out the concertina of scale from the tiny to the global, as well as the significance of futurity to planning. In this part, Elen Stokes and Maria Lee turn more explicitly to these questions.

Planning is inherently future-oriented, imagining the playing out of time and space for a territory or a specific site; it also relies on the past to control the future, creating models and maps of the future from assessments of the past. And planning is inherently scalar, self-consciously utilising and attempting to organise different scales not only of governance, but also of interests and actors, sometimes with short-term instrumental objectives, sometimes with the aim of achieving more profound shifts of power. Law's relation with time and scale is not fixed or natural; law contributes to constructing time and scale, just as law attempts to make use of temporal and scalar understandings of the world. The complexity and dynamism of time and scale in planning is often buried beneath instrumental and detailed doctrinal developments in planning law.

In this part, we ostensibly deal with time and space separately, vulnerable to the criticism that analysis of scale is static,[1] a moment in time captured as lines on a map. But both time and space reverberate through each contribution. In her exploration of the complex dimensions of planning for housing, Maria Lee highlights the constant interplay and shifting of scale, the constant efforts to fix perceived problems by scalar institutions, bringing out the (temporal) dynamism of scale. Elen Stokes brilliantly and more explicitly brings out the connections between time and scale. Her examination of the call-in of fracking developments reveals the ways in which different imaginations and regularisations of the future resonate through lenses that we might otherwise think of as scalar.

Note

1. Massey 2005; Valverde 2015.

References

Massey, Doreen (2005). *For Space*. Oxford: Sage.
Valverde, Mariana (2015). *Chronotopes of Law: Jurisdiction, Scale and Governance*. Abingdon: Routledge.

8
Futurescapes of planning law: Some preliminary thoughts on a timely encounter

Elen Stokes[*]

Introduction

It is uncontroversial to say that land use planning is a temporal field, concerned as it is with issues of sustainability, change, conservation, growth, regeneration and 'the possibilities that time offers space'.[1] Equally uncontroversial is the suggestion that planning involves a particular orientation to the future and that, even if it falls short of expectations, it is motivated by 'a belief that action now can shape future potentialities'.[2] Planning is variously described as a form of 'persuasive storytelling about the future',[3] as 'anticipatory',[4] and as 'the specification of a proposed future coupled with systemic intervention and/or regulation in order to achieve that future'.[5] Both as an ideal and as a practice, planning is future-bound.[6] Yet while the relationship between planning and the future has long been accepted as foundational, and has proved fertile ground for critical scholars in land use management and planning theory, there has been little express consideration in this context of the part played by law.

My aim in this chapter is to give planning law, and law generally, a greater prominence in research on the future. Modern futures studies began life as an applied science aimed at developing computational tools for forecasting and prediction. It has since grown in disciplinary scope and gained a sharper critical edge in the social sciences and humanities, setting new agendas for engaging with the future not as a fixed object 'out there' to be measured, managed and moved into, but instead as a continuous process, always in flux, not separate from but immanent in the present. Pioneers in the field have accorded particular analytic significance to futures-in-the-making (rather than futures already 'made' through statistical modelling, for example),[7] and to the need for inventive ways of studying the empirically elusive realm of the not-yet.[8] This has been taken in several directions, opening up new avenues of inquiry into anthropologies of the future,[9] geographies of the future,[10] futurescapes of urban regeneration,[11] speculative research methods,[12] and sociotechnical imaginaries.[13] Those are just a few areas where explicit efforts have been made to build a fuller picture of what specific imaginations of the future 'do' – how they configure power relations, serve ideological goals, and determine which/whose futures are deemed possible, plausible, probable and preferable – in the here and now.

This type of research has not been pursued, at least not directly or systematically, in legal scholarship, despite the future's pervasiveness in all aspects of legal process and doctrine. The future's inescapability and diffuseness are the very features, however, that seem to have contributed to the lack of targeted legal engagement. Although there are notable exceptions, the future has generally been subservient to other related frames and issues in the study of law – such as sustainable development, risk, and intergenerational justice – meaning that futurity has been poorly tended as a *legal* problem. This is true of planning law, the most self-evidently future-oriented of all the legal fields. The purpose here, then, is to offer a means of foregrounding the future-making practices of planning law, so that closer attention may be paid to the various ways in which planning law imagines and regularises certain futures and future possibilities.

A 'futurescapes' framework adapted from the work of social theorist Barbara Adam brings a heightened sensitivity to the traces of futurity in law, and to the futures rendered meaningful in distinctively legal ways. One of the important qualities of the relationship between planning law and the future is that it can appear fixed and inert, and not up for debate. Yet that obscures the difference that law makes in actively producing the future rather than just passively encountering it. An advantage of a futurescapes approach is that it can be used to examine legal future-making in terms of specific modes – for example, the timeframes, temporalities, tempos, timings and time sequences of planning law that shape how futures are anticipated and *'lived and felt* as inevitable'.[14] The approach also helps to illustrate that while planning law is always 'futural', it is not uniformly or consistently so. The relationship is dynamic and manifests itself in many ways, through different combinations of temporal structures and processes, and this is fundamental to the effects that law is able to achieve in the present. To begin to address these issues, the chapter draws on two specific aspects of English planning law that apply to the onshore exploration and development of unconventional oil and gas: the application of local development plans; and the Secretary of State's statutory powers to call-in planning applications and recover planning appeals.

About time: futures theory and law

Law is sometimes depicted as the ultimate custodian or venerator of the past,[15] especially in common law jurisdictions where the invocation of precedent 'perpetually reclaims the past for the present'.[16] Examples of law's path dependence, status quo bias and respect for tradition, for example, have tended to feed overgeneralised claims, however, that law is innately past-oriented. So much so that it can be difficult to avoid resorting to platitudes about law being backward-looking, nostalgic even, and too slow to keep pace with social transformation.[17] I too have used such caricatures in my research and teaching, because even though they leave little room for complexity, they have at least a ring of truth. Ask any law student to describe the discipline, and it is unlikely that they would respond with 'progressive', 'innovative' or 'modern'. Still, these ideas are in danger of overestimating the importance of the past in law.[18] One consequence of the prominence of historical time is that the problem of the future tends to have been overlooked.[19]

Any notion that law's relationship with time is lodged only in history has been comprehensively dispelled by a significant and insightful body of work in socio-legal and critical legal studies, which has brought a new level of precision to the field, detailing the varying temporalities that contemporary legal systems and techniques use or construct.[20] The scholarship has done much to broaden the focus beyond historical context by illuminating the diversity of ways in which law discursively and practically shapes what we interpret and experience as time. It goes against the commonly held and often tacit view that law and time are analytically distinct, providing original concrete analyses of them as mutually dependent entities that interact and shape each other. Whereas legal scholars, like social theorists generally, have tended to treat questions of law separately from those of time, the recent line of work focuses on their interconnections and shows how we gain explanatory power by thinking of legal processes, institutions and doctrine as fundamentally temporalised.[21] Law is full of temporal structures – for instance, it determines when (for example sunset clauses), in what order (for example consultation and pre-decision matters), how quickly (for example determination deadlines) and for how long (for example injunctions, temporary stop notices) action can be taken.[22] Law also operates more subtly, though, to construct a particular sense of time, such as rhythm, intensity, potential and accentuation, in the moment. It is through the richer, more finely textured accounts of law's temporal dynamics that these felt-realities of time have come to be regarded as a form of legality.[23] Time is not just an object of legal intervention – it is also a mode of legal reasoning; a means of marshalling evidence, framing interactions and stabilising powerful normative frameworks; a medium through which social relations, values and meanings become embedded in legal and regulatory practices. Law's relationship with time is anything but uniform and one-directional.

Yet although the literature has made major conceptual inroads into the temporalities and temporalising effects of law, and prompted a much greater engagement with other disciplinary and interdisciplinary studies of time, there has been no sustained engagement, as there has been in other fields, with the future. There are some brilliant exceptions to this, for example the work of Emily Grabham on the futures conceived, and critically the futures excluded, under the UK's Gender Recognition Act 2004;[24] Annelise Riles on 'placeholders' for resolving ambiguity about the near future;[25] Renisa Mawani on the significance of certain, envisioned colonial futures to the claimed authority, sovereignty and legitimacy of British imperial law;[26] Sarah Keenan on title registration as a means of protecting the transcendental, future entitlement of white settler subjects to indigenous land;[27] Davina Cooper on prefigurative institutional action;[28] and Christos Boukalas on the emptying of futures and suppression of potential change in security and economic law and policy.[29] Still, these examples are not typical of the discipline overall and it is fair to say that legal scholarship generally has viewed the future in 'shreds and patches', so to speak.[30] This is in contrast to legal history, which has become its own sub-genre.

It would be a mistake, though, to regard legal *history* and legal *futurity* as direct opposites. As many works on temporality have shown, the present is always infused with both pasts and futures – with both 'experience' and 'expectation',[31] with both 'retentions' and 'protentions'.[32] The past, present and future cannot be disentangled because they are integral to each other. 'All our pasts,' says Dipesh Chakrabarty, 'are futural in orientation.'[33] In Nancy Munn's words: 'Ways of attending to the past also create modes of apprehending certain futures or of reconstructing a particular sense of the past in the present that informs the treatment of "the future in the present".'[34] However self-contained the past, present and future might appear, the research reveals porousness and fluidity, opening the door to more processual understandings of temporality as a sphere of 'dynamic simultaneity'.[35] For Adam, 'There is no single time, only a multitude of times which interpenetrate and permeate our lives'.[36]

What this means is that the future, and its manifestations in the present, cannot be satisfactorily understood or explained in isolation from the multiple, intersecting historical trajectories that are also implicated in the framing of times yet to come. The treatment of the future as a simultaneous co-presence of temporal features is elaborated by Adam in her conceptualisation of 'timescapes',[37] and latterly 'futurescapes'.[38] The suffix 'scape' – as in landscape or cityscape – signals that thinking about time necessarily has implications for how we imagine space and spatial relations.[39] It has further significance because it says something about the approach to analysis, which is to see time as a domain that is always in formation, always incomplete and open to being re-formed. Adam explains that a landscape, and by extension a timescape, 'tells a story of immanent forces, of interdependent, contingent interactions that have given rise to its existence'.[40]

A futurescape is similarly conceived, though it reflects a deeper frustration over the lack of sociological tools and methods, and until relatively recently the lack of enthusiasm, for taking the social reality of futures seriously. Social scientists are well-equipped to study 'present-futures', that is, the realm of prediction, plans, promises, models, strategies and other rational instrumentalities for deciphering what the future 'will be'. By contrast, 'future-presents' are less amenable to empirical investigation by conventional means because they occupy 'the inaccessible, invisible, latent world of processes'.[41] A futurescapes perspective enables a more nuanced account of the future as a 'precarious achievement'[42] that is continually being made in everyday practices, not only through individual acts of projection but also through iterative, emergent processes that are 'imperceptible as events'[43] but nonetheless have future-making effects. Significantly, because the approach attends to *how* futures and their socio-political effects are achieved (rather than assuming their coherence or stability), it is open to diverse and often contradictory possibilities. Thus the futurescape is not simply a list of temporal features to be ticked off one-by-one. Instead, it describes a critical sensibility that invites us to question how the future animates the contemporary condition without reducing away its more elusive qualities. For example, the future may be encountered as a particular mood, feeling, ambience or other collective affect that presses upon the present. Hence the terms 'futurescape' and 'futurity' are used not as academic-speak for 'the future' but to signify the actual diversity and messiness of temporal features that are often assumed to be straightforwardly accounted for.[44]

Futurescapes and other integrative approaches like it have been influential beyond their disciplinary origins,[45] but they have yet to find their way into the bulk of legal research.[46] Here, I want to suggest planning law as one possible entry point. There are already examples of critical engagement with futures in planning theory.[47] A logical next step is to ensure that planning rules and regulations figure more prominently in those debates to avoid the law being treated as an incidental issue or afterthought.

It is not a new problem that legal analysis can be weakly represented in or missing altogether from multidisciplinary spaces for social inquiry. That is certainly the case with futures studies, and it is also a claim made about the philosophical and theoretical foundations of planning. Patrick McAuslan began his seminal book *The Ideologies of Planning Law* with the observation that: 'Alone of all the disciplines involved in land use planning in the United Kingdom, law is considered to be, at least by its practitioners and publicists, in no need of a fundamental examination.'[48] More than 40 years on, it remains a motivating force for planning law scholarship. And so, one reason for encouraging critical reflection on planning law from a futures-perspective is that it arises out of a commitment among academics to chip away at planning law's reputation for being too technical, or worse, too mundane, to be of interest to theorists. There is something be gained from 'taking on the technicalities',[49] as Riles compellingly puts it, so that legal doctrine and argumentation may be reclaimed or rediscovered for theory.[50] In that spirit, connecting planning law and futures theory is not an occasion for lament, but rather an opportunity for exploring the possibilities that the two fields offer each other.

Finding futures in planning law

To illustrate how the approach just outlined could be put to use, I will draw on two different aspects of the English planning regime as applied to hydraulic fracturing, or 'fracking', for unconventional oil and gas such as shale gas. They are: the role of the statutory development plan in determining planning applications, and the scope of the Secretary of State's powers to call-in applications and recover appeals. Although the illustrations differ in their legal particularities, each addresses the future not as a passive object of governance, but as an active form of legality that produces legal meaning and effect. The purpose is not to claim any generalisable findings, as that would be impossible from such a narrow base. Instead the example is intended to raise more questions, and by doing so, to start a conversation about the directions that this type of analysis could take.

The development of unconventional oil and gas, typically shale gas, provides an intensely futural context in which to ground the discussion, because it involves 'heroic' future narratives of technological innovation;[51] promises of a cleaner, cheaper and more secure energy supply;[52] fears about the short- and long-term consequences of the drilling technique itself and of prospective shale gas exploitation;[53] and framings of shale gas a key part of the UK's efforts to meet its 2050 emissions reduction target and interim carbon budgets,[54] and as a 'bridging fuel' to a greener future.[55] This is borne out in conflicts over the siting of shale gas operations, which expose the diverging ways in which participants in the planning process make sense of time. As Anna Szolucha demonstrates, the grant of planning permission for exploratory shale gas works at Preston New Road, Lancashire, invoked very different modes of time-reckoning – for example, an accelerated capitalist temporality built on the promise of a new future of progress and growth, compared with the temporal tactics adopted by protestors to slow down the construction and operation of the drilling site.[56]

Planning disputes can be especially revealing of the multiple and competing futures of any given place. It is more usual, however, to see disputes characterised as conflicts between localised 'not-in-my-backyard' politics and the broader public interest. No doubt, a critical source of disagreement in the planning and regulation of shale gas fracking has been the different scalar frames employed in defining the problem and proposing its resolution. Chris Hilson has carefully examined how certain scalar frames have come to dominate (for example the local risks of fracking weighed against the national need for energy supply) while other such frames have been repressed or filtered out of the system altogether (for example the global climate consequences of fossil fuel extraction).[57] In this sense, planning law serves as a 'funnel'[58] for arguments about which scales are most important for any given decision. But planning law also funnels and filters different temporal relations, including of course different orientations to, imaginations of and engagements with possible futures.

An obvious meeting point for planning law and the future is the statutory development plan. The drilling operations associated with fracking amount to 'development' and therefore require planning permission from the local mineral planning authority.[59] It is a central tenet of the local planning regime that applications for planning permission must be determined in accordance with the development plan, unless material considerations indicate otherwise.[60] As discussed in Chapter 2, the development plan is prepared by the local planning authority (LPA), and sets out a vision and a framework for development in the authority's area. The development plan must include policies on the LPA's strategic priorities,[61] and make 'sufficient provision'[62] for a number of key land uses, such as housing, community facilities, the conservation and enhancement of the natural, built and historic environment, and, importantly for current purposes, the provision of minerals and energy.

A question that has arisen in the determination of planning applications for fracking operations is how to apply development plans which include policies on mineral resources, but which make no specific provision for the development of shale gas. The issue in such circumstances is whether relevant policies in the development plan are to be regarded as 'absent', 'silent' (the terminology used in previous planning policy[63]) or 'out-of-date'.[64] If so, a weighted balance, commonly referred to as a 'tilted' balance (discussed in the context of housing by Carolyn Abbot and by Maria Lee in their chapters), applies, whereby permission should be granted unless protective policies in the National Planning Policy Framework (NPPF) provide a 'clear reason' for refusal, or the adverse impacts would 'significantly and demonstrably outweigh the benefits'.[65] This tilted approach seems both to sidestep the development plan and to require something more demanding than the standard balancing exercise to displace the presumption in favour of sustainable development.

Whether the tilted balance is triggered is a matter of planning judgment, not of legal reasoning, although the courts have clarified how the triggers operate. For example, a development plan that lacks policies *specifically* targeted at the type of development under consideration (such as fracking) is not automatically considered out-of-date (or absent or silent, as in previous policy), and provided the policies of the development plan are still 'relevant' to the decision to grant or refuse planning permission, the tilted balance will not apply.[66] Thus, in a decision on fracking, a development plan may be considered relevant where it includes policies on mineral resources and development management generally, which do not explicitly address shale gas or fracking but which nevertheless have a real role to play in the determination of the application.[67] Those general policies can be seen as offering a future-proof framework to deal with technological innovation not envisaged or planned at the time of their inception. For example, it has been noted that 'although a local development document is intended to present as a coherent suite of policies, that objective is not inconsistent with the inclusion of some environmental policies being intended and designed to operate on a longer time scale than that which may be contemplated by the plan period'.[68]

There is a further point, which is that judgments over the relevance of a local development plan, including through its classification as in-date or out-of-date, shape how the future is ushered into the present. Such classificatory practices determine whether and with what consequence future risks and benefits are assessed against each other, through the application of either a standard or tilted balance. These different future-oriented logics operate with powerful performative force to organise how planning decisions are made and reasoned; they govern the 'knowledge moves'[69] entailed in determining the consistency or otherwise of a development with the plan; they set the threshold for tipping the balance against approval (for example whether adverse impacts 'significantly and demonstrably' outweigh, or just outweigh, the benefits); and they influence the forms of reasoning that decision-makers offer. In this regard, the future enters the present as an organising epistemology,[70] or 'epistemological ordering frame',[71] constraining or enabling certain ways of imagining, projecting and acting ahead of time. This opens up to investigation an array of questions about the contingent interpretive processes (for example 'relevance') and pragmatic steps (for example the engagement or disengagement of the 'presumption in favour') through which certain representations of the future are made effective. In particular, it shows the future not as a category of analysis so much as a category of practice, highlighting the need to account for the processes through which specific configurations of the future are assembled.[72]

It is these processual features of future-making – for instance, the sense-making practices and discursive resources relied upon in applying non-specific policies of a statutory local development plan to proposals for new technological developments – that a futurescapes approach takes as its starting point. The approach is less concerned with what we 'know' as the future, than with the work – in this context, the often-routine legal work – that goes into producing and sustaining particular ideas about the future in social and legal consciousness and practice. As the discussion so far has suggested, a concept as rudimentary as 'relevance' creates a particular temporal dynamic, in that the applicability of the tilted balance depends on the relationship between the proposed future development and pre-existing policies of the local plan. It offers at least a sense of the past, present and future as aspects of each other, rather than as contrasting 'types' of time, which offers a promising broadening of the temporal features examinable in planning law.

Opening up planning law studies to broader conceptualisations of futurity raises the possibility that futures are envisioned, regularised and practised in a wider range of planning law provisions than has been appreciated. As a result, provisions which are not explicitly futural, or which are so routine and unremarkable that their futures-work goes without saying, become new contenders for analysis. Therefore, in order to take planning law seriously as a site of future-making, there is a case for focusing on the numerous less obvious ways that futures are anticipated and acted upon.

In that respect, a useful illustration is offered by the Secretary of State's statutory powers to call-in planning applications and recover planning appeals for her own determination, specifically in the context of shale gas operations involving fracking. The illustration is historical, given that the UK Government has now withdrawn its support for fracking, but it gives an idea of some of the avenues waiting to be explored in investigating how – by which legal mechanisms and temporal modes – planning law operates through futures that, by definition, may never actually happen. In Juliet Davis's words, planning histories 'are inescapably histories of futures'.[73] As will be shown, the Secretary of State's intervention in planning decisions has come to be understood predominantly in terms of jurisdictional scale, even though the administration and exercise of such ministerial power can also involve rather specific invocations and institutionalised practices of future-making. The discussion below begins to bring out some of the distinctive insights that a futurescapes perspective can offer legal analysis in this setting.

Supplementing scalar analyses with a futurescapes approach

The Secretary of State has various statutory powers to intervene in the planning process. They include default powers enabling the Secretary of State to prepare or revise a local development plan, if she considers that the LPA is failing properly to carry out its functions in that regard.[74] In respect of planning applications, the Secretary of State may give a direction restricting the grant of permission by an LPA, for a specified period or until the direction is lifted.[75] She may give a direction for a development to be treated as a project of national significance requiring a development consent order, as opposed to local planning permission.[76] She may issue guidance on matters such as the community infrastructure levy – a tax on development to fund the infrastructure it will rely on, which LPAs must take into account in adopting the levy.[77] This is just to name a few of the devices that allow for ministerial involvement in local policy formulation and decision-making, and the list could go on. The existence of such powers reflects central government's historical importance in securing consistency in the execution of national planning policy at the local level, as well as its continued role in providing strategic direction, oversight and coordination across the planning system.[78] It explains why the planning system has been described as hierarchical,[79] because although LPAs operate with a degree of autonomy, that autonomy is restricted by parameters set centrally.

My focus here is on one aspect of central government intervention: the ability of the Secretary of State to exercise jurisdiction over individual decisions, by 'calling-in' planning applications[80] and 'recovering' planning appeals[81] for her own determination. It may seem odd to include this example at all, given that the powers of call-in and recovery are intended to be used only sparingly. In the vast majority of cases, planning applications are determined by the LPA, and appeals are determined by the Planning Inspectorate (PINS).[82] Even at their height, the overall proportions of called-in applications and appeals recovered by the Secretary of State have been small.[83] The data reveal a more complicated picture – for instance, ministerial intervention has a higher prevalence in respect of certain types of development (for example onshore wind turbines),[84] and likewise can fluctuate depending on the minister in charge.[85] An example of a called-in application can be seen in Abbot's chapter in this volume. Altogether, though, the incidence of call-in and recovery is low, and the Secretary of State's invocation of those powers has aroused little academic interest among both lawyers and planners, except as a general indication of the relationship between central and local government.

The reason that call-in and recovery are viewed in this manner – as a proxy for central-local relations – is that they raise questions about the appropriate balance of power in the planning process, and meet with strong criticism when the balance is felt to have tipped too much in the direction of central government.[86] This has intensified in recent years, following the passage of the Localism Act 2011 and repeated calls for call-in and recovery to be used only in exceptional circumstances, for cases involving significant national or wider than local issues.[87] Controversy surrounding ministerial intervention is seen as epitomising a deep tension in the scalar logics of planning, discussed in more detail in Lee's chapter, in particular the 'vertical topography of power'[88] and the difficulties of reconciling different spatial orders operating within the same system – 'national', 'local', 'neighbourhood', 'grassroots'. Therefore, the Secretary of State's rights of call-in and recovery, when discussed at all, are treated as specific aspects of a broader debate about demarcations of space and scale.

Taken in the context of pathbreaking studies in geography and allied areas (such as legal geography and political ecology) on the scalar structuration of the state,[89] the call-in of planning applications and recovery of appeals can be understood as scalar practices that organise power relations between different layers of government. From that angle, it might be observed that there is nothing innate about a project's classification as a development of 'major importance' and 'more than local significance' – those designations are constructed; that is, they are conceptualised and made effective through routine bureaucratic practices (for example Written Ministerial Statements, planning guidance) and uses of discretionary authority (provided for by statute) to secure the legitimacy of 'top-down' state actions. Focusing on the separation and hierarchy between 'higher' and 'lower' scales of practice, and more precisely on the work that scale does as a politico-legal device, considerably enriches the analysis of contemporary practices of government. But there are other ways of approaching the matter, which can supplement spatial and scalar perspectives.

In particular, the powers of call-in and recovery may lend themselves, in as yet untested ways, to an analysis of the *futures* they envision and act upon. Call-in and recovery are not intuitively the most obvious example for thinking about how planning law operates through different future-orientations – that is a deliberate move on my part to show that non-obvious sites are also where futures take shape, in ways that may otherwise escape scrutiny.

Future-orientations of jurisdiction

To begin with, a futures-perspective may help to bring clarity to the ways in which the Secretary of State's statutory powers to determine planning applications and appeals can induce or amplify particular orientations towards the future. The focus here is on the future-orientations that give the jurisdiction its form, setting the conditions of possibility for the distribution of governing authority and the manner of its use. These future-orientations are an additional dimension of what might be described as the 'often hidden architectures . . . of discretion',[90] structuring the operations of law and imposing limits to legal order, yet kept out of the analytical frame because of the tendency in this context, and more generally, to conceptualise jurisdiction in terms of administrative boundaries and the territorial allocation of authority between different levels of government.[91] The point is that the assertion of jurisdiction can also be viewed as an act of constructing, giving meaning to, and orienting towards futures that are perceived as inevitable and experienced as 'real', regardless of whether those futures actually come to pass.

Continuing with the example of shale gas operations involving fracking, a futurescapes approach – one that involves seeing the future not just as an outcome but also a process and an affective state – provides a useful addition to analyses of jurisdiction and power that are shaped onto the more conventional axis of scale. In September 2015, in a Written Ministerial Statement to Parliament, the Secretary of State for Communities and Local Government announced two temporary changes to the criteria for call-in and recovery. First, where an LPA was identified as 'underperforming' in respect of planning applications for onshore oil and gas, including shale gas, the Secretary of State would 'actively consider exercising the power under section 77 of the Town and Country Planning Act (TCPA) 1990 to call-in the applications'. Secondly, the recovery criteria were expanded so that the Secretary of State could give 'particular scrutiny' to appeals against refusals of planning permission for exploring and developing shale gas.[92] Such appeals would be 'treated as a priority for urgent resolution'.[93]

It is noteworthy that the amendments created separate and distinct criteria for shale gas projects, because such changes were not strictly necessary. The Secretary of State's prior discretion to call-in applications and recover appeals was already very wide, and arguably unspecific enough to encompass shale gas projects without any need for amendment. The general criteria list the sorts of situations where a decision may be called-in or recovered because it involves issues of 'more than local significance' – for instance, where the project gives rise to substantial regional or national controversy, or where it raises important or novel issues of development control and/or legal difficulties. Although these are not exhaustive of the factors that motivate and legitimate ministerial intervention, it is not a stretch to claim that shale gas operations could easily have come within the scope of the criteria in their original form.[94] So there was clearly a perceived need to signal that planning decisions regarding shale gas projects were exceptional, even more so than other called-in applications and recovered appeals – which, given their generally low incidence, were themselves an exceptional feature of the normal planning process. The singling out of shale gas projects made them doubly aberrant, *doubly exceptional*, and as an expression of the potency and reach of the

Secretary of State's jurisdiction, this instituted a particular relation to the future – one organised around the temporal logics of emergency.

A range of work in critical geography, political theory and related fields has charted the role of emergency as an indispensable technique of governance in contemporary liberal democratic states.[95] One reason the notion of governing through emergency holds appeal is that it offers an alternative to accounts of the future as an abstract, other or even absent time. This is especially pertinent in the context of land use planning, where the future is encountered in innumerable ways and does not comfortably fit narratives of a future 'out there', waiting to be measured, commodified, inhabited. Emergencies scholarship looks instead at how the future is already emergent in the present, full of tendencies and just-forming potential, building affective registers or 'atmospheres'[96] that induce or compel action in the current moment. In this light, emergency does not denote a single temporal sequence, rather it depends on the co-existence of multiple temporalities through which the future is disclosed and related to.

Exceptionality is one such temporality, which works by diagnosing events as rare, time-limited, atypical and therefore in need of some sort of extraordinary governance response. As Ben Anderson and colleagues have comprehensively shown, the 'state of exception' has become so frequently invoked that it is often not exceptional at all, and yet it remains an insistent force in the expression, exercise and legitimation of political and legal authority.[97] In part that force stems from the idea that without intervention the future might be otherwise, but it can be further intensified by a sense of urgency that necessitates action now. Together the temporalities of exceptionality and urgency are characterised by the presence of what Anderson describes as an 'on-rushing future'[98] and an imperative to act quickly, creating the conditions for 'lightning strikes'[99] of state power. They are inseparable from a temporality of hope that the future is alterable, and that 'though the outcome of an event of situation is uncertain, correct action may make a difference, and that which is threatened might be averted'.[100] These insights offer a different take on styles of governing, in that they capture how particular futures and futural dispositions – not just scales and spatialities – become folded into claims of jurisdiction.

This provides a basis for revisiting the example of the Secretary of State's powers of call-in and recovery – as a way of exemplifying the broader contention that there is scope for planning law to feature more centrally in efforts to understand the future as an integral, rather than an additional, part of any analysis of power. Indeed the re-assertion of the

Secretary of State's jurisdiction in respect of shale gas operations could be read as contributing to the performative constitution and experience of the future – or rather of multiple, disparate (urgent, exceptional, hopeful) futures, 'held together'[101] by their not-yet-ness and given real-time purpose by becoming the locus of debate.[102] The prefix 're' (re-assertion of jurisdiction) is intentional, to remind that planning legislation already conferred on the Secretary of State very wide discretionary powers of intervention, wide enough to cover shale gas operations – not just in principle but also in practice. Hence the simple bureaucratic act of extending the call-in and recovery criteria explicitly to include shale gas operations offered a means through which ministerial power could be symbolically re-affirmed. Thereafter, the debate became not about whether, but about when and under what circumstances shale gas exploration would be approved.[103] The fact that the shale gas industry did not, in the end, develop as the UK Government had planned is of little consequence. It does not alter the fact that, whether or not anticipated futures materialise, their effects can still be felt in the present.[104]

The suggestion here is that greater scrutiny of the involvement of distinctively legal mechanisms (jurisdiction being a classic example) in engagements with the future may open up some promising lines of inquiry into the forms of authority and legality that follow from invoking specific future-orientations. The 'double exceptionality' of shale gas projects, for instance, is justified on the basis of emergency claims that time for action is running out, through what Adi Ophir calls 'discursive means of catastrophization' which work to 'designate objects to be observed, described, measured and analysed, predicted and interfered with'.[105] These discursive processes construct the future, an imminently catastrophic or threatening future, as the thing to be governed, but more than that they provide powerful narratives and rhetorical devices that 'tacitly authorize those in power to respond'.[106] In this context, the thing to be governed is the 'underperforming' LPA that is perceived to be too slow in deciding shale gas applications,[107] and so ministerial intervention is seen as a necessary means of averting threats of national energy insecurity, missed economic opportunity and so on. But the earmarking of shale gas projects as not just a legitimate but also as a necessary target for the Secretary of State's exercise of her statutory powers helps to create the conditions in which particular future-orientations (exceptionality, urgency, hope) take hold, becoming institutionally stabilised and publicly performed.[108]

One way of taking this further might be to examine the future-making effects of the Secretary of State's jurisdiction on decision-making in the local planning regime, before the powers of call-in and recovery have even been exercised. The question this raises, which can be addressed empirically, is whether and in what ways the potential for ministerial intervention influences how an LPA determines a planning application, or how PINS determines an appeal. It is clear that the Government's policy on shale gas, expressed in the same Written Statement that amended the criteria for calling-in applications and recovering appeals, is capable of being a material consideration when deciding permission.[109] Less clear are the more subtle ways in which the *prospect* of call-in or recovery might shape how local planning decisions are taken, as suggested also in Chapter 2. These effects are more likely to be missed when the powers of call-in and recovery are addressed as issues of jurisdictional scale. The trouble with conventional scalar analysis, Mariana Valverde has observed,[110] is that it is underpinned by a zero-sum understanding of jurisdiction, which in this context means that *either* the Secretary of State has jurisdiction *or* the LPA does. But the realities of governance are not so clear-cut, as is also apparent from Lee's chapter below. Central and local government may often be in tension or conflict but they are not opposites – their functions and powers can combine, overlap and interact in various ways. Thus there may be value in examining the consequences of the Secretary of State's powers of call-in and recovery for local planning, specifically when those powers are not exercised but are anticipated, pre-empted and experienced as 'looming or pressing in'.[111] It suggests at least that the Secretary of State's jurisdiction can also be studied as a temporal realm of expectation and imminence.

Concluding remarks

The purpose here has been to think about the sorts of questions and areas of investigation that may be opened up by approaching the analysis of planning law from a futures perspective. Too often the future is treated as an incidental aspect of law, as a backdrop against which legal rules and processes play out. Yet there is work to be done to understand the many ways in which law actively engages, and oftentimes *produces*, various expectations, promises and fears about what will come. By making futures an explicit focus of attention, it becomes possible to trace the different roles of planning law in drawing the future into the present, whether through practices of seeing and knowing (for example assessing costs and benefits), evidential thresholds (for example 'significantly and demonstrably outweigh'), ideational frames (for example sustainable development), material trajectories (for example the presumption in favour of development), affective experiences (for example urgency, hope), or some other future-oriented modality. The reason for using a futurescapes approach in this context is that it nudges us away from any idea that the relationship between planning law and the future is a straightforward one. Indeed, the '-scape' element gets at the multi-layered complexity of future-making, which is as evident in law as it is in other socio-political domains – the difference being that mainstream legal research on futures is limited and sporadic.

My aim in not only highlighting but also pulling together these various strands is to encourage a move away from the definitional question 'what or when is the future?' and to focus instead on how the future – as a logic, a reason, an orientation, an affect – is made effective and authoritative through specific legal means. In this respect, the discussion of planning law provisions applicable to shale gas operations suggests that it may be just as important to look at the routine or less obviously futural aspects of legal practice as it is to consider the headline acts. For example, there is nothing self-evident about the relevance of non-specific policies of a development plan to a proposed fracking site. As a matter of planning judgment it entails a degree of temporal organisation, to establish whether the new development falls within the remit of the plan, and this determines how the future is related to – as a continuity of experience or sharp rupture with the past-present, for instance. Similarly, shale gas-specific amendments to the criteria for calling-in applications and recovering appeals involve contestable future claims. The point, however, is not to suggest that characterisations of shale gas projects as exceptional, urgent and hopeful are necessarily a distortion of reality. It is to show that those characterisations also carry out some of the jurisdictional work of 'bringing' shale gas projects 'to law',[112] by framing such development as not just amenable to ministerial intervention but in need of it. These are among planning law's unmarked practices of future-making.

Notes

* I am very grateful for the help and encouragement of Barbara Adam and Antonia Layard.
1. Abram and Weszkalnys 2011, 3. See also e.g. Abram 2014; Zhang 2018; Windemer 2019.
2. Healey 2010, 19.
3. Throgmorton 1992, 17.
4. Davis and Groves 2019.
5. Byrne 2003, 174.
6. Rydin 2011, 9.
7. Adam and Groves 2007. See also e.g. Massumi 2015; Adams, Murphy and Clarke 2009; Anderson 2017.
8. Selin 2008; Coleman 2017.

9. See e.g. Appadurai 2013; Pels 2015; Bryant and Knight 2019; Valentine and Hassoun 2019. For an early, influential call for more focused attention on the future in cultural anthropology, see Munn 1992, esp. 112–16.
10. See e.g. Anderson 2010; Jeffrey and Dyson 2021.
11. See e.g. Davis 2019.
12. Wilkie, Savransky and Rosengarten 2019.
13. Jasanoff and Kim 2015.
14. Adams, Murphy and Clarke 2009, 248.
15. Posner 2000, 573.
16. Greenhouse 1989, 1640.
17. On the descriptive inaccuracies of the 'law lag', for example, see Jasanoff 2007.
18. For critique see Wistrich 2012.
19. For the same observation in anthropology see Munn 1992.
20. Standout examples include Greenhouse 1989; Mawani 2014; Valverde 2015; Grabham 2016; Johns 2016; Corrias and Francot 2018; Beynon-Jones and Grabham 2019; Hilson 2019; Keenan 2019; Chowdhury 2020. This list is by no means exhaustive but it gives a flavour of the rich writing on the topic.
21. See especially Valverde 2015.
22. Khan 2017.
23. See especially Mawani 2014; Valverde 2015; Grabham 2016.
24. Grabham 2010.
25. Riles 2011.
26. Mawani 2014.
27. Keenan 2016; Keenan 2019.
28. Cooper 2020.
29. Boukalas 2021.
30. Munn 1992, 116.
31. Pickering 2004.
32. Husserl 1983; Tavory and Eliasoph 2013.
33. Chakrabarty 2000, 250.
34. Munn 1992, 115.
35. The phrase is borrowed from Massey 1994, 4.
36. Adam 1995, 12.
37. Adam 1998.
38. Adam 2008.
39. See also Massey 2005; Valverde 2015.
40. Adam 1998, 54.
41. Adam 2006.
42. The phrase is borrowed from Graham 2010, 10.
43. Anderson et al 2020, 631.
44. For inspiration in a different context see McLeod 2017, 13.
45. See e.g. Rindova and Martins 2021.
46. See, however, note 20 above.
47. See e.g. Abram and Weszkalnys 2011; Abram 2014; Zhang 2018; Davis 2019; Davis and Groves 2019; Windemer 2019.
48. McAuslan 1980, 1.
49. Riles 2005.
50. See also Valverde 2009.
51. Janda and Topouzi 2015, 517.
52. Davey 2013.
53. Committee on Climate Change 2016.
54. Department for Business, Energy and Industrial Strategy (DBEIS) 2019.
55. Parliamentary Office of Science and Technology 2011.
56. Szolucha 2018.
57. Hilson 2015.
58. Valverde 2012, 12.
59. Town and Country Planning Act (TCPA) 1990, section 57.
60. Planning and Compulsory Purchase Act (PCPA) 2004, section 38(6); see also TCPA 1990, section 70(2).

61. PCPA 2004, section 19(1B)–(1C).
62. NPPF 2021, [20].
63. Department for Communities and Local Government (DCLG) 2012, [14].
64. Ministry of Housing, Communities and Local Government (MHCLG) 2021, [11(d)].
65. MHCLG 2021, [11(d)].
66. *Paul Newman New Homes Ltd v Secretary of State for Housing, Communities and Local Government* [2021] EWCA Civ 15, Andrews LJ, [37]–[40]. In *Hopkins Homes Ltd v Secretary of State for Communities and Local Government* [2017] UKSC 37; [2017] 1 WLR 1865 the Supreme Court also clarified that even if the relevant policies are out-of-date, they may still be relevant as a matter of planning judgment.
67. DCLG 2016, [24].
68. *Peel Investments (North) Ltd v Secretary of State for Housing, Communities and Local Government* [2020] EWCA Civ 1175; [2021] 2 All ER 581, Baker LJ, [68].
69. Valverde 2007, 83.
70. Moore 2008.
71. Marston, Jones and Woodward 2005, 420.
72. See e.g. Davis and Groves 2019.
73. Davis 2019, 878.
74. PCPA 2004, section 27.
75. Town and Country Planning (Development Management Procedure) (England) (Order) 2015, regulation 31(1).
76. Planning Act 2008, section 35.
77. Planning Act 2008, section 41.
78. See e.g. House of Commons Library 2016.
79. Moore 1997, 10; Mark Tewdar-Jones 1999, 244.
80. TCPA 1990, section 77.
81. TCPA 1990, section 79.
82. See e.g. Planning Inspectorate (PINS) 2021–2.
83. For instance, the number of called-in applications reached 34 in April–June 2021 (provisional data at time of writing), and the number of recovered appeals peaked in 2013/14 at 163 applications. To put that into context, PINS made 16,980 appeal decisions between May 2020 and May 2021. See PINS 2021.
84. See e.g. Cowell and Devine-Wright 2018, 510.
85. See e.g. Wilding 2019.
86. See e.g. Willmore 2017.
87. Barker 2006, [3.41] and [3.55].
88. Ferguson and Gupta 2002, 983.
89. See e.g. Brenner 2001; Ferguson and Gupta 2002; Swyngedouw and Heynen 2003; Moore 2008; Valverde 2009; MacLeavy and Harrison 2010; MacKinnon 2011; Bennett and Layard 2015.
90. Khan 2017, 6.
91. See especially Kaushal 2015.
92. See Hansard 2015.
93. Rudd 2015.
94. In fact, the Secretary of State in recovering an appeal on shale gas exploration has previously justified the recovery of jurisdiction on the basis of the 'more than local significance' criterion, not the criterion specific to shale gas. See DCLG 2016, [2].
95. See e.g. Hussain 2003; Aradau and van Munster 2011; Adey, Anderson and Graham 2015; Massumi 2015; Anderson 2017.
96. McCormack 2015.
97. Anderson et al 2020.
98. Anderson 2017, 470.
99. Massumi 2015.
100. Anderson 2017, 470–1.
101. Brown et al 2012.
102. Weszkalnys 2014.
103. Stokes 2016.
104. Adams, Murphy and Clarke 2009.
105. Ophir 2010.

106. Vázquez-Arroyo 2013, 742.
107. Hansard 2015.
108. Jasanoff 2015, 4.
109. See e.g. DCLG 2016, [28].
110. Valverde 2009; Valverde 2021. See also Blomley 2016.
111. Bryant 2020, 21.
112. The phrasing here is adapted from Dorsett and McVeigh 2012, particularly chapter 6.

References

Abram, Simone (2014). 'The Time it Takes: Temporalities of Planning', *Journal of the Royal Anthropological Institute* 20: 129–47.
Abram, Simone and Gisa Weszkalnys (2011). 'Anthropologies of Planning – Temporality, Imagination, and Ethnography', *Focaal – Journal of Global and Historical Anthropology* 61: 3–18.
Adam, Barbara (1995). *Timewatch: The Social Analysis of Time*. Cambridge: Polity Press.
Adam, Barbara (1998). *Timescapes of Modernity: The Environment and Invisible Hazards*. Abingdon: Routledge.
Adam, Barbara (2006). 'Futurescapes: Challenge for Social and Management Sciences'. Retroscapes and Futurescapes – Temporal Tensions in Organizations International Conference, Palazzo d'Aumale, Terrasini, 21–23 June.
Adam, Barbara (2008). 'Of Timescapes, Futurescapes and Timeprints'. Lüneburg University, 17 June.
Adam, Barbara and Chris Groves (2007). *Future Matters: Action, Knowledge, Ethics*. Leiden: Brill.
Adams, Vincanne and Michelle Murphy and Adele E. Clarke (2009). 'Anticipation: Technoscience, Life, Affect, Temporality', *Subjectivity* 28: 246–65.
Adey, Peter, Ben Anderson and Stephen Graham (2015). 'Governing Emergencies: Beyond Exceptionality', *Theory, Culture and Society* 32: 3–17.
Anderson, Ben (2010). 'Preemption, Precaution, Preparedness: Anticipatory Action and Future Geography', *Progress in Human Geography* 34: 777–98.
Anderson, Ben (2017). 'Emergency Futures: Exception, Urgency, Interval, Hope', *The Sociological Review* 65: 463–77.
Anderson, Ben et al (2020). 'Slow Emergencies: Temporality and the Racialized Biopolitics of Emergency Governance', *Progress in Human Geography* 44(4): 621–39.
Appadurai, Arjun (2013). *The Future as Cultural Fact: Essays on the Global Condition*. London: Verso.
Aradau, Claudia and Rens van Munster (2011). *Politics of Catastrophe: Genealogies of the Unknown*. Abingdon: Routledge.
Barker, Kate (2006). *Barker Review of Land Use Planning. Final Report – Recommendations*. London: HMSO.
Bennett, Luke and Antonia Layard (2015). 'Legal Geography: Becoming Spatial Detectives', *Geography Compass* 9: 406–22.
Beynon-Jones, Siân and Emily Grabham (eds) (2019). *Law and Time*. Abingdon: Routledge.
Blomley, Nicholas (2016). 'What Sort of a Legal Space is a City?'. In *Urban Interstices: The Aesthetics and the Politics of the In-Between*, edited by Andrea Mubi Brighenti, 1–20. Abingdon: Routledge.
Boukalas, Christos (2021). 'No Future: Pre-emption, Temporal Sovereignty and Hegemonic Implosion', *Constellations* 28: 252–68.
Brenner, Neil (2001). 'The Limits to Scale? Methodological Reflections on Scalar Structuration', *Progress in Human Geography* 25: 591–614.
Brown, Gavin et al (2012). 'Holding the Future Together: Towards a Theorisation of the Spaces and Times of Transition', *Environment and Planning A* 44: 1607–23.
Bryant, Rebecca (2020). 'The Anthropology of the Future', *Etnofoor* 32: 11–22.
Bryant, Rebecca and Daniel M. Knight (2019). *The Anthropology of the Future*. Cambridge: Cambridge University Press.
Byrne, David (2003). 'Complexity Theory and Planning Theory: A Necessary Encounter', *Planning Theory* 2: 171–8.
Chakrabarty, Dipesh (2000). *Provincializing Europe: Postcolonial Thought and Historical Difference*. Princeton, NJ: Princeton University Press.

Chowdhury, Tanzil (2020). *Time, Temporality and Legal Judgment*. Abingdon: Routledge.
Coleman, Rebecca (2017). 'A Sensory Sociology of the Future: Affect, Hope and Inventive Methodologies', *The Sociological Review* 65: 525–43.
Committee on Climate Change (2016). *Onshore Petroleum: The Comparability of UK Onshore Petroleum with Meeting the UK's Carbon Budgets*.
Cooper, Davina (2020). 'Towards an Adventurous Institutional Politics: The Prefigurative "As If" and the Reposing of What's Real', *Sociological Review* 68: 893–916.
Corrias, Luigi and Lyana Francot (eds) (2018). *Temporal Boundaries of Law and Politics: Time Out of Joint*. Abingdon: Routledge.
Cowell, Richard and Patrick Devine-Wright (2018). 'A "Delivery-Democracy Dilemma"? Mapping and Explaining Policy Change for Public Engagement with Energy Infrastructure', *Journal of Environmental Policy and Planning* 20: 499–517.
Davey, Ed (2013). 'Speech: The Myths and Realities of Shale Gas Exploration'. The Royal Society, London.
Davis, Juliet (2019). 'Futurescapes of Urban Regeneration: Ten Years of Design for the Unfolding Urban Legacy of London's Olympic Games, 2008–2018', *Planning Perspectives* 34: 877–901.
Davis, Juliet and Chris Groves (2019). 'City/Future in the Making: Masterplanning London's Olympic Legacy as Anticipatory Assemblage', *Futures* 109: 13–23.
Department for Business, Energy and Industrial Strategy (n.d.). Guidance on Fracking: Developing Shale Gas in the UK, available at https://www.gov.uk/government/publications/about-shale-gas-and-hydraulic-fracturing-fracking/developing-shale-oil-and-gas-in-the-uk (accessed 12 June 2022).
Department for Communities and Local Government (2012). *National Planning Policy Framework*.
Department for Communities and Local Government (2016). Recovered Appeals: Cuadrilla Bowland Ltd and Cuadrilla Elswick Ltd, available at https://assets.publishing.service.gov.uk/government/uploads/system/uploads/attachment_data/file/778144/16-10-06_DL_Cuadrilla.pdf (accessed 12 June 2022).
Dorsett, Shaunnagh and Shaun McVeigh (2012). *Jurisdiction*. Abingdon: Routledge.
Ferguson, James and Akhil Gupta (2002), 'Spatializing States: Toward an Ethnography of Neoliberal Governmentality', *American Ethnologist* 29: 981–1002.
Grabham, Emily (2010). 'Governing Permanence: Trans Subjects, Time, and the Gender Recognition Act', *Social and Legal Studies* 19: 107–26.
Grabham, Emily (2016). *Brewing Legal Times: Things, Forms, and the Enactments of Law*. Toronto: University of Toronto Press.
Graham, Stephen (2010). 'When Infrastructures Fail'. In *Disrupted Cities: When Infrastructure Fails*, edited by Stephen Graham, 1–26. New York: Routledge.
Greenhouse, Carol J. (1989). 'Just in Time: Temporality and the Cultural Legitimation of Law', *Yale Law Journal* 98: 1631–51.
Hansard (2015), House of Commons Debates, 16 September, vol 599 c32WS.
Haughton, Graham and Phil Allmendinger (2013). 'Spatial Planning and the New Localism', *Planning Practice and Research* 28: 1–5.
Healey, Patsy (2010). *Making Better Places: The Planning Project in the Twenty-First Century*. London: Red Globe Press.
Hilson, Chris (2015). 'Framing Fracking: Which Frames Are Heard in English Planning and Environmental Policy and Practice?', *Journal of Environmental Law* 27: 177–202.
Hilson, Chris (2019). 'Framing Time in Climate Change Litigation', *Oñati Socio-Legal Series* 9, 361–79.
House of Commons Library (2016). *Comparison of the Planning Systems in the Four UK Countries*.
Hussain, Nasser (2003). *The Jurisprudence of Emergency: Colonialism and the Rule of Law*. Ann Arbor, MI: University of Michigan Press.
Husserl, Edmund (1983). *Ideas Pertaining to a Pure Phenomenology and to a Phenomenological Philosophy*. Translated by F. Kersten. The Hague: Martinus Nijhoff.
Janda, Kathryn B. and Marina Topouzi (2015). 'Telling Tales: Using Stories to Remake Energy Policy', *Building Research and Information* 43: 516–33.
Jasanoff, Sheila (2007). 'Making Order: Law and Science in Action'. In *Handbook of Science and Technology Studies*, edited by Edward J. Hackett et al, 761–86. Cambridge, MA: MIT Press, 3rd edn.
Jasanoff, Sheila (2015). 'Future Imperfect: Science, Technology, and the Imaginations of Modernity'. In *Dreamscapes of Modernity: Sociotechnical Imaginaries and the Fabrication of Power*, edited by Sheila Jasanoff and Sang-Hyun Kim, 1–33. Chicago, IL: University of Chicago Press.

Jasanoff, Sheila and Sang-Hyun Kim (eds) (2015). *Dreamscapes of Modernity: Sociotechnical Imaginaries and the Fabrication of Power*. Chicago, IL: University of Chicago Press.

Jeffrey, Craig and Jane Dyson (2021), 'Geographies of the Future: Prefigurative Politics', *Progress in Human Geography* 45: 641–58.

Johns, Fleur (2016). 'The Temporal Rivalries of Human Rights', *Indiana Journal of Global Legal Studies* 23: 39–60.

Kaushal, Asha (2015). 'The Politics of Jurisdiction', *Modern Law Review* 78: 759–92.

Keenan, Sarah (2016). 'Smoke, Curtains and Mirrors: The Production of Race Through Time and Title Registration', *Law and Critique* 28: 87–108.

Keenan, Sarah (2019). 'From Historical Chains to Derivative Futures: Title Registries as Time Machines', *Social and Cultural Geography* 20: 283–303.

Khan, Jeffrey S. (2017). 'Geographies of Discretion and the Jurisdictional Imagination', *Political and Legal Anthropology* 40: 5–27.

MacKinnon, Danny (2011). 'Reconstructing Scale: Towards a New Scalar Politics', *Progress in Human Geography* 35: 21–36.

MacLeavy, Julie and John Harrison (2010). 'New State Spatialities: Perspectives on State, Space, and Scalar Geographies', *Antipode* 42: 1–11.

McAuslan, Patrick (1980). *The Ideologies of Planning Law*. Oxford: Pergamon Press.

McCormack, Derek (2015). 'Governing Inflation: Price and Atmospheres of Emergency', *Theory, Culture and Society* 32: 1–24.

McLeod, Julie (2017). 'Marking Time, Making Methods: Temporality and Untimely Dilemmas in the Sociology of Youth and Educational Change', *British Journal of Sociology of Education* 38: 13–25.

Marston, Sallie A., John Paul Jones III and Keith Woodward (2005). 'Human Geography without Scale', *Transactions of the Institute of British Geographers* 30: 416–32.

Massey, Doreen (1994). *Space, Place and Gender*. Cambridge: Polity Press.

Massey, Doreen (2005). *For Space*. London: Sage.

Massumi, Brian (2015). *Ontopower: War, Powers, and the State of Perception*. Durham, NC: Duke University Press.

Mawani, Renisa (2014). 'Law as Temporality: Colonial Politics and Indian Settlers', *UC Irvine Law Review* 4: 65–95.

Ministry of Housing, Communities and Local Government (2021). *National Planning Policy Framework*.

Moore, Adam (2008). 'Rethinking Scale as a Geographical Category: From Analysis to Practice', *Progress in Human Geography* 32: 203–25.

Moore, Victor (1997). *A Practical Approach to Planning Law*. Oxford: Blackstone, 6th edn.

Munn, Nancy D. (1992). 'The Cultural Anthropology of Time: A Critical Essay', *Annual Review of Anthropology* 21: 93–123.

Ophir, Adi (2010). 'The Politics of Catastrophization: Emergency and Exception'. In *Contemporary States of Emergency: The Politics of Military and Humanitarian Interventions*, edited by Didier Fassin and Mariella Pandolfi, 59–88. New York: Zone Books.

Parliamentary Office of Science and Technology (2011). *Unconventional Gas*. PostNote Number 374 April.

Pels, Peter (2015). 'Modern Times: Seven Steps toward an Anthropology of the Future', *Current Anthropology* 56: 779–96.

Pickering, Michael (2004). 'Experience as Horizon: Kosselleck, Expectation and Historical Time', *Cultural Studies* 18: 271–89.

Planning Inspectorate (2021–2). *Quarterly and Annual Volume Statistics Q1 2021 to 2022*, available at https://www.gov.uk/government/statistics/planning-inspectorate-statistics (accessed 12 June 2022).

Posner, Richard A. (2000). 'Past-Dependency, Pragmatism, and Critique of History in Adjudication and Legal Scholarship', *University of Chicago Law Review* 67: 573–606.

Riles, Annelise (2005). 'A New Agenda for the Cultural Study of Law: Taking on the Technicalities', *Buffalo Law Review* 53: 973–1033.

Riles, Annelise (2011). *Collateral Knowledge: Legal Reasoning in the Global Financial Markets*. Chicago, IL: University of Chicago Press, chapter 4.

Rindova, Violina P. and Luis L. Martins (2021). 'Futurescapes: Imagination and Temporal Reorganization in the Design of Strategic Narratives', *Strategic Organization*: 1–25.

Rudd, Amber (2015). Shale Gas and Oil: Policy Statement of the Secretary of State for Energy and Climate Change, 16 September.

Rydin, Yvonne (2011). *The Purpose of Planning: Creating Sustainable Towns and Cities*. Bristol: Policy Press.

Selin, Cynthia (2008). 'The Sociology of the Future: Tracing Stories of Technology and Time', *Sociology Compass* 2: 1878–95.

Stokes, Elen (2016). 'Regulatory Domain and Regulatory Dexterity: Critiquing the UK Governance of "Fracking"', *Modern Law Review* 79: 961–86.

Swyngedouw, Erik and Nikolas C. Heynen (2003). 'Urban Political Ecology, Justice and the Politics of Scale', *Antipode* 35: 898–918.

Szolucha, Anna (2018). 'Anticipating Fracking: Shale Gas Developments and the Politics of Time in Lancashire, UK', *The Extractive Industries and Society* 5: 348–55.

Tavory, Iddo and Nina Eliasoph (2013). 'Coordinating Futures: Toward a Theory of Anticipation', *American Journal of Sociology* 118: 908–42.

Tewdwr-Jones, Mark (1999). 'Discretion, Flexibility and Certainty in British Planning: Emerging Ideological Conflicts and Inherent Political Tensions', *Journal of Planning Education and Research* 18: 244–56.

Throgmorton, James A (1992). 'Planning as Persuasive Storytelling About the Future: Negotiating an Electric Power Rate Settlement in Illinois', *Journal of Planning Education and Research*: 17–31.

Valentine, David and Amelia Hassoun (2019). 'Uncommon Futures', *Annual Review of Anthropology* 48: 243–60.

Valverde, Mariana (2007). 'Theoretical and Methodological Issues in the Study of Legal Knowledge Practices'. In *How Law Knows*, edited by Austin Sarat, Lawrence Douglas and Martha Merrill Umphrey, 72–92. Stanford, CA: Stanford University Press.

Valverde, Mariana (2009). 'Jurisdiction and Scale: Legal "Technicalities" as Resources for Theory', *Social and Legal Studies* 18: 139–57.

Valverde, Mariana (2012). *Everyday Law on the Street: City Governance in an Age of Diversity*. Chicago, IL: University of Chicago Press.

Valverde, Mariana (2015). *Chronotopes of Law: Jurisdiction, Scale and Governance*. Abingdon: Routledge.

Valverde, Mariana (2021). 'Games of Jurisdiction: How Local Governance Realities Challenge the "Creatures of Province" Doctrine', *Journal of Law and Social Policy* 34: 21–38.

Vázquez-Arroyo, Antonio Y. (2013). 'How Not to Learn From Catastrophe: Habermas, Critical Theory and the "Catastrophization" of Political Life', *Political Theory* 41: 738–65.

Weszkalnys, Gisa (2014). 'Anticipating Oil: The Temporal Politics of a Disaster Yet to Come', *The Sociological Review* 62: 211–35.

Wilding, Mark (2019). 'Proportion of Permissions Following Secretary of State Intervention Drops Sharply Under Brokenshire', available at https://www.planningresource.co.uk/article/1589918/proportion-permissions-following-secretary-state-intervention-drops-sharply-brokenshire (accessed 12 June 2022).

Wilkie, Alex, Martin Savransky and Marsha Rosengarten (eds) (2019). *Speculative Research: The Lure of Possible Futures*. Abingdon: Routledge.

Willmore, Chris (2017). 'Planning Law Reform and reconceptualising the Regulation of Land Use'. In *Modern Studies in Property Law: Volume 9*, edited by Heather Conway and Robin Hickey, 257–75. Oxford: Hart Publishing.

Windemer, Rebecca (2019). 'Considering Time in Land Use Planning: An Assessment of End-of-Life Decision Making for Commercially Managed Onshore Wind Schemes', *Land Use Policy* 87: 104024.

Wistrich, Andrew J. (2012). 'The Evolving Temporality of Lawmaking', *Connecticut Law Review* 44: 737–826.

Zhang, Amy Y. (2018). 'Thinking Temporally When Thinking Relationally: Temporality in Relational Place-Making', *Geoforum* 90: 91–9.

9
Slippery scales in planning for housing

Maria Lee

Introduction

Housing is centrally important to the lives of individuals and communities, as well as an extraordinarily complex social and legal challenge. Whilst planning is only part of housing's story, housing is at the centre of planning and debate about planning. Housing has also been at the heart of contests over the appropriate scale of planning, including scale-shifting 'regionalism' and 'localism', and the fluctuating and contested relationship between local and central government. As well as bringing out the complexity and dynamism of scale, housing illustrates both instrumental uses of scale to find 'right' answers, and the limitations of such approaches.

'Scale' is the subject of rich literatures, with a range of concerns and approaches.[1] The social construction (and contestedness) of scale is a key theme:[2] scale is not given, but made. Scale is relational,[3] so that scales must be understood through (including constructed by) their relations to one another (and with other phenomena across scales). Hierarchy, where the local is necessarily secondary to the national, is rendered complex by this social constructedness and relationality,[4] which also confound the metaphor of scales 'nesting' within each other, so that the local is comfortably encompassed within the national.[5]

My primary interest is in planning law and policy, rather than space, capital or even state power, all key issues in scale. Legal scholars are perhaps more accustomed to addressing 'levels' of governance rather than scale,[6] and my language may reflect that, as may my scale choices: local, regional, national, international/transnational/global. These familiar, abstract terms should not imply that the scales should be understood as fixed physical and legal spaces, always neatly separated and hierarchical. The scale at which authority is held in planning for housing is not clearly articulated in English law, but is effortlessly constructed and contested. The spatial constructs the legal, as well as vice versa.[7] For lawyers, scale also resonates with the spatial or territorial[8] and hierarchical[9] aspects of jurisdiction. Jurisdiction is multi-faceted, and does not necessarily map neatly onto scale.[10] It usefully captures, however, the sharing or division of authority within or between scales, and the assertion of decision-making authority by actors at a particular scale.

Discussion of housing commonly pitches a *national* crisis against *local* amenity, with a resulting tension between national need and local resistance. This captures some useful truth, but, as will be discussed below, housing escapes any simple dichotomy of scalar interests. Over-reliance on this dichotomy has led to increased central or national intervention,[11] and relentless pressure on local delivery. One important conclusion (or even starting point) for this chapter is that whilst the local has apparent decision-making responsibility over planning for housing, the central exercises primary authority. Again, this scalar mismatch contains some useful truth, and reflects local planning structures subject to the longstanding centralisation of political power in England. It fails, however, to capture the elusiveness of *both* local place-shaping *and* national control, as well as the irremediable intertwining of local and national, their plurality and their relations with other scales (for example the 'more than' local, 'more than' national).

This chapter interrogates scaling of planning for housing through three categories: interests and impacts; law and policy; and actors. There are no hard lines between these categories, which contribute to the construction of scale for each other. Their purpose is to provide a route through the complexity of the terrain, and to highlight the inadequacy of simple scalar descriptions or prescriptions.

In addition to readings of academic and policy documents, and the general legal framework, I have sought insights from the decision-making process leading to the Supreme Court decision in *Dover v CPRE*.[12] The context is a local authority eager for development, by contrast with the focus of much of the literature on local resistance (although a pro-development local authority does not preclude local resistance). A wealth of documentation is available on the Dover District Council (DDC) website, including the 'remarkable'[13] *Report of the Head of Regeneration and Development to the Planning Committee* ('Report'),[14] and on request, DDC provided me with hard copies of public consultation responses.[15] Outline planning permission was granted in 2013 for development on two sites. One site was in an Area of Outstanding Natural Beauty (AONB) and included 521 residential units, a 90-apartment retirement development, and associated commercial and other developments. The other was Western Heights, a scheduled monument and conservation area, where there would be 40 residential units and a hotel and conference centre. A contribution of £5 million would be made to DDC, with the intention of providing a museum and visitor centre at the Drop Redoubt, which is a Napoleonic fort at Western Heights. In addition, £1.8 million would be made available for infrastructure, and £500,000 for bus services. Officers recommended granting outline planning permission subject to mitigation of the impact on the AONB by reducing the amount of housing and imposing conditions on phasing development, and to conditions that would increase the likelihood of the promised benefits materialising. The Council granted the outline permission without these changes. The Supreme Court upheld the Court of Appeal's decision to quash the permission for failure to provide adequate reasons. An amended application was re-submitted afresh after the litigation. *Dover* is a very significant development, and methodologically, a different story might emerge were I to select a more modest residential application. Large-scale housing developments are, however, influential in driving English planning law, and the case provides a useful perspective on the ways in which such applications proceed.

There is no such thing as a 'natural' scale at which housing (or anything else) *should* be governed, and no single scale can be assumed to be preferable.[16] So the purpose of this chapter is not to argue for a re-scaling. Scale, however, has a real impact on both planning outcomes, and on planning's role as a forum for debate.[17] Space for the messy construction of an understanding of the public interest needs to be found at different scales.[18]

Interests and impacts

The housing 'crisis' is a familiar trope, implying an urgency that adds a temporal dimension (on which Elen Stokes focuses in the previous chapter) to our discussion of space,[19] as well as an expectation (often not fulfilled) of strong action. The crisis is found in at least a lack of decent, affordable homes (on which see Edward Mitchell's chapter below) of the right type (including appropriate tenure), in the right place.

Central government policy has over many years attributed this crisis to too few new homes being built, so a supply-side problem, in turn largely attributed to the regulatory 'barriers' created by the (local) planning system.[20] The idea of planning as barrier is not unique to either recent policy or to housing.[21] Although planning may indeed restrict the availability of land for new housing, and a planning application is inherently uncertain,[22] this is a very partial picture. First, the starting point for analysis has often been London and the south-east, and, although affordability problems are widely shared (and the attention has not solved London's problems), this neglects regional and spatial diversity and inequalities.[23] Second, the 'narrow quantitative logic' disregards the quality of housing, as well as place-specific locational appropriateness.[24] Third, this framing also neglects individual inequalities and perspectives (homeless people, professionals unable to get on the 'housing ladder', insecure private tenants). These issues have multiple scalar dimensions, from individual or household need,[25] to local demographic patterns (for example a need for multi-generational family homes or homes for older people), to regional economic demands (for example in 'travel to work' areas), to national design or safety standards.

The limitations of the singular national framing of planning as barrier are increasingly recognised by central government.[26] Long delays in the building of houses for which permission has been granted, the related over-dependence on a few volume house-builders, and even the exit of the public sector from housebuilding[27] have all been acknowledged over recent years. The so-called 'levelling-up' agenda should be inherently sensitive to regional diversity, and Michael Gove, who became Secretary of State at the Department for Levelling Up, Housing and Communities (DLUHC) in 2021, has acknowledged many of the criticisms of the single and purely quantitative approach to housing.[28] The scaled articulation of a national housing crisis, however, is remarkably resilient, and local planning is likely to continue to present 'the softest target for policy reform',[29] both cause and potential solution.[30]

There are broader and more intractable issues beyond the *supply* of decent houses. On the demand side, housing is an investment commodity, often supporting the broader economy, even if high prices have their own negative economic impacts.[31] This is frequently seen as a national interest, but is potentially pervasive through and across scales. Housing as investment embeds housing in global markets, and a global 'wall of money'[32] shapes the English and local residential property markets.[33] International purchasers invest in residential property (which is rented, occupied occasionally, or never occupied at all[34]) in London and other cities. Credit flows at all scales fund small landlords and second home-owners, as well as those who live in the property they own.[35] The financialisation of housing, its embedding in and shaping by the practices and narratives of the financial sector,[36] is profound. It affects the way individuals and institutions think and behave, for example local authorities and housing associations viewing land as an asset rather than for its use value and managing rent to secure future credit,[37] and individuals relying on their homes to support retirement.

Efforts to institutionalise the conscious and simplistic scaling of housing along a national need/local resistance dichotomy fail to do justice to issues that assert themselves at multiple scales. This is even clearer when we turn to an actual housing development, located in a particular place. The attractions of the *Dover* application seem to be largely economic, with a strong focus on the local, albeit in a competitive national and international context. Councillors speaking in favour of granting permission emphasise general regeneration of the town, including especially the expected tourism and associated benefits from the heritage work on the Drop Redoubt, together with the hotel and conference centre. The local economic pressure is clear, even in the sparse minutes of the Council meeting.

Landscape dominates discussion of the negative impact of the application, falling within the 'amenity' issues generally attributed to the 'local'. There are also expressions of concern from local people about traffic and local services. The emphasis on landscape indicates how patterns of legal protection (local, national, international),[38] and prior institutional knowledge (created in a multi-scale forum),[39] shape debate and construct 'local' publics to engage in particular ways on particular issues.[40] Environmental impacts by contrast receive relatively little attention, largely from the local Wildlife Trust. When there are different patterns of environmental law protection and prior institutional knowledge, as well as different 'official' expert determinations of the impact of the proposal, a different sort of engagement may be stimulated. Environment and landscape are location-specific, yet the focus is shaped (not determined) by broader legal and policy frameworks, across scales, discussed below.

For DDC's expert advisors, the contribution of the proposal to filling the shortfall of housing land in the local development plan (constructed as a 'shortfall' by the central government policy discussed below) is part of the 'finely balanced exceptional justification for this major AONB development'.[41] The tight link between national and local housing need ('while housing land supply is important at the local level it also has a national dimension'[42]) is not unique to *Dover*.[43] As well as illustrating a simple exercise of hierarchy over outcomes, this exposes central government's shaping of the very nature of the problem, through the scaling of the very meaning of housing need. There is a striking silence, throughout the *Dover* documentation, on the possible benefits of the proposed housing as a place for people to live.

Impacts and interests are difficult to 'sort' in a scalar fashion, spilling into different scales. Most importantly for current purposes, the local does not necessarily stick with the interests it is assigned.[44] The national need for housing (or for *this* housing), and the ability of this development to contribute to meeting that need, is not taken for granted. The hierarchical policy 'cascade', with contestation supposedly reducing as we go down the spatial hierarchy,[45] is resisted. This general phenomenon is clear in *Dover*. Some public contributions to the consultation express doubts about the contribution of the housing to 'local' need, raising the possibility that they will become second homes. Those organising a petition against the development describe the look of 'hopelessness' of those in need of housing when told that the housing 'was for Executives'.[46] Both the CPRE and the National Trust challenge any claim that local 'need' for the housing has been established by the applicant. The CPRE (boldly in retrospect) asserts that the local plan is up to date and should be applied. We see these arguments rehearsed in processes around the country, dramatically if ambiguously with the partial attribution of the 2021 Chesham and Amersham by-election result to proposed planning reform.[47]

Local resistance to the central narrative may have a limited impact on individual decisions, given the ability of the legal and policy framework to channel decisions, discussed next. It can nevertheless contribute to the contestation of assumptions underpinning dominant approaches.[48] We may even be witnessing the evolution of dominant assumptions about the link between planning and housing in the (for now only rhetorical) change of tone from the Secretary of State.[49]

Law and policy

Before turning to law and policy of planning, we should note that the 'global wall of capital' seeks a home in English residential property in part because national laws make it a safe place for that capital; and it is enabled to do so by a complex system of local, national and transnational rules.[50]

The local dominates the legal planning framework for housing. Housing is subject to 'normal' Local Planning Authority (LPA) processes of town and country planning. As discussed in Chapter 2, LPAs set out their vision for their local area in the local or development plan, and grant or refuse permission for individual developments. Chris Willmore tells a compelling story of increasing central control over planning, whilst this basic structure remains unchanged.[51] As in other areas, central policy-setting, the examination of development plan documents, the Secretary of State's call-in powers and the developer's right to appeal on the merits all ensure considerable central scrutiny throughout planning.[52] The manner and strength of the exercise of that authority in housing are, however, distinctive.

The longstanding allocation of blame for 'the' national housing crisis squarely with supply-side restrictions in local planning has led central government to a national, 'place-neutral' approach[53] to housing. A national target of 300,000 new homes a year seems to have survived any recent shift in the appreciation of the complexity of housing and housing need.[54] This national target feeds into numerical targets for local housing, beginning with the allocation of housing land in local plans.

The National Planning Policy Framework (NPPF) requires LPAs to allocate a five-year supply of 'specific, deliverable' sites, 'taking into account their availability, suitability and likely economic viability', plus a 'buffer', in local strategic policies.[55] Local need should be 'objectively assessed'.[56] A slim exception to the obligation to provide the objectively assessed five-year supply applies if protective policies in the NPPF (including green belt and AONB policies) provide a 'strong reason' for restricting development, or the adverse impacts would 'significantly and demonstrably outweigh the benefits'.[57] This exception has been narrowly drawn, but provides scope for shifts in emphasis that could dramatically affect outcomes.[58]

A national 'standard method' for calculating the 'objectively assessed' housing 'need' was introduced in 2018, further diminishing local distinctiveness.[59] The calculation depends on projected household growth, a local 'affordability' adjustment, and a cap on the increase. In 2020, a 35 per cent uplift was added for 20 cities. The hidden assumptions and technical complexity of objectively assessed need (and viability, discussed further by Mitchell in this volume) tend to exclude particular groups and individuals and limit the issues open to debate.[60] The challenge of engaging with technical assessments is not limited to members of the public, but extends to LPAs and their elected members.[61]

A single, nationally acceptable technical method for the objective assessment of housing need changes not only the nature of the debate, reinforcing a market rather than public interest narrative, but also its scale. Before the introduction of the 'standard method', debates over the appropriate methodology locally[62] provided (limited) means to engage multiple, including local, perspectives on housing need.[63] When central government proposed changes to the standard method for calculating housing need in 2020, the threat of higher allocations in the south-east led to scale boundaries being crossed as MPs (actors on the national and local stage, responding to local knowledge and local concerns, at the national level), forced a retreat. The 35 per cent uplift for 20 cities, mentioned above, was an alternative way to reach the *national* housing target. As well as rendering visible the politics of 'objectively' assessed need, this changing approach to calculation raises questions of which localities are heard, and which neglected.[64] Even for those areas welcoming development, the uplift implies greenfield housing.[65]

The independent examination of local development plans prevents the adoption of a plan that is not 'sound'.[66] A sound plan is, inter alia, consistent with national policy and 'seeks to meet the area's objectively assessed needs', included on housing.[67] An adopted plan (allocating sufficient land to housing) then feeds into applications for planning permission, granted swiftly for applications in accordance with the plan.[68] In the absence of 'up-to-date' relevant local plan policies, the NPPF takes us to the 'tilted balance'.[69] The tilted balance requires permission to be granted unless protective policies in the NPPF (including green belt and AONB policies) provide a 'clear reason' for refusal, or the adverse impacts would 'significantly and demonstrably outweigh the benefits'.[70] A successfully adopted local plan can quickly become out-of-date. An inability to evidence a five-year supply of deliverable housing land explicitly renders policies out-of-date.[71] The failure of an LPA to meet the 'housing delivery test', through which central government monitors the actual building (not just permitting) of housing in the area, also renders policies out-of-date.[72] This is one way in which the recognition of private sector house builders' failure to 'build out' planning permission (because of their own market interests) has increased rather than reduced pressure on LPAs. LPAs' ability to shape their space is reduced, as the tilted balance makes it difficult to refuse planning permission for housing on commercially attractive greenfield sites, even if brownfield sites have been identified in the plan.[73] Quintin Bradley describes a move from 'planning by appeal' to 'planning by surrender'.[74]

The scaling described here is to some extent straightforwardly hierarchical, central above local. There are, however, complexities.[75] In *Hopkins Homes*, the leading case on the tilted balance, the Supreme Court emphasises the priority of statute over policy. As discussed in Chapter 2, decisions on applications 'must' under section 38(6) of the Planning and Compulsory Purchase Act (PCPA) 2004 'be made in accordance with the plan unless material considerations indicate otherwise'. Soft as that requirement can be, given the range of material considerations and discretion of the LPA, *Hopkins Homes* emphasises the continued statutory 'primacy' of the local plan,[76] and the centrality of planning judgment to deciding the weight of (even out-of-date) local policies when applying the tilted balance.[77] The Court of Appeal has reinforced this decision, upholding the relevance of restrictive local policies and the weight given to them by decision-makers, even when there is no five-year supply of housing.[78] Further, although I am anxious not to overstate the case,[79] the Planning Inspectorate (PINS) also confirms the continued relevance of restrictive local policies even in the absence of sufficient allocation of land to housing: 'the supply of housing is not the be all and end all'.[80]

This renders the hierarchy between central and local power more ambiguous, suggesting the possibility of greater local assertiveness. But that too is far from straightforward. Local and central policy point in different directions. Since the courts rarely interfere with the exercise of planning judgment, the weight given to different elements of policy by the decision-maker is crucial. The decision-maker could be the LPA or PINS (or the Secretary of State in a recovered appeal). The Supreme Court has described inspectors as being 'required to exercise their own independent judgment . . . within the framework of national policy as set by government'.[81] There is an expectation that the LPA prefers its policy, but PINS (acting 'instead of' the Secretary of State on appeal[82]) generally prefers central policy. Although central policy contains important protective policies and is not always pro-development, *objectors* to planning permission have no right of merits appeal (and the Secretary of State will call-in only rarely). Developers will only appeal when a shift of approach to policy may work in their favour. Planning law shows that outcomes are determined not just by which scale is allocated ultimate legal or jurisdictional authority, but also by who gets to invoke that authority.[83]

It is difficult to conclude that we have unambiguous or entirely predictable local or central control. Neither central nor local can simply ignore the other's policy or exercise untrammelled authority. An insistence on local specificity may subtly feed into central approaches, and central policy rather less subtly intervenes in local decision-making.

Beyond the policy framework on housing specifically, national (and international[84]) legal designations can focus attention on local places. For example, the Countryside and Rights of Way Act 2000 requires the LPA to 'have regard to the purpose of conserving and enhancing the natural beauty of the [AONB]'.[85] The NPPF, central policy, is more demanding: 'planning permission should be refused for major development [in an AONB] other than in exceptional circumstances, and where it can be demonstrated that the development is in the public interest'.[86] The protection of AONBs (and other designations, such as green belts, conservation areas, sites of special scientific interest) gets force from *central* insistence on local specificity; sensitivity to context is multi-scalar.

We see this in the *Dover* case, where the impact of the proposed development on an AONB was crucial. Categorisation as 'AONB' might imply a single set of understandings of sites across the country.[87] That national framework, however, contributes to shaping meaning in a particular place and brings complex multi-scalar understandings of land into local decisions.[88] AONBs defy a neat nesting of scales: the local reaches out, for example with the particular national resonance of the 'white cliffs' of the Kent Downs AONB.[89]

This gives us a different perspective on central intervention, highlighting the 'local trap', that is, the danger of assuming that the local is a preferable scale for decision-making.[90] The exclusionary potential of the local, and its incentives to ignore broader impacts or impacts on other localities, should not be ignored. Rather than (or as well as) a mistrust of local power and democracy, increased central control might be prompted by concerns to protect broader interests. Local decision-making is subject, for example, to legally guaranteed rights to participate in decision-making, legally supported limits on harm to protected habitats and species, and various legally mandated assessments. Many legal rights of this character are found in EU law, sometimes with roots in international law. Bypassing the national, the supranational forced an intense empirical focus on local places and people, as well as bringing the more conventionally transnational (such as cross-border pollution or migratory birds) to local attention. When EU law was also domestic law, it complicated hierarchy, expanding scale up and down. Now that it is 'foreign' law, it exists in 'retained' domestic law[91] but is far more fragile to the priorities of central government.

The national and local are not neatly self-contained, but deeply intertwined.[92] In housing, clear divisions have been eroded by central authority reaching into local discretion, coupled with the resilience of local interests, as well as by repeated calls on scales greater and smaller than the LPA. The 'Regional Spatial Strategies' introduced by the Planning and Compulsory Purchase Act 2004, building on earlier policy and institutional priorities,[93] may have emerged out of a new-found enthusiasm for 'spatial' planning over its regulatory role.[94] But they were also about increasing housing development, feeding housing targets and a growth-focused agenda to LPAs, via this new scale between local and national.[95] The rise and fall (and rise?) of regional planning is discussed in Chapter 2 above. Regional plans were abolished by the Localism Act 2011, removing both statutory spatial (more than buildings) and statutory regional (more than local) planning. The Act allows parish councils and neighbourhood forums, a smaller and less formal scale than the LPA, to create 'neighbourhood development plans'.[96] The Act does not define localism, or rationalise its prioritisation, and it uses different conceptualisations and definitions of the local[97] (local authority, neighbourhood, communities, 'not regional'). Like the regionalism it rejected, localism was somewhat predicated on housing. Local communities were said to have resisted housing in part because they lacked the opportunity to influence it.[98] But in the immediate aftermath of the Localism Act, rather than 'bottom up' growth, 'local authorities saw reduced housing numbers as a legitimate expression of localism'.[99] It was soon made clear that neighbourhood planning would be subject to the same objectively assessed housing need requirements as the LPA.[100] The central is apparently inescapable, notwithstanding the rhetoric of anti-centralism.

These interludes indicate how planning (and other) law plays its part in the social construction of scale.[101] This is a little more complex than simply creating new steps in the central-local hierarchy. As well as adding a level between local and national hierarchy, regional planning made new space for LPAs at a different scale. It was also more amenable to national control, and changed the political opportunities for external actors.[102] The abolition of regional planning, removing these new spaces, was achieved by the central exercise of authority, but partially responding to local concerns. The mutual dependence of the different scales comes through.[103] Finally, the re-emergence of regional forms of governance, through the 'disorganised' patchwork of combined authorities and city regions discussed in Chapter 2,[104] and even the LPA duty to cooperate,[105] suggests a continued search for scalar solutions. Perennial change reinforces the dynamism and construction of scale, the fragility of scalar fixes, and the impossibility of isolating either different scales or one 'local' from another.

Unsurprisingly, given the rhetoric of planning as barrier, housing has also been part of the deregulation of planning. A loss of regulatory capacity might be glimpsed in policies like the tilted balance, but is clearest in amendments to the Use Classes Order and permitted development rights, which have removed the requirement to seek planning permission from certain residential conversions.[106] Analysis of these changes has been highly critical.[107] It is part of the relentless focus on numbers, which means that quantity takes priority over the quality of the homes, or the broader amenity of new and existing residents. The belated introduction in 2020 of a requirement for natural light in all homes and minimum space standards only emphasises the disregard of broader questions of quality.[108] There is no opportunity for community consultation, and elected local representatives are able to address only limited issues through prior approval. In terms of scale, this deregulation could be understood as part of a longstanding mistrust of local planning, and the institutions and processes that go along with it. Rather than centralising government control, however, government is reduced, leaving the shaping of public space to the market, with its own open-ended questions of scale.

Centralisation pervades law and policy in our case, but although that centralisation is meaningful, it is complicated. We become aware of the complexity, not only by thinking in terms of scale theory, but also in the 'almost perpetual whirl of spatial configurations' apparent in the legal framework governing planning for housing.[109]

Actors

In this discussion of the scale of actors in planning for housing, I do not wish to suggest either that the scale of actors can be clearly distinguished or that 'actors' can be separated from the other categories. Actors are engaged by interests and impacts, enabled or excluded by law and policy, and they act across supposedly pre-determined scales.

The LPA is a key actor in planning for housing, representing and governing a space that is formally defined by lines on a map and by boundaries to powers. If the local is socially and legally constructed, it is somewhat (although not exhaustively) constructed by the scale of the LPA, itself somewhat constructed by ideas and practices of the 'local'. In Chapter 2, I discussed the inelegance and dynamism of 'the' LPA. Further, LPAs reach beyond their boundaries, and not just in the ubiquity of the 'global' city.[110] They adapt to new manifestations of scale, such as combined authorities or neighbourhood planning, or in the role played in the *Dover* permission by Dover's *national* historic significance.

Chapter 2 also briefly discusses what this thing, 'the' LPA, is, setting out the divide in understanding between those who see local authorities as service providers (for central government), and those who see them as democratic bodies with broader responsibilities for the life of a place.[111] This partially maps onto a divide between planning as a technocratic or a democratic process: implementing the public interest as defined by experts, or working out democratically what the public interest might be.[112] Elected local councillors have the final say, but their role is constrained by legal and policy obligations.[113] Professional advisers and LPA officers have a significant role to play in meeting these obligations, including assessments from environment to viability, as well as advising on the ultimate planning judgment.

Turning more concretely to the *Dover* decision, the Report provided the overall planning judgment of professionals within the council, building on the advice of other experts, internal and external. The Kent Downs AONB executive is a local body, but at a different, overlapping scale from DDC, and with specific objectives. It concluded that the scheme 'is wholly contrary to national and local policy', slipping between scales and challenging both local and national need for housing. LPAs also receive expert input from official government advisors. These are national actors, and because of their status and expertise they are often privileged in the decision-making process.[114] In *Dover*, Natural England recommended refusal on AONB grounds, and made detailed criticisms of the applicant's technical assessment of landscape impact.

Commissioned advice is often crucial.[115] DDC and English Heritage, for example, jointly commissioned a financial viability review of the £5 million contribution to the regeneration of the Drop Redoubt, and a second economic consultant assessed the other claimed economic benefits. These reports provide an important alternative perspective on the applicant's case, in particular clarifying the uncertainties surrounding the delivery of benefits. The use of consultants, whose reputation and expertise depends on work across the country and internationally, 'will inevitably reduce the "localness" of decisions',[116] and keeps us firmly in largely context-independent market thinking. The use of commissioned expertise is primarily driven by limited resources of expertise within the authority, discussed below. External professionals can also enhance credibility with outsiders (including the applicant) and protect individual officers. For example, although DDC probably had sufficient internal legal expertise to reach its own view,[117] it sought advice from a QC on the legality of the proposed section 106 agreement.[118] Ultimately, the LPA disagreed with the mitigation measures recommended by its officers, and approved the application as submitted.

Beyond 'official' actors, broader publics are entitled to be involved in both plan-making and permitting. Local interests are diverse in any single place and localities are similarly diverse and complex. Groups and publics are not a simple input into the process, ready and waiting to take part in a consultation process. They are partially constructed (for example as insider/outsider, silent majority, NIMBY) by the regulatory and political activity that they are engaging in.[119] The limitations of public participation are well-known.[120] Publics face significant challenges, including inconvenient, daunting and time-intensive processes and the need to master inaccessible technical evidence. These disadvantages are shared, but not evenly, so that the already marginalised may be further disadvantaged. Also excluded are potential future occupiers of new housing, who are elsewhere in space or time, and so unlikely to speak directly to the process.[121] Whether or not housing is built in one locality affects other localities, who lives, works and seeks services there. In *Dover* on the other hand, the LPA expressly sought 'higher skill/income households' from elsewhere, without addressing the impact of this demographic change on existing residents, and without any provision for affordable housing.

Local consultation also opens opportunities for NGOs, including business organisations, with different scalar manifestations. *Local* NGOs might include bodies constituted for the purpose of the application, as for example discussed in the chapters by Carolyn Abbot and Chiara Armeni above. NGOs provide expertise in exchange for influence, and their ability to engage with important technical detail can set them apart from other local actors.[122] Kent Wildlife Trust, a local branch of a national NGO, objected strongly in Dover, and national NGOs (the National Trust and the CPRE) engaged vigorously for protection of the local (and more than local) landscape.

Like the 'official' local, the central or national is also fragmented. The 'national' is essentially English, acting through UK-wide institutions in Whitehall and Westminster, raising bigger questions about the UK's ambiguous territorial constitution. There is no spatial planning at a national level in England.[123] Government does, though, have a strong hand on planning, and 'the planning Acts' give the Secretary of State 'overall responsibility for oversight of the planning system'.[124] Housing was added to the title of the Ministry of Housing, Communities and Local Government in 2018, renamed and refocused again as the DLUHC in 2021. The website suggests that housing dominates the work of the Department.[125] There is no planning minister; planning reform, tellingly, is the responsibility of the housing minister, and planning 'casework' sits with two ministers. Cabinet involvement in housing policy is also likely to be intense, and the Chief Secretary to the Treasury has 'housing and planning' listed in his responsibilities.[126]

Parliament and individual parliamentarians provide an important link between central and local government.[127] Parliament's formal role is greatest in respect of primary legislation. Much planning law, however, from procedure to permitted development rights, is contained in statutory instruments, with limited formal parliamentary input. Policy change may have dramatic effects whilst sidestepping Parliament altogether, although consultation is often expected and sometimes required. In any event, the executive is usually dominant in the Westminster Parliament, even if Parliament can influence government informally, beyond visible 'defeats' of government.[128] On housing specifically, we might note the changes to the government's 'standard method' of calculating housing need, discussed above. These were largely the result of protests made by MPs, acting as members of central institutions (and membership of the parliamentary Conservative Party might have been as significant as membership of Parliament) and as representatives of local constituencies.

PINS, introduced in Chapter 2, plays an immense role in appeals, call-ins and examinations. Inspectors 'have primary responsibility for resolving disputes between planning authorities, developers and others, over the practical application of the policies, national or local'.[129] Whilst they decide at the centre, 'within the framework of national policy as set by government',[130] local specificity can be unavoidable. By comparison with judicial review, merits review places inspectors in an intensely context-specific situation, dealing with local land case by case, and applying the statutory requirement to decide 'in accordance with the [local] plan unless material considerations indicate otherwise'.[131] Inspectors, however, certainly see their role as primarily to ensure the correct application of ministerial policy,[132] and their statutory role on appeal is to act 'instead of' the Secretary of State.[133]

Central government allocation of resources can play an important redistributive role between different areas, as well as reducing competition between localities.[134] The potential for central government to control local authorities through financing is raised in Chapter 2. LPAs are notoriously and increasingly poorly funded from the centre, constraining capacity and risking permanent 'institutional degradation'.[135] Centrally mandated tight and inflexible schedules intensify resource constraints.[136] Government control of resources fundamentally affects how different actors are involved in planning, and accordingly the influence of different scales. Good consultation processes, not to mention proper community participation, require LPA resources. Poor resourcing of LPAs increases the influence of major developers, with their superior capacity – perhaps another subtle form of deregulation; and fewer internal resources of expertise intensify dependence on external private-sector consultants.

The role of the applicant, its advisors, and organisations representing developers is considerable. Our planning system depends on private-sector developers to provide the public goods identified by local people and the LPA, from affordable housing, as discussed by Mitchell below, to more general economic investment and the tax revenue and jobs that come with it.[137] Their resources of expertise, discussed in the chapters by Mitchell and Abbot in this volume, compared with both the relatively under-resourced public sector and other actors, give them considerable advantages. Large developers act across scales, and the market thinking they bring with them may escape the local context. Smaller local businesses often share the disadvantages of other local residents in planning participation,[138] and smaller local builders can find the system difficult to navigate.[139] Larger economic interests are also most able to adapt to changes to scale, for example 'regionalising' themselves to match new governance structures.[140]

This has been a necessarily incomplete and brief overview.[141] It illustrates the fragmentation and overlapping of scale by individual actors, and the incorporation of actors at all scales. Official and unofficial actors in planning shape themselves to scale, and attempt to shape scale to their interests, emphasising local impacts or national policy.

Conclusions

The centre reaches deeply into local places and local processes. Central definitions of acceptable methodology cut short debate, and central supervision of processes enhances implementation of central priorities and policies. Central power cannot, however, escape the complexities and meshing of scales. Hierarchy (with the central at the top) does assert itself, but hierarchy is complicated, with central requirements sometimes intensifying attention to grounded local issues, and local debate sometimes challenging central command.[142] Perhaps this is self-evident: the scales we construct are connected and complicated.

Without suggesting that governance challenges can be resolved by simply transferring power from one scale to another,[143] Willmore raises the possibility of honestly addressing the central dominance of planning simply by centralising decision-making.[144] I have some sympathy with the wish to clarify the exercise of authority and lines of accountability. Maintaining local responsibility is presumably in part a political tactic to devolve conflict.[145] But centralised decisions would come at the cost of local voices, heard most clearly at the project-specific level, and of careful attention to the local impact of development. Central decision-making would anyway be unable to sidestep the complexity of scale; the local awkwardly reasserts itself outside of the hierarchy, within and beyond centralised processes.[146]

More importantly, limitations on the rejection of housing by LPAs has not made their role meaningless. They retain some agency over the location and even the quantity of housing. And if 'how-not-whether' governance is problematic, it does at least allow mitigation of negative impacts and enhancement of benefits.[147] Along with immediate outcomes, the scrutiny and debate of central policy by local experts, politicians and publics has its own value. Susan Owens and Richard Cowell illustrate how planning's spaces for resistance to dominant narratives can sometimes, and slowly, contribute to changing what is 'thinkable'.[148] The change in governance scale for major onshore wind in England, from local to national and back again (and from pro- to anti-development), may be an example of the ways in which local objections escape their local parameters, to confront the national approach.[149] Similarly, changes to the 'standard method' for objectively assessing housing need proposed in 2020 were amended to reflect concern of certain local areas. The re-scaling of wind farms did not, however, empower local people, unless their views were consistent with the new suspicion of onshore wind;[150] and the centralised approach to determining housing need remains in place.

The continued *legal* relevance of local policy, notwithstanding non-compliance with national housing demands,[151] is differently interesting. Alongside sustained local resistance to central demands, it lessens the dominance of the central, albeit without replacing it with the local. How that plays out depends on the exercise of planning judgment by PINS and LPAs. And in their exercise of planning judgment, they may also pick up on any possible softening of the national policy environment.[152] Even if the narrative of local planning as a cause of the housing crisis persists, that narrative has become more complex.[153]

The tensions around housing are deep, and re-scaling will not resolve them. Scale does, however, prioritise, legitimise or marginalise certain voices and priorities. A familiar rhetorical privileging of the local, through routine participation, as well as the 'morally charged' language of localism,[154] is under considerable pressure in planning for housing, and belied in practice. Imposition of central demands reduces the political opportunities for 'ordinary' people, who are more able to participate in processes around specific local projects than higher level strategy – projects which are also more likely to resonate in local than national elections. It also reduces the space for NGOs seeking to preserve environmental or landscape goods, with literally fewer formal opportunities to bring their expertise to bear, and greater difficulty mobilising publics.

But although reduced space for 'the local' is concerning, the local should not be uniquely privileged in housing. Localism could have a pernicious role in normalising spatial inequalities and defining fairness.[155] LPAs and existing residents may have incentives to limit housing, and local decision-making excludes those perceived as outsiders beyond and within the local 'boundary'.[156] This suggests a role for the centre, or at least the more than local, to reduce negative impacts on *other* localities, and the otherwise excluded, as well as on national interests. Neither national nor local is innately better qualified to deliver either inclusive or socially and environmentally progressive outcomes. But housing highlights the importance of opportunities to contest. Many of those opportunities are in LPA planning. If planning is not just a space for implementing a pre-defined version of the public interest, but also for working out that public interest, a powerful (but not all-powerful) local is important.

Notes

1. Cox 2009; Brenner 2009. And it is contested: see Purcell 2003 on the Marston 2000/Brenner 2001 'non-debate'.
2. Marston 2000; Delaney and Leitner 1997. Also of jurisdiction: Ford 1999.
3. Brenner 2001; Purcell 2006; Massey 2005.
4. Marston 2000; Brenner 2001.
5. Delaney and Leitner 1997; Brenner 2001.
6. Particular terminology and approaches are said to be too capacious, too hierarchical or otherwise inadequate; each has the potential to adjust.
7. Bennett and Layard 2015.
8. Ford 1999.
9. Valverde 2009; Valverde 2015; Bennett and Layard 2015.
10. Kaushal 2015.
11. Whilst I equate the national with the 'centre' in this chapter, that is always a question of perspective: Smith 2004.
12. *Dover District Council v CPRE* [2017] UKSC 79; [2018] 1 WLR 108. Note that the CPRE is now known as 'the Countryside Charity': https://www.cpre.org.uk/ (accessed 12 June 2022).
13. *Dover*, [5] per Lord Carnwath.
14. Dover District Council (DDC) 2013.
15. Approximately 1.7 kilogrammes.
16. See e.g. Purcell 2006; Valverde 2009.

17. Owens and Cowell 2011; Allmendinger and Haughton 2010; Inch 2012.
18. Armeni and Lee 2021.
19. For criticism of approaching space and time in isolation see Massey 2005; Valverde 2015.
20. Prime Minister's Office 2021.
21. See e.g. Lord and Tewdwr-Jones 2014.
22. Gallent et al 2021 refer to a 'sub-crisis'.
23. Gray and Barford 2018; McGuinness et al 2018; UK2070 Commission 2020; Ferm and Raco 2020.
24. Most pressingly in respect of permitted development rights, Ferm et al 2020, 4.
25. This chapter does not go 'down' to the individual. On the household see Marston 2000.
26. Inch and Shepherd 2020 argue that the blaming of planning has been destabilised since the 2017 General Election, citing especially Department for Communities and Local Government (DCLG) 2017 and Letwin 2018. See now Gove 2021.
27. On recent slight increases in council house building see Marshall 2021, 199; Gove 2021.
28. Gove 2021.
29. Gallent et al 2021.
30. DCLG 2017; Ministry of Housing, Communities and Local Government (MHCLG) 2020.
31. Barker 2004.
32. Aalbers 2016.
33. The global is no more abstract than the local. Massey 2005 highlights the disappearance of the 'western' in the de-spatialised 'global'; the globals in this paragraph of the text are dynamic and varied. On global financial markets see Aalbers 2016; Bradley 2021.
34. On the complex picture see Glucksberg 2016; Edwards 2016.
35. Gallent 2018.
36. Aalbers 2016; Bradley 2021.
37. Edwards 2016.
38. Lee 2017; Beebeejaun 2018 on policy.
39. Lee 2017.
40. Rydin et al 2018a; Pieraccini 2015.
41. DDC 2013, [2.447].
42. DDC 2013, [2.39].
43. For example Lord Gill noting the *local* plan's '[failure] properly to contribute to the national housing requirement': *Suffolk Coastal District Council v Hopkins Homes* [2017] 1 WLR 1865, [80].
44. Rydin et al 2018a; Pieraccini 2015; Beebeejaun 2018.
45. Owens and Cowell 2011.
46. Letter from Lorrain Senicicle to DDC, 13 July 2012.
47. See e.g. BBC 2021; Marshall 2021 on local elections, 204.
48. Owens and Cowell 2011.
49. Gove 2021.
50. Cox 2009 emphasises that rescaling the state is partial and contradictory.
51. Willmore 2017.
52. The Secretary of State can also 'designate' a poorly performing (assessed by delay and appeal outcomes) LPA under the Town and Country Planning Act (TCPA) 1990, section 62B, so that applications for certain planning permissions can be made directly to the Secretary of State (section 62A).
53. McGuinness et al 2018; Willmore 2017 refers to 'fungibility'.
54. Gove 2021.
55. MHCLG 2021, [68]. A similar approach dates back to the first edition of the NPPF in 2013, and before.
56. MHCLG 2021, [11], [23].
57. MHCLG 2021, [11(b)].
58. See the Secretary of State's suggestion that protective policies might in some cases make the local numbers 'unrealistic': Gove 2021, Q85. The interpretation of the NPPF is ultimately for the court (see chapter 2), but the language provides room for this sort of shift of emphasis.
59. MHCLG 2015, as amended.
60. Layard 2019; Mitchell 2020; Bradley 2021.

61. Layard 2019; Mitchell 2020; Bradley 2021.
62. DCLG 2017; Hickman and Boddy 2018; on technical assessments as a limited space for deliberation see Lee et al 2018.
63. On the challenges for the Planning Inspectorate (PINS) see Hickman and Boddy 2018.
64. Schragger 2001. This is the most visible space for local interests; other lobbying (e.g. by local government or business) will take place.
65. See Ferm and Raco 2020 on how 'viability' can prioritise greenfield development even in areas seeking more development. The Secretary of State has suggested that he may 'look again' at this: Gove 2021, Q86.
66. Planning and Compulsory Purchase Act (PCPA) 2004, section 20(5)(b); see Chapter 2.
67. Plans are sound if they are 'positively prepared' (incorporating objectively assessed needs), 'justified', 'effective' and 'consistent with national policy': MHCLG 2021, [35].
68. MHCLG 2021, [11(c)].
69. *Hopkins Homes*.
70. MHCLG 2021, [11(d)].
71. MHCLG 2021, footnote 8; see the potential for nuance in [14].
72. MHCLG 2021, footnote 8.
73. Ferm and Raco 2020.
74. Bradley 2021, 395.
75. See Cox 2009 on the complexity of loss of 'national' authority.
76. [21]. See the discussion in chapter 1.
77. [55], [56].
78. *Gladman Developments Ltd v Secretary of State for Housing, Communities and Local Government and Corby Borough Council* [2021] EWCA Civ 104; *R (on the application of Monkhill) v Secretary of State for Housing, Communities and Local Government and Waverley Borough Council* [2021] EWCA Civ 74.
79. Since a perusal of planning appeals indicates plenty of cases that continue to apply central pro-development policy over local restrictive policies.
80. *Gladman*, [17], quoting the Inspector.
81. *Hopkins Homes*, [21].
82. TCPA 1990, Schedule 6, 1(1).
83. By contrast with Valverde 2009.
84. European Landscape Convention, Council of Europe (2000).
85. Section 85.
86. MHCLG 2021, [177].
87. Layard 2021.
88. Lee 2017.
89. Readman 2014.
90. Purcell 2006.
91. European Union (Withdrawal) Act 2018.
92. A lesson of the scale literature from Marston 2000 to Brenner 2009.
93. Marshall 2002.
94. Lord and Tewdwr-Jones 2014; Allmendinger and Haughton 2010.
95. Allmendinger and Haughton 2010.
96. Schedule 9; PCPA 2004, section 38A.
97. Layard 2012b; on the longstanding, complex political ideologies of localism see Tait and Inch 2016.
98. Creating NIMBYs: Inch 2012.
99. Boddy and Hickman 2013, 761.
100. See now MHCLG 2021, [24], footnote 18.
101. Layard 2012a.
102. Marshall 2002 and 2004. On political opportunity theory see Abbot and Lee 2021.
103. Cox 2009.
104. Shaw and Tewdwr-Jones 2017.
105. McGuinness et al 2018.
106. Town and Country Planning (Use Classes) Order 1987 SI 1987/764, amended by SI 2020/757; Town and Country Planning (General Permitted Development) (England) (Order)

SI 2015/596, amended by SI 2020/755 and 756. For a useful discussion of how this fits together, see *R (on the application of Rights: Community: Action) v Secretary of State for Housing, Communities and Local Government* [2021] EWCA Civ 1954.
107. Ferm et al 2020.
108. Clifford 2020.
109. Lord and Tewdwr-Jones 2014, 357.
110. See e.g. Massey 2007; Philippopoulos-Mihalopoulos 2007.
111. Loughlin 1996; Jones and Stewart 2012.
112. Marshall 2021; McAuslan 1980; Owens and Cowell 2011.
113. Town and Country Planning Association 2018.
114. Lee et al 2018.
115. See e.g. Ferm and Raco 2020; Tait and Inch 2016.
116. Raco 2018. This is not to say that they are without their own 'places' and their own interests: Massey 2005.
117. The DDC solicitor provided detailed advice.
118. The applicant provided a 'briefing note' in support from Pinsent Masons: see DDC Solicitor's Advice (no 4).
119. Rydin et al 2018a; Pieraccini 2015; Inch 2012.
120. Armeni and Lee 2021; Natarajan et al 2019; Beebeejaun 2018; Town and Country Planning Association 2018.
121. Seeing things temporally as well as spatially, Schragger 2001.
122. Lee 2017.
123. Town and Country Planning Association 2018.
124. *Hopkins Homes*, [19].
125. https://www.gov.uk/government/organisations/department-for-levelling-up-housing-and-communities/about/our-governance (accessed 12 June 2022).
126. https://www.gov.uk/government/ministers/chief-secretary-to-the-treasury (accessed 12 June 2022).
127. Loughlin 1996.
128. Russell and Cowley 2016.
129. *Hopkins Homes*, [25].
130. *Hopkins Homes*, [21].
131. PCPA 2004, section 38(6); *Hopkins Homes*; *Gladman*.
132. See e.g. the interviews in Hickman and Boddy 2020.
133. TCPA 1990, Schedule 6, 1(1).
134. Cox 2009.
135. Gray and Barford 2018.
136. Marshall 2002.
137. Rydin 2013.
138. Rydin 2018b.
139. Town and Country Planning Association 2018; MHCLG 2020.
140. Marshall 2004.
141. In particular, global/transnational financial institutions and regulators reinforce the complexity of scale.
142. Marston 2000; Brenner 2001; Bennett and Layard 2015.
143. Owens and Cowell 2011, 7.
144. Willmore 2017.
145. Inch 2021.
146. Rydin et al 2018a.
147. Rydin et al 2015.
148. Owens and Cowell 2011.
149. Lee 2017.
150. Armeni 2016.
151. *Hopkins Homes*.
152. Just as it is plausible that the rejection of Navitus offshore wind farm was made more likely not by a formal change to policy on offshore wind, but by a general shift of the policy environment from enthusiasm to hostility towards wind: Lee 2017.
153. Inch and Shepherd 2020.

154. Tait and Inch 2016.
155. See e.g. Tait and Inch 2016; Purcell 2006; more generally see Ford 1999.
156. Layard 2012a; Schragger 2001.

References

Aalbers, Manuel (2016). *The Financialisation of Housing: A Political Economy Approach*. Abingdon: Routledge.

Abbot, Carolyn and Maria Lee (2021). *Environmental Groups and Legal Expertise: Shaping the Brexit Process*. London: UCL Press. https://www.uclpress.co.uk/products/155996 (accessed 12 June 2022).

Allmendinger, Phil and Graham Haughton (2010). 'Spatial Planning, Devolution, and New Planning Spaces', *Environment and Planning C: Government and Policy* 28: 803–18.

Armeni, Chiara (2016). 'Participation in Environmental Decision-making: Reflecting on Planning and Community Benefits for Major Wind Farms', *Journal of Environmental Law* 28: 415–41.

Armeni, Chiara and Maria Lee (2021). 'Participation in a Time of Climate Crisis', *Journal of Law and Society* 48: 549–72.

Barker, Kate (2004). *Delivering Stability: Securing our Future Housing Needs* London: HMSO.

BBC (2021). *Chesham and Amersham By-Election Defeat a Warning Shot, Says Tory Co-Chairman*, 19 June, https://www.bbc.co.uk/news/uk-politics-57535928 (accessed 12 June 2022).

Beebeejaun, Yasminah (2018). 'Public Participation and the Declining Significance of Planning'. In *Planning Practice: Critical Perspectives from the UK*, edited by Jessica Ferm and John Tomaney, 85–100. Abingdon: Routledge.

Bennett, Luke and Antonia Layard (2015). 'Legal Geography: Becoming Spatial Detectives', *Geography Compass* 9: 406–22.

Boddy, Martin and Hannah Hickman (2013). 'The Demise of Strategic Planning? The Impact of the Abolition of Regional Spatial Strategy in a Growth Region', *The Town Planning Review* 84: 743–68.

Bradley, Quintin (2021). 'The Financialisation of Housing Land Supply in England', *Urban Studies* 58: 389–404.

Brenner, Neil (2001). 'The Limits to Scale? Methodological Reflections on Scalar Structuration', *Progress in Human Geography* 25: 591–614.

Brenner, Neil (2009). 'Open Questions on State Rescaling', *Cambridge Journal of Regions, Economy and Society* 2: 123–39.

Clifford, Ben (2020). 'Can Deregulation Free Up the Market in the Public Interest'. In *The Wrong Answers to the Wrong Questions*, edited by the Town and Country Planning Association, 22–8. London: Town and Country Planning Association.

Cox, Kevin (2009). 'Rescaling the State in Question', *Cambridge Journal of Regions, Economy and Society* 2: 1–15.

Delaney, David and Helga Leitner (1997). 'The Political Construction of Scale', *Political Geography* 16: 93–7.

Department for Communities and Local Government (2017). *Fixing our Broken Housing Market*.

Dover District Council (2013), *Report of the Head of Regeneration and Development to the Developer Contributions Executive Committee and Planning Committee*, available at https://publicaccess.dover.gov.uk/online-applications/search.do?action=simple&searchType=Application (Reference 12/00440) (accessed 12 June 2022).

Edwards, Michael (2016). 'The Housing Crisis and London', *City* 20: 222–37.

Ferm, Jessica and Mike Raco (2020). 'Viability Planning, Value Capture and the Geographies of Market-Led Planning Reform in England', *Planning Theory & Practice* 21: 218–35.

Ferm, Jessica, Ben Clifford, Patricia Canelas and Nicola Livingstone (2020). 'Emerging Problematics of Deregulating the Urban: The Case of Permitted Development in England', *Urban Studies*: 1–19.

Ford, Richard T. (1999). 'Law's Territory (A History of Jurisdiction)', *Michigan Law Review* 97: 843–930.

Gallent, Nick (2018). 'Planning for Housing: The Global Challenges Confronting Local Practice'. In *Planning Practice: Critical Perspectives from the UK*, edited by Jessica Ferm and John Tomaney, 205–19. Abingdon: Routledge.

Gallent, Nick, Claudio de Magalhaes and Sonia Freire Trigo (2021). 'Is Zoning the Solution to the UK Housing Crisis?', *Planning Practice & Research* 36: 1–19.

Glucksberg, Luna (2016). 'A View from the Top: Unpacking Capital Flows and Foreign Investment in Prime London', *City* 20: 238–55.

Gove, Michael (2021). *Oral Evidence: Work of the Department 2021*. London: House of Commons Housing, Communities and Local Government Select Committee.

Gray, Mia and Anna Barford (2018). 'The Depth of the Cuts: The Uneven Geography of Local Government Austerity', *Cambridge Journal of Regions, Economy and Society* 11: 541–63.

Hickman, Hannah and Martin Boddy (2018). '"Between a Rock and a Hard Place": Planning Reform, Localism and the Role of the Planning Inspectorate in England', *Planning Theory & Practice* 19: 198–217.

Hickman, Hannah and Martin Boddy (2020). '"If Independence Goes, the Planning System Goes": New Political Governance and the English Planning Inspectorate', *The Town Planning Review*: 21–45.

Inch, Andy (2012). 'Creating "A Generation of NIMBYs"? Interpreting the role of the State in Managing the Politics of Urban Development', *Environment and Planning C: Government and Policy* 30: 520–35.

Inch, Andy and Edward Shepherd (2020). 'Thinking Conjuncturally about Ideology, Housing and English Planning', *Planning Theory* 19: 59–79.

Jones, George and John Stewart (2012). 'Local Government: The Past, the Present and the Future', *Public Policy and Administration* 27: 346–67.

Kaushal, Asha (2015). 'The Politics of Jurisdiction', *Modern Law Review* 78: 759–92.

Layard, Antonia (2012a). 'Law and Localism: The Case of Multi-Occupancy Housing', *Legal Studies* 32: 551–76.

Layard, Antonia (2012b). 'The Localism Act 2011: What is "Local" and How do we (Legally) Construct It?', *Environmental Law Review* 14: 134–44.

Layard, Antonia (2019). 'Planning by Numbers: Affordable Housing and Viability in England'. In *Planning and Knowledge: How New Forms of Technocracy are Shaping Contemporary Cities*, edited by Mike Raco and Frederico Savini, 213–24. Bristol: Bristol University Press.

Layard, Antonia (2021). 'Law, Place and Maps'. In *Handbook on Space, Place and Law* edited by Robin Bartel and Jennifer Carter, 129–40. Cheltenham: Edward Elgar.

Lee, Maria (2017). 'Landscape and Knowledge in Nationally Significant Wind Energy Projects', *Legal Studies* 37: 3–24.

Lee, Maria et al (2018). 'Techniques of Knowing in Administration: Co-production, Models, and Conservation Law', *Journal of Law and Society* 45: 427–56.

Letwin, Oliver (2018). *Independent Review of Build Out*. London: HM Government.

Lord, Alex and Mark Tewdwr-Jones (2014). 'Is Planning "Under Attack"? Chronicling the Deregulation of Urban and Environmental Planning in England', *European Planning Studies* 22: 345–61.

Loughlin, Martin (1996). *Legality and Locality. The Role of Law in Central-Local Government Relations*. Oxford: Clarendon Press.

McAuslan, Patrick (1980). *The Ideologies of Planning Law*. Oxford: Pergamon Press.

McGuinness, David, Paul Greenhalgh and Paul Grainger (2018). 'Does One Size Fit All? Place-Neutral National Planning Policy in England and its Impact on Housing Land Supplies and Local Development Plans in North East England', *Local Economy* 33: 1–18.

Marshall, Tim (2002). 'The Re-Timing of English Regional Planning', *The Town Planning Review* 73: 171–95.

Marshall, Tim (2004). 'Regional Planning in England: Progress and Pressures Since 1997', *The Town Planning Review* 75: 447–72.

Marshall, Tim (2021). *The Politics and Ideology of Planning*. Bristol: Bristol University Press.

Marston, Sallie (2000). 'The Social Construction of Scale', *Progress in Human Geography* 24: 219–42.

Massey, Doreen (2005). *For Space*. London: Sage.

Massey, Doreen (2007). *World City*. Cambridge: Polity.

Ministry of Housing, Communities and Local Government (2015). *Guidance: Housing and Economic Needs Assessment* (updated 2020), https://www.gov.uk/guidance/housing-and-economic-development-needs-assessments (accessed 12 June 2022).

Ministry of Housing, Communities and Local Government (2018). *The Planning Inspectorate Framework Document*.

Ministry of Housing, Communities and Local Government (2020). *White Paper: Planning for the Future*.

Ministry of Housing, Communities and Local Government (2021). *National Planning Policy Framework*.

Mitchell, Edward (2020). 'Financial Viability Modelling in Urban Property Development', *Northern Ireland Legal Quarterly* 71: 35–55.

Natarajan, Lucy et al (2019). 'Participatory Planning and Major Infrastructure: Experiences in REI NSIP Regulation', *Town Planning Review* 90: 117–38.

Owens, Susan and Richard Cowell (2011). *Land and Limits: Interpreting Sustainability in the Planning Process*. Abingdon, Routledge, 2nd edn.

Philippopoulos-Mihalopoulos, Andreas (2007). *Law and the City*. Abingdon: Routledge.

Pieraccini, Margherita (2015). 'Rethinking Participation in Environmental Decision-Making: Epistemologies of Marine Conservation in South-East England', *Journal of Environmental Law* 27: 45–67.

Prime Minister's Office (2021). *The Queen's Speech 2021: Background Briefing* available at https://assets.publishing.service.gov.uk/government/uploads/system/uploads/attachment_data/file/986770/Queen_s_Speech_2021_-_Background_Briefing_Notes..pdf (accessed 12 June 2022).

Purcell, Mark (2003). 'Islands of Practice and the Marston/Brenner Debate: Toward a More Synthetic Critical Human Geography', *Progress in Human Geography* 27: 317–32.

Purcell, Mark (2006). 'Urban Democracy and the Local Trap', *Urban Studies* 43: 1921–41.

Raco, Mike (2018). 'Private Consultants, Planning Reform and the Marketisation of Local Government Finance'. In *Planning Practice: Critical Perspectives from the UK*, edited by Jessica Ferm and John Tomaney, 123–37. Abingdon: Routledge.

Readman, Paul (2014). '"The Cliffs are not Cliffs": The Cliffs of Dover and National Identities in Britain, c.1750-c1950', *History* 99: 242–69.

Russell, Meg and Philip Cowley (2016). 'The Policy Power of the Westminster Parliament: The "Parliamentary State" and the Empirical Evidence', *Governance* 29: 121–37.

Rydin, Yvonne (2013). *The Future of Planning: Beyond Growth Dependence*. Bristol: Policy Press.

Rydin, Yvonne, Maria Lee and Simon Lock (2015). 'Public Engagement in Decision-Making on Major Wind Energy Projects', *Journal of Environmental Law* 27: 139–50.

Rydin, Yvonne et al (2018a). 'Local Voices on Renewable Energy Projects: The Performative Role of the Regulatory Process for Major Offshore Infrastructure in England and Wales', *Local Environment* 23: 565–81.

Rydin, Yvonne et al (2018b). 'Do Local Economic Interests Matter When Regulating Nationally Significant Infrastructure? The Case of Renewable Energy' *Local Economy* 33: 269–86.

Schragger, Richard C. (2001). 'The Limits of Localism', *Michigan Law Review* 100: 371–472.

Shaw, Keith and Mark Tewdwr-Jones (2017). '"Disorganised Devolution": Reshaping Metropolitan Governance in England in a Period of Austerity', *Raumforschung und Raumordnung* 75: 211–24.

Smith, Neil (2004). 'Scale Bending and the Fate of the National'. In *Scale and Geographic Inquiry: Nature, Society and Method*, edited by Eric Sheppard and Robert B McMaster, 192–212. Oxford: Blackwell.

Tait, Malcolm and Andy Inch (2016). 'Putting Localism in Place: Conservative Images of the Good Community and the Contradictions of Planning Reform in England', *Planning Practice & Research* 31: 174–94.

Town and Country Planning Association (2018). *Planning 2020: Raynsford Review of Planning in England*.

UK2070 Commission (2020). *Make No Little Plans: Acting at Scale for a Fairer and Stronger Future*.

Valverde, Mariana (2009). 'Jurisdiction and Scale: Legal "Technicalities" as Resources for Theory', *Social & Legal Studies* 18: 139–57.

Valverde, Mariana (2015). *Chronotopes of Law: Jurisdiction, Scale and Governance*. Abingdon: Routledge.

Willmore, Chris (2017). 'Planning Law Reform and reconceptualising the Regulation of Land Use'. In *Modern Studies in Property Law: Volume 9*, edited by Heather Conway and Robin Hickey, 257–75. Oxford: Hart Publishing.

Part V
Planning at the intersections
Maria Lee and Carolyn Abbot

The very genesis of this book is in the relative neglect of planning law by legal scholars, and some possible reasons for that neglect are raised in Chapter 1. One additional possibility lies in the ways in which planning law works within and across other legal sub-disciplines. All of our disciplinary building blocks (property, obligations, criminal law) are connected with other legal sub-disciplines, and are inherently overlapping. The difference is perhaps an informal (and mistaken in our view) hierarchy, with the dominance of those other scholarly sub-disciplines intensifying the risk that planning law will be overlooked.

In this part, our authors skilfully explore the intersections between planning and contract law, administrative law and property law, centring planning law. There is much still to be said, and we could have chosen other areas, most obviously planning and environmental law,[1] or planning and tort.[2] Our contributors in this part provide three quite different ways of engaging with the intersections between planning and other sub-disciplines. Edward Mitchell demonstrates very directly how contract law scholarship can inform planning law scholarship, and what the details of planning law might have to offer to the understanding of contract; resonating with other parts of the book, his chapter also demonstrates the distributive impact of highly complex and demanding legal mechanisms. Joanna Bell takes a slightly different tack, demonstrating clearly and with painstaking care the space for planning in the fundamentals of administrative law. Along the way, she illustrates the fascination of the wealth of planning case law. Last but by no means least, Kim Bouwer and Rachel Gimson re-evaluate Patrick McAuslan's influential thesis setting property and planning apart from and in opposition to each other. This also provides a significant challenge to the robustness of the public/private divide more broadly.

Notes

1. See e.g. Holder 2006.
2. See e.g. Lee 2014.

References

Holder, Jane (2006). *Environmental Assessment: The Regulation of Decision-Making*. Oxford: Oxford University Press.

Lee, Maria (2014). 'Private Nuisance in the Supreme Court: *Coventry v Lawrence*', *Journal of Planning and Environmental Law*: 705–13.

10
Contracting affordable housing delivery? Residential property development, section 106 agreements and other contractual arrangements

Edward Mitchell

Introduction

Most development of land in England requires planning permission granted by the relevant local planning authority (LPA).[1] LPAs tend to grant planning permission subject to 'conditions' that control how, when and where development can be carried out.[2] Alongside this, section 106(1) of the Town and Country Planning Act (TCPA) 1990 gives LPAs the power to enforce 'planning obligations' that a developer has entered into and that apply further controls on how that developer uses and develops their land. These obligations typically seek to impose different requirements than those that would be sought through conditions attached to a planning permission,[3] and developers can enter into these obligations either by agreement with the relevant LPA or by making a 'unilateral undertaking'.[4] This chapter focuses on planning obligations entered into by agreement and refers to these as 'section 106 agreements'. These agreements involve a convergence, as Matthew White has put it, of 'general contractual principles ... modified and supplemented by statutory provisions'.[5] They also play an essential role in shaping the built environment in England, so are an important subject for further analysis.

LPAs and developers applying for planning permission usually negotiate and sign section 106 agreements before the LPA has decided whether to approve the developer's application.[6] This raises a question, therefore, about the extent to which proposed planning obligations can lawfully influence an LPA's decision-making when it is considering an application for planning permission. To that end, regulation 122(2)(a) of the Community Infrastructure Levy Regulations 2010 states that an LPA can only consider proposed planning obligations when determining a planning application if the obligations are necessary to address impacts that would make a proposed development 'unacceptable' in planning terms and that would thus compel the LPA to withhold the grant of planning permission.[7] Moreover, if a prospective developer does propose to provide planning obligations in a section 106 agreement, regulation 122(2)(b) and (c) of the 2010 Regulations states that the LPA can only take the proposed obligations into account if those obligations relate both 'directly' and 'fairly and reasonably ... in scale and kind' to the development. This is to provide clarity for developers, before they begin negotiating with an LPA, about the contributions that they might be expected to provide, and to ensure that those contributions genuinely relate to appropriate town planning matters.[8] In practice, many LPAs have longstanding formal policies stating that they will seek to use section 106 agreements to impose controls on what those developers build or to secure contributions from them towards the preservation or enhancement of local infrastructure, services, facilities and amenities that either would be newly required or would otherwise be adversely affected as a result of a development.[9] These section 106 agreements are often intensely negotiated contracts containing a 'tightly drafted' and intricate web of highly detailed arrangements designed to govern how the developer delivers its obligations.[10]

The system described above is not the only method currently used in England for securing developer contributions to infrastructure or other public policy goals. The government introduced a discretionary levy in April 2010, called the Community Infrastructure Levy, which LPAs can also use to fund local infrastructure projects by charging developers a locally set fixed-rate tariff.[11] This levy sits alongside the system for securing planning obligations through section 106 agreements, although fewer than half of English LPAs had adopted it by the end of 2019.[12] Moreover, the levy cannot be used to secure the delivery of so-called 'affordable housing'.[13] LPAs seeking to secure affordable housing delivery by property developers primarily do this through planning obligations contained in section 106 agreements.[14] However, the government is, at the time of writing, proposing to change this by creating a new Infrastructure Levy that LPAs will use to fund the delivery of affordable housing and other types of infrastructure.[15] Nonetheless, the contractual arrangements relating to affordable housing in section 106 agreements will continue to shape the places where ordinary people live for some years to come, as this chapter demonstrates. Studying these agreements also provides novel and important insights into the substance of the contractual arrangements that LPAs and developers make when negotiating what a developer will build.

To investigate how section 106 agreements operate in practice, this chapter presents a case study of the interlinked contractual arrangements relating to affordable housing that were created for three residential development projects. The projects studied here are unremarkable developments that happen all the time, everywhere in England, and were chosen because of their everydayness. The developments are located in the author's home town and the author stumbled across their most striking features by accessing the relevant LPA's online planning database and by reading documents relating to the developments. Nevertheless, the interlinking contractual arrangements governing affordable housing delivery in these developments are, as this chapter shows, surprising because of their complexity and their effect. This chapter reveals, therefore, that mundane and small-scale housing delivery can produce highly technical and highly formal legal agreements. By drawing upon Ian Macneil's relational contract theory, this chapter asks why LPAs and private-sector developers create this type of contractual arrangement and examines the power dynamics that are visible in the contractual arrangements studied here.

The chapter proceeds as follows. The first section outlines existing academic scholarship on the role of section 106 agreements in securing the delivery of planning obligations. It then discusses scholarship that critiques the use of private contracting to deliver public policy objectives. It goes on to introduce and consider some applications of Macneil's relational contract theory before explaining how Macneil's ideas have already been used to analyse some aspects of contemporary planning practice. The second section examines the policy basis for affordable housing delivery in England and shows how current delivery methods cause instability and tension. Against this background, the third section introduces the contractual network that links affordable housing delivery at the three developments studied here. It goes on to reveal how the private sector developers constructing those developments used these contractual arrangements to shape when, where and how they delivered affordable housing. The fourth section illustrates how those arrangements created a contractual network that had a 'quality of bindingness'[16] that was skewed in favour of the private developers delivering the developments. The final section concludes by noting that, while it is well known that contractual arrangements between private companies and public bodies do not always deliver underlying public policy objectives, this chapter provides a means to understand why such uneven outcomes occur.

Critiquing the role of contract in delivering planning obligations

Much of the scholarship over the last 30 years relating to section 106 agreements and planning obligations has focused on the theoretical justifications and policy rationales for extracting planning obligations from property developers.[17] That scholarship examines how landowners, planners and developers establish 'negotiating frameworks' within which they shape development trajectories and determine the planning obligations that a developer will provide.[18] Other work takes a more critical approach, explaining that the negotiated nature of planning obligations can create a tendency amongst councillors and planners to pursue vote-winning developer contributions rather than obligations with a robust planning justification.[19] Recent critical commentary has also questioned the prominence of 'viability' modelling and how this shapes the content and delivery of planning obligations.[20] This work emphasises how viability modelling often produces outputs that developers use to secure significant reductions in the amounts of affordable housing that LPAs will expect those developers to deliver and thus provides an important contextual basis on which this chapter builds.[21]

This chapter also develops another recent line of enquiry in legal and town planning scholarship that examines the turn to private contracting as the primary mode for the delivery of various public services and that points to serious and longstanding deficiencies in those contracting regimes. Mike Raco, for example, highlights how contracting practices enable private companies to shape and then govern the implementation of urban development and town planning goals.[22] According to Raco, this form of governance 'has become a more technical process, managed by contract-writers, lawyers and accountants'.[23] The contracts that emerge from this process tend often to be highly complex, opaque instruments that 'lock' public bodies into relationships that do not always deliver intended public policy objectives.[24] This chapter offers a new perspective on the turn to private contracting for the delivery of public services by analysing both the content of particular contractual arrangements and how those arrangements work in practice. Doing so provides a rare insight into the granular details of interlinked section 106 agreements and reveals how LPAs and developers use contracts to establish how, when and where those developers provide affordable housing.

The approach adopted in this chapter uses Macneil's relational contract theory to examine how these section 106 agreements actually work. Macneil suggests that all contractual arrangements involve an interplay of 'common contract behavioral patterns and norms'.[25] He also explains that all contractual arrangements inhabit a point on a spectrum that has more 'discrete' and 'presentiated' contractual behaviour at one pole and entirely 'relational' contractual behaviour at the other.[26] A fully discrete arrangement will exist when contracting parties plan their relations in full and then consent to and achieve the complete implementation of that plan.[27] Presentation is related to 'discreteness' and is 'the bringing of the future into the present', which means that a fully presentiated contract would entirely fix the contracting parties' future dealings.[28] However, Macneil explains that the concept of a fully discrete, fully presentiated contract 'is *entirely* fictional' because more 'relational' behaviours such as solidarity, reciprocity and trust inevitably intervene whenever contracting parties seek to create complex and long-term contractual relations.[29] Macneil's work shows, therefore, that it can be informative to analyse the balance, in any given contractual arrangement, between more discrete behaviour and more relational behaviour.[30]

Relational contract theory thus provides a framework for analysing many types of contractual arrangements. For example, Peter Vincent-Jones has used Macneil's ideas to study contracting regimes that the UK government created in pursuit of specific public policy objectives.[31] These regimes involved administrative contracts designed to regulate the behaviour of central government departments and agencies, economic contracts related to outsourcing and the quasi-market restructuring of central and local government service provision, or social control contracts imposed to regulate the behavioural interactions between state agencies and 'deviant' citizens.[32] Vincent-Jones shows that these contracting regimes rarely enabled the government to achieve its underlying policy objectives.[33] A reason for this failure, according to Vincent-Jones, was central government's 'top-down' imposition of these contracting regimes, which produced destabilising weaknesses in the relationships between the contracting parties.[34] These weaknesses flowed, Vincent-Jones suggests, from the absence of more relational contractual behavioural norms relating to fairness and reciprocity and a consequent lack of trust or cooperation between the contracting parties.[35] This chapter draws on Vincent-Jones's insights to examine both matters of trust and dependency in section 106 agreements and the unevenness of the relationships that shape and that are re-established in those agreements.

Relational contract theory has also already been utilised in scholarship examining aspects of urban development and planning practice. Menno van der Veen and Willem Korthals Altes, for example, use Macneil's ideas as a framework to offer important insights into the interaction between formal contractual arrangements and the need for flexibility in the delivery of complex urban development projects.[36] In addition, this author has used relational contract theory to analyse contracts that oblige LPAs to use their powers of 'compulsory purchase' to redistribute ownership of private land and thus facilitate property development by private developers.[37] This work has illustrated how a type of 'one-sided flexibility' in these contracts embeds an asymmetric power dynamic in which LPAs become tied to a pre-determined course of action over which their private-sector development partners exercise tight control.[38] By applying a similar approach to the analysis of the contractual arrangements used to secure affordable housing delivery, this chapter shows that those arrangements can appear to embody contractual behavioural norms connected to discreteness and presentation but that this appearance can mask the complex dealings that take place behind the scenes to shape how, when and where developers deliver affordable housing.

Planning policy, affordable housing and section 106 agreements

It is generally accepted that a sizeable proportion of households in England require subsidised housing because they would otherwise be unable to access homes of an acceptable standard via the private housing market.[39] The Government has sought to address this by using its National Planning Policy Framework (NPPF) to advocate the delivery of this 'affordable housing' by private property developers rather than public bodies. The NPPF currently defines the concept of affordable housing by reference to different ownership types, ranging from social rented[40] and affordable rented[41] through to mechanisms designed to enable occupiers either to acquire private 'for-sale' housing at discounted prices or to rent that housing at discounted rates that are nonetheless higher than those set for social or affordable rented housing.[42] The current NPPF uses definitions of affordable housing that are similar to those contained in previous versions[43] and which LPAs have largely incorporated into their planning policies.[44]

The approach to affordable housing delivery advocated in the NPPF relies upon property developers incorporating some affordable housing alongside private market housing into the development projects they build.[45] It has also enabled successive governments to pursue the creation of 'mixed communities' through affordable housing delivery alongside private market housing while simultaneously replacing public spending on affordable housing with privately funded provision. This delivery method draws upon the additional value created when a developer receives planning permission for and constructs a new residential development but depends, therefore, on the developer being able to project a profit from a development before it will agree to provide affordable housing.[46] Moreover, to ensure that LPA affordable housing policies do not prevent new residential development proposals coming forward, the NPPF contains detailed guidance on how LPAs should formulate those policies.

To establish the specific amount of affordable housing that they will expect any given development to provide, the NPPF recommends that LPAs should assess the overall need for housing of different sizes, types and tenures in their areas.[47] However, the current NPPF then advises LPAs that they should only require affordable housing delivery where a proposed development will provide 10 or more dwellings in total.[48] The basis for this seems to be the government's concern that the costs, in terms of lost profit, of requiring smaller developments to provide affordable housing would make many of those developments 'unviable'.[49] Where a developer does seek planning permission for a development of 10 or more dwellings, the NPPF advises that LPAs should require the developer to make at least 10 per cent of the total number of dwellings available as affordable housing.[50] LPAs should then, according to the NPPF, expect developers to provide that amount of on-site affordable housing unless the developer can 'robustly justify' either off-site provision or a financial contribution to the LPA instead of providing actual affordable housing.[51]

The use of the phrase 'robustly justified' in the NPPF points to two sources of tension in the formulation and implementation of affordable housing policies. On the one hand, the NPPF states that all LPA policies, including those relating to affordable housing, 'should be underpinned by relevant and up-to-date evidence' that 'take[s] into account relevant market signals' and that supports the proposed policies.[52] The focus, moreover, is on ensuring the 'deliverability' of an LPA's development plan for its area.[53] This focus on 'market signals' and 'deliverability' has been present in every NPPF.[54] The original NPPF, however, went further and expressly advised LPAs to conduct 'viability' modelling to assess how their policy proposals would affect the profitability of notional development projects.[55] While the NPPF is now less explicit about the need for viability modelling to assess the prospect of competitive economic returns to notional property developers, the effect of these practices has often been to compel LPAs to prioritise private profit-making over public housing need when formulating their affordable housing policies.[56] Alongside this, controversies involving viability modelling practices have also arisen from the ways that LPAs have implemented those policies in response to individual applications for planning permission.[57] The NPPF has stated, in all its iterations since 2012, that LPAs should not expect a specific development to provide affordable housing if the developer produces verifiable evidence showing that affordable housing delivery would reduce the development's profit-making potential to an extent that would threaten overall delivery.[58] At times, this has created what Antonia Layard calls a 'duel of the spreadsheets' when developers and LPAs separately seek to establish the mix of housing that a given development should provide.[59]

LPAs create the contested policy framework for affordable housing delivery in their development plan documents and, as should be expected given that LPAs use assessments of both local housing need and local economic conditions when formulating their policies, the content of affordable housing policies tends to vary from one LPA to the next. Nevertheless, LPA policies have consistently stated that, when a development proposal does trigger a requirement to provide affordable housing, LPAs will usually only grant planning permission if the developer signs a section 106 agreement that purports to impose binding duties on the developer to provide that housing.[60] Studying the actual commitments contained in section 106 agreements thus sheds new light on the processes through which LPAs and developers establish how, when and where to deliver affordable housing.

Affordable housing delivery: contracting options for people in housing need

Recent legal and planning scholarship on affordable housing delivery has tended to overlook the actual content and operation of clauses relating to affordable housing in section 106 agreements. By examining three interlinked residential development projects, this chapter demonstrates the extent to which the contractual arrangements between private developers and LPAs can grant those developers control over affordable housing delivery. The first development studied here involved the construction of 110 dwellings on land adjacent to Brook Street, in the centre of Colchester (the Brook Street development).[61] Brook Street is a narrow residential street that acts as a major thoroughfare for vehicular traffic.[62] It is also an Air Quality Management Area, which means that required air quality standards are neither being nor are likely to be achieved in the area.[63] Colchester Borough Council (Colchester Council) granted Mersea Homes Limited (Mersea Homes)[64] planning permission for the Brook Street development in April 2006.[65] Prior to the grant of planning permission, Colchester Council and Mersea Homes had made a section 106 agreement, which, among other things, stated that Mersea Homes would provide four affordable homes as part of the Brook Street development.[66] The Brook Street planning permission was originally due to expire in April 2011 but, in 2010, Mersea Homes applied for, and Colchester Council approved, an extension of that expiry date to April 2014. The reasons for this extension are outside this chapter's scope, but contractual arrangements made for the Brook Street development following that extension shaped affordable housing delivery both at Brook Street and elsewhere in Colchester.

On 29 May 2013, Colchester Council, Mersea Homes and Hills Residential Construction Limited (Hills)[67] signed a supplementary section 106 agreement for the Brook Street development (the first Brook Street 2013 agreement). This agreement noted that Mersea Homes owned the Brook Street site at that time, but that Hills would soon acquire ownership of 55 per cent of it. The agreement then stated that the two developers had agreed to provide an extra 21 affordable homes at Brook Street. These extra dwellings were, however, only part of an overall commitment by the two developers to provide an additional 68 affordable homes at Brook Street.[68] This would increase the total amount of affordable housing to 72 dwellings, which would represent 65 per cent of the total number of dwellings to be constructed. Colchester Council's local development plan documents state that developments of this size should provide 20 per cent affordable housing,[69] so the council and the two developers had agreed an affordable housing amount that was far higher than that required in the council's affordable housing policies.

However, on 29 May 2013, Colchester Council, Mersea Homes and Hills had also signed a separate contract made pursuant to section 1(1) of the Localism Act 2011 (the second Brook Street 2013 agreement).[70] The reference here to the Localism Act 2011 is striking because it indicates that the second agreement was probably *not* a section 106 agreement. Local authorities derive their power to make contracts from statute. Section 111 of the Local Government Act 1972 permits local authorities to make contracts that enable them to perform their statutory functions, whereas section 106 of the TCPA 1990 gives LPAs more specific powers to make contracts securing the delivery of planning obligations. Section 1(1) of the Localism Act 2011 confers a much broader power, allowing local authorities to 'do anything that individuals may generally do'. Subsequent case law confirms that this entitles local authorities to make contracts that do not relate directly to the performance of their statutory functions.[71] Since the second Brook Street 2013 agreement was probably not a section 106 agreement, the council could not consider the obligations therein when determining applications for planning permission relating to either the Brook Street development or any other developments. This also means that the duties imposed on the developers in the second Brook Street 2013 agreement would be enforceable against Mersea Homes and Hills but not against anyone who subsequently acquired ownership of the development site from them.[72] Similarly, it means that the rights created in the second agreement were personal to the two developers but were nonetheless binding on Colchester Council. Finally, it also means that Colchester Council was not obliged to keep a public record of the second agreement and, since the council also appears to have chosen not to include it in its online planning database, the second agreement's existence was seemingly hidden from view.[73]

Despite Colchester Council's decision not to publish the second Brook Street 2013 agreement, it is possible to piece together its purpose by examining the other developments discussed in this case study. The second development considered here is called 'Chesterwell'.[74] It is significantly larger than the Brook Street development and will provide around 1,600 new residential dwellings, a new primary school, a new secondary school and other local services, facilities and amenities on the edge of Colchester.[75] Mersea Homes and Countryside Properties (UK) Limited are constructing the development in a series of phases. The whole development, according to Mersea Homes, 'combines beautiful green spaces, timeless design and modern amenities to offer the perfect backdrop to family life'.[76] Mersea Homes and Countryside Properties jointly applied for 'outline' planning permission for Chesterwell in 2012. Developers often seek outline rather than 'full' planning permission when they want to obtain confirmation from an LPA that it regards a development proposal as acceptable 'in principle'.[77] A developer seeking to proceed with a development that has outline planning permission must, however, make subsequent 'reserved matters' applications before they can start building.[78] In those reserved matters applications, the developer usually seeks approval for the specific details of either a phase of a development or a whole development, so an application for outline planning permission is a logical early step for a developer proposing to build a large project in a series of phases. A developer applying for full planning permission should, by contrast, provide all the reports, drawings, plans and other documents that an LPA needs to permit a developer to start building.[79]

Mersea Homes and Countryside Properties jointly made a section 106 agreement with Colchester Council for Chesterwell in June 2014 (the Chesterwell agreement),[80] and the council then granted outline planning permission. The Chesterwell agreement contains affordable housing obligations alongside a wide range of other planning obligations. While the agreement governs the delivery of obligations for the whole Chesterwell development, Mersea Homes obtained reserved matters approvals for, and has been constructing, phases one and two. Mersea Homes is also constructing phase four but has, at the time of writing, been in dispute with Colchester Council over vehicular access for that phase. Countryside Properties is constructing phase three. This chapter focuses on phase two, which would provide 146 dwellings in total, of which, according to the Chesterwell agreement, 22 should have been affordable homes.

The third development discussed here is taking place at the disused Rowhedge port (the Rowhedge development).[81] On 11 March 2016, Hills applied to Colchester Council for permission to construct 86 dwellings on part of that site. Hills describes this development as 'an idyllic riverside village' encapsulating 'all the finer details of everyday life'.[82] Colchester Council's planning committee approved the grant of planning permission subject to the council, the developer and Essex County Council signing a section 106 agreement obliging the developer to provide on-site affordable housing alongside various other planning obligations. In November 2016, Colchester Council, the county council, a company that is part of the Hills group[83] and other interested parties duly signed a section 106 agreement (the Rowhedge agreement)[84] and Colchester Council granted planning permission.

The Rowhedge agreement's affordable housing clauses provide a key insight into the network of contractual arrangements that link affordable housing delivery at these developments. The Rowhedge agreement obliges Hills to provide affordable housing but creates a contractual right for the developer to elect either to provide the 17 affordable homes that Colchester Council's planning policies would ostensibly require, or to provide only two affordable homes.[85] An outsider trying to understand this contractual right to elect must follow a series of cross-references leading from the Rowhedge agreement back to the second Brook Street 2013 agreement. The Rowhedge agreement states that, in the second Brook Street 2013 agreement, the council and the two developers agreed that the over-supply of affordable housing at Brook Street meant that the two developers had earned something called 'the Brook Street Affordable Housing Allowance'. This allowance derived from the actual floorspace of the additional Brook Street affordable housing and would be allocated to the two developers in separate portions equivalent to their respective land interests on the Brook Street site.[86] Mersea Homes and Hills could thus apply their respective shares of the allowance to other developments in Colchester Council's area, meaning that the developers had a contractual right to deviate from the council's affordable housing policies on those other developments.

Nicky Morrison and Gemma Burgess have suggested that one of the advantages to LPAs of the use of section 106 agreements is that they can secure affordable housing delivery in places where that type of housing would not otherwise be available.[87] This principle underpins current affordable housing policy in England and is designed to ensure the creation of mixed communities consisting of housing of different types and tenures. The effect of the contractual arrangements discussed here, by contrast, was to enable two private developers to supply extra affordable housing on one of the most polluted streets in Colchester in exchange for the opportunity to elect to supply less of that housing at more upmarket developments elsewhere in the area. Consequently, the arrangements discussed here seem to have produced a contraction in the range of potential living spaces available in Colchester for people in housing need while granting private developers significant freedom to choose when, where and how they would deliver that housing.

Prescription and choice in contracts for affordable housing delivery

The contractual arrangements discussed here gave the respective developers a right to elect when, where and how they would deliver affordable housing. This section now shows how that right interacted with the complex and technical clauses relating to affordable housing delivery in the Chesterwell and Rowhedge section 106 agreements. It does this by first analysing the affordable housing provisions in the Chesterwell agreement and then examining the equivalent provisions in the Rowhedge agreement.

Mersea Homes chose to apply its share of the Brook Street allowance to the second phase of the Chesterwell development.[88] However, the Chesterwell agreement does not indicate that Mersea Homes had this option available to it. Instead, the Chesterwell agreement states that the developer of any phase of the development should ensure that at least 15 per cent of the total number of dwellings to be constructed for that phase should be affordable housing. Of that 15 per cent, the agreement states that two-thirds should be affordable rented and that the remainder should be available for purchase or rent at prices or rates that are higher than affordable rented housing but lower than market prices or rates. To achieve this, the agreement obliges the developer to confirm the number and sizes of affordable homes to be provided in a phase whenever they make a reserved matters application for that phase. The agreement then states that the council can respond by either commenting upon, amending or approving an affordable housing proposal within 60 working days of receipt, or the council can request a monetary contribution from the developer towards off-site provision of some, but not all, of the required on-site affordable housing. If the council does request a monetary contribution, the agreement states that the developer must provide it. On the other hand, the agreement expressly states that the council cannot require an alternative affordable housing mix that would 'adversely affect' the viability of either a phase of the development or the whole development.

Once the developer and the council agree an affordable housing proposal for a Chesterwell phase, the Chesterwell agreement also contains further obligations that manifest as a series of staging posts. Stage one of the affordable housing delivery mechanism in the Chesterwell agreement states that the developer will not permit the occupation of more than 40 per cent of the market dwellings in a phase until it has exchanged a contract with a registered affordable housing provider for the transfer to the provider of half the affordable housing in that phase. Stage two states that the developer will not permit the occupation of more than 80 per cent of those dwellings until it has arranged the transfer of the remainder of that phase's affordable housing. Finally, the agreement states that the developer will not begin a new phase of the development until all the affordable housing in an earlier phase is ready for occupation. However, if the developer fails to reach an agreement with a registered affordable housing provider for the transfer of the affordable housing for a phase on terms that the developer deems acceptable, the developer can instead sell all the affordable housing required for that phase at full price on the open market. In those circumstances, the agreement states that the developer should pay a 'fallback' monetary contribution to the council in an amount equivalent to 20 per cent of the market value of those dwellings before it permits the occupation of more than 85 per cent of the market dwellings in that phase.

If, as Macneil suggests, contractual behaviour inhabits a point on a spectrum between highly relational behaviour and highly discrete behaviour,[89] the affordable housing delivery mechanism described above looks like an attempt to maximise the 'discreteness' of the contractual arrangements for the Chesterwell development. Morrison and Burgess have noted that attempting to secure affordable housing delivery through section 106 agreements causes tension between LPAs and property developers,[90] so it is perhaps unsurprising that Colchester Council and Mersea Homes tried to plan mechanisms that had a strong 'quality of bindingness'[91] and that left very little room for 'tacit assumptions' about how each party would behave.[92] However, this reveals a contracting regime in which the parties seem to have been unwilling to place trust in the choices that their partners might make. While Vincent-Jones explains that individuals and organisations usually create contractual arrangements to achieve mutually beneficial outcomes,[93] he also argues that those arrangements that do not support contractual behavioural norms relating to trust and cooperation can tend to minimise the potential for any joint welfare maximisation.[94] Moreover, this author has shown elsewhere that the 'quality of bindingness' running through the contractual arrangements made for town planning processes is often skewed against LPAs.[95] This unbalanced power dynamic also emerges here in the way that the Chesterwell agreement purports to control precisely what Colchester Council can do when it receives an affordable housing proposal for a Chesterwell phase. The express prohibition in the Chesterwell agreement of any action that might undermine development viability is particularly striking, and reflects a broader mismatch in the way that the contractual arrangements used in town planning processes tend to reduce the range of actions open to LPAs while giving private developers the tools to predict and control precisely what an LPA will do. On the other hand, where there is flexibility in the contractual arrangements for the Chesterwell development, that flexibility favours the developer. According to the terms of the Chesterwell agreement, phase two should have provided 22 affordable homes, of which 14 would be affordable rented and eight would be for purchase or rent at prices or rates that are higher than affordable rented housing but lower than market prices or rates. Instead, Colchester Council agreed that

Mersea Homes, by applying its share of the Brook Street allowance to the second Chesterwell phase, was entitled to provide only eight affordable homes, of which none would be affordable rented.[96] Consequently, there is a striking contrast between the substance of the Chesterwell agreement and the actual effect of the contractual arrangements between Mersea Homes and Colchester Council. The existence of this substantial freedom to choose was thus largely hidden from public view.

Hills elected to apply its share of the Brook Street allowance to the Rowhedge development,[97] although the Rowhedge agreement does expressly acknowledge that Hills had this choice available to it. The Rowhedge agreement states that, if Hills did choose to use its allowance, it would need to provide two affordable homes instead of the 17 affordable homes that would otherwise be required. Alongside this, the agreement then contains affordable housing clauses that would apply regardless of the amount of affordable housing that the developer elected to deliver. These clauses create a series of staging posts akin to those described above in the Chesterwell agreement and appear to have been carefully planned to restrict the future choices available to the parties. By comparison, the cross-references in the Rowhedge agreement to the Brook Street allowance are jarringly imprecise. For example, the agreement states that the Brook Street allowance

> effectively provides [the two developers] with the opportunity to transfer all or part of their affordable housing requirement from [their] other development sites (one of which is [the Rowhedge development]) to their development at Brook Street, Colchester.

The language used in section 106 agreements tends to be 'tightly drafted' and, where possible, based on wording that has been tested in earlier agreements and incorporated into standard clauses which are then available for subsequent agreements.[98] However, the use of the word 'effectively' in the Rowhedge agreement in relation to the Brook Street allowance suggests that Colchester Council and Hills were either unable or unwilling to speak directly about what they had created. They may have been unable to speak directly about the implications of the allowance because they had created a novel network of contractual arrangements and were grappling to find the appropriate words to describe it. Alternatively, this may have been a product of reflexive hesitancy flowing from an awareness that the arrangements reshaped affordable housing delivery in ways not envisaged in either central government guidance or Colchester Council's planning policies.

This discussion of affordable housing delivery at the Chesterwell and Rowhedge developments shows that aspects of the contractual arrangements did allow the developers more flexibility than might have been expected given the rigid structure of the formal contract documents. Macneil has observed that reciprocal flexibility is essential for durable contractual relations,[99] and Tom Dobson has explained that effective town planning often requires LPAs to be willing to use planning obligations and section 106 agreements in creative ways.[100] The network of contractual arrangements studied here suggests that Colchester Council does take a flexible approach to what it can do with its formal contracts. However, this creative contractual behaviour produced an over-supply of affordable housing on a polluted street in the centre of Colchester and an under-supply at more upmarket developments elsewhere in the area. The contracting regime within which these arrangements were created is also one which, using Marc Galanter's well-known terminology, favours those developers who are 'repeat players' and who can use the longevity of their relationship with an LPA to influence the implementation of affordable housing policies.[101] These findings thus show how developers can use contractual arrangements to establish control over when, where and how they provide affordable housing. They also demonstrate how dependency, mistrust and the pursuit of this control can shape the contracts used in town planning processes and enable developers to manipulate contemporary town planning decision-making.

Conclusion

In simple quantitative terms, the loss of affordable housing at the Rowhedge and Chesterwell developments may not seem too serious. After all, the developers involved in those developments had to deliver extra affordable housing elsewhere before Colchester Council would permit a deviation from its policies on affordable housing delivery. However, the point of this chapter is to highlight the small things that different types of contractual arrangements do to shape the places where ordinary people live. It is well known that private property developers attempt to use viability modelling practices to ensure that they do not have to provide affordable housing as part of their development projects.[102] The developments discussed in this case study now show that well-connected developers can also deploy a complex network of partially hidden contractual arrangements to create a type of one-sided flexibility that enables them to compel LPAs to bend their rules relating to affordable housing. This unbalanced power dynamic is a familiar consequence of the contractual arrangements used in contemporary planning practices.[103] The outcomes are also an inevitable product of the turn to quasi-market solutions to deliver public policy goals and are part of a trend that Raco,[104] Linda Fox-Rogers and Enda Murphy[105] and this author[106] have already analysed in relation to planning and that Vincent-Jones has examined in relation to public contracting more generally.[107] Macneil, albeit in a different context, also notes that specialisation often begets a relationship of dependency that can shape contractual behaviour.[108] It is thus unsurprising that, when LPAs rely on private developers to provide affordable housing, those developers will seek to create contractual arrangements that enable them to choose when, where and how they fulfil their public policy obligations. Nevertheless, this case study provides new perspectives on opportunism and the pursuit of control in town planning processes and shows how developers can create flexibility even amidst highly formal contractual behaviour. It also highlights the need for a robust study of both the contractual arrangements that other LPAs make to secure affordable housing delivery and the granular details of section 106 agreements produced for other types of property development.

Notes

1. Town and Country Planning Act (TCPA) 1990, section 57(1).
2. TCPA 1990, section 70(1).
3. Cunliffe 2001, 33 (see also Mole 1996, 183). For example, planning obligations might require the delivery of complex infrastructure and the details of that delivery would be beyond the scope of a condition attached to a planning permission.
4. A developer might make a unilateral undertaking if an LPA refuses to agree a negotiated planning obligation (e.g. *R (on the application of Millgate Developments Ltd) v Wokingham Borough Council* [2011] EWCA Civ 1062; [2012] 3 EGLR 87).
5. White 2013, 1232.
6. Crook 2016, 68.
7. Community Infrastructure Levy Regulations 2010 SI 2010/948.
8. Crook 2016, 95–6.
9. The government's National Planning Policy Framework (NPPF) states that LPAs should use their local development plans to specify the developer contributions they will seek: Ministry of Housing, Communities and Local Government (MHCLG) 2021a, [34].
10. White 2013, 1244.
11. Dobson 2012 and Amodu 2020 provide a detailed discussion of this levy.
12. Lord et al 2020, 9.
13. Planning Act 2008, section 216 and Community Infrastructure Levy Regulations 2010, regulation 59 list the matters to which LPAs can apply levy funds. They do not include affordable housing. See also MHCLG 2020a, [144].
14. The government estimates that 52 per cent of new affordable housing in 2019–20 in England was delivered through section 106 agreements: MHCLG 2020b, 5.
15. MHCLG 2020c, 60–7.
16. Vincent-Jones 2006, 158.
17. Healey, Purdue and Ennis 1996; Mole 1996; Cunliffe 2001; Amodu 2008.
18. Claydon and Smith 1997; Ennis 1997.

19. Fox-Rogers and Murphy 2015.
20. Christophers 2014; Layard 2019; Mitchell 2020; Ferm and Raco 2020.
21. Christophers 2014; Mitchell 2020.
22. Raco 2012. See also Campbell and Henneberry 2005.
23. Raco 2012, 454, resonating in a very different context with Carolyn Abbot's discussion of legal expertise in planning inquiries.
24. Raco 2012, 453. See also Fox-Rogers and Murphy 2015, Mitchell 2021 and, in relation to other public contracting regimes, Vincent-Jones 2006.
25. Macneil 2000, 879.
26. Macneil 2000, 894–5.
27. Macneil 1980, 60.
28. Macneil 1980, 60.
29. Macneil 1980, 11 (emphasis in original). Macneil explains that behaviours such as contractual solidarity and reciprocity are more 'relational contract norms': Macneil 1983–4, 361–6.
30. Mitchell 2013, 178.
31. Vincent-Jones 2006; Vincent-Jones 2007.
32. Vincent-Jones 2006, 21–5.
33. Vincent-Jones 2007, 267.
34. Vincent-Jones 2007, 269.
35. Vincent-Jones 2006, 352; Vincent-Jones 2007, 269.
36. Van der Veen and Korthals Altes 2011; Van der Veen and Korthals Altes 2012.
37. Mitchell 2021.
38. Mitchell 2021, 10.
39. Bramley 2019. For a broader discussion of housing in this volume see Maria Lee's chapter.
40. Rents for social rented housing are set nationally: MHCLG 2021b, [3.4]–[3.7]. LPAs and registered social housing providers generally own and manage social rented housing.
41. LPAs or registered providers usually own affordable rented housing. It can be let at a rent up to 80 per cent of local market rent: MHCLG 2021b, [3.10]–[3.14].
42. MHCLG 2021a, Annex 2.
43. See e.g. Department for Communities and Local Government (DCLG) 2012, Annex 2.
44. See e.g. Colchester Borough Council (Colchester Council) 2011, [3.1]–[3.5].
45. Tony Crook explains how this approach emerged and its current manifestations: Crook 2016, 74–83. See also Morrison and Burgess 2014, 426–9.
46. Morrison and Burgess 2014.
47. MHCLG 2021a, [61]–[62]. The original NPPF contained similar guidance: DCLG 2012, [47] and [50].
48. MHCLG 2021a, [64] states that LPAs should only seek affordable housing from 'major' developments. A residential development is a major development if it provides 10 or more homes: MHCLG 2021a, Annex 2.
49. Crook 2016, 78.
50. MHCLG 2021a, [65].
51. MHCLG 2021a, [63].
52. MHCLG 2021a, [31].
53. MHCLG 2021a, [34].
54. See e.g. DCLG 2012, [173].
55. DCLG 2012, [173].
56. Mitchell 2020, 41; see also Layard 2019 and Christophers 2014. The current NPPF now simply notes that viability assessments are necessary in some circumstances, and it provides generic guidance on how LPAs should conduct these: MHCLG 2021a, [58].
57. Crosby, McAllister and Wyatt 2013; Ferm and Raco 2020.
58. DCLG 2012, [50]; MHCLG 2021a, [63].
59. Layard 2019, 217. The courts considered viability disputes in *Kensington and Chelsea RLBC v Secretary of State for Communities and Local Government* [2010] EWCA Civ 1466 (also known as *Vannes KFT v Kensington and Chelsea RLBC*) and *Parkhurst Road Ltd v Secretary of State for Communities and Local Government* [2018] EWHC 991 (Admin); [2019] JPL 855.
60. See e.g. Colchester Council 2011, sections 4 and 5.
61. Colchester is the largest town in the Borough of Colchester, a local government area that includes neighbouring towns and villages in part of Essex, eastern England. Colchester Borough Council (Colchester Council) and Essex County Council share local government

administrative responsibilities in the area. For example, Colchester Council formulates and implements area-wide planning policies whereas the county council administers various highways and transport matters and state education provision: see https://www.colchester.gov.uk/info/cbc-article/?catid=our-services&id=KA-02065 (accessed 12 June 2022).
62. Colchester Council 2020, 2–3.
63. Colchester Council illustrates local Air Quality Management Areas on a plan available at https://cbccrmdata.blob.core.windows.net/noteattachment/Air%20Quality%20Management%20Area%20Map%20-%202018.pdf (accessed 12 June 2022). The underlying law on air quality standards and local authority reviews is in the Environment Act 1995, sections 80–91.
64. Mersea Homes Limited is a regional property developer: https://www.merseahomes.co.uk/the-experience (accessed 12 June 2022).
65. Colchester Council published the planning documents referred to in this chapter on its online planning database https://www.colchester.gov.uk/planning-search-results/ (accessed 12 June 2022). The author has copies available for inspection on request. Documents relating to the Brook Street development are also available on the council's planning database under reference numbers F/COL/04/1747 and 101983.
66. Colchester Council 2016, [14.1].
67. Hills Residential Construction Limited is a regional property developer that is part of a wider group of companies: https://www.hillsgroup.co.uk/construction/projects/ (accessed 12 June 2022). This chapter uses the shorthand 'Hills' to refer to all companies in the group.
68. Colchester Council 2017, [4.2].
69. Colchester Council 2014, policy H4.
70. The statutory basis of the second Brook Street 2013 agreement is recorded in schedule 4B of the Rowhedge agreement, as discussed later in this chapter. Its existence is also recorded in Colchester Council 2016, [14.1] and Colchester Council 2017, [4.1].
71. *Hussain v Sandwell Metropolitan Borough Council* [2017] EWHC 1641 (Admin); [2018] PTSR 142, [125].
72. Section 106 agreements are automatically enforceable against the person making the obligation and any person deriving ownership of the affected land from that person (TCPA 1990, section 106(3)).
73. Section 106 agreements are local land charges (TCPA 1990, section 106(11)). Local land charges are recorded on a searchable register (Local Land Charges Act 1975, section 3). Article 40(3)–(4) of the Town and Country Planning (Development Management Procedure) (England) Order 2015 No 595 (DMPO 2015) also requires LPAs to place a copy of section 106 agreements on their planning registers. DMPO 2015 article 40(3)–(4) replaces the Town and Country Planning (Development Management Procedure) (England) Order 2010 No 2184, article 36(3)–(4), which contained similar provisions. This legislation does not apply to agreements made under section 1(1) of the Localism Act 2011.
74. Documents discussed here from Colchester Council's planning database for Chesterwell are available under reference numbers 121272 (outline planning permission) and 161593 (phase two reserved matters approval).
75. David Lock Associates 2012, [1.02].
76. Publicity material downloaded from https://www.merseahomes.co.uk/ on 29 November 2021 and held on file by the author. Countryside Properties (UK) Limited is a subsidiary of Countryside Properties plc, which is another regional property developer: https://www.countrysidepartnerships.com/about-us (accessed 12 June 2022).
77. MHCLG 2021c, [005].
78. MHCLG 2021c, [006]. See also TCPA 1990, section 92(1)–(2) and DMPO 2015, articles 2(1) and 5(1).
79. MHCLG 2021c, [004]. See also TCPA 1990, section 62 and DMPO 2015, article 7(1). The developers constructing the other developments discussed here sought and obtained full planning permission.
80. The Chesterwell agreement records that Mersea Homes and Countryside Properties owned most of the Chesterwell site at the time of the agreement. The other individuals who owned the remainder were also signatories. Essex County Council was a signatory so that it could secure transport and education obligations detailed in the agreement.
81. Rowhedge is a village situated approximately three miles south-east of Colchester. Documents on the council's planning database for the Rowhedge development are available under reference number 160551.

82. Publicity material downloaded from https://www.hills-residential.co.uk/ on 15 November 2021 and held on file by the author.
83. The company that signed the Rowhedge agreement is called Grange Marsh Properties Limited (Grange Marsh). The agreement does not state that Grange Marsh is part of the Hills group but company records downloaded on 14 December 2021 from Companies House and held on file by the author show that Grange Marsh and other Hills companies have the same registered office address, company secretary, directors and shareholders. The reasons why Grange Marsh but not another Hills company signed the Rowhedge agreement are beyond this chapter's scope. As stated above, this chapter uses the shorthand 'Hills' to refer to all companies in the group.
84. The county council entered into the agreement because it required the developer both to provide new access roads that the county council would then adopt and maintain and to make financial contributions to address local education needs. The individuals who owned the development site also signed the agreement. The agreement records that Hills had agreed a separate contract with those landowners for the purchase of the development site.
85. Colchester Council's Core Strategy states that developments of this size should provide 20 per cent affordable housing (Colchester Council 2014, policy H4). Providing 17 affordable housing dwellings, of which the agreement states that 14 would be affordable rented and three would be for purchase or rent at prices or rates that are higher than social rented housing but lower than market prices or rates, would satisfy this policy goal.
86. See also Colchester Council 2016, [14.1] and Colchester Council 2017, [4.3]–[4.4]. The allowance amounted to 2,046 square metres of affordable housing. Since Hills owned 55 per cent of the Brook Street site, it was entitled to an allowance of 1,125 square metres. Mersea Homes received the remainder.
87. Morrison and Burgess 2014, 430.
88. Colchester Council 2017, [4.7]–[4.8].
89. Macneil 2000, 894.
90. Morrison and Burgess 2014, 432.
91. Vincent-Jones 2006, 158.
92. Macneil 1980, 25.
93. Vincent-Jones 2007, 269.
94. Vincent-Jones 2007, 269.
95. Mitchell 2021.
96. Colchester Council 2017, [4.9].
97. Colchester Council 2017, [4.3].
98. White 2013, 1244.
99. Macneil 1983–4, 363.
100. Dobson 2012. See also Healey, Purdue and Ennis 1996, 158.
101. Galanter 1974.
102. Layard 2019; Mitchell 2020.
103. Mitchell 2021 provides another example.
104. Raco 2012.
105. Fox-Rogers and Murphy 2015.
106. Mitchell 2021.
107. Vincent-Jones 2006.
108. Macneil 1980, 32.

References

Amodu, Tola (2008). '"For the Record"? Understanding Regulatory Processes through Archival Materials: The Example of Planning Agreements', *Journal of Law and Society* 35: 183–200.

Amodu, Tola (2020). 'Revisiting the Rules. The Pervasiveness of Discretion in the Context of Planning Gains: The Case of the Community Infrastructure Levy', *Public Law*: 643–60.

Bramley, Glen (2019). *Housing Supply Requirements across Great Britain for Low-Income Households and Homeless People: Research for Crisis and the National Housing Federation; Main Technical Report*. Edinburgh: Heriot-Watt University. Available at https://core.ac.uk/download/pdf/287503808.pdf (accessed 12 June 2022).

Campbell, Heather and John Henneberry (2005). 'Planning Obligations, the Market Orientation of Planning and Planning Professionalism', *Journal of Property Research* 22: 37–59.

Christophers, Brett (2014). 'Wild Dragons in the City: Urban Political Economy, Affordable Housing Development and the Performative World-Making of Economic Models', *International Journal of Urban and Regional Research* 38: 79–97.

Claydon, Jim and Bryan Smith (1997). 'Negotiating Planning Gains through the British Development Control System', *Urban Studies* 34: 2003–22.

Colchester Borough Council (2011). *Supplementary Planning Document. Affordable Housing.* Available at https://cbccrmdata.blob.core.windows.net/noteattachment/Adopted_AH_SPD_Aug11.pdf (accessed 12 June 2022).

Colchester Borough Council (2014). *Core Strategy.* Adopted December 2008. Selected policies revised July 2014. Available at https://cbccrmdata.blob.core.windows.net/noteattachment/Core%20Strategy.pdf (accessed 12 June 2022).

Colchester Borough Council (2016). *Report to Planning Committee in Respect of Application no.: 160551 Related to Development at Rowhedge Wharf, High Street, Rowhedge, Colchester.* Available in Colchester Borough Council's planning database for planning application 160551 (accessed 20 December 2021).

Colchester Borough Council (2017). *Affordable Housing at the Chesterwell Development (formerly known as North Growth Area Urban Extension) and the use of the Brook Street Affordable Housing Allowance.* Available at https://colchester.cmis.uk.com/colchester/Document.ashx?czJKcaeAi5tUFL1DTL2UE4zNRBcoShgo=KcTnJhsdk9t50U%2BkbpmYbKRf9yKEeOScGRgrmq6Pf3KAk3H6O6DOnw%3D%3D&rUzwRPf%2BZ3zd4E7Ikn8Lyw%3D%3D=pwRE6AGJFLDNlh225F5QMaQWCtPHwdhUfCZ%2FLUQzgA2uL5jNRG4jdQ%3D%3D&mCTIbCubSFfXsDGW9IXnlg%3D%3D=hFflUdN3100%3D&kCx1AnS9%2FpWZQ40DXFvdEw%3D%3D=hFflUdN3100%3D&uJovDxwdjMPoYv%2BAJvYtyA%3D%3D=ctNJFf55vVA%3D%3D&FgPlIEJYlotS%2BYGoBi5olA%3D%3D=NHdURQburHA%3D&d9Qjj0ag1Pd993jsyOJqFvmyB7X0CSQK=ctNJFf55vVA%3D&WGewmoAfeNR9xqBux0r1Q8Za60lavYmz=ctNJFf55vVA%3D&WGewmoAfeNQ16B2MHuCpMRKZMwaG1PaO=ctNJFf55vVA%3D (accessed 12 June 2022).

Colchester Borough Council (2020). *Findings for the Clean Air for Colchester Community Engagement.* Available at https://cbccrmdata.blob.core.windows.net/noteattachment/CBC-Environment-Clean-Air-Survey-Findings-2020-Findings%20report%20from%20Clean%20Air%20for%20Colchester%20Community%20Engagement.pdf (accessed 12 June 2022).

Crook, Tony (2016). 'Planning Obligations Policy in England: *De Facto* Taxation of Development Value'. In *Planning Gain: Providing Infrastructure and Affordable Housing,* edited by Tony Crook, John Henneberry and Christine Whitehead, 63–114. Chichester: John Wiley.

Crosby, Neil, Pat McAllister and Peter Wyatt (2013). 'Fit for Planning? An Evaluation of the Application of Development Viability Appraisal Models in the UK Planning System', *Environment and Planning B: Planning and Design* 40: 3–22.

Cunliffe, Michael (2001). 'Planning Obligations – Where are We Now?', *Journal of Planning and Environment Law* Supp (Occasional Papers No. 29): 31–63.

David Lock Associates (2012). *Colchester North Outline Planning Application. Planning Statement.* Available in Colchester Borough Council's planning database for planning application 121272 (accessed 20 December 2021).

Department for Communities and Local Government (2012). *National Planning Policy Framework.*

Dobson, Tom (2012). 'Community Infrastructure Levy: Will it Deliver?', *Journal of Planning and Environment Law* 13 Supp: OP117-OP138.

Ennis, Frank (1997). 'Infrastructure Provision, the Negotiating Process and the Planner's Role', *Urban Studies* 34: 1935–54.

Ferm, Jessica and Mike Raco (2020). 'Viability Planning, Value Capture and the Geographies of Market-Led Planning Reform in England', *Planning Theory & Practice* 21: 218–35.

Fox-Rogers, Linda and Enda Murphy (2015). 'From Brown Envelopes to Community Benefits: The Co-option of Planning Gain Agreements under Deepening Neoliberalism', *Geoforum* 67: 41–50.

Galanter, Marc (1974). 'Why the "Haves" Come Out Ahead: Speculations on the Limits of Legal Change', *Law & Society Review* 9: 95–160.

Healey, Patsy, Michael Purdue and Frank Ennis (1996). 'Negotiating Development: Planning Gain and Mitigating Impacts', *Journal of Property Research* 13: 143–60.

Layard, Antonia (2019). 'Planning by Numbers: Affordable Housing and Viability in England'. In *Planning and Knowledge: How New Forms of Technocracy are Shaping Contemporary Cities,* edited by Mike Raco and Federico Savini, 213–24. Bristol: Policy Press.

Lord, Alexander et al (2020). *The Incidence, Value and Delivery of Planning Obligations and Community Infrastructure Levy in England in 2018–19*. Available at https://assets.publishing.service.gov.uk/government/uploads/system/uploads/attachment_data/file/907203/The_Value_and_Incidence_of_Developer_Contributions_in_England_201819.pdf (accessed 12 June 2022).

Macneil, Ian R. (1980). *The New Social Contract: An Inquiry into Modern Contractual Relations*. New Haven, CT: Yale University Press.

Macneil, Ian R. (1983–4). 'Values in Contract: Internal and External', *Northwestern University Law Review* 78: 340–418.

Macneil, Ian R. (2000). 'Relational Contract Theory: Challenges and Queries', *Northwestern University Law Review* 94: 877–908.

Ministry of Housing, Communities and Local Government (2020a). *Guidance. Community Infrastructure Levy*. Available at https://www.gov.uk/guidance/community-infrastructure-levy (accessed 12 June 2022).

Ministry of Housing, Communities and Local Government (2020b). *Affordable Housing Supply: April 2019 to March 2020, England*. Available at https://assets.publishing.service.gov.uk/government/uploads/system/uploads/attachment_data/file/940517/AHS_2019-20.pdf (accessed 12 June 2022).

Ministry of Housing, Communities and Local Government (2020c). *White Paper: Planning for the Future*.

Ministry of Housing, Communities and Local Government (2021a). *National Planning Policy Framework*.

Ministry of Housing, Communities and Local Government (2021b). *Guidance. Rent Standard – April 2020 (Updated 15 November 2021)*. Available at https://www.gov.uk/government/publications/rent-standard/rent-standard-april-2020 (accessed 12 June 2022).

Ministry of Housing, Communities and Local Government (2021c). *Guidance. Making an Application*. Available at https://www.gov.uk/guidance/making-an-application (accessed 12 June 2022).

Mitchell, Catherine (2013). *Contract Law and Contract Practice: Bridging the Gap between Legal Reasoning and Commercial Expectation*. Oxford: Hart Publishing.

Mitchell, Edward (2020). 'Planning, Property and Profit: The Use of Financial Viability Modelling in Urban Property Development', *Northern Ireland Legal Quarterly* 71: 35–55.

Mitchell, Edward (2021). 'Compulsory Purchase and the State Redistribution of Land: A Study of Local Authority-Private Developer Contractual Behaviour', *Journal of Property, Planning and Environmental Law* 13: 1–16.

Mole, David (1996). 'Planning Gain After the Tesco Case', *Journal of Planning and Environment Law* Mar: 183–93.

Morrison, Nicky and Gemma Burgess (2014). 'Inclusionary Housing Policy in England: The Impact of the Downturn on the Delivery of Affordable Housing Through Section 106', *Journal of Housing and the Built Environment* 29: 423–38.

Raco, Mike (2012). 'The Privatisation of Urban Development and the London Olympics 2012', *City* 16: 452–60.

Van der Veen, Menno and Willem K. Korthals Altes (2011). 'Urban Development Agreements: Do They Meet Guiding Principles for a Better Deal?', *Cities* 28: 310–19.

Van der Veen, Menno and Willem K. Korthals Altes (2012). 'Contracts and Learning in Complex Urban Projects', *International Journal of Urban and Regional Research* 36: 1053–75.

Vincent-Jones, Peter (2006). *The New Public Contracting: Regulation, Responsiveness, Relationality*. Oxford: Oxford University Press.

Vincent-Jones, Peter (2007). 'The New Public Contracting: Public Versus Private Ordering?', *Indiana Journal of Global Legal Studies* 14: 259–78.

White, Matthew (2013). 'Renegotiating Planning Obligations: An Overview of the Law', *Journal of Planning and Environment Law* 10: 1232–54.

11
Embracing the unwanted guests at the judicial review party: Why administrative law scholars should take planning law seriously

Joanna Bell

Introduction

Reading judicial review case law is a bit like mingling at a party filled with an eclectic mix of guests. Put simply, there is no such thing as an archetypal judicial review challenge.[1] Judicial review case law arises in many administrative contexts and varies across many metrics.[2] The conversation therefore varies considerably from one to the next.

Some guests at the judicial review party generate more excitement among administrative law scholars than others.[3] Judicial reviews of prerogative powers,[4] human rights challenges raising morally or politically contentious issues[5] and claims in which ambitious barristers press arguments for the advancement of general grounds of review,[6] for instance, are all known to make for lively conversation. Perhaps the guests at the dinner party that administrative law scholars most hope to avoid sitting next to, however, are the planning law judicial reviews. One commentator recently joked that while 'as a self-styled judicial review connoisseur'[7] he enjoys reading case law of all kinds, this does not extend to planning cases.

Part of the problem is that, to engage with these party guests, one needs to understand the distinctive 'grammar'[8] of planning law. Without understanding the intricate legal and administrative background, planning case law can appear impenetrable. Becoming lingual in planning law, however, requires a significant investment of time and intellectual energy. Put simply, there is a lot to master. The field has a long history.[9] The modern statutory framework is characterised by numerous interlocking layers, which have changed and continue to change with frequency. Understanding many planning law judicial reviews also requires an understanding of other things, including different forms of policy, numerous environmental law regimes[10] and the non-legal planning concepts that underpin legal developments.[11]

This chapter argues, however, that administrative law scholars have a lot to gain from becoming lingual in planning law. There are, it argues, at least three reasons why close study of planning challenges can generate essential insights into the nature of judicial review itself. First, the planning regime is one of the most established, developed and commonly litigated areas of administration in England and Wales. Courts have had ample opportunity to develop judicial review doctrine in this field. Planning case law therefore provides a useful study, offering valuable insights into what highly developed judicial review doctrine looks like and potentially the directions in which judicial review may evolve in other areas. Secondly, planning law judicial reviews are not peculiar. Many of the features of planning case law which perhaps deter closer intellectual engagement are widespread features of much administrative law adjudication. Scholars must take these characteristics seriously and factor them into their understanding of judicial review. Thirdly, planning judicial reviews are a proven source of broader judicial review principle. It continues to be important to look to planning judicial reviews for potential legal developments which may have application in other areas.

The discussion is organised into five parts. The first part offers a brief introduction to practical intersections between planning law and judicial review. The second, third and fourth parts articulate the chapter's three arguments for administrative law scholars taking planning law more seriously. The chapter's final part concludes with a broader plea to scholars to embrace the 'vertical', as well as the 'horizontal', dimensions of judicial review more warmly.[12]

The intersections between planning law and judicial review

Before articulating the various benefits of administrative law scholars paying closer attention to planning law, it is useful to briefly highlight the main sites of practical interaction between judicial review and planning law. A good place to begin is the Town and Country Planning Act

(TCPA) 1947. The 1947 Act fundamentally altered the face of planning law – and indeed public law more broadly – in England and Wales. Although legal regulations on the use of land had long existed,[13] this Act made planning permission a *general* requirement for the 'development'[14] of land. The result was a major shift in the balance of public and private decision-making responsibility. Broadly, a jurisdiction without any planning control leaves decisions concerning the development of land solely in the hands of property owners. The TCPA 1947, however, introduced a major oversight role for a range of both local and central public authorities, equipping them with powers to make a range of planning decisions. Those decision-making powers persist, in amended forms, today.

The overlapping relationship between planning law and judicial review arises for a primary, simple reason: when it comes to legally challenging planning decisions in England and Wales, the routes are varied and have changed over time[15] but they all ultimately lead to the same destination: judicial review before the High Court. Judicial review of planning decisions takes broadly two procedural forms. First, in some places, legislation creates what are commonly called 'statutory review'[16] processes. These empower parties with a requisite interest[17] to make an appeal on points of law to the High Court, sometimes as a first step[18] and sometimes following other procedural stages.[19] Legislative provision for appeals is, however, 'piecemeal'[20] and does not offer comprehensive coverage. In other places, challengers are therefore left to fall back on the application for judicial review (AJR) procedure. Introduced in the late 1970s, this procedure functions as a 'remedy of last resort',[21] enabling challenges to be brought before the High Court[22] where there is no other procedural route available.[23] The AJR plays an especially important role in the planning context in facilitating challenges to *grants* of permission.

Importantly, across both statutory reviews and AJRs, and aside from a few minor peculiarities,[24] the nature of the legal inquiry undertaken by the High Court is the same. The core question to be addressed is not whether the decision was 'wrong'[25] but whether it was lawful. 'Disagreement in the absence of any identifiable legal error',[26] as the Court of Appeal recently put it, 'cannot ground'[27] a successful challenge. The courts, in other words, review planning decisions on 'ordinary public law grounds',[28] against the general principles of review.[29]

Judicial review of planning decisions has created sites through which planning law and administrative law have influenced one another. The primary focus of this chapter is on what *administrative law scholars* stand to gain from engaging more closely with planning law. Specifically, the next three parts identify three benefits of administrative law scholars becoming 'lingual' in planning law.

These points connect with a broader lesson for administrative law scholars: the importance of embracing what Mark Aronson has usefully termed judicial review's both 'horizontal' and 'vertical' aspects.[30] As Aronson emphasises, no judicial review case is one-dimensional. Any given judicial review challenge has *horizontal* dimensions. These arise because the applicant will usually seek to rely on one or more established general grounds of review.[31] In a planning challenge, this horizontal aspect is reflected in the list of grounds on which the applicant relies: misinterpretation of law or policy; failure to consider a material matter; procedural unfairness; etc. Judicial review challenges, however, also have a *vertical* dimension, in the sense that any given judicial review challenge focuses on a particular power or area of decision-making: planning, immigration, social security, etc. The conclusion of this chapter will call upon scholars to reflect more deeply on the intersection between these different dimensions of judicial review.

It is also worth emphasising, however, that implicit in the chapter are a series of reasons why scholars interested in planning law would benefit from engaging deeply with judicial review. For one, this chapter highlights that courts are important forums in which planning law is developed. Planning law is not a product only of legislatures and policy-makers. It is also made by judges, and fundamentally important features of the planning regime have been shaped by legal rulings. To understand both the practical forces in play and what is legally possible in the planning law regime it is, in other words, essential to engage with the role of courts. Planning law scholars could also usefully see themselves more firmly as part of a broader intellectual conversation about public administration and accountability. Debates about legitimacy and reform in judicial review would benefit immeasurably from a stronger planning perspective. Planning law scholars, in other words, should not view *themselves* as the unwelcome guests at the judicial review party. They are valuable contributors to debates about public power with a wealth of experience to bring to bear.

An image of highly evolved judicial review doctrine

Several decades ago, it was common for leading administrative scholars to take an active interest in planning law.[32] Now, despite the practical points of intersection between the two fields, administrative law scholars in England and Wales[33] are generally as guilty of neglecting planning law as others.[34] A first reason why this is unfortunate is that planning judicial reviews have generated a highly developed body of judicial review doctrine. Planning judicial reviews have a long history, the foundations of the modern system having been laid in the late 1940s.[35] Planning issues also continue to arise with considerable frequency. A recent study of Administrative Court case law, for instance, identified planning challenges as a common category of judicial review case at both Administrative and Court of Appeal level,[36] and the Supreme Court regularly determines planning issues of major importance.[37] A useful resource created jointly by Landmark Chamber and Town Legal LLP[38] at the inception of the Planning Division[39] records 493 planning judgments, across all courts, since 2014.

This large body of case law has afforded the courts a great many opportunities to develop judicial review doctrine in the planning context. Planning judicial reviews, in other words, offer a valuable case study in how judicial review doctrine is implemented and evolved in an administrative area which courts have engaged with regularly. Courts judicially review decisions taken in a broad variety of administrative contexts.[40] Few of these administrative schemes are as established, or as commonly litigated, as planning.[41] The study of planning challenges not only highlights a different side to judicial review, firmly emphasising that, although challenges to novel schemes may be interesting,[42] they are not the norm.[43] It may also afford a helpful glimpse into possible directions for judicial review doctrine in other areas.

One feature of planning judicial review is particularly worth highlighting:[44] the high level of *particularisation* which characterises doctrine in this area. As any student of administrative law knows, judicial review involves assessing the lawfulness of public authority decision-making against a series of well-established, general grounds of review. To be lawful, public authority decisions must, among other things, be based on a proper understanding of the law, conform to the principles of procedural fairness and be rational.[45] Across the large body of planning case law, the courts have come to articulate clear and context-specific guidance on how the general grounds of review apply in the *specific context* of planning administration. There are leading authorities on probably close to all aspects of how judicial review doctrine applies to various aspects of the planning system.[46] Substantial bodies of case law have built up, for instance, on the difference between irrelevant and relevant considerations in determining planning applications,[47] and on what it means for a grant or refusal of permission or environmental impact assessment[48] to be rational. In consequence, the proper formulation of general grounds of review and the 'landmark'[49] cases that established them are rarely mentioned in planning judicial reviews nowadays. Planning law has *its own* landmarks.[50] What, after all, is the point in retracing the origin story of procedural fairness[51] when there is Court of Appeal guidance specifically stating how its demands bear out in a planning inquiry?[52]

Two examples illustrate neatly the highly refined form judicial review doctrine has taken. First, the clusters of principles of interpretation through which courts ascertain the meaning of the various legal texts which may be relevant to a planning decision. In the case of planning policy, for instance, case law stresses the importance of *objective* interpretation.[53] Planning policy is 'intended to guide . . . behaviour . . . [and] to secure consistency and direction in the exercise of discretionary power',[54] making it important to consider the perspective of the reader, not that of the drafter. At the same time, the Supreme Court has repeatedly warned against the 'dangers of over-legalisation'.[55] Planning policy is often shot through with broad concepts and ambiguous language. Judges are warned against the temptation to use interpretation to rewrite policy to afford clearer, better guidance to decision-makers. Broad language, rather, must sometimes be understood as conferring a broad discretion, even if this means decision-makers may sometimes adopt different approaches.[56] There are also separate and well-established legal principles on the interpretation of officer reports to local planning committees,[57] the construction of planning inspector and ministerial decision letters,[58] reports by neighbourhood plan examiners,[59] advice from statutory consultees[60] and existing planning permissions.[61]

A second example concerns the rules on bias. It is a longstanding principle of the common law that decisions should be reached by decision-makers who both are and appear to be impartial.[62] The principle, however, was largely developed across challenges to *judicial* decisions.[63] Its application in other contexts continues to give rise to significant legal and normative questions.[64] In the local planning context, judicial review on the ground of bias has taken a highly distinctive form. The courts have drawn a distinction between permissible *predispositions* towards a particular planning outcome, and unlawful *predeterminations*.[65] Establishing predetermination requires evidence of a closed mind, and therefore sets a high bar.[66] This highly adapted approach to review for bias reflects the fact that, at the local level, planning decisions are taken by those who have been elected to take them.[67] It is therefore to be *expected*, rather than a source of concern as it may well be in other decision-making contexts, that councillors responsible for planning decisions will have expressed views, perhaps in a campaign context,[68] and engaged in communications with interested constituents.[69]

The highly particularised form judicial review doctrine has assumed in the planning context is well deserving of careful thought by administrative law scholars, not least because studies have suggested that similar patterns may well have emerged in other areas of judicial review.[70] Administrative law scholars do not tend to think of different parts of judicial review as being in different phases of doctrinal evolution: judicial review doctrine, rather, is commonly imagined as a set of *general legal principles* which are applied equally across all areas of administration.[71] Perhaps, however, the time has come to better recognise the different doctrinal forms judicial review takes in different areas. In the planning context, it is uncommon for courts to apply general judicial review principle *directly* to the facts.[72] Most areas are governed by case law which acts as a sort-of 'doctrinal mediator', offering context-specific guidance on what the grounds of review require of a *planning* decision-maker.

The non-peculiarity of planning challenges

It is interesting to posit why administrative law scholars now show relatively little interest in planning law, despite the obvious practical overlaps with judicial review. Addressing the question is necessarily a speculative exercise. Perhaps the single biggest factor, however, is that scholars see planning law as too specialist or exceptional to be of broader interest. Many planning challenges turn on narrow points of construction, often concerning the meaning of intricate legislation or policy. There is a well-established planning bar[73] and now a specialist Planning Court.[74] All of this perhaps adds up to a sense that planning judicial reviews are too niche to be of broader interest.

To dismiss planning judicial reviews on this basis would, however, be a mistake. Even if it were true that planning challenges are, in some sense, a deviation from the judicial review norm, that would not justify disregarding them. A comprehensive understanding of judicial review must consider *all* instances of judicial review, especially those so numerically significant as planning challenges. Judicial review, furthermore, is replete with instances which may be thought of as peculiarities.[75] This is a reflection both of its non-monolithic nature[76] and of the 'adaptability and contextually enhanced level of scrutiny which judicial review can deliver, where necessary in the interests of justice'.[77] The complexity and variety inherent in judicial review is something to be embraced by scholars, not explained away.[78]

More fundamentally, it is difficult, perhaps impossible, to pinpoint a feature of planning judicial reviews which makes them truly unique. Rather, close reflection shows that even the features of planning challenges that perhaps most deter closer scholarly engagement are, in fact, widespread features of much judicial review case law which it is important for scholarship to engage with. Three examples will suffice to illustrate.

First, consider perhaps the most off-putting feature of planning law: the complexity and 'piecemeal'[79] nature of its legislative backdrop. Modern planning law is not characterised by a single, consolidating master statute[80] in which all its significant powers, duties and procedures can be found.[81] Its legal basics are spread across numerous interlocking Acts of Parliament,[82] all created in different political contexts,[83] and supplemented by reams of oft-changing[84] delegated legislation[85] and policy.

Legislative complexity, however, is far from an issue peculiar to planning law challenges. The comments above, for instance, apply equally to tax legislation and many regulatory regimes. The legal intricacy of planning law, furthermore, pales in comparison to the most commonly litigated[86] administrative area: immigration.[87] Immigration legislation has been described by serving judges as 'asbtruse',[88] characterised by 'rebarbative drafting'[89] and as posing 'real obstacles to achieving predictable consistency'.[90] Drawing on a metaphor which is particularly apt in a book about planning, Beatson LJ said of the Immigration Rules in *Khan* that they were 'not the grand design of Lutyens' Delhi or Hausmann's Paris, but more that of the organic growth responding to the needs of the moment that is a feature of some shanty towns'.[91] In 2020 the Law Commission called for wholesale statutory overhaul.[92]

Grappling with complex, oft-amended and inelegant statutory structures is, in other words, part-and-parcel of being a practising administrative law judge or lawyer. Sometimes courts in judicial review are faced with 'skeleton'[93] legislation or non-statutory powers, and invited to decide how the general grounds of review apply. But, equally, much judicial review involves the careful untangling of many different layers of legislation.[94] It is important that the challenges of working with complex legislative frameworks, such as those which govern planning and immigration decision-making, stay on the administrative law scholarship radar. To disregard cases characterised by a complex legislative backdrop would be to paint a false picture of judicial review. The complexity of legislative frameworks, furthermore, gives rise to important questions, concerning for instance the extent to which the legal system complies with rule of law values,[95] on which public law scholars are especially well placed to comment.

Secondly, planning judicial reviews are characterised by several context-specific *procedural* features. As mentioned, there is a highly established and specialised planning bar. Since 2014 there has been a specialist Planning Division within the Administrative Court, meaning that most planning judicial reviews are now heard by a small handful of expert judges.[96] There are specialist mechanisms for resolving planning disputes, before we get to judicial review, in the form of planning inquiries and paper hearings. There are also particularised time-limits for initiating,[97] and timescales for resolving,[98] planning judicial reviews. These context-specific procedural characteristics perhaps feed into a sense of planning law exceptionalism.

The procedural adaptation of judicial review is again, however, not a phenomenon confined to planning challenges. Procedural diversification is a longstanding and important feature of the administrative law landscape in England and Wales, and elsewhere.[99] Immigration challenges again provide an important example. There has long been concern that, if immigration challenges were left to proceed through the AJR, the High Court would become swamped with challenges.[100] There is an important, context-specific modern history of legislative amendments targeting this concern[101] which is presently managed by diverting large swathes of challenges through the tribunals, by conferring both broad rights of appeal on the First-tier Tribunal and judicial review powers on the Upper Tribunal.[102] An older example concerns housing judicial reviews, which generated similar case-load concerns in the 1990s.[103] Most housing challenges[104] are now dealt with through a statutory review process[105] carried out by county courts.

The procedural modification of planning judicial reviews is, in other words, part of a much longer history.[106] English and Welsh administrative law has struck different balances between, on the one hand, resolving disputes through general legal procedures and, on the other, the creation of specialist forums and processes. Several decades ago, Harry Arthurs[107] framed this tension as one between a traditional Diceyan insistence on the primacy of the ordinary courts[108] and administrative law 'pluralism'.[109]

The place of specialist forums and processes within the broader court system raises ongoing conceptual, normative and practical questions.[110] It is important that administrative law scholarship remains alive to them. A striking feature of the recent Independent Review of Administrative Law[111] was its exclusive focus on the application for judicial review (AJR) procedure. A result of the terms of reference, this was a shame. The AJR is one part of a much broader administrative-adjudication landscape, and it is important that the question of whether legal challenges are being dealt with in the most suitable forum is kept in mind.

Thirdly, and more briefly, a final striking characteristic of many planning law judicial reviews is the dominance of policy. Planning decision-making is structured by various kinds of policy. In determining an application for planning permission, for instance, decision-makers are required to adhere to the local plan – including neighbourhood plan – documents,[112] unless material considerations indicate otherwise.[113] This requires close engagement with all relevant documents within what are often lengthy adopted plans and the adoption of a view on whether, read as a whole,[114] the plan is or is not supportive of proposed development. Central government planning policy, including the National Planning Police Framework (NPPF)[115] and supplementary planning policy guidance,[116] is also recognised as a material consideration to be weighed in the planning balance.

It is common, therefore, for planning judicial reviews to give rise to intricate legal questions concerning the meaning, application and relationship between different forms of policy. If an example is needed, a recent Planning Court challenge turned almost entirely on whether the planning authorities had properly carried out a 'footnote 37 review'.[117] The dominance of policy in legal argument and reasoning can add to the sense that planning judicial reviews are the domain of specialists only.

It is important to recognise again, however, that the centrality of policy does not make planning administration distinct or exceptional. Policy is, or is becoming, a major feature of many areas of administration:[118] tax,[119] immigration,[120] housing,[121] to name a few. Indeed, US scholars Metzger and Stack have argued that policy is best understood as a form of 'internal'[122] law which should prompt a reconceptualisation of how administrative law is imagined, taught and studied.

The role of policy in both planning and other areas of administrative decision-making, furthermore, gives rise to a host of important issues. Is there a danger, for instance, that policy is becoming an avenue through which central government is able to introduce major shifts in policy direction without detailed parliamentary scrutiny?[123] Does the informality of much policy,[124] and the speed with which it can be changed,[125] pose a threat to rule of law values?[126] If so, do the courts, and indeed Parliament,[127] possess the necessary tools to ensure policy is used responsibly?[128] There is a growing literature examining questions of this sort.[129] Any detailed discussion of planning policy is, however, strikingly absent from it. This is lamentable. Planning administration is perhaps the area of decision-making with the greatest experience with different kinds of policy. It provides a neat case study into the values, pitfalls and legal challenges to which policy can give rise.

Planning judicial reviews are certainly characterised by many striking features including legislative complexity, context-specific procedural mechanisms and the dominance of policy, which pose challenges for those who seek to become 'lingual' in planning law. None of these characteristics, however, make planning challenges unique. On the contrary, each is connected with themes or challenges which apply more broadly across administrative law. Administrative law scholars should, therefore, avoid the temptation of concluding that planning case law is simply too specialist or exceptional to be of interest. While there is no such thing as a paradigm judicial review, planning challenges are in many ways typical of large swathes of administrative law adjudication.

Planning case law and broader judicial review principle

A third and final benefit of administrative law scholars engaging closely with planning law is that challenges to planning decisions have proven themselves to be fertile ground for the emergence of broader judicial review principle. The origin story of many of the general grounds of review involves the evolution of legal principle in judicial review of a particular area, or areas, of administrative decision-making,[130] which is later expanded into wider territory.[131] As David Feldman has put it, the evolution of modern administrative law is therefore in large part due to practitioners and academics with 'fingers on the living pulse of public law as a whole',[132] inviting the courts to connect the dots between different areas of review.

Planning case law has played an important role in this process. In *South Bucks DC v Porter*,[133] for instance, Lord Brown famously explained that a planning inspector is expected to give reasons for a decision which are

> [i]ntelligible . . . and adequate. [Reasons] must enable the reader to understand why the matter was decided as it was and what conclusions were reached on the 'principal important controversial issues', disclosing how any issue of law or fact was resolved. Reasons can be briefly stated, the degree of particularity required depending entirely on the nature of the issues falling for decision . . .

> The reasons need refer only to the main issues in the dispute, not to every material consideration.[134]

This passage has been cited countless times. Indeed, Lord Brown's words have become the blueprint for assessing the adequacy of reasons not only across other parts of the planning system[135] but also in many areas of administrative law adjudication.[136]

A similar point can be made about Lord Hoffmann's characterisation of the courts' role in assessing whether a grant of planning permission is unlawful due to failure to consider a material consideration in *Tesco*.[137] His Lordship explained:

> ... the law has always made a clear distinction between the question of whether something is a material consideration and the weight which it should be given. The former is a question of law and the latter is a question of planning judgment, which is entirely a matter for the planning authority. Provided that the planning authority has regard to all material considerations, it is at liberty (provided that it does not lapse into *Wednesbury* irrationality) to give them whatever weight the planning authority thinks fit or no weight at all.[138]

Lord Hoffmann's distinction between the question of whether a consideration is (ir)relevant and the weight it should be given is used as an explanatory device to capture the courts' general approach in many administrative law textbooks.[139] *Tesco* is, furthermore, frequently cited in both planning[140] and non-planning[141] judicial reviews.

There are further examples. Mid-twentieth-century estoppel challenges to planning authorities,[142] for instance, laid important foundations for the later emergence of the doctrine of legitimate expectations.[143] The distinction between lawful predispositions and unlawful predeterminations, discussed above, has been applied in non-planning contexts.[144] The impact of Article 6 of the European Convention on Human Rights on administrative law,[145] following the coming into effect of the Human Rights Act, was heavily shaped by early challenges in the planning context.[146]

The potential of planning challenges to contribute to the broader administrative law landscape, furthermore, is not confined to the past. It continues to be important to look to planning challenges for legal principles which may prove to be important in other fields.

In *Gallaher*,[147] for instance, the Supreme Court determined that, while not recognisable as a freestanding general principle of judicial review, lack of consistency in approach may be an indicator that a public authority has acted unreasonably. This, however, gives rise to a host of questions. What kinds of inconsistency indicate unreasonableness? If a public authority offers reasons for the inconsistency, when will this diffuse the appearance of unreasonableness? *Gallaher* was a non-planning challenge. In the planning context, however, the courts have long recognised consistency as a freestanding principle of good decision-making[148] and have grappled with some of these questions.[149] Planning challenges may therefore offer useful insights into the types of inconsistency that may or may not point to unreasonableness in other contexts.

The Supreme Court in the planning case *Dover DC*[150] also oversaw a major extension of the principle of open justice. Developed in the court context, open justice had been applied in *Kennedy*[151] to an inquiry conducted under the Charities Act. The Supreme Court reasoned in *Dover DC* that the principle must accordingly be applicable to planning inquiries and, by extension, to local planning authority decision-making. The full ramifications of this opening of the door to open justice to play a broader role in administrative law remain to be seen.

Conclusion

To repeat a point made above, no judicial review case is solely a judicial review case. As Mark Aronson put it, judicial review has both horizontal and vertical dimensions.[152] Most challenges involve the application of generally applying legal principles (the horizontal) in the context of a specific, often highly detailed, legislative regime (the vertical). Judicial review case law is, in other words, inherently legally *intra*disciplinary: arguing, deciding and understanding a challenge usually requires an appreciation of overlapping bodies of law.

However, remarkably little legal scholarship is published at the intersection(s) between judicial review's horizontal and vertical components. There is no shortage of judicial review commentary[153] but contributions tend to cluster around 'silos'[154] situated along one or other of these planes. Some grounds of review have been 'endlessly debated'.[155] There are also sophisticated scholarly discourses in fields such as social security and housing law. It has not, however, been common for scholarship to explore the operation of the grounds of judicial review *in specific administrative areas*.

There are signs that things are beginning to change. Imaginative inquiries have been undertaken in recent years into topics such as judicial review of development consent for wind turbines,[156] ombuds,[157] NHS rationing[158] and institutions of the criminal justice system.[159] Though their subjects are diverse, what these contributions have in common is that they all offer a new perspective on the role and operation of judicial review: they present a 'different view of the cathedral'.[160]

This chapter is similarly situated at the intersection between the horizontal and the vertical. It has argued that administrative law scholars stand to gain a great deal from engaging more closely with judicial review's operation in the planning context. Planning challenges should not be seen as the unwanted guests at the judicial review party. They represent a highly evolved body of judicial review doctrine[161] and have proven to be fertile ground for the evolution of broader judicial review principle.[162] Many of planning law's most off-putting features are, furthermore, intimately connected with broader administrative law themes and challenges.[163] This chapter, however, not only reveals the importance of administrative law scholars taking *planning law* seriously; it is an illustration of the importance of embracing *both* the horizontal and vertical dimensions of judicial review. Administrative law adjudication in practice involves the fusion of general grounds of review with legislative, policy and administrative particulars. Both the process and the results of this fusion would benefit from more scholarly engagement.

Notes

1. Nason 2016.
2. Bell 2020.
3. Tomlinson 2020, 297–300.
4. See e.g. *Miller v Prime Minister* [2019] UKSC 41; [2020] AC 373.
5. See e.g. *R (Nicklinson & another) v Ministry of Justice* [2014] UKSC 38; [2015] AC 657.
6. See e.g. *R (Keyu) v Secretary of State for Foreign and Commonwealth Affairs* [2015] UKSC 69; [2016] AC 1355.
7. Tan 2021.
8. To borrow helpful language from Gee and Webber 2013.
9. Hall 2014.
10. See e.g. Town and Country Planning (Environmental Impact Assessment) Regulations 2017 SI 2017/571.
11. For a useful discussion of the planning concepts underlying the community infrastructure levy see e.g. Amodu 2020.
12. To borrow language from Aronson 2021, 9.
13. Sheppard and Peel 2017. See e.g. the Town Planning Act 1909.
14. Now defined in the Town and Country Planning Act 1990, section 55.
15. For instance, the application for judicial review procedure was introduced in the late 1970s and placed on a statutory footing in the Senior Courts Act 1981, section 31. Prior to these reforms, planning challenges, like others for which there was not a legislative route of challenge, would be brought as an application for prerogative writ (see e.g. *Smith v East Elloe Rural District Council* [1956] AC 736 (HL); [1956] 1 All ER 855) or declaration/injunction (see e.g. *Gregory v London Borough of Camden* [1966] 2 All ER 196 (QB)). For a helpful discussion of the resulting procedural complexity see Law Commission 1976.

16. Reflected in e.g. the Civil Procedure Rules 1998 of which the title is 'Judicial Review and Statutory Review'.
17. A concept that has generated debate and on which judicial thinking has changed over time. Compare e.g. *Gregory* with *Walton v Scottish Minister* [2012] UKSC 44; [2013] PTSR 51.
18. See e.g. Planning and Compulsory Purchase Act 2004, section 113; Planning Act 2008, section 13.
19. As in the case of the TPCA 1990, section 288 which provides a right of appeal against ministerial or Planning Inspectorate decisions, including on appeal from local authorities (see TCPA 1990, section 72).
20. *Dover DC v CPRE Kent* [2017] UKSC 79; [2018] 1 WLR 108, [58].
21. *Glencore Energy UK Ltd v HMRC* [2017] EWHC 1476 (Admin); [2017] STC 1824, [40].
22. Note also that the Upper Tribunal has jurisdiction to hear judicial reviews, primarily in the immigration context, pursuant to the Tribunals, Courts and Enforcement Act 2007, section 15, and related delegated legislation.
23. See Bell and Fisher 2021, 519.
24. For instance, the requirement to refuse relief where substantially the same outcome is 'highly likely' introduced by the Criminal Justice and Courts Act 2015, section 84 applies only in AJRs. Statutory reviews continue to be subject to the inevitability threshold created by *Simplex GE (Holdings) Ltd v Secretary of State for the Environment* [1988] 3 PTSR 1041 (CA).
25. Compare other statutory rights of appeal governed by the Civil Procedure Rules 1998 and those which apply for instance in the extradition (Extradition Act 2003, section 27(3)) and professional discipline (for instance Medical Act 1980, sections 40–40A) contexts. See Bell and Fisher 2021, 509.
26. *Smith v Castle Point BC* [2020] EWCA Civ 1420; [2021] Env LR 20, [51].
27. *Smith*, [51].
28. See e.g. *Fuller v Secretary of State for Communities and Local Government* [2015] EWHC 142 (Admin), [4].
29. Woolf et al 2017.
30. Aronson 2021, 9.
31. A possible exception is in areas of judicial review in which courts have developed particularised principles. Note, for instance, the role of the *Hardial Singh* principles in challenges to immigration detention: *R (Lumba) v Secretary of State for the Home Department* [2011] UKSC 12; [2012] 1 AC 245.
32. See e.g. Jowell 1977; McAuslan 1980; Loughlin 1981.
33. The same is not true of other jurisdictions, including Australia, where it is more common for scholars to work at the intersection of administrative and planning law. See e.g. Weeks and Pearson 2017; Groves 2021.
34. A notable exception is Fisher 2018.
35. Notable earlier case law includes *Local Government Board v Arlidge* [1914] AC 120 (HL); [1914–15] All ER 1 (famously discussed in Dicey 1915a).
36. Bell and Fisher 2021, 510 and 517.
37. Notable recent examples include *R (Fylde Coast Farms Ltd) v Fylde BC* [2021] UKSC 18; [2021] 1 WLR 2794; *R (Friends of the Earth) v Heathrow Airport Ltd* [2020] UKSC 52; [2021] 2 All ER 967; *R (Wright) v Resilient Energy Severndale Ltd* [2019] UKSC 53; [2019] 1 WLR 6562; *R (Lancashire CC) v Secretary of State for the Environment, Food and Rural Affairs & another* [2019] UKSC 58; [2021] AC 194.
38. https://www.landmarkchambers.co.uk/planning-court-case-explorer/ (accessed 12 June 2022).
39. Elvin 2014.
40. Nason 2016, 87–93.
41. Indeed, sometimes wholly new decision-making systems are created. See e.g. *Citizens UK v Secretary of State for the Home Department* [2017] EWHC 2301 (Admin); [2018] 4 WLR 123 and *R (Help Refugees) v Secretary of State for the Home Department* [2017] EWHC 2727 (Admin); [2018] 4 WLR 168 (both concerning the system created to implement the Immigration Act 2016, section 67 (the 'Dubs amendment')).
42. *Miller*.
43. See Bell and Fisher 2021, 511.
44. The discussion in this section benefits heavily from an ongoing research project with Professor ACL Davies and Professor Elizabeth Fisher, to whom I owe my thanks.

45. As Lord Diplock famously expressed in *Council of Civil Service Unions v Minister for the Civil Service* [1985] AC 374 (HL); [1984] 3 WLR 1174, 510.
46. Note, however, that legislative reform is relatively common in the planning context and can give rise to novel legal questions. The Planning Act 2008 is a case in point. See e.g. *Friends of the Earth; R (ClientEarth) v Secretary of State for Business, Energy and Industrial Strategy* [2021] EWCA Civ 43; [2021] PTSR 1400.
47. *Stringer v Minister of Housing and Local Government* [1970] 1 WLR 1281 (QB); *Newbury DC v Secretary of State for the Environment* [1981] AC 578 (HL); [1980] 1 All ER 731.
48. *Derbyshire Waste Ltd v Blewett* [2004] EWCA Civ 1508; [2005] Env LR 15.
49. Juss and Sunkin 2017.
50. Incorporated Council of Law Reporting 2020. See also *Practice Direction (Citation of Authorities)* [2012] 1 WLR 180.
51. *Ridge v Baldwin* [1964] AC 40 (HL).
52. *Secretary of State for Communities and Local Government v Hopkins Development Ltd* [2014] EWCA Civ 470; [2014] PTSR 1145.
53. *Tesco Stores Ltd v Dundee City Council* [2012] UKSC 13; [2012] PTSR 983.
54. *Tesco Stores Ltd*, [18].
55. *Hopkins Homes Ltd v Secretary of State for Communities and Local Government* [2017] UKSC 37; [2017] 1 WLR 1865, [23]–[34]; *R (Samuel Smith Old Brewery (Tadcaster)) v North Yorkshire CC* [2020] UKSC 3; [2020] 3 All ER 527, [22]–[23].
56. See e.g. *Oxton Farm v Harrogate BC* [2020] EWCA Civ 805 (emphasising the diversity of approaches permissible to the calculation of housing need).
57. *Mansell v Tonbridge and Malling Borough Council* [2017] EWCA Civ 1314; [2019] PTSR 1452, [42].
58. *St Modwen Developments Ltd v Secretary of State for Communities and Local Government* [2017] EWCA Civ 1643; [2018] PTSR 746, [6].
59. *R (Wilbur Developments Ltd) v Hart DC* [2020] EWHC 227 (Admin); [2020] PTSR 1379, [65]–[66].
60. *Thorpe Hall Leisure Ltd v Secretary of State for Housing, Communities and Local Government* [2020] EWHC 44 (Admin).
61. *Trump International Golf Club Scotland Ltd v Scottish Ministers* [2015] UKSC 74; [2016] 1 WLR 85.
62. *Dimes v Proprietors of Grand Junction Canal* 10 ER 315 (HL).
63. See e.g. *R v Bow Street Metropolitan Stipendiary Magistrate, ex parte Pinochet* [2000] 1 AC 119 (HL); *Locabail v Bayfield Properties Ltd* [2000] QB 451 (CA).
64. See e.g. *Halliburton Company v Chubb Bermuda Insurance Ltd* [2020] UKSC 48; [2020] 3 WLR 1474.
65. *R v Amber Valley DC, ex parte Jackson* [1985] 1 WLR 298 (QB); *R (Lewis) v Redcar and Cleveland BC* [2008] EWCA Civ 746; [2009] 1 WLR 83; *R (Island Farm Development Ltd) v Bridgend County BC* [2006] EWHC 2189 (Admin).
66. For a rare example see *R (Kind) v Secretary of State for the Home Department* [2021] EWHC 710 (Admin); [2021] ACD 66.
67. Endicott 2018, 189–94.
68. See e.g. *Island Farm*.
69. *R (Holborn Studios Ltd) v London Borough of Hackney* [2020] EWHC 1509 (Admin); [2021] JPL 17, [76]–[79].
70. See e.g. Kirkham and O'Loughlin 2020.
71. Daly 2017.
72. Although see note 46.
73. Planning & Environment Bar Association, http://peba.org.uk (accessed 1 June 2022).
74. Elvin 2014.
75. For example, judicial review on the *Hardial Singh* principles has been described as a 'radical departure from the usual approach in a public law challenge' (*R (SB (Ghana)) v SSHD* [2020] EWHC 668 (Admin), [71]). In *R (Din) v Secretary of State for the Home Department* [2018] EWHC 1046 (Admin), Fordham J introduced a refusal to recognise British citizenship as 'no conventional judicial review': [2].
76. Bell 2020.

77. *Din*, [2].
78. Bell 2020.
79. *Dover DC*, [58].
80. Compare, for instance, the Housing Act 1996.
81. Town and Country Planning Association 2018.
82. Among others: TCPA 1990; PCPA 2004; Localism Act 2011; Planning Act 2008.
83. See the useful summary affixed to Lord Carnwath's response to the Planning White Paper Consultation 2020.
84. See e.g. *R (Rights: Community: Action) v Secretary of State for Housing, Communities and Local Government* [2020] EWHC 3073 (Admin) (concerning recent changes to general permitted development rights).
85. See e.g. Town and Country Planning (Use Classes) Order 1987 SI 1987/764 (as amended); Town and Country Planning (General Permitted Development Order) 1995 SI 1995/418 (as amended); Town and Country Planning (Development Management Procedure) Order 2015 SI 2015/595 (as amended).
86. Independent Review of Administrative Law 2021, 161–2.
87. Much immigration case law is now handled by the tribunals system, although see Thomas and Tomlinson 2019.
88. *R (Iqbal) v Secretary of State for the Home Department* [2015] EWCA Civ 838; [2016] 1 WLR 582, [49].
89. *Singh v Secretary of State for the Home Department* [2015] EWCA Civ 74, [59]; [2015] WLR (D) 66.
90. *Hossain v Secretary of State for the Home Department* [2015] EWCA Civ 207, [30].
91. *Secretary of State for the Home Department, ex parte Khan* [2016] EWCA Civ 137; [2016] 4 WLR 56, [40].
92. Law Commission 2020.
93. House of Lords Select Committee on the Constitution 2017–19.
94. See e.g. Neale 2019.
95. Beatson 2021.
96. Civil Procedure Rules 1998, 54.22; Practice Direction 54D, 3.2 (on significant claims which must be heard by nominated judge).
97. Civil Procedure Rules 1998, 54.5(5).
98. Practice Direct 54D, rule 3.4.
99. See e.g. Preston 2014.
100. *R (Cart) v Upper Tribunal* [2011] UKSC 28; [2012] 1 AC 663; Elliott and Thomas 2012.
101. *R (G) v Immigration Appeal Tribunal* [2004] EWCA Civ 1731, [2005] 1 WLR 1445.
102. Tribunals, Courts and Enforcement Act 2007, section 15.
103. Law Commission 1994.
104. Some, such as challenges to housing allocation schemes, proceed via judicial review: see e.g. *R (Gullu) v London Borough of Hillingdon* [2019] EWCA Civ 682; [2019] PTSR 1738.
105. Housing Act 1996, section 204.
106. Arthurs 1985, 404–7.
107. Arthurs 1979.
108. Dicey 1915b.
109. Arthurs 1979.
110. See e.g. *R (Privacy International) v Investigatory Powers Tribunal* [2019] UKSC 22; [2020] AC 491, where the different judgments are underpinned by different conceptualisations of the relationship between the High Court and the Investigatory Powers Tribunal.
111. Independent Review of Administrative Law 2021.
112. Localism Act 2011, Schedule 9 paragraph 6.
113. PCPA 2004, section 38(6).
114. See e.g. *R (Corbett) v Cornwall Council* [2020] EWCA Civ 508.
115. Ministry of Housing, Communities and Local Government (MHCLG), *National Planning Policy Framework* (July 2021); Mills 2018.
116. Planning Practice Guidance, https://www.gov.uk/government/collections/planning-practice-guidance (accessed 12 June 2022).

117. *Wainhomes (North-West) v Secretary of State for Housing, Communities and Local Government* [2020] EWHC 2294 (Admin).
118. Weeks 2016.
119. Daly 2020.
120. Law Commission 1994.
121. See e.g. *Nzolameso v Westminster CC* [2015] UKSC 22; [2015] 2 All ER 942, [39]–[40].
122. Metzger and Stack 2017.
123. Scotford and Robinson 2013, 395–401.
124. See e.g. the discussion in *Suffolk Coastal DC v Hopkins Homes Ltd* [2017] UKSC 37; [2017] 1 WLR 1865, [19]–[21] of the non-statutory basis of the NPPF.
125. See e.g. *R (Patel) v General Medical Council* [2013] EWCA Civ 327; [2013] 1 WLR 2801.
126. Beatson 2021, chapter 4.
127. For a related discussion of scrutiny of delegated legislation see e.g. Pywell 2019; King 2020.
128. See e.g. *Lumba*.
129. See e.g. Perry 2017; McHarg 2017.
130. *R v Inland Revenue Commissioners, ex parte MFK Underwriting Agents Ltd* [1990] 1 WLR 1545 (QB); *R v Inland Revenue Commissioners, ex parte Unilever* [1996] STC 681 (CA).
131. See for instance the discussion in Woolf et al 2017, [5-090]–[5-091] on the origins of review for extraneous purposes.
132. Feldman 2019.
133. *South Buckinghamshire DC v Porter* [2004] UKHL 33; [2004] WLR 1953.
134. *South Buckinghamshire*, [36].
135. *Dover DC*, [37] discussing reasons offered by local planning authorities.
136. Elliott and Thomas 2020, 538. See e.g. *Thilakawardhana v Office for Independent Adjudicator for Higher Education* [2018] EWCA Civ 13, [54] and *Cheatle v General Medical Council* [2009] EWHC 645 (Admin) (concerning the standard of reasons expected of fitness to study and professional disciplinary panels).
137. *Tesco Stores Ltd v Secretary of State for the Environment* [1995] 1 WLR 759 (HL).
138. *Tesco Stores*, [56].
139. Elliott and Varuhas 2017.
140. See e.g. *Friends of the Earth*, [121].
141. See e.g. *R (Albion Water Ltd) v Water Services Regulation Authority* [2012] EWHC 2259 (Admin), [63].
142. *Lever (Finance) Ltd v Westminster Corporation* [1970] 3 All ER 496 (CA); Craig 1977.
143. *R (Reprotech (Pebsham) Ltd) v East Sussex CC* [2002] UKHL 8; [2003] 1 WLR 348, [34]–[35].
144. See e.g. *Kind*.
145. Craig 2003.
146. *Bryan v UK* (1995) 21 EHRR 342; *R (Alconbury Developments Ltd) v Secretary of State for the Environment* [2001] UKHL 23; [2003] 2 AC 295.
147. *R (Gallaher Group Ltd) v Competition and Markets Authority* [2018] UKSC 25; [2019] AC 96.
148. *North Wiltshire DC v Secretary of State for the Environment* (1993) 65 P & CR 137 (CA).
149. See *DLA Delivery Ltd v Baroness Cumberledge of Newick* [2018] EWCA Civ 1305; [2018] PTSR 2063; *Hallam Land Management Ltd v Secretary of State for Communities and Local Government* [2018] EWCA Civ 1808; [2019] JPL 63.
150. *Dover DC*.
151. *Kennedy v Charity Commission* [2014] UKSC 20; [2015] AC 455.
152. Aronson 2021, 9.
153. Indeed, it has been said that judicial review unhealthily dominates administrative law scholarship: see e.g. Richardson and Genn 2007.
154. Kirkham and O'Loughlin 2020, 680.
155. Tomlinson 2020, 297.
156. Fisher 2018.
157. Kirkham and O'Loughlin 2020.
158. Wang 2017.
159. Feldman 2020.
160. To borrow an image from Calabresi and Melamed 1972.
161. Part 2.
162. Part 4.
163. Part 3.

References

Amodu, Tola (2020). 'Revisiting the Rules. The Pervasiveness of Discretion in the Context of Planning Gains: The Community Infrastructure Levy', *Public Law* 643–60.

Aronson, Mark (2021). 'Judicial Review of Administrative Action: Between Grand Theory and Muddling Through', *Australian Journal of Administrative Law* 28: 6–19.

Arthurs, Harry (1979). 'Rethinking Administrative Law: A Slightly Dicey Business', *Osgoode Hall Law Journal* 17: 1–45.

Arthurs, Harry (1985). *"Without the Law": Administrative Justice and Legal Pluralism in Nineteenth Century England*. Toronto: University of Toronto Press.

Arvind, TT et al (eds) (2021). *Executive Decision-Making and the Courts: Revisiting the Origins of Modern Judicial Review*. Oxford: Hart Publishing.

Beatson, Jack (2021). *The Rule of Law and the Separation of Powers*. Oxford: Hart Publishing.

Bell, Joanna (2020). *The Anatomy of Administrative Law*. Oxford: Hart Publishing.

Bell, Joanna and Elizabeth Fisher (2021). 'Exploring a Year of Administrative Law Adjudication in the Administrative Court', *Public Law* 505–22.

Calabresi, Guido and A. Douglas Melamed (1972). 'Property Rules, Liability Rules, and Inalienability: One View of the Cathedral', *Harvard Law Review* 85: 1089–128.

Craig, Paul (1977). 'Representations by Public Bodies', *Law Quarterly Review* 93: 398–420.

Craig, Paul (2003). 'The Human Rights Act, Article 6 and Procedural Rights', *Public Law* 753–73.

Daly, Paul (2017). 'The Signal and the Noise in Administrative Law', *University of New Brunswick Law Journal* 68: 68–86.

Daly, Stephen (2020). *Tax Authority Advice and the Public*. Oxford: Hart Publishing.

Dicey, Albert Venn (1915a). 'The Development of Administrative Law in England', *Law Quarterly Review* 31: 148–53.

Dicey, Albert Venn (1915b). *Introduction to the Study of the Law of the Constitution*. London: Macmillan, 8th edn.

Elliott, Mark and Robert Thomas (2012). 'Tribunal Justice, *Cart* and Proportionate Dispute Resolution', *Cambridge Law Journal* 71: 297–324.

Elliott, Mark and Robert Thomas (2020). *Public Law*. Oxford: Oxford University Press, 4th edn.

Elliott, Mark and Jason N.E. Varuhas (2017). *Administrative Law*. Oxford: Oxford University Press, 5th edn.

Elvin QC, David (2014). 'The Planning Court', *Judicial Review* 19: 98–102.

Endicott, Timothy (2018). *Administrative Law*. Oxford: Oxford University Press, 4th edn.

Feldman, David (2019). 'Changing Boundaries: Crime, Punishment and Public Law'. In *The Frontiers of Public Law*, edited by Jason Varuhas and Shona Wilson Stark, 277–96. Oxford: Hart Publishing.

Fisher, Elizabeth (2018). 'Law and Energy Transitions: Wind Turbines and Planning Law in the UK', *Oxford Journal of Legal Studies* 38: 528–56.

Gee, Graham and Gregoire Webber (2013). 'A Grammar of Public Law', *German Law Journal* 14: 2137–55.

Groves, Matthew (2021). 'Standing Outside: An Environment of Challenge and Withheld Cures', *Environmental and Planning Law Journal* 38: 111–31.

Hall, Peter (2014). *Cities of Tomorrow: An Intellectual History of Urban Planning and Design Since 1880*. Oxford: Wiley-Blackwell, 4th edn.

House of Lords Select Committee on the Constitution (2017–19). *The Legislative Process: The Delegation of Powers*. 16th Report of Session.

Incorporated Council of Law Reporting (2020). *Leading Planning Case Law*. London: Wildy & Sons.

Independent Review of Administrative Law (2021). *The Independent Review of Administrative Law*.

Jowell, Jeffrey (1977). 'The Limits of Law in Urban Planning', *Current Legal Problems* 30: 63–83.

Juss, Satvinder and Maurice Sunkin (eds) (2017). *Landmark Cases in Public Law*. Oxford: Hart Publishing.

King, Jeff (2020). 'The Province of Delegated Legislation'. In *The Foundations and Future of Public Law: Essays in Honour of Paul Craig*, edited by Elizabeth Fisher, Jeff King and Alison Young, 145–71. Oxford: Oxford University Press.

Kirkham, Richard and Elizabeth O'Loughlin (2020). 'Judicial Review and Ombuds: A Systematic Analysis', *Public Law* 680–700.

Law Commission (1976). *Report on Remedies in Administrative Law*. Law Comm No 73.

Law Commission (1994). *Administrative Law: Judicial Review and Statutory Appeals*. Law Comm No 226.

Law Commission (2020). *Simplifying the Immigration Rules*. Law Comm No 388.

Loughlin, Martin (1981). 'Planning Gain: Law, Policy and Practice', *Oxford Journal of Legal Studies* 1: 61–97.

McAuslan, Patrick (1980). *Ideologies of Planning Law*. Oxford: Pergamon Press.

McHarg, Aileen (2017). 'Administrative Discretion, Administrative Rule-Making and Judicial Review', *Current Legal Problems* 70: 267–303.

Metzger, Gillian E. and Kevin Stack (2017). 'Internal Administrative Law', *Michigan Law Review* 115: 1239–307.

Mills, Alistair (2018). *Interpreting the NPPF: The New National Planning Policy Framework*. Bath: Bath Publishing.

Nason, Sarah (2016). *Reconstructing Judicial Review*. Oxford: Hart Publishing.

Neale, David (2019). 'The Ghost of Human Rights Claims Past: Immigration Appeal Rights after *Robinson*', *Judicial Review* 24: 183–96.

Perry, Adam (2017). 'The Flexibility Rule in Administrative Law', *Cambridge Law Journal* 76: 375–98.

Preston, Brian (2014). 'Characteristics of Successful Environmental Courts', *Journal of Environmental Law* 26: 365–93.

Pywell, Stephanie (2019). 'Something Old, Something New: Busting Some Myths about Statutory Instruments and Brexit', *Public Law*: 102–20.

Richardson, Genevra and Hazel Genn (2007). 'Tribunals in Transition: Resolution or Adjudication', *Public Law* 116–41.

Scotford, Eloise and Jonathan Robinson (2013). 'UK Environmental Legislation and its Administration in 2013 – Achievements, Challenges and Prospects', *Journal of Environmental Law* 25: 383–409.

Sheppard, Adam and Deborah Peel (2017). *The Essential Guide to Planning Law: Decision-Making and Practice in the UK*. Bristol: Policy Press.

Tan, Gabriel (2021). 'A Robust Defence of Freedom of Expression in Local Government – Let the NIMBYs Speak'. Administrative Court Blog (20 July), available at https://administrativecourtblog.wordpress.com/2021/07/20/a-robust-defence-of-freedom-of-expression-in-local-government-let-the-nimbys-speak/ (accessed 12 June 2022).

Thomas, Robert and Joe Tomlinson (2019). 'A Different Tale of Judicial Power: Administrative Review as a Problematic Response to the Judicialisation of Tribunals', *Public Law* 537–62.

Tomlinson, Joe (2020). 'Do We Need a Theory of Legitimate Expectations?', *Legal Studies* 40: 286–300.

Town and Country Planning Association (2018), *Planning 2020 – Final Report of the Raynsford Review of Planning in England*.

Wang, Daniel Wei L. (2017). 'From Wednesbury Unreasonableness to Accountability for Reasonableness', *Cambridge Law Journal* 76: 642–70.

Warnock, Ceri (2017). 'Reconceptualising Specialist Environment Courts and Tribunals', *Legal Studies* 37: 391–417.

Weeks, Greg (2016). *Soft Law and Public Authorities*. Oxford: Hart Publishing.

Weeks, Greg and Linda Pearson (2017). 'Planning and Soft Law', *Australian Journal of Administrative Law* 24: 252–70.

Woolf, Harry et al (2017). *De Smith's Judicial Review*. London: Sweet & Maxwell, 8th edn.

12
Provoking McAuslan: Planning law and property rights

Kim Bouwer and Rachel Gimson[*]

Introduction

It is an accepted truism that 'every [person] . . . [has] a right to use his own land by building on it as he thinks most to his interest'.[1] This sentiment reflects a prevailing belief that common law protections exist solely to protect private interests in land, including against encroachment of private land rights by third parties, the latter being the primary focus of this chapter. Thus, the law governing land and property relations has traditionally been classified as 'private', being concerned with rights and priority interests in estates in land as fundamentally constitutive of private property relations. In contrast, administrative regimes, such as those involving planning and environmental issues, are typically defined as 'public'. These public regimes are commonly seen as presenting an incursion on private rights,[2] rather than as being part of an intertwined and complementary body of property law principles.

Despite these entanglements, the role and impact of planning law continues to be neglected in academic analysis of land law. It is telling that few property law textbooks give planning law a distinct treatment,[3] despite its growing importance in modern-day land use. Indeed, an increasing number of the decisions discussed therein refer to, or turn on, the regime of planning control.[4] Moreover, where it is discussed, planning law is very much perceived as something that is *imposed* on private property law protections, rather than being a *part of* property law principles.[5] By recognising that property law also exists to protect the social utility of land, discussed next in this chapter, it is possible to reconcile planning law principles as being part of the foundational principles of land law.

If there is a planning law canon, central to it is Patrick McAuslan's thesis that argues that there is an ideological tension between the private values of property rights and the quasi-democratic nature of public land administration.[6] McAuslan discusses three ideologies. First, the traditional common law (private) approach, in which courts mediate between competing parties, frequently for the protection of private property and its institutions.[7] Second, the administrative (public) approach, which characterises planning law as existing to advance land management goals, if necessary against the interests of private property, and in the public interest. In this way, he argues that planning law can be seen as both imposing constraints on private property rights and existing for the legal preservation of the public interest. The third ideology is that of public participation. Participation can inform and legitimise decision-making within planning processes; for instance, Eloise Scotford and Rachael Walsh highlight how privileged property rights-holders frequently are in planning processes.[8] This gives property rights-holders a 'distinctive voice' in land use decisions,[9] and a greater capacity for influence in democratised decision-making processes. However, understanding the potential and shortcomings of these processes lies beyond the scope of this chapter, although these issues are explored throughout this volume.

The purpose of the chapter is to analyse McAuslan's assumed opposition between private land rights and public administrative regimes. Interestingly, even as McAuslan asserts the competition between these ideologies, a recognition of their entanglement is to some extent implicit in his work. He explains that these seemingly opposing regimes are in essence different aspects of the same legal and political establishment. The legal status quo, according to McAuslan, is preserved by systemic protection of property rights within an administrative system which purports to represent the public interest.[10] Despite its publication over 40 years ago in a breathtakingly dynamic area of policy and practice, McAuslan's analysis of this tension still informs scholarly practice in planning,[11] even if the balance between the competing ideologies can be understood to shift over time.[12]

Our project here is to interrogate McAuslan's understanding of public and private ideologies as being fundamentally opposed. While we do not dispute his thesis entirely, we argue that the public and private aspects of property governance are more entangled – and, at times, more complementary – than he suggests. We argue that the idea that private property rights are necessarily entirely deployed for selfish purposes[13] is to some extent misconceived. We motivate for a better understanding of the social contribution and role of property, which includes a recognition of its 'symbiotic' relationship with land planning law.[14] Our concept of the social utility of land challenges the idea of a law of property concerned solely with the protection of private rights and interests. We also argue, using the example of compulsory purchase, that planning law can shape and determine property rights. By so doing we emphasise two points. First, the concept of 'public interest' reflected in administrative planning frequently does not resemble the ordinary meaning of the term. Second, the concept of the 'public interest' planning regime and 'private rights' property law are more intertwined than supposed. We use the term 'social utility' when discussing a public ethos in land law, and the term 'public interest' to describe the purported goal of planning. Whilst so doing it is important to note that the terms we use are not terms of art and are not precise; this is because these principles are not clearly defined or used consistently in practice.

The chapter is structured as follows. In the next section, we challenge the notions of strictly private concepts of property in land by arguing that the courts also consider the promotion of the social utility of land in their decision-making. Subsequently, we discuss compulsory purchase and compensation in planning, arguing that these do not always advance the public interest. Finally, we conclude.

Land as a social utility

By presenting private interests and public rights as competing ideologies, our concern is that McAuslan's theory leads to an overfocus on property law's role in the protection of private interests. A private interest approach would see the courts settle property disputes purely on the basis of who has the better title claim. We are not disputing that the legal protection of property in land centres largely on the protection of private interests. Certainly, examples such as *Bradford Corporation v Pickles*[15] demonstrate the capacity of the courts to focus purely on the private interest, at the expense of everything else. Here, the title holder's right to siphon off water running through his land was upheld, despite the fact that it limited the water access to the entire city of Bradford, which was rapidly expanding at the time. Similarly, in *Phipps v Pears*[16] the title owner was perfectly entitled to pull down his house, even though it exposed his conjoined neighbour's property wall to the elements when it had not been properly rendered. Focusing on cases such as these, it is no wonder that public interests in land are seen as incompatible with – or somehow alien to – orthodox understandings of land law. However, we argue here that public interests are more entangled with the foundational principles of property law protecting private interests, and that land law has a clear interest in protecting public rights, particularly when considering more recent property cases.

The protection of individual rights has never been the sole focus of the courts; land law has never sought *solely* to protect private rights. Title disputes do not exist in a vacuum and property law has historically sought to ensure that land remains useful and does not stagnate when determining property disputes, even if this is at times at the expense of the private right. We loosely describe this phenomenon as the social utility approach in land law. The implicit endorsement of the social utility of land grew during the Second Industrial Revolution through the creation of devices such as restrictive covenants and the recognition of recreational easements. These rights in rem, as part of a general law of servitudes, sought to manage property interests and can be described as a precursor to modern planning law.[17] It is important to note that we are not arguing that social utility always takes priority over private interests, but rather we seek to establish here that the courts, when seeking to resolve land disputes, do not simply consider who has better claim. Therefore, the protection of property rights is not always the 'selfish' endeavour suggested by McAuslan. Acknowledging a social utility approach to land can illustrate how the courts have sought to mediate disputes taking public interest considerations into account.

Although protecting the social utility of land is an inherent consideration in the protection of property rights, it is not a novel concept. Curiously, whilst it is extensively debated in the literature in the US,[18] this concept is largely ignored in English academic discourse. Kevin Gray and Susan Francis Gray are a fairly lone voice in explicitly acknowledging the protection of the social utility of land,[19] but they never directly advocate it or develop it as a thesis. Other academic texts touch on the concept, but do not discuss it fully.[20] There is clearly more to be said about the theoretical underpinnings of the social utility approach to land law, but this is beyond the scope of this chapter. Rather, this section seeks to establish that there is case law that reflects the concept of social utility. In particular, we argue here that it has gained increasing prominence in recent property law decisions. In doing so we suggest that the recognition and protection of public interests in land, such as planning law, is not at direct odds with the protection of private rights as McAuslan supposes.

So, to provide some examples of the existence of the social utility approach: a stark reminder of the social utility of land occurred 20 years before Lord Cranworth's statement, cited in the first sentence of this chapter, in the seminal judgment of *Tulk v Moxhay*.[21] Even though the Court of Chancery acknowledged that 'the price [of the land] would be affected by the covenant' to 'keep and maintain . . . Leicester Square garden',[22] it nonetheless recognised that an equitable restrictive covenant could run with the land. This decision can demonstrate how land law recognises, and also implicitly protects, the social utility of the land. Decided during the Second Industrial Revolution, when increasing urbanisation resulted in a greater need for land control,[23] the restrictive covenant provided an important tool through which competing land use could be resolved.[24] *Tulk v Moxhay* went against the *laissez-faire* instincts present in much of Europe at this time, where land obligations were largely seen as a contract between two parties.[25] However, where 'modern patterns of high-density land use have necessarily placed a premium on neighbourly co-operation and the avoidance of foreseeable harm to adjacent occupiers', the law of contract was seen as inadequate protection for neighbours.[26] Thirty years after *Tulk v Moxhay*, Leicester Square was donated to the local government authority to be used as a public square, which undoubtedly played an important role in maintaining this area of central London as open and public. Nevertheless, had the restrictive covenant not been created in *Tulk v Moxhay*, Leicester Square would look very different today.[27] Although the scope of the restrictive covenant remains narrow,[28] it provides a powerful tool in ensuring social utility, where the preservation of open space and gardens 'uncovered with buildings' took precedence over the private rights of a developer.[29] Indeed, its very existence demonstrates how controls over land are not purely public in nature but can also occur through private land controls.

The post-Second World War period has seen a growing, albeit somewhat implicit, desire to ensure land's social utility. For example, although restrictive covenants have been confirmed, reluctantly,[30] as having only equitable status,[31] their presence in property titles is ubiquitous. Approximately 79 per cent of households are subject to a restrictive covenant,[32] demonstrating the impact that protecting the social utility of land can have on private interests. Moreover, the durability of such covenants has been expanded due to the presumption that the benefit of the covenant passes with the land, as a result of *Federated Homes*'[33] interpretation of section 78 Law of Property Act 1925. In determining a dispute about future development as part of a convoluted land acquisition, the court created a presumption that the benefit of a covenant would run with the land unless there was an express contrary intention. Although *Federated Homes* remains controversial,[34] it has significantly increased the ease with which the benefit of a restrictive covenant, and its associated promotion of land's social utility, can pass with the property. There are also growing calls for the expansion of covenants, to allow them to operate in law and to impose a positive burden, with the Law Commission stating that 'the market has made its own case'[35] for positive covenants. This statement is equally applicable to the equitable status of restrictive covenants.

The desire of the courts in recent times to protect the social utility of land can be more keenly seen in easements, specifically recreational easements. Despite the fact that the courts have repeatedly stressed the need for easements to remain flexible, the notion that recreational rights can run with the land has historically been anathema to the courts.[36] The problem with recreational rights running in rem is twofold. Firstly, recreational rights often lack the necessary definition to satisfy the criteria for being an easement.[37] Secondly, and more importantly for this chapter, they have the potential to substantially curtail the private rights of the title holder by affording an enduring right of use of land for what could be seen as relatively trivial activities. As a result, recreational easements are seen to be at odds with the need to protect private interests.

These somewhat dramatic consequences are reflected in *Ellenborough Park*,[38] significant here for its recognition that a recreational right, here a right to access a shared garden, can amount to an easement. Prior to *Ellenborough Park* the dicta relating to recreational rights in rem conflicted.[39] However, the courts, in deciding that the *Ellenborough Park* right operated in rem, were at pains to state that recreational rights were a long-established property law principle. In the High Court, Judge Dankwerts pointed out that 'the enjoyment of amenities [considered here] is no modern novelty',[40] while the Court of Appeal also looked to the importance of parks such as St James' Park and Kew Gardens for public enjoyment.[41] As a result, it is possible to conclude that whilst *Ellenborough Park* is perceived to be a seminal judgment, it simply consolidated existing discourse and practice. Indeed, the Supreme Court recently reiterated that the *Ellenborough Park* criteria had been 'well-established . . . by the 1950s'.[42] The fact that *Ellenborough Park* situated its judgment in current practice reinforces our argument that social utility has been a thread running through the law (and commentary) for some time.

Recently, the Supreme Court in *Regency Villas* went even further, holding that a right of 'mere recreation and amusement'[43] – here involving access to leisure and sporting facilities from one holiday complex to another – can operate in rem, and amount to an easement. At first glance, *Regency Villas* might be read as another instance of land law's determination of competing private interests. After all, the fundamental issue to be decided in this case was whether the interests of the freeholders of Regency Villas prevailed over the interests of Diamond Resort. However, this case is also an interesting demonstration of the social utility approach, for two interlinked reasons. First, *Regency Villas* explicitly recognised the value recreational rights could have for society to justify why such rights should operate in rem.[44] This goes beyond simply ensuring that the land does not become stagnant; it is an explicit recognition of how property rights can be used to benefit society as a whole. Such a recognition goes against a historical reticence to create new categories of easements.[45] Moreover, by compelling the owners of the servient land to pay for the upkeep of the easements over their land, recreational 'social utility' was prioritised at the expense of the private interests in this case. Second, the justices were 'well-aware of the novelty and reach' of their decision, and the decision was carefully drafted to ensure the precedential value of the case.[46] This means that *Regency Villas* is not specific to the unique facts but is an explicit acknowledgment that recreational rights can operate in rem precisely because of their benefit to society; the court clearly had in contemplation the protection of a wider range of 'social' interests. Although the implication of this decision has not been universally accepted by land lawyers,[47] nevertheless it provides an interesting example of our assertion that property law seeks to protect the social utility of land.

Land law has never existed to simply protect private interests in land as McAuslan supposes. This section aimed to demonstrate that promotion of social utility is a foundational and enduring approach in land law. Our argument that land law protects the social utility of land is not to undermine the need for clear, consistent and coherent definitions of land rights and obligations.[48] We do not argue that the recognition of social utility changes the definitions of easements or restrictive covenants, for example. Nor do we argue that social utility is at the heart of every judicial decision. Rather, we argue here that the need to protect the social utility of land is an often overlooked but fundamental component of English land law's *modus operandi*. Recognising this is not only vital to fully understanding modern judgments such as *Regency Villas*, but it also helps us to appreciate considerations of the public interest as embedded in the determination of private rights in land. We continue to consider this entanglement of public and private considerations in the next section, when we question how these supposedly competing ideologies are reflected in one area of planning law.

Entangled ideologies in planning and land use

The tension between public interest considerations and property rights is a constitutive feature of planning law. As a starting point, it might be said that powers of compulsory purchase represent a 'serious invasion of proprietary rights' of property owners.[49] Property rights are subject to and shaped by regulatory incursions through planning law. Therefore, the effect of planning law is to constrain private property rights 'in the public interest'. In short, inherent in planning law is the idea that it is legitimate for the state to regulate land use, although in effect this is already done through the common law of property – extensively codified and streamlined through statute. Compulsory purchase is a fruitful starting point for a study of this nature, because it certainly does represent an area in which supposedly inalienable private property rights are overridden in the furtherance of (a perception of) the public interest, through planning law.

Thus, the concept of absolute inalienability of owned land is in itself challenged by an administrative regime that can commandeer property, albeit purportedly for the purpose of the common good. Orthodox property theory prescribes that rights in estates in land confer on the owner a right to control access to the property in question and to exclude others from it.[50] Below, we first argue that a state's capacity to reclaim land is not just created through regulatory imposition; it constitutes an inherent part of land ownership. We go on to discuss statutory compulsory purchase in more detail, illustrating how perceptions of public good and private (or privatised) gain are thoroughly entangled in this exercise of state power in the 'public interest'.

The right or power of the state to reassert fundamental domain over property,[51] to force a sale and to curtail owners' rights through regulation is recognised as inherent in property ownership.[52] Even if notional, in such instances the basis on which property is returned or reclaimed forms part of the property right. The concept of the right to compensation in cases of expropriation is recognised in most legal systems, which allow 'market rate compensation' when rights in land are acquired for public purposes.[53] This is demonstrated by the extent to which peaceful possession of property is protected as a human right. In *James v UK*,[54] the applicants challenged their tenants' right to purchase the freehold estates of their leasehold properties. In spite of the protection of property under Article 1, Protocol 1 of the European Convention on Human Rights, the European Court of Human Rights (ECtHR) reinforced the legitimacy of compulsory purchase. The entitlement of the state to compulsorily acquire land was part of the protected right, and not 'distinct' from the general principle of peaceful possession.[55] In short, the right of a state to legislate for forced sales in the public interest – seemingly anathema to a concept of private property rights – is inherent in the concept and protection of property.

The ECtHR recognised that compulsory purchase that reallocated land between private parties could be in the public interest.[56] It stated that 'the fairness of a system of law governing the contractual or property rights of private parties is a matter of public concern and therefore legislative measures intended to bring about such fairness are capable of being "in the public interest" '.[57] The right inherently requires compensation 'reasonably related to its value',[58] but nevertheless the legislation was considered not to offend human rights protection despite the calculation methodology of the value of the freehold transfer frequently resulting in a considerable windfall for transferees.[59] For the most part, planning compulsory purchase will differ from the factual matrix in *James*, as it is more likely to consolidate land ownership than serve redistributive purposes. However, this decision is relevant because it clarifies the concept of rights in private property. Furthermore, the court's characterisation of the wider distribution of privately owned land as being in the public interest (as conceptualised by English courts) stands in significant contrast to the way land is redistributed using planning compulsory purchase.

McAuslan was writing during the post-war shift towards development-friendly policies that formed part of the rebuild and regeneration agenda after World War Two. In England and Wales, compulsory purchase for land management purposes has always been regulated by statute.[60] At the time, the Compulsory Purchase Act 1965, McAuslan argued, reflected the interests of private property. In particular, the regime ensured that private landowners were sufficiently compensated if their property needed to be acquired for development.[61] He argued further that the procedural and administrative provisions of the Act, whilst having as their goal the protection of private property, also significantly reflected the need to encourage development.[62] Julie Adshead recognises that these 'are areas of planning law firmly underpinned by the fundamental ideology of society', which in addition to shaping the law also 'shape politics and society'. On the face of it, these are most closely aligned to McAuslan's public interest ideology.[63] But as we illustrate below, developments in the way compulsory purchase has been dealt with over the years paint an interesting picture in terms of how and why the regulatory regime intrudes on individual property rights. The rationales for property taking, and permitted compensation calculation methodology, also raise questions about the values underpinning the 'public interest'. We explain this in more depth below, but first we need to clarify briefly how compulsory purchase works.

Compulsory purchase in the planning sense is a statutory right afforded to a local authority to acquire land in their area if it is needed for development, redevelopment or 'improvement',[64] or is necessary in 'the interests of the proper planning of the area'.[65] This must be done with due regard to the development plan, and if and as 'the public interest decisively so demands',[66] but does not have to be carried out by the local authority itself. As such, decisions about compulsory purchase are, at least in theory, required to be made in accordance with what has been determined to be in the public interest for that particular area, at that particular time.[67] This also 'must not' be done unless it is likely to contribute to any or all of the 'promotion or improvement' of the economic, social and environmental well-being of the relevant area.[68] Similar provisions are made in relation to nationally significant infrastructure projects,[69] and arise in cases where publicly owned land is acquired (or de facto acquired) for some purpose.[70] Objections to compulsory purchase are afforded to holders of private rights, who have significant participatory rights in relation to proposed development plans.[71]

The above can be associated with, although is distinct from, 'reverse compulsory purchase',[72] where under Part VI of the Town and Country Planning Act 1990 (TCPA) landowners are permitted to serve purchase notices on local authorities requesting acquisition of their land.[73] These fall into two categories – adverse decisions and adverse proposals. Taking these in turn: where an adverse planning decision (or the failure to obtain planning permission) either requires that a land owner discontinues using the land,[74] or otherwise constrains their capability to put their land to 'reasonably beneficial use',[75] any owner of land can request a purchase of their own property.[76] Although not uncontroversial and not conclusive, it has become permissible to calculate the question of what constitutes 'reasonably beneficial use' by having regard to the land's value had it been granted planning permission.[77] Adverse planning proposals – also called 'planning blight' – arise where the threat of compulsory purchase implicit in a planning proposal depreciates the value of land, or makes it unsaleable. This could include circumstances where provision in a development plan suggests that the land may be designated for 'relevant public functions', including the development of new towns or highways.[78] Under such circumstances any person with proprietary rights 'qualifying for protection'[79] can serve 'blight notices' on the relevant public authority. Where the specific conditions are met,[80] owners can require the local authority to purchase the blighted land.[81]

Thus, the various assumptions about planning permission that we outline below are deployed to determine when a piece of land may no longer be said to be available for beneficial use. One of these assumptions relates to how compensation for the extinguishment of proprietary rights (but not other forms of property rights, for instance licenses[82]) is calculated in cases of compulsory purchase (including reverse compulsory purchase). Where land is acquired by a local planning authority or the Secretary of State 'for some public purpose', the compensation paid for the interest acquired is normally based on its 'market value'.[83] However, the determination of a property's market value is 'fraught with complexity and obscurity'.[84] The broad picture is that the Land Compensation Act 1961 permits the market value to be calculated with the assumption that, 'were it not for the acquisition, planning permission would have been granted for development of a specific kind'.[85] The practicalities determining this have always been quite difficult, because the 'no-scheme rule' prohibits the consideration of the impact of the proposed scheme on the land's value at the relevant time,[86] but doing so requires the calculation of an uncertain counterfactual. The line between compensating the owner for their property's value in the 'real world',[87] which should include its development potential,[88] and not providing a windfall was difficult to draw.

The solution has been the progressive introduction of assumptions about planning permission on the land. The so-called 'planning assumptions' specify that account 'may' be taken not only of extant planning permission,[89] but also of the prospect of permission being granted.[90] As such, these assumptions to some extent take account of permissions that were already contemplated when the acquisition was set in train. Newer amendments permit such assumptions to be made on the basis of a *possibility* that planning permission might have been approved. The effect of the amended Act is that 'in relation to land where there was only the prospect of the grant of planning permission, if that prospect amounts to a reasonable expectation, the reasonable expectation is transformed, for the purposes of assessing compensation, into a certainty'.[91] The planning assumptions permit the identification of 'appropriate alternative development' – planning permission which 'could . . . reasonably have been expected to be granted on an application',[92] and which may be assumed to be in force at valuation.[93] Certification of 'appropriate alternative development' (a CAAD) can be sought from the relevant local authority.[94] This requires the relevant authority to determine hypothetical applications for the purpose of certifying planning permission (or development consents) that had never previously been sought. Also, the extent to which local authorities can take proper account of factors that would almost certainly be material considerations in 'real' applications is constrained.[95] It is difficult to understand the justification for placing a burden on a public authority to determine hypothetical planning applications, for the sole purpose of inflating the cost of acquisition which they – at least in theory – have to pay. While it is a stretch to say that the state funds this transfer of property – due to the use and structuring of section 106 agreements with developers – local authorities at least notionally fund compulsory purchase, and are largely forced to underwrite the risk of future development.[96]

This presents a conundrum: the supposedly inalienable rights in land can be corroded, or extinguished entirely, if deemed in the public interest or if forming part of a broader programme of spatial development. Yet this deprivation of rights could result in a considerable windfall for the (forced) seller, where the planning regime constructs fictions about the property.[97] It is difficult to justify the interpretation of 'development potential' into a fiction of actual planning permission.[98] In many cases such assumptions serve to justify an inflated 'market value' of the acquired land, resulting in the sorts of windfalls that the 'no scheme rule' was intended to prevent. This inflation of 'market value' is emblematic of the valorisation of capital accumulation and continued property price inflation, making it difficult to argue that compulsory purchase operates entirely in the 'public interest'.

Furthermore, despite frequent assertions of the 'public interest' in compulsory purchase, the *benefit* of compulsory acquisitions is not always public, or at least not entirely so. This brings us to an important distinction – that between the protection of private property rights or interests through law, and concepts of the public interest which seek to protect (and bolster) the property *market*. These are not the same thing. The distinction can be difficult to draw, not least for those of us whose concept of the public interest does not include value inflation or capital consolidation for the benefit of a small (and shrinking) group of property developers and investors.[99] The point, however, is that this is not the same as the protection of a private right through law. In addition, as we explain above, this cannot be seen as in favour of *individual* (private) property rights, as any rights in property would have been forcibly acquired and thereby extinguished. Certainly, both approaches to social utility in common law decisions and regimes for compulsory acquisition of land reflect an understanding that land serves a public function in part, and that sometimes private rights in land must cede to the needs of the common good if an area requires development. So much for the eradication of private rights through compulsory purchase.

More generally, an analysis of the scholarship and cases discussed in this chapter reveals a pattern of community-led and community-serving spaces being transformed into 'retail-led regeneration projects', with very low percentages of 'affordable' housing or accessible space not dedicated to consumerism.[100] In the scholarship, Antonia Layard identifies the homogenising effects of spatial restructuring, where diversity and multiplicity are sanitised out of existing community spaces, to be replaced with corporatised uniformity.[101] A feature of these 'malls without walls' and the cession of land management to private entities frequently results in little public space that is not devoted to retail consumerism.[102] The loss of such public space entails the loss of community assets such as libraries, public playing fields and allotments, which are rarely replaced once lost.[103] It is ironic that we are losing these community assets at the same time as the scope for recreational easements is broadening. The planning applications discussed by Edward Mitchell in his examination of projects in Winchester and north London feature the acquisition of community assets including bus stations, doctors' surgeries, local businesses, sheltered accommodation and day-care centres, all for the purpose of homogenised retail development.[104]

In the case law we find *Burgos*, an unsuccessful challenge to permission for the reconstruction of a housing development with its own market space.[105] This would inevitably eradicate the existing Latin American market in Seven Sisters. The contribution made by community members to this asset was dismissed both by the London Borough of Haringey in granting permission and by the High Court.[106] In this volume, although they do not discuss compulsory purchase directly, Steven Vaughan and Brad Jessup describe how the safety and sense of community offered by queer spaces are eroded by the provision of sanitised 'replacements'.

The extent to which applications for compulsory purchase reflect a genuine commitment to the fulfilment of 'the public interest' is therefore questionable. Increased state licence for private developers and a monetisation of property seems to underlie a focusing of planning policy that supports swift and under-scrutinised development, for instance by relaxing scope for local participation.[107] While not universally the case, compulsory purchase land acquisition is increasingly employed to implement 'the delineation, characterization, and commodification of "retail-led" development sites flourishing in city centres'.[108] This happens through the transformation of property, including housing, into 'high-quality collateral, supported by deregulation, by [lending practices], and by new patterns and opportunities for investment'.[109] These issues of financialisation of property and planning recur throughout this volume, especially in Vaughan and Jessup, Maria Lee and Mitchell's chapters. Theoretically, the role of the public body, in these instances frequently the local authority, can be seen to favour the interests of corporate capital accumulation over genuine notions of the public benefit.[110] The transfer of land from one private owner to another can be seen to rest on 'the desire of states to help capitalists overcome barriers to accumulation'.[111] This does not, in itself, protect or advance *individual property rights*; rather it protects and advances the accumulation of private wealth, including by facilitating profit-taking from commodified assets.[112] The extent to which this is genuinely in the public interest is questionable.

Conclusion

Our chapter aimed to demonstrate the entanglement between the so-called public and private aspects of the legal regime that governs land and land use. There exists a continuing perception that planning is governed by ideologically distinct legal regimes, namely the protection of private rights through the courts and the advancement of the public interest through administrative planning law. We argue that this division is not always so stark.

As we explain in our discussion of social utility, private property protections are not simply designed for individualised and 'selfish' property rights. The social utility approach demonstrates that the courts do not always seek to promote private interests above all else. Judges have considered the public interest in interpreting property entitlements, for instance in recreational easements and restrictive covenants. We have also argued that the nature of estate ownership in English land law entails that forced acquisition is 'built into' the property right itself.

Using the example of compulsory purchase, we challenge two ideas: that planning law advances the public interest through administrative processes; and that the owners of estates in land can counter these public benefits by enforcing their private property rights through the courts. Indeed, as we argue, neither of these presents a definitive account of what is done through these processes, and how. As such, our discussion of compulsory purchase and social utility in land demonstrates the ways in which public and private ideologies are entangled in the space between administrative and private rights protections in the planning law regime.

Notes

* We are grateful to everyone present at the Property Law Stream of the Society for Legal Scholars Conference at Durham Law School for their interest in and feedback on our work. We are also grateful to Chris Bevan for his helpful comments on the written draft. Mistakes are ours.
1. *Tapling v Jones* (1865) 11 HL Cas 290, [311].
2. But see Scotford and Walsh 2013.
3. The most prominent textbook to consider planning law in any depth is Gray and Gray's seminal *Elements of Land Law*, although it must be noted that in this behemoth of books, comprising 1,434 pages, the planning law chapter is a mere 8 pages long.
4. For instance, in *Cuckmere Brick v Mutual Finance* [1971] EWCA Civ 9; [1971] Ch 949, the mortgagee's breach of duty was determined by its failure to capture a sufficient price, taking the planning permission into account.
5. See e.g. Gray and Gray 2009, 1378–86; Cowan et al 2012, 138–44.
6. McAuslan 1980.
7. McAuslan 1980, 2.
8. Scotford and Walsh 2013, 1012.
9. Scotford and Walsh 2013.
10. McAuslan 1980, 268–9.
11. See for instance Lees and Shepherd 2015; Adshead 2014; Davy 2020.
12. Willmore 2017.
13. McAuslan 1980, 3.
14. We rely heavily on Scotford and Walsh 2013.
15. *Bradford Corporation v Pickles* [1895] AC 587.
16. *Phipps v Pears* [1965] 1 QB 76.
17. This is something that Bevan argues in relation to restrictive covenants: Bevan 2020, 456.
18. See e.g. Caldwell 1974; Freyfogle 1999; Alexander 2009; Foster and Bonilla 2011; Shoked 2014.
19. See e.g. Gray and Gray 2003, 253–65; Gray and Gray 1998.
20. For example by reframing property rights as going beyond the right to exclude, as seen in Penner 1997. See also France-Hudson 2017; Lucy and Mitchell 1996; Becker 2017; Austin 2018.
21. (1848) 2 Philips 774.
22. [779], per Lord Cottenham.
23. Duxbury 2018, [1.01]–[1.04].
24. McCarthy 1973.
25. McCarthy 1973.
26. Gray and Gray 2003, 255.
27. See Smith 2009.
28. *Austerberry v Oldham Corp* (1885) 29 ChD 750; *Rhone v Stephens* [1994] 2 WLR 429.
29. *Tulk v Moxhay*, 777.
30. See e.g. *Thamesmead Town Ltd v Allotey* (2000) 79 P & CR 557.
31. *Rhone v Stephens* [1994] UKHL 3; [1994] 2 AC 310.
32. Law Commission 2008.
33. *Federated Homes Ltd v Mill Lodge Property Ltd* [1980] 1 All ER 371.
34. Snape described the law as 'traumatised' by *Federated Homes*: Snape 1994, 68.
35. Law Commission 2008.
36. See e.g. Fraewell J's decision in *International Tea Stores v Hobbes* [1903] 2 Ch 165.
37. For further detail see Bray 2017.
38. *Re Ellenborough Park* [1956] Ch 131 (CA).
39. In *Duncan v Lounch* (1845) 6 QB 904 a right to walk for pleasure was an easement, whilst in *Mounsey v Ismay* (1865) 3 H & C 486 a customary public right to hold horse races was not.

40. *Re Ellenborough Park* [1955] 3 WLR 91 (Ch), [150].
41. Moreover, the characteristics for an easement set out in *Ellenborough Park* were not judicial invention, rather both the High Court and the Court of Appeal relied on academic commentary, specifically on Cheshire 1954. Per Danckwerts J [140] (for the High Court) and per Eversham MR [163] and [170] (for the Court of Appeal).
42. *Regency Villas Title Ltd v Diamond Resorts (Europe) Ltd & Others* [2018] UKSC 57; [2019] AC 553, [35].
43. *Regency Villas*, [59].
44. *Regency Villas*.
45. Bray 2017; Baker 2012.
46. Bevan 2019, 62.
47. See Bevan 2019; McLeod 2019; Pratt 2017.
48. Which, as Gray and Gray note, is a consistent theme within land law: Gray and Gray 1998, 32.
49. *Prest v Secretary of State for Wales* (1982) 81 LGR 193, 211. See also Scotford and Walsh 2013.
50. Penner 1997.
51. George and Layard 2019, 30–33. Of course, we are not suggesting that forfeiture or escheat constitutes part of the day-to-day of land regulation. The point is that property repossession by the state is inherent in the very structure of (English) land law. This is emblematic of the relationship between private property rights and the state and goes well beyond the private social sharing discussed by Penner 1997.
52. Gray and Gray 1998, 37.
53. Seng Wei Ti 2019.
54. *James v United Kingdom* [1986] ECHR 2.
55. *James*, [37].
56. *James*, [40]–[41].
57. *James*, [40].
58. Bevan 2020, 611.
59. *James*, [27]–[29], [54]–[57].
60. *R (on the application of Sainsbury's Supermarkets Ltd) v Wolverhampton City Council* [2010] UKSC 20; [2011] 1 AC 437, [9].
61. Prior to 1991 protection was even more extensive. These protections were terminated due to a (not entirely fair) perception that they were widely abused. See Bowes 2019.
62. McAuslan 1980.
63. Adshead 2014.
64. TCPA 1990, section 266(1)(a).
65. TCPA 1990, section 266(1)(b). Similar provisions exist for the acquisition of land by the Secretary of State: see section 268.
66. *Prest v Secretary of State for Wales* (1982) 81 LGR 193, [198].
67. The extent to which the formulation of neighbourhood plans can be said to be democratic is questionable. See Willmore 2017; Bogusz 2018.
68. TCPA 1990, section 226(1)(a).
69. Planning Act 2008, section 122.
70. De facto acquired refers to the granting of very long leases to private management companies, which Layard 2019 argues is an effective transfer to private ownership. The acquisition of publicly owned land for private purposes entails specific processes and has particular implications, not least because when the land is transferred into private ownership the public law framework for land management is lost.
71. Acquisition of Land Act 1981, section 12 specifies that notice be given only to holders of rights in land – specifically freeholders and leaseholders (under section 12(2)(a)) and under limited circumstances to those with interests in property (see section 12(2)(b) read with section 5 Compulsory Purchase Act 1965).
72. Seng Wei Ti 2019, 141. Further details as to the process may be found in Duxbury 2018, [14.34]–[14.69].
73. TCPA 1990, sections 137(2)/150(2) respectively.
74. TCPA 1990, section 137(1)(c).
75. TCPA 1990, section 137(1)(a) and (b). See Duxbury 2018, [14.01]–[14.33].
76. As defined in TCPA 1990, section 366.
77. Under the amended TCPA 1990, section 138. See Duxbury 2018, [14.07]–[14.22].

78. TCPA 1990, section 149(1) and Schedule 13. This also covers land that is affected by development consent for a Nationally Significant Infrastructure Project, granted under Schedule 13 Planning Act 2008, [24].
79. TCPA 1990, section 49(2) and (3), section 168(4), but not property speculators: see Duxbury 2018, [14.60]. The position in relation to adverse decisions is altogether narrower: see TCPA 1990, section 336.
80. TCPA 1990, section 149 read with Schedule 13.
81. TCPA 1990, section 150(1).
82. In *DHN Food Distributors v Tower Hamlets LBC* [1976] 1 WLR 852 Lord Denning was willing to find that the contractual licensees were entitled to compensation for disruption to their businesses as a consequence of compulsory purchase. This approach has not been followed: see George and Layard 2019, 292. It is probably more often the case that licensees and occupiers face the inevitable end of their businesses due to rent increases in the new development. See the discussion in *Burgos v Secretary of State for Housing, Communities and Local Government* [2019] EWHC 2792 (Admin) – the claimants as licensees had no right to compensation, and the court endorsed the inspector's finding that the 'retention of the market is not dependent on the existing traders' [17], despite quite clear evidence that the market was embedded in a community.
83. Land Compensation Act (LCA) 1961, section 5(2). See also the principles outlined by Lord Collins in *Transport for London v Spirerose Ltd* [2009] UKHL 44; [2009] 1 WLR 1797, [89]–[95].
84. *Waters and another v Welsh Development Agency* [2004] UKHL 19; [2004] 2 All ER 915, [2]. This decision, however, predates the Localism Act 2011, which amended section 14 assumptions about planning permission and introduced section 17 Certificates.
85. Bowes 2019, [4.84].
86. LCA 1961, section 6A(3).
87. The 'reality principle' is the 'starting point' – see *Secretary of State for Transport v Curzon Park and others* [2021] EWCA Civ 651, [43]; [2021] WLR(D) 260.
88. See the comments of Lord Nicholls in *Spirerose*, [89]–[95]; [2009] 1 WLR 1797.
89. LCA 1961, section 14(2)(a).
90. LCA 1961, section 14(2)(b). This includes conditional, deemed and outline planning permission – see LCA 1961, section 14(9). The previous section allowed a claimant the actual or assumed value of the land with planning permission – see discussion in *Waters v Welsh Development*.
91. *Curzon Park*.
92. LCA 1961, section 14(4)(b).
93. LCA 1961, section 14(3). Localism Act 2011, section 232(2), section 240(2) read with section 232(8) amended this from a 'reasonable expectation' to a 'permitted assumption'.
94. The process and significance of CAADs, and the scope and process of appeal to the Upper Tribunal, are set out in LCA 1961, sections 17 and 18 respectively. This process is entirely hypothetical and exists solely for the purpose of determining the 'market value of expropriated land': *Grampian Regional Council v Secretary of State for Scotland* [1983] 1 WLR 1340, [1343]; *Fletcher Estates Ltd v Secretary of State for the Environment* [2000] 2 AC 307, [316].
95. See the discussion in *Curzon Park*. Here the relevant authority was the Secretary of State for Transport, seeking compulsory acquisition to clear space for HS2. All four respondents sought CAADs in relation to *hypothetical* developments that would never all have been granted, as the local authority would have been entitled to take account of the other applications as material considerations. The Court of Appeal determined that CAADs are not 'notional planning applications' such that other CAADs could be material planning considerations: [69].
96. Mitchell 2020.
97. Indeed, even where the windfall for the seller arises from the strict application of statutory assumptions, leading to a result that would not be granted in the 'real world' – see *Curzon Park*.
98. In *Spirerose*, Lord Nicholls emphasised that the value of property to the owner must include its 'development potential': [89]–[95].
99. Gallent et al 2017.
100. Layard 2010, 418.
101. Layard 2010, 419 and generally; see also Vaughan and Jessup, this volume.
102. Layard 2019, 161.
103. Layard 2019.

104. Mitchell 2020. In the Brent Cross application, the proposed development did include a new bus station – although it is difficult not to assume that this was intended to service the shopping centre.
105. See *Burgos*.
106. See *Burgos*.
107. This is observed in Adshead 2014.
108. Layard 2010, 415 and generally.
109. Gallent et al 2017.
110. Mitchell 2020.
111. Levien 2011, cited in Mitchell 2020, section 2.
112. See generally Dorling 2014; Mitchell 2020, section 2.

References

Adshead, Julie (2014). 'Revisiting the Ideologies of Planning Law: Private Property, Public Interest and Public Participation in the Legal Framework of England and Wales', *International Journal of Law in the Built Environment* 6: 176–94.
Alexander, Gregory (2009). 'The Social-Obligation Norm in American Property Law', *Cornell Law Review* 94: 745–819.
Austin, Lisa (2018). 'The Public Nature of Private Property'. In *Property Theory: Legal and Political Perspectives*, edited by James Penner and Michael Otsuka, 1–22. Cambridge: Cambridge University Press.
Baker, Adam (2012). 'Recreational Privileges as Easements: Law and Policy', *Conveyancer and Property Lawyer* 1: 37–54.
Becker, Lawrence (2017). *Property Rights: Philosophic Foundations*. Abingdon: Routledge.
Bevan, Chris (2019). 'Opening Pandora's Box? Recreation Pure and Simple', *Conveyancer and Property Lawyer* 1: 55–70.
Bevan, Chris (2020). *Land Law*. Oxford: Oxford University Press.
Bogusz, Barbara (2018). 'Neighbourhood Planning: National Strategy for "Bottom up" Governance', *Journal of Property, Planning and Environmental Law* 10: 56–68.
Bowes, Ashley (2019). *A Practical Approach to Planning Law*. Oxford: Oxford University Press.
Bray, Judith (2017). 'More than just a Walk in the Park: A New View on Recreational Easements', *Conveyancer and Property Lawyer* 6: 418–39.
Caldwell, Lynton (1974). 'Rights of Ownership or Rights of Use? The Need for a New Conceptual Basis for Land Use Policy', *William and Mary Law Review* 15: 759–75.
Cardwell, Michael (2019). 'Recreational Easements: A Right to Have Fun?', *Cambridge Law Journal* 78: 506–10.
Cheshire, G.C. (1954), *The Modern Law of Real Property*. London: Butterworth, 7th edn.
Cowan, David, Lorna Fox O'Mahony and Neil Cobb (eds) (2016). *Great Debates in Land Law*. London: Palgrave.
Davy, Benjamin (2020). '"Dehumanized Housing" and the Ideology of Property as a Social Function', *Planning Theory* 19: 38–58.
Dorling, Danny (2014). *All that is Solid: The Great Housing Disaster*. London: Penguin.
Duxbury, Robert (ed.) (2018). *Telling & Duxbury's Planning Law and Procedure*. Oxford: Oxford University Press.
Foster, Sheila and Daniel Bonilla (2011). 'The Social Function of Property: A Comparative Law Perspective', *Fordham Law Review* 80: 101–13.
France-Hudson, Ben (2017). 'Surprisingly Social: Private Property and Environmental Management', *Journal of Environmental Law* 29: 101–27.
Freyfogle, Eric (1999). 'The Particulars of Owning' *Ecology Law Quarterly* 25: 574–90.
Gallent, Nick, Dan Durrant and Niel May (2017). 'Housing Supply, Investment Demand and Money Creation: A Comment on the Drivers of London's Housing Crisis', *Urban Studies* 54: 2204–16.
George, Martin and Antonia Layard (2019). *Thompson's Modern Land Law*. Oxford: Oxford University Press.
Gray, Kevin and Susan Francis Gray (1998). 'The Idea of Property in Land'. In *Land Law: Themes and Perspectives*, edited by Sue Bright and John Dewar, 15–51. Oxford: Oxford University Press.

Gray, Kevin and Susan Francis Gray (2003). 'The Rhetoric of Realty'. In *Rationalising Property, Equity and Trusts: Essays in Honour of Edward Burn,* edited by Joshua Getzler, 204–80. London: Butterworth.

Gray, Kevin and Susan Francis Gray (2009). *Elements of Land Law.* Oxford: Oxford University Press.

Law Commission (2008). *Easements, Covenants and Profits à Prendre.* Consultation Paper No. 186.

Layard, Antonia (2010). 'Shopping in the Public Realm: A Law of Place', *Journal of Law and Society* 37: 412–41.

Layard, Antonia (2019). 'Privatising Land in England', *Journal of Property, Planning and Environmental Law* 11: 151–68.

Lees, Emma and Edward Shepherd (2015). 'Incoherence and Incompatibility in Planning Law', *International Journal of Law in the Built Environment* 7: 111–26.

Levien, Michael (2011). 'Special Economic Zones and Accumulation by Dispossession in India', *Journal of Agrarian Change* 11: 454–83.

Lucy, William and Catherine Mitchell (1996). 'Replacing Private Property: The Case for Stewardship', *Cambridge Law Journal* 55: 566–600.

McAuslan, Patrick (1980). *Ideologies of Planning Law.* Oxford: Pergamon Press.

McCarthy, Paul (1973). 'The Enforcement of Restrictive Covenants in France and Belgium: Judicial Discretion and Urban Planning', *Columbia Law Review* 73: 1–57.

McLeod, Gavin (2019). 'The Traditional Concept Hits the Bunker: Easements after *Regency Villas Title Ltd v Diamond Resorts (Europe) Ltd*', *Conveyancer and Property Lawyer* 3: 250–73.

Mitchell, Edward (2020). 'Compulsory Purchase and the State Redistribution of Land: A Study of Local Authority-Private Developer Contractual Behaviour', *Journal of Property, Planning and Environmental Law* 13: 1–16.

Penner, James (1997). *The Idea of Property in Law.* Oxford: Oxford University Press.

Pratt, Natalie (2017). 'A Proprietary Right to Recreate', *Conveyancer and Property Lawyer* 4: 312–21.

Scotford, Eloise and Rachel Walsh (2013). 'The Symbiosis of Property and English Environmental Law – Property Rights in a Public Law Context', *Modern Law Review* 76: 1010–45.

Seng Wei Ti, Edward (2019). 'Compensating Regulation of Land: UK and Singapore Compared', *Journal of Property, Planning and Environmental Law* 11: 135–50.

Smith, James (2009). '*Tulk v Moxhay*: The Fight to Develop Leicester Square'. In *Property Stories,* edited by Gerald Korngold and Andrew Morris, 171–88. New York: Foundation Press.

Snape, John (1994). 'The Benefit and Burden of Covenants – Now Where are We?', *Nottingham Law Journal* 3: 68–94.

Shoked, Nadav (2014). 'The Duty to Maintain', *Duke Law Journal* 64(3): 437–514.

Willmore, Chris (2017). 'Planning Law Reform and Reconceptualising the Regulation of Land Use'. In *Modern Studies in Property Law: Volume 9,* edited by Heather Conway and Robin Hickey. London: Bloomsbury.

13
Concluding thoughts
Carolyn Abbot and Maria Lee

In the introduction to this collection, Maria talked about our wish for this book 'to create space for planning law scholarship in all its variety, and for curiosity about law in all its complexity'. We are confident that our authors have achieved this ambition; if nothing else, they have demonstrated that planning law is fascinating, diverse and meaningful. It impacts us in every way, from the houses we live in, to the highways we walk, drive and cycle down, to the energy infrastructure that supplies our electricity.

We do not claim here to be able to reach any final conclusions 'about' planning law, or even to be able to summarise the wonderful work of our contributors. It is perhaps tautologous to say that law is a key theme of this book, and we do not hope to be able neatly to summarise its role or significance. Instead, we highlight two key themes: the complexity of planning and planning law; and the deeply political nature of planning and planning law.

We doubt we need to labour any further the complexity of planning law: the chapters of this book tease out in multiple ways the challenge of navigating the tangled and extensive web of planning and planning law, in practice and in scholarship. Maria suggested in the introduction that complexity, dense detail and constant reform may be part of the explanation for the relative neglect of planning law by English legal scholars over recent decades. We well recognise the anxiety of overlooking crucial, and yet almost invisible, detail and the painstaking nature of the work. We do not even deny that the technicalities can be tedious. And yet, looked at differently, and thinking again about the well-known work of Anneliese Riles (discussed in the introduction and in Elen Stokes' chapter),[1] this complexity provides a rich context within which to study questions from the heart of legal scholarship. Planning law, and this book, raise fundamental legal questions, such as the exercise of constraints on discretionary powers, the pursuit of justice and fairness in decision-making, the division of power between different scales of authority and different communities, and the relative space for expert/technical and democratic/political decisions. Our authors raise questions about lines between public and private law, between property rights and public interest goals, between the exercise of state power and private contractual arrangements, about the way resources of knowledge and expertise distribute goods and bads. They raise equally interesting and significant questions about the substantive contribution of law to shaping understandings of acceptable development, and hence of place – how places work, as well as how they look.[2]

Expanding on this theme, the authors illuminate the multiple roles and responsibilities of local authorities in the planning sphere. Alongside and within their responsibilities for plan making and regulatory decision-making, they have powers of compulsory purchase, they designate low traffic neighbourhoods, they determine future housing need, they enter into contracts with developers; and their role does not end with planning permission – their oversight role can extend for years into the future. In the introduction, Maria reflected upon the confused identity of local planning authorities (LPAs) in England, and associated ambiguity around their, and planning's, proper role: local authorities and planning as democratic spaces for deliberating and deciding on the future of a place, or as a technocratic space for the provision of services whose values are determined elsewhere. And yet little attention is paid in the legal scholarship to either the tensions between or the interconnectedness of these roles; the chapters in this book nicely reflect the dual roles of LPAs. LPAs negotiate and contribute to the construction of the meaning and values of a place and the communities who seek to use it; they also operationalise the day-to-day routines of plan making and planning permission, and everything that goes along with those tasks. Planning provides a perfect illustration of the impossibility of separating the technical and the political, the expert and the political.

And turning to disagreement, planning law is a space where conflicts are aired, and resolution (although not necessarily consensus) is reached. Planning is both founded on and illuminates deep conflicts about property and land use, about fairness and democracy, about what matters in creating good places and good lives. The uneven distribution of the resources that enhance power within planning is a theme of many of the chapters above.[3] The advantages of well-resourced, large corporate developers over other actors (from the LPA to local or interest communities) recurs in numerous chapters. The privileging of central government, including central government's visions of the future, is also clear, although so is the complexity of that privileging and the danger of assuming that the local is necessarily a better place for decision-making.

These are not new observations; the pervasiveness of power and politics in planning is perhaps more of a starting point than a conclusion. Nor does it need to be overemphasised: perennial and profound disagreements do not preclude routine outcomes that everybody can agree to live with. Conflict, however, is not only more visible than quiet agreement, but can also illuminate day-to-day practice.

How disagreement manifests itself, and the decision reached, both depend to some extent on who and what is part of the process. The chapters in this volume reveal and explore the multiple ways in which law shapes these issues. Whilst planning law is more than 'a scaffolding to support a process',[4] the processes provided by planning law are central, distributing power and shaping substance. Susan Owens and Richard Cowells' work on the importance of the 'apertures' for deliberation or debate provided by planning is important here.[5] Planning and planning law provide for scrutiny of proposals and refinement of argument, for challenges to established ways of doing things, and opportunities to think afresh. And this is not a theoretical exercise – decisions must be reached, and they have impacts that really matter.[6] As well as providing spaces to speak, law also affects what is properly relevant for a decision. We see a frustration in some of the chapters above at the failure of the planning system adequately to 'see' or 'hear' certain concerns, especially those that are not expressed in a technical or expert frame. Even when there is sympathy for and acknowledgment of these concerns by decision-makers, this can be overtaken by an uneasiness about reflecting lived experience (for example) in decision-making.

Which brings us to law's role in ensuring attention to or even protection of cherished values in the face of disagreement. The generosity of 'material' or 'relevant' 'considerations' provides a wide scope for what may lawfully drive a decision.[7] But law, alongside planning practice and routines, as discussed in Chapter 2 and seen elsewhere in this volume, incentivises caution and a particular type of tried and tested reasoning. LPAs, for example, seek to avoid appeals, which intensifies the presumption in favour of (sustainable) development, and incentivises reliance on only the best-established planning grounds for any refusal of permission.

Law can shape the issues that dominate the reasoning for a decision, where specific values, interests or places are singled out in legislation, and defined and understood in a particular way through prior institutional knowledge or expert responses to a particular case. But there are limits to law. A discretionary, more or less democratic (but in any event intensely political) system leaves space for disagreement, debate and deliberation. The apparent, and sometimes real, inconsequentiality of law, and the paradoxical role of legal frameworks in that,[8] is as important for legal scholars as its strength.

Finally, the detail and density of planning law is nothing to be scared of – or bored by – and nor is perennial reform. On the contrary, whether we step back from that detail or launch ourselves into it, planning law asks many of the practical, conceptual and doctrinal questions that most preoccupy legal scholars. Planning offers a major conceptual and analytical resource to scholars, grounded in rich sets of materials through which political and legal disagreement plays out. As policy priorities and legal provisions change, the underlying tensions and fascinations remain, extending beyond the particular framing of the moment.

Notes

1. Riles 2005.
2. Rydin 2011.
3. See also Abbot 2020.
4. Booth 2007, 143.
5. Owens and Cowell 2011.
6. Owens and Cowell 2011.
7. Town and Country Planning Act 1990; Planning Act 2008.
8. Chapter 2.

References

Abbot, Carolyn (2020). 'Losing the Local? Public Participation and Legal Expertise in Planning Law', *Legal Studies* 40: 269–85.
Booth, Philip (2007). 'The Control of Discretion: Planning and the Common Law', *Planning Theory* 6: 127–45.
Owens, Susan and Richard Cowell (2011). *Land and Limits: Interpreting Sustainability in the Planning Process*. Abingdon: Routledge, 2nd edn.
Riles, Anneliese (2005). 'A New Agenda for the Cultural Study of Law: Taking on the Technicalities', *Buffalo Law Review* 53: 973–1033.
Rydin, Yvonne (2011). *The Purpose of Planning: Creating Sustainable Towns and Cities*. Bristol: Policy Press.

Index

Aarhus Convention 115
Abbot, Carolyn 7, 20, 27, 30, 43, 109, 164, 167, 193, 195, 224
Abbot, Carolyn and Maria Lee 135, 139, 147, 148, 149
Adam, Barbara 158, 161
Administrative Court 223, 237
Administrative law 205, 236–9, 240–2, 244
   pluralism 237
   scholarship 229–32, 235, 237, 239, 242, 246
Affordable housing 193, 195
   definition 212–13
   definition in NPPF 212
   delivery methods 209, 213, 224
   effect on delivery of agreements made under Localism Act 2011 215–16
   financial contributions in lieu of 208, 219–20
   NPPF guidance on 212–14
   private developer control over delivery of 209, 212–13, 215, 221–3
   provision by private developers 209
   and Section 106 Agreements 208–9, 211, 214–18, 220, 223
   use of contractual arrangements to manipulate supply of 218–23
   and viability 214, 222, 224
Agenda 2030 88
Air quality 5
Amenity 39, 44, 45, 181, 184, 191
Anderson, Ben 170
AONB 119, 121–3, 182, 184, 186, 187, 189, 192
   Kent Downs. *See* Kent Downs AONB
Appleyard, Donald 72
Applicants 139
   See also Developers; House builders
Area of Outstanding Natural Beauty. *See* AONB
Armeni, Chiara 7, 26, 27, 101, 109, 110, 133, 145, 193
Asset of Community Value 35, 41

Backstreet 36, 44–6, 49, 50–2, 54
Beauty 26, 112, 119, 122, 123, 189
Bell, David and Jon Binni 44
Bell, Joanna 7, 20, 138, 205
Bias, Rules on 234

Biodiversity 15, 22, 92, 142, 147
   See also Habitats protection; Nature protection
Bird, Simon 90
Blomley, Nick 70
Bolton MBC 141–5, 147
Boukalas, Christos 160
Bouwer, Kim and Rachel Gimson 7, 27, 205
Bristol City Council 13
Brook Street development (Colchester) 215–16
   obligations in section 106 agreement 215
   effect of agreement made under Localism Act 2011 215–16
Buchanan, Colin 78
Burchiellaro, Olimpia 39, 52

Call in 23, 146, 151, 156, 167–8, 172, 194
   Secretary of State powers to 20, 159, 162, 166, 168–71, 186, 188
Campkin, Ben and Lo Marshall 39, 40, 49
Cars 69, 70, 73, 78, 80
Casey, Edward 113, 114
Chakrabarty, Dipesh 160
Chesterwell development (Colchester) 216
   obligations in section 106 agreement 217, 219–21, 225
   effect of agreement made under Localism Act 2011 215–16
Climate change 6, 21, 100, 112, 118, 124, 125, 126
   crisis 112, 119, 125
Colchester
   See also Brook Street development; Chesterwell development; Rowhedge development
Colchester Borough Council 215, 224–5
   See also Brook Street development; Chesterwell development; Rowhedge development.
   Air Quality Management Areas 215
   affordable housing policies
      flexible approach to application of 218–22
   Core Strategy 226
Collins, Alan 39
Colum, Claire 44
Combined Authority 14
Common law 67–8, 73–4, 79, 159, 234, 249, 250, 256, 260

Community Infrastructure Levy 19, 144, 166, 208, 242
  Complexity, planning law 5, 8, 26, 135–9, 144, 236, 239, 268. *See also* local government complexity; scale complexity.
Compulsory purchase 27, 33, 38, 212, 251, 256–63, 265, 269
Conservation 21, 86, 93, 94, 119, 124, 157, 164. *See also* nature; habitats protection.
Conservation Areas 42, 43, 182, 189
Consistency 4, 15, 18, 118, 165, 167, 234, 236, 241
Consultation 7, 15, 21, 22, 38, 64, 66, 73, 75–6, 95, 115–18, 121–2, 127, 141, 146, 160, 181, 185, 191, 193, 194, 195
  See also Public participation; Statutory consultees
Cooper, Davina 160
Corburn, Jason 113
Councillors 12, 13, 184, 192, 210, 235
  See also Elected members
County councils 12, 13, 217, 225, 226
Countryside Properties (UK) Limited 216, 217, 225
Covid–19 80, 151, 155
Cowell, Richard and Patrick Devine-Wright 118
Cowell, Richard. *See* Owens, Susan and Richard Cowell
CPRE 185, 193, 197
Cresswell, Tim 113
Cross–examination 145, 146, 147
Cycling 64, 65, 70, 73, 113
Cyclists 65, 66, 68, 69, 73, 74, 77–8, 79

de Lucia, Vito 92, 93
Department for Levelling Up, Housing and Communities 20, 183
Democratic process
  and planning 3, 5, 6, 15, 109, 112, 115–16, 204, 269, 291
  and local government 10, 12, 13, 14, 16, 18, 192, 269
Designated areas. *See also* AONB and WHS
  national 119
  international 119–20
Developers 11, 19, 21, 27, 38, 51, 100, 104, 109, 134, 138, 148, 149–50, 188, 195, 207, 208–11, 212, 214, 215, 216, 218, 220, 222–3, 260, 261, 269
  See also Applicants; House builders; Mersea Homes Ltd; Hills Residential Construction Ltd.
Development, definition of 17
Development order 17
Development plan 18–19, 20–2, 55, 127, 136–8, 162, 173, 184, 186, 187, 190, 213, 223, 258
  Independent examination of 22, 186, 187
  See also Local plan
District Councils 12, 127
DIY urbanists 72
Douek, Samuel 39
Dover 191, 193

Dover District Council (DDC) 181–2, 184, 192
Drivers 65, 66, 69–70, 75, 77, 79
Drop Redoubt, the 182, 184, 192

Ealing 64
East Marine Plans 95, 99–102
Ecosystem 91, 93. *See also* Marine Plan; Marine Policy Statement.
  approach 33, 85–7, 91–4, 99, 101–2, 103
  services 100, 101, 103
Elected members 15, 27, 186
  See also councillors
Energy 6, 7, 112, 114, 116–19, 127–8, 163, 164, 171, 268
  See also Wind energy; Fracking
Environmental law 86, 91, 92, 93, 96, 102, 134, 184, 205, 230
Epistemology 92, 98, 165
Equality 6, 55
  duty 22, 38, 75
Escobar, Arturo 89, 92
Examining Authority (ExA) 117–18, 121–3, 124
Experience. *See* Legal Expertise; Place experience
Expertise
  legal expertise 133–5, 143–4, 147–50, 192
  of consultants 192
  of NGOs 193, 197
  of planning officers 15, 24, 74, 126, 192, 195
  of RVT Future 43, 54
  Technical 116
Expert witnesses 142, 145, 146
Expropriation 256

Financialisation. *See* Housing
Fisher, Elizabeth 8
Fracking 156, 162–4, 166, 169, 173
Futurescapes 158, 161–2, 165, 166, 169, 173
Futures theory
  and law 159–62
Futurity 155, 158, 160, 162, 166

Galanter, Marc 148, 222
Galliard Homes 44, 45
Gentrification 39, 44
Gimson, Rachel. *See* Bouwer, Kim and Rachel Gimson
Grabham, Emily 160
Green Belt 134, 137, 140–6, 151, 186, 187
Gregory, Julia (Planning Inspector) 45–6

Habitats protection 5
  See also conservation; Nature conservation; Biodiversity
Hackney Council 64
Hartog, Hendrik 76
HEART 134, 139, 141–9, 152
Heritage
  assets 41, 119–20, 129, 137, 140, 142, 144
  LGBT+ 42, 53–4
  setting of 38, 40, 41, 73, 74, 119–20, 121, 122
  World Heritage Site 119, 122–3

INDEX   273

Highway
  as a place 65, 70–3
  as a resource 33, 64–5, 73–9, 80
  as a right 65, 67–70
Highway Code 68, 77–8
Hills Residential Construction Limited 215, 225
Hilson, Chris 163
Holder, Jane and Donald McGillivray 146
Horrendous Hackney Road Closures 64
House builders 183
  See also Developers; Applicants
Housing See also Affordable Housing
  complexity 186, 209
  crisis 182, 183
    causes of 182, 186, 196
  complexity 186, 209
  demand 183, 196
  financialisation of 184, 262
  land allocation for 186–8
  need for
    objective assessment of 186–7
    standard method for calculating 187
  quality 183, 191
  quantity 191, 196
  standard method of calculating need 186–7
  supply 137, 151, 183, 184, 186–8, 218, 222
  tenure 213, 218
  and the tilted balance 187–8
  units 44, 182
Hulton Park 134, 136–7, 139–42, 144–6, 150, 151
Human Rights 69, 117, 229, 240, 256–7

Ideology 250, 257
Immigration
  legislative complexity 236, 238
  procedural adaptation 237
Immovate 40, 42
Independent Review of Administrative Law 237
Inspector. See Planning inspector

Jessup, Brad. See Vaughan, Steven and Brad Jessup.
Jilg, Karl 72
Judicial review
  grounds of 232, 233
  horizontal and vertical dimensions 232, 241–2
  landmark cases in 233, 234
  particularisation of 233–5, 237–8, 242
  in planning law 20, 24, 117, 138, 194, 231–2
  reform of 232. See also Independent Review of Administrative Law
  as remedy of last resort 231
Jurassic Coast WHS 121, 122–3

Keenan, Sarah 160
Kent Downs AONB 189, 192
Kent Wildlife Trust 193
Knowledge 74–5, 91, 92, 98, 101, 113–16, 122, 186, 187, 269, 271
  See also Expertise

Lame, Amy (Night Czar) 43, 48
Landscape 26, 73, 74, 93, 111, 113–14, 119, 120, 121–4, 141, 147, 161, 184, 192, 193, 197
  See also AONB
Layard, Antonia 7, 13, 27, 33, 155, 214, 261, 264, 265
Leach, William MP 69
Lee, Maria 7, 17, 19, 20, 21, 27, 39, 74, 114, 116, 118, 134, 136, 137, 148, 149, 155, 164, 167, 172, 262. See also Abbot, Carolyn and Maria Lee
Legal expertise. See also Expertise
  Experience 143, 145, 148, 149
  skill 109, 133–4, 143, 145–9
Legitimate expectations 70, 240
Levelling up 15, 183
LGBT+
  heritage. See Heritage
Listing
  Historic England 41, 42, 53–4, 141
  National Heritage List for England 41, 54
Local government 12–15
  complexity 10. 12, 14, 26
  funding 15, 16, 65, 75
  Purpose
    Conflict over 16–17
Local
  meaning of 113
  planning. See Local planning
  prioritisation of the 190
    environmental groups. See Local environmental groups
  NGOs 193
  See also Localism; Local Planning Authority; Scale
Local elections 12
Local environmental groups 133, 138, 139, 145, 158, 149
Local Plan 21, 24, 30, 149–50, 165, 238
  affordable housing policies in 187
  Lambeth 43, 49
  NPPF guidance on 187–8
  Tower Hamlets 49
  See also Development plan
Local planning
  processes 116–17
  vilification of 6
Local Planning Authority (LPA)
  role of 13–17
  NPPF definition of
Localism 180, 190, 197
Lockdown 7, 8, 64, 66
London Mayor. See Mayor of London
London Plan 2021 13, 45, 50
Loughlin, Martin 4, 16
Low Traffic Neighbourhoods. See LTNs
LTNs 64–7, 70–1, 73–6, 78–80

Macneil, Ian 211, 220, 222, 223, 224
Malawi Principles 92, 93, 97, 98, 102, 103
Malpas, Jeff 114
Marine Management Organisation (MMO) 94–5, 97–8, 101, 103
Marine Plan 85, 95
Marine Policy Statement 85, 127

Marine spatial planning 33, 85–7, 93–4, 98, 102, 103
  legal framework 94–6
Marples, Ernest 66
Material considerations 18–19, 50, 112, 115, 125, 129, 136, 143, 164, 188, 194, 238, 260, 265. *See also* Relevant considerations
Mawani, Renisa 160
Mayors
  Mayor of London 12, 13, 38–9, 42, 43, 45, 47, 48, 53
  Metro–Mayors 13
  Mayoral Combined Authority 14–15
McAuslan, Patrick 162, 205, 250, 252, 255, 257
McGillivray, Donald. *See* Holder, Jane and Donald McGillivray
Mersea Homes Limited 215–17, 218, 219, 220–1, 225, 226
Methodology 7, 36, 37–8, 147, 187, 195, 257
MHCLG 193
Ministry of Housing, Communities and Local Government. *See* MHCLG
Ministry of Transport 78
Mitchell, Edward 7, 19, 27, 51, 109, 155, 182, 186, 195, 205, 261, 262
Mixed communities 213, 218
MPs
  central/local status 187
  role in planning 25, 187
Motor Vehicles 64, 68, 72, 73, 76–80
Munn, Nancy D. 160

Natarajan, Lucy 8
Natarajan, Lucy et al 135
National Planning Policy Framework (NPPF) 2012 151, 212, 214, 224, 238, 246
National Planning Policy Framework (NPPF) 2013 198
National Planning Policy Framework (NPPF) 2019 144, 151
National Planning Policy Framework (NPPF) 2021 11, 23–4, 95, 198
  and affordable housing 212–14
  and AONBs 189
  and definition of local planning authority 12
  and heritage 41, 120
  and plans 22, 136
    housing allocation 186
  and presumption in favour of sustainable development 20, 85, 90, 137–8, 142–3, 164, 165, 173, 270
  and tilted balance 20, 138, 143, 164–5, 187
  and World Heritage Sites 119
National Policy Statement (NPS)
  Overarching for energy 117, 119, 127
  For Renewable Energy Infrastructure 117–19
National Trust 185, 193
Nationally Significant Infrastructure Project (NSIP) 112, 135, 148, 152
  Consenting process for 116–17, 124–5
  Onshore wind, withdrawal 118
  See also Navitus Bay Wind Park; Table of Legislation (Planning Act 2008)

Nature 86, 87, 89, 91, 92, 93, 97, 98, 101, 103, 141
  See also biodiversity; conservation; habitats protection
Navitus Bay Wind Park 109, 112, 120–3, 124, 148, 200
Neighbourhood plan 13, 21, 22, 30, 55, 190, 234, 238, 264
Neighbourhood planning forum 13, 22, 190
Newman, Lyda 72
NIMBY 163, 193
Northern Ireland 13
Northern Powerhouse 140

Officers 7, 15, 24, 44, 51, 88, 182, 192–3
Open justice 241
Ophir, Adi 171
Owens, Susan and Richard Cowell 196, 270

Parish council 13, 22, 190
Participation. *See* Public participation
Pedestrianism 70
Pedestrians 64, 66, 68–9, 72, 73, 74, 77–9, 80
Peel Holdings 134, 140, 141, 143, 145, 147, 150
Permitted development rights 17, 19, 191, 194
Pieraccini, Margherita 7, 20, 27, 33, 155
Pill, Malcolm 146
PINS 20, 24, 116, 117, 139, 143, 145, 147, 149, 188, 194, 196, 239
  and special measures 24
  and Role in appeal 23, 51, 167, 172, 175, 188
  See also Development plan, independent examination of
'Placescapes' 114
Place attachment 101, 113, 114
  See also Place experience; Sense of place
Place experience 110, 112–15, 118, 119, 120, 124–6, 145
Place–making 5, 71, 72
Planning agreements. *See* Section 106 agreements; planning obligations
Planning blight 258
Planning Court 235, 238
Planning for the Future. *See* Planning White Paper
Planning inquiries 20, 45, 117, 133, 134, 135, 142, 148, 149, 241
  Cross–examination 145, 146, 147–8
  Procedure 139, 143–4, 145–6, 148, 151, 234
  and Rule 6 parties 135, 144, 146
Planning Inspectorate. *See* PINS
Planning inspectors. *See* PINS
Planning judgment 5, 15, 18, 23, 24, 125, 164, 173, 188, 192, 196, 240
Planning obligations 19, 45, 141, 144, 207–10, 216, 217, 222, 223
  See also Section 106 agreements
Planning permission 11, 17–20, 21, 23–4, 38, 163–4, 187, 191, 231, 259–60, 269
  and Backstreet 44, 45, 46, 50
  and Colchester 215–17
  and Dover 182
  and fracking 163, 164, 169
  and Peel Holdings 140, 143
  and XXL 47, 49

INDEX **275**

Planning policy. *See* Development plan; Local plan; National Planning Policy Framework (2021)
Planning, reform of 6, 11, 12, 13, 25–6, 136, 183, 185, 194, 208, 268, 271. *See also* Planning White Paper
Planning White Paper 6, 8, 11, 25–6, 30, 90, 138, 149
Pluriversality 89, 92, 98
Prior institutional knowledge 74–5, 184, 271
Prior, Jason 49
Private rights 3, 249, 251–2, 253, 254, 255, 258, 261, 262–3
Property rights 250, 251, 252, 255, 256–8, 260, 262
PropTech 26
Public interest 5, 16, 90, 163, 182, 187, 189, 192, 197, 250–2, 255, 256–8, 260, 261, 262, 269
Public participation 12, 18, 25, 109, 117–18, 133, 139, 149, 195, 250, 261, 269–70
   Challenges of 115, 134, 135, 193
   In marine planning 95, 98, 101–2
   And place experience 112, 124, 126
   Value of 115–16

Queer communities 40, 42, 45, 46, 49, 50, 51, 53–5
Queer heritage 42, 53–4
Queer legal theory 36
Queer spaces 33, 35–6, 37–8, 39–40, 41, 49, 50, 51–2, 54–5, 261
Queer theory 36–7, 50

Raco, Mike 210
Raynsford Review 6, 11
   And presumption in favour of sustainable development 90
Reasons for planning decisions 15, 95, 124, 125, 137, 144, 164, 165, 186, 187, 271
   Adequacy of 182, 239–40
Referenda 13–14, 22, 28
Reform. *See* Planning reform
Regional Assemblies 13–14
Regional planning 13–14, 38, 85, 138, 140, 183, 190
Regional Spatial Strategies 13, 190
Registered Park and Garden 134, 140–1, 142, 143, 144, 146
Relational contract theory 209, 211–12, 220
Relational ontology 88, 89, 92, 93, 97, 98, 102–3
Relationship between planning policy and law 23–24
Relevant considerations 50, 95, 233. *See also* Relevant considerations
Resources
   of developers 19, 109, 148, 195, 270
   of LPAs 16, 18, 21, 22, 148, 192, 194–5
   of local community groups 43, 55, 115, 146, 148
Riegl, Alois 53
Right. *See* Highway; Human rights; Private rights; Permitted development rights; Property rights. *See* Right of passage

Right of passage 33, 64, 66, 67–70. *See also* Highway
Riles, Anneliese 4, 5, 160, 162, 268
Road tax. *See* Vehicle Excise Duty
Rooney, David 68
Rowhedge development (Colchester) 217–18, 221
   obligations in section 106 agreement 218–19, 221
Royal Vauxhall Tavern (RVT) 40–3, 49, 50, 54, 55
Rule 6 parties. *See* planning inquiries
Rydin, Yvonne 8

Sandford, Mark 16
Scale
   of actors 191–5
   complexity 155, 172, 173, 180, 191, 195, 196
   of interests and impacts 182–5
   jurisdiction of. *See* Scale, of law and policy
   layers of government 168–9, 172, 180–2, 196, 269
   of law and policy 185–91
   spatial 19, 93, 155–6, 163, 180–2
   temporal 163, 165, 166, 169, 237
Scotland 13
Seamon, David 111, 113
Section 106 agreements 19, 38, 143, 145, 192, 208, 210–12, 225, 260
   and Affordable housing. *See* Affordable housing. *See also* Viability
   as part of network of contractual arrangements 208, 218–22
   and Localism Act 207
   and Queer spaces 44, 45, 51–2
Sense of place 113, 114, 121
Social norms 65, 71, 77, 79
Social utility 249, 260, 262
   Land as 251–5
Soininen, Niko and Froukje Platjouw 93
South Marine Plans 86, 99–102
Spatial Development Strategy. *See* London Plan
Statutory consultees 18, 116, 234
Statutory review 20, 138, 231, 237
Stokes, Elen 4, 7, 17, 19, 20, 155, 156, 182, 268
Streetspace 69
Sustainable development 21, 29, 33, 85, 86, 87–94, 96, 97, 100, 101, 102
   See also National Planning Policy Framework; Raynsford Review
Szolucha, Anna 163

Tafon, Ralph 102
Tarlock, Dan 93
Technical evidence 112, 115, 116, 121–3, 124, 145, 146, 148, 186–7, 192, 193, 269, 270
Technicalities of planning law 4, 7, 17, 26, 135–9, 162, 186, 209, 210, 218, 268
Thatcherism 16
Tilted balance. *See* Housing; National Planning Policy Framework (2021)
Tripp, Alker 78, 80

Troubworst, Arie 91
Tuan, Yi-Fu 112, 113
Two-tier councils 12

Unitary authority 12–13
Upper Tribunal 237, 243, 265
Uthwatt Committee 80

Valverde, Mariana 172
Vaughan, Steven and Brad Jessup 13, 22, 27, 33, 155, 261, 262
Vehicle Excise Duty 69
Viability 142, 143, 146, 186, 199, 210
   and affordable housing delivery 214, 220, 222
   and delivery of planning obligations 192, 219
   NPPF guidance in respect of 186, 224

View 113–114, 120, 122, 123. *See also* Landscape
Vincent-Jones, Peter
Vorspan, Rachel 68, 70

Wales 13, 127
Willmore, Chris 186, 196
Wind energy 6, 95, 109, 112, 114, 116, 124, 127, 167, 196. *See also* Navitus Bay Wind Park
Woonerf 65
World Heritage Site (WHS) 119
   See also Jurassic Coast WHS

XXL 36, 46–9, 50, 51–2, 54, 55, 56

Yes, Minister 66

CPSIA information can be obtained
at www.ICGtesting.com
Printed in the USA
BVHW010151190423
662613BV00006B/11